discover
FRANCE

NICOLA WILLIAMS
OLIVER BERRY, STEVE FALLON, EMILIE FILOU,
CATHERINE LE NEVEZ, DANIEL ROBINSON, MILES RODDIS

BRITTANY & NORMANDY p129

PARIS & ITS DAYTRIPS p53

CHAMPAGNE & THE NORTHEAST p101

BORDEAUX & THE SOUTHWEST p287

THE LOIRE & CENTRAL FRANCE p167

LYON & THE FRENCH ALPS p203

THE SOUTH OF FRANCE p235

DISCOVER FRANCE

Paris & Its Day Trips (p51) A riverside city bursting with iconic sights, world-class museums and Chanel-chic shopping.

Champagne & Northeast France (p101) Inject a bit of fizz into your French travels with France's most northerly wine region.

Brittany & Normandy (p129) Bracing clifftop walks make Brittany unique. Monet preferred next-door Normandy.

The Loire & Central France (p167) Renaissance châteaux, Burgundy reds and prehistoric art is what this region is about.

Lyon & the French Alps (p203) Dine fine in France's gastronomic capital en route to Mont Blanc and its outdoor playground.

The South of France (p235) Provence markets, Roman relics, lavender fields, Riviera glamour: what a riot of pleasures!

Bordeaux & the Southwest (p287) Some of France's finest wine, the Pyrenees and gateway to spirited French Basque Country.

↘CONTENTS

BRITTANY &
NORMANDY
p129

PARIS & ITS
DAYTRIPS
p51

CHAMPAGNE
& THE
NORTHEAST
p101

BORDEAUX
& THE
SOUTHWEST
p287

THE LOIRE &
CENTRAL
FRANCE
p167

LYON & THE
FRENCH
ALPS
p203

THE SOUTH OF
FRANCE p235

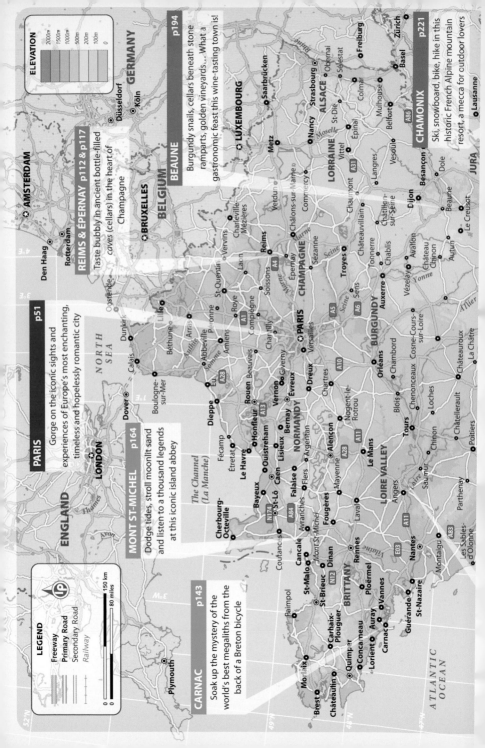

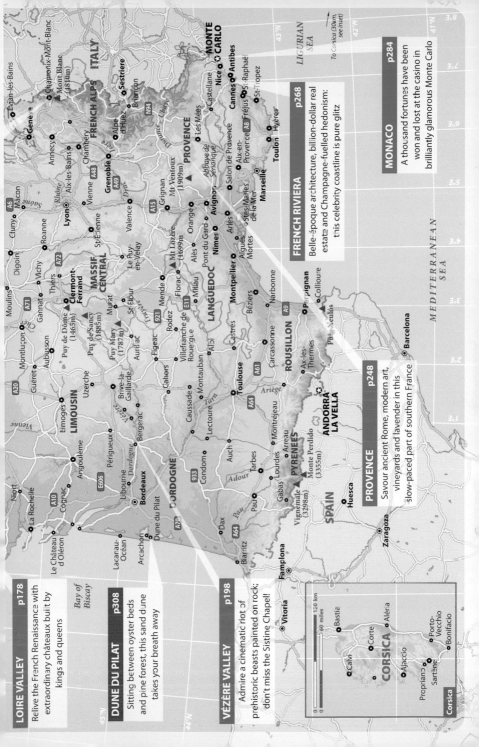

LOIRE VALLEY p178

Relive the French Renaissance with extraordinary châteaux built by kings and queens

DUNE DU PILAT p308

Sitting between oyster beds and pine forest, this sand dune takes your breath away

VÉZÈRE VALLEY p198

Admire a cinematic riot of prehistoric beasts painted on rock; don't miss the Sistine Chapel!

PROVENCE p248

Savour ancient Rome, modern art, vineyards and lavender in this slow-paced part of southern France

FRENCH RIVIERA p268

Belle-époque architecture, billion-dollar real estate and Champagne-fuelled hedonism: this celebrity coastline is pure glitz

MONACO p284

A thousand fortunes have been won and lost at the casino in brilliantly glamorous Monte Carlo

⬐ THIS IS FRANCE

Be it mooching between vines in a Citroën 2CV, cycling through lavender or taking it all in with walking stick in hand, France is a land of languid moments laced with soul, a zesty spirit and more culture than you can shake a baguette at.

Its capital alone requires more than a lifetime to absorb. Paris is chic and sexy, understatedly elegant and impossibly romantic, with endless world-class art, attitude and a rebellious cigarette brazenly poised between manicured nails. Paris is outrageously feminine and a right madam everyone wants to meet.

Paris (Pa-*ree*) to the French, this city meets for Sunday ice cream on Pont St-Louis, quaffs cocktails Seine-side, shops for 1950s Chanel vintage in the 9th, dines hip in the Marais, grabs a bike for riverbank rides, buys fruit and vegetables at the local street market and occasionally catches a late-night opening at the Louvre. It is overtly urban, passionate, obnoxious, arrogant, irresistible, officious and downright maddening at times. But in true French fashion, life is approached at a deeply humbling, sacrosanct

pace that means every last moment is really savoured. Its holy trinity, as old as the Seine that flows through this ancient city built by Celtic Gauls, is good food, wine and *joie de vivre*.

The rest of France is no short straw. It is the world's top tourist destination, a place everyone wants to visit. The only hitch is pinning down which chunk of the hexagon to savour first. Modern art buffs swear the hot south, with an intensity of light absolutely unknown elsewhere in Europe, is best: Renoir, Matisse and Picasso certainly thought so. In the French Alps, winter skiers and summer hikers

> **'It is the world's top tourist destination, a place everyone wants to visit'**

thrive on Europe's highest peak and its outdoor adventures, while gourmets find the cider trails, oyster beds and Champagne cellars of northern France quite intoxicating. Countrywide, ancient churches, sea-splashed abbeys and old stone châteaux quietly safeguard 1001 tales of deep tradition and inventive passion. *This*, at the end of the day, is France.

↘ FRANCE'S TOP
25 EXPERIENCES

1

⬂ EIFFEL TOWER, PARIS

I'd taken a Parisian bus tour, losing myself in the amazing sights and scents of this lovely city. It took my breath away. I squealed when I finally saw the sparkling lights of the **Eiffel Tower** (p76).

Lisa Larkin, Traveller, Australia

↘ THE SEINE, PARIS

2

Going on a cruise at night along the **Seine** (p77) and seeing all the sights lit up, the couples strolling along the river bank. It was so romantic even if we are a couple of old folks.

Irene Poulton, Traveller, Australia

3

↘ AV DES CHAMPS-ÉLYSÉES, PARIS

I've loved Paris' broadest and most famous **boulevard** (p77) ever since I was a student and my boyfriend and I stood beneath the Arc de Triomphe on New Year's Eve and shouted 'C'est pour nous! C'est pour nous!' (It's for us! It's for us!) as the cars raced around, blowing their horns and flashing their headlights.

Steve Fallon, Lonely Planet Author, UK

1 JAN ETROMM; 2 GLENN BEANLAN; 3 WILL SALTER

1 Eiffel Tower (p76), Paris; **2** Cruisebnat and sunset on the Seine (p77), Paris; **3** Arc de Triomphe on av des Champs-Élysées (p77), Paris

↘ MONTMARTRE, PARIS

You will find the atmosphere of **Montmartre** (p77) is simply charming! The little shops with all their trinkets, the artists lining the streets and the crêpes galore create an environment one can't help but enjoy. And then there are the street performers who you could enjoy for hours, sitting in the sun. Montmartre definitely has the old Parisian feel and is a must see when in Paris.

Crystal Wilkinson, Traveller, Canada

↖ CHÂTEAU DE VERSAILLES

Château de Versailles (p95) is ludicrously large and the queues for a ticket or the toilet test the patience of a saint. But garden-meander between love temple and grotto, orange tree and scented rose, 1001 sculpted stones and fountains, and suddenly it really doesn't matter.

⬎ ADRENALINE KICK, CHAMONIX

Sure, 007 did it, but so can you: the **Vallée Blanche** (p225) is a once in a lifetime experience. You won't regret the €70-odd it costs to do it because every minute of the five hours it takes to go down will pump more adrenaline in your body than anything else you've ever done.

Emilie Filou, Lonely Planet Author, UK

6

4 RACHEL LEWIS; 5 JOHN ELK III; 6 JEFF CANTARUTTI

4 Painter, Montmartre (p77), Paris; 5 Château de Versailles (p95); 6 Vallée Blanche (p225) from Aiguille du Midi, French Alps

⬏ MONT ST-MICHEL

At **Mont St-Michel** (p164) the tide goes out 10km, so far until you cannot see it which is quite amazing. The difference between low tide and high tide is 15m – equally amazing.

Jack Lecoq, Guide in Baie de St-Michel, France

7

8

⬊ THE HEART OF THE LOIRE VALLEY

The Loire Valley (p178) drive from Blois to Saumur, via Amboise and Tours, is one of the loveliest drives in the world, down rustic lanes past farmhouses, vineyards and châteaux. It feels like nothing has changed here in 100 years.

stoml, Traveller

⬊ CHARTRES BLUE

Chartres Cathedral (p98) raises your eyes to the heavens and defies belief that man can make such a masterpiece. I spent a whole day here, taking the excellent guided tour then exploring on my own. The stained glass grabs the headlines, but the ornate carvings on the outside reward a detailed examination. If this was in nearby Paris, no other church would get a look in.

Tom Hall, Lonely Planet Staff

9

7 DENNIS JOHNSON; 8 DIANA MAYFIELD;; 9 CHRISTOPHER WOOD

7 Sheep grazing by Mont St-Michel (p164), Normandy; 8 Château de Chambord (p182), Loire Valley; 9 Carved figures in Royal Portal, Cathédrale Notre Dame de Chartres (p98)

10

⇖ CHAMPAGNE TASTING

We drove the Route Touristique du Champagne from Reims, stopping in gorgeous villages and drinking in the views. At **Épernay** (p117) we toured Moët & Chandon – once you know the story of how it's made, you realise that Champagne really *is* worth the money!

Janine Eberle, Lonely Planet Staff

⇖ CARNAC MEGALITHS

11

Cycling past Carnac's fields full of thousands of otherworldly **megaliths** (p143) is an otherworldly reminder of Brittany's ancient human inhabitation. You can even stop for crêpes in a traditional long Breton house right in the middle of a 70-strong *cromlech* (circle of menhirs). Amazing!

Catherine Le Nevez,
Lonely Planet Author, France

↘ CROIX ROUSSE, LYON

I cannot think of a finer spot to be Sunday morning than sitting on a pavement terrace in **Croix Rousse** (p218), sipping white Côtes du Rhône and watching a man with briny hands and blue plastic apron shuck oysters before my very eyes. *Quelle joie!*

Nicola Williams,
Lonely Planet Author, France

↘ WINE TASTING

Winding through country lanes, golden fields stretching as far as the eye could see, we drove…searching for a family-run vineyard for a spot of **wine tasting** (p366). There, a jovial man told stories about his vineyard as he served us his favourite vintages. We picnicked in a flower-filled clearing nearby.

Caroline Thresher, Traveller, UK

10 OLIVER STREWE; 11 JOHN ELK III; 12 OLIVER STREWE; 13 OLIVER STREWE

10 Tower rising above vineyard, Champagne; 11 Carnac megaliths (p143), Brittany; 12 Rooftops of Croix Rousse (p218), Lyon; 13 Vineyard worker among vines

14

↘ DIPPING BENEATH THE PONT DU GARD

Don't forget your trunks at the **Pont du Gard** (p261) in Languedoc – the perfect place to be a big kid. The waters of the Gard are perfect for daredevil diving and high-level jumps off the rocks under the *pont* itself. A post-history-binge plunge will keep even the most reluctant young historian happy.

Tom Hall, Lonely Planet Staff

↘ CARCASSONNE'S LA CITÉ AT DUSK

I spent the day wandering around Carcassonne's La Cité (p260), walking across the medieval drawbridge and admiring the pennant-capped towers. I was impressed, but it wasn't until later that the awe-inspiring beauty of the citadel took hold. Bathed in pink light, it appeared like a magic castle in a fairy tale.

James McMurray, Traveller, South Africa

15

14 BILL WASSMAN; 15 GLENN BEANLAND

14 Pont du Gard (p261), Languedoc; 15 La Cité, Carcassonne (p260), Languedoc

⬎ THE THREE CORNICHES

It's quite impossible to motor along these **coastal roads** (p283) without imagining Grace Kelly, Hitchcock, the glitz of Monaco, the tragic end of the fairytale Hollywood queen – to the standing ovation of big view after big view of sweeping blue sea caressing Europe's most mythical coastline.

Nicola Williams, Lonely Planet Author, France

16

⬎ CASINO DE MONTE CARLO, MONACO

17

The world's most famous belle époque casino (p286) is a must. The slot machines are something of a letdown and it's the type of place you feel you need dough to enter. But simply lingering at the entrance, watching everyone ogling at everyone, instantly fires the imagination.

⬎ DUNE DU PILAT

Not only is the view amazing from the top of the Dune du Pilat (p308), Europe's largest sand dune – taking in the Banc d'Arguin bird reserve and even Cap Ferret across the bay – but the nearby beaches have some of the best surf along the French Atlantic coast.

18

Catherine Le Nevez,
Lonely Planet Author, France

16 DAVID TOMLINSON; 17 DAVID TOMLINSON; 18 ANDREW BAIN

16 Corniches passing through Roquebrune (p284), Provence; 17 Casino de Monte Carlo (p286), Monaco; 18 Dune du Pilat (p308)

↘ FESTIVAL MADNESS

Festival time in the **Pays Basque** (p309) is an amazing street party. The streets are full of people in traditional white clothes with neck scarves, fireworks, live music, dancing and games. Bars sell sangria to drink in the streets. It's impossible not to get caught up in it all.

Vanessa Collins, Traveller, UK

19

CHAMBRES
Chez
l'Habitant

20

🐚 SHOPPING AT THE MARKET

For me, a visit to France is all about the **markets** (p364) – sometimes it's an ancient covered market, sometimes it's an alfresco affair in the town square. I love eyeing the pristinely stacked vegetables, pondering the mounds of perfectly ripened cheese and chatting with the fruit-sellers while I assemble my picnic.

Caroline Sieg, Lonely Planet Author, London

19 St-Jean-Pied-de-Port (p313), French Basque Country; 20 Rue Mouffetard food market (p85), Paris

21

◄ ABBAYE DE SÉNANQUE, PROVENCE

Visiting this abbey (p266) is something of a soulful experience, but what sets it apart from the rest of Provence's lovely countryside abbeys is the row after row of sweet-smelling lavender that frames it purple in early summer. *This* is why most people come here.

◄ MONET'S GARDEN, GIVERNY

22

Everyone knows Monet's waterlilies. And there is something quite magical about standing on a bridge inside a painting that you know so well. But, for me, the most interesting part was Monet's house (p159): on the brightly painted walls hung not Impressionist masterpieces but Japanese woodcuts, making me suddenly curious about the artist's life.

Suzannah Shwer,
Lonely Planet Staff

⇖ FRENCH RIVIERA BEACHES

What makes the **Riviera beaches** (p268) so special for me is the sea's mesmerising colour and the intense light: it's not called Côte d'Azur for nothing. And there's something for everyone, whether you're after long sandy beaches, intimate rocky coves or somewhere to bare it all!

Emilie Filou,
Lonely Planet Author, UK

⇖ PROVENÇAL LIVING

The landscape reminds one of Tuscany: bright warming sunshine, lush green hills, and streams and springs. Small villages cling to the hillsides. The area is dominated by **Mont Ventoux** (p265) – everywhere you go it lingers on the horizon. And did I mention the wine?

Andrew Briffett, Traveller, UK

21 Abbaye de Sénanque (p266), Provence; 22 Monet's house (p159), Giverny; 23 Sunbathers on beach, Nice (p268); 24 Mont Ventoux (p265) behind Vaison-la-Romaine, Provence

⇲ EXTREME EMBROIDERY

You enter a dimly lit hall, walk up to a long **strip of linen** (p158) behind glass and peer at embroidered figures – and suddenly, you're back in 1066, helping William the Conqueror build his ships, crossing the Channel under striped sails, and watching the Norman horsemen rout the Saxons at Hastings.

Daniel Robinson, Lonely Planet Author, Israel

25

DONALD C. & PRISCILLA ALEXANDER EASTMAN

25 Bayeux Tapestry (p158)

FRANCE'S TOP ITINERARIES

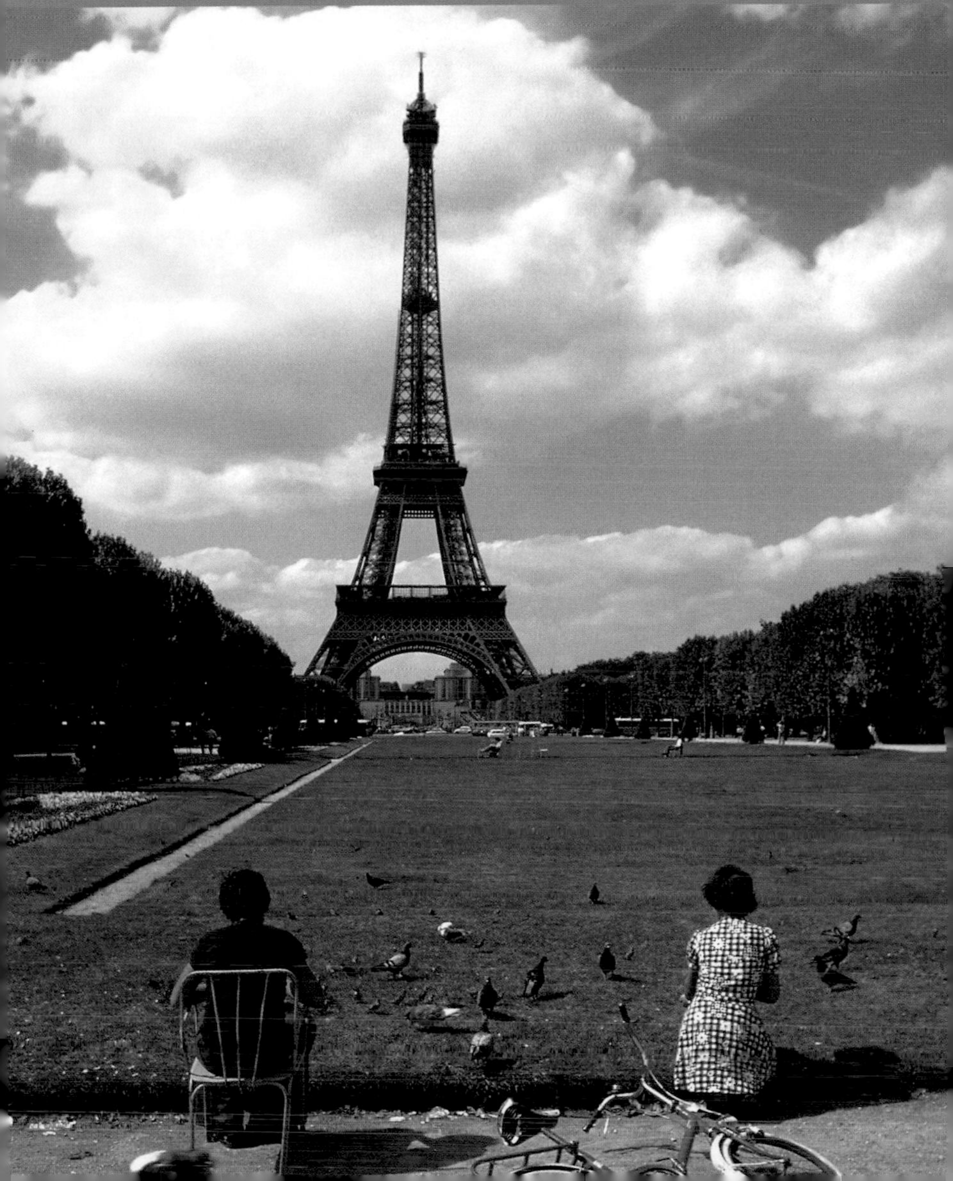

A JOURNEY OF MAGNIFICENCE

FIVE DAYS PARIS TO TOURS

It might not seem very long, but it is astonishing what marvels and majesty you can squeeze into five smart days. Start in the capital, from where a journey of magnificent French icons, Renaissance châteaux and sought-after sparkling wines fans out.

❶ PARIS

Spend a day being seduced by France's soulful capital, a hike up the **Eiffel Tower** (p76) being something of a pilgrimage on a sunny day. City view done, don your walking shoes or pedalling legs (grab a **Vélib' bike**; p94) and embark on a sensual meander east along the Seine to the magnificent art-packed **Musée d'Orsay** (p74) and beyond to the god of all art museums, the **Louvre** (p63). Consider lunch at **Chez La Vieille** (p82) before taking the plunge inside. Come dusk, explore a different part of the city: **Montmartre** (p77) perhaps, with its bohemian heritage and bevy of charming bistros; or the trendy **Marais** (p67) with its feast of fantastic places to eat, drink and hang out.

❷ REIMS

It is a mere 45-minute train trip from Paris to this regal city in the heart of the Champagne region. Savour the soul-stirring Romanesque **Basilique St-Rémi** (p112) and scale the **cathedral** (p113) for dazzling views of one of France's finest wine-producing areas before tucking into the serious business of **tasting bubbly** (p115). **Le Foch** (p104) is an exceptional lunch or dinner address. Overnight in Reims and

Château de Chenonceau (p186), Loire Valley

ADINA TOVY AMSEL

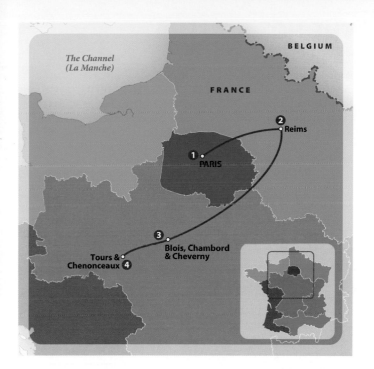

next day catch a train to neighbouring **Épernay** (p117) to continue the Champagne fest.

❸ BLOIS, CHAMBORD & CHEVERNY
Day three train it to **Blois** (p180) in the châteaux-studded Loire Valley where you can make the most of the limited time you have by hooking up with an **organised chateaux tour** (p181): queen of all castles **Château de Chambord** (p182) and the charmingly classical **Château de Cheverny** (p183) with its hound-packed kennels (watch them being fed) form a great combination. Back in Blois, dine medieval at **Le Castelet** (p182) or romantically beneath the stars at **L'Orangerie** (p182).

❹ TOURS & CHENONCEAU
Continue southwest along the Loire, France's longest river, to solidly bourgeois **Tours** (p185), from where **Château de Chenonceau** (p186), beautifully strung across the River Cher 34km east, is an easy hop. Allow plenty of time at this idyllic retreat with a history as exotic and colourful as the women who created it. Back in Tours **L'Adresse** (p185) is *the* address to cap such a magnificent journey.

THE HOT SOUTH

10 DAYS NICE TO BIARRITZ

Whet the appetite with Nice, Riviera queen, from where Europe's most mythical coastline unfurls in an extravagant pageant of belle époque palaces and celebrity sands. Head west across the Pyrenees and the humble rhythm of pilgrims making their way on foot to Spain kicks in.

❶ NICE & MONACO

Flop on a corn-blue chair on **Promenade des Anglais** (p270) to contemplate the Mediterranean. Shop at the **Cours Saleya market** (p273), get lost in **Vieux Nice** (p270) and eat **socca** (p273) – and at **La Merenda** (p273) – at least once. Day two, catch the train to glitzy **Monaco** (p284) to watch the **changing of the guard** (p284), pay homage to a **Hollywood queen** (p286), flutter in **Monte Carlo** (p286) and celebrity-watch.

❷ ST-TROPEZ

Play the star in this mythical fishing port where millionaire yachts jostle in the limelight with peddling street artists and flash Harries on Harleys. Grab *un café* at the **Vieux Port** (p279), admire art at the **Musée de l'Annonciade** (p279) and hike to the **citadel** (p279). Frolic away the afternoon on **Plage de Pampelonne** (p280). Next morning rise early to beat the crowds at **Place des Lices market** (p281).

❸ AIX-EN-PROVENCE

Meet bourgeois Provence in this graceful canvas of elegant 19th-century architecture, chic café terraces and secret fountain-clad squares. Visit a

LEFT: BARBARA VAN ZANTEN; RIGHT: BETHUNE CARMICHAEL

Left: Vieux Nice (p270), Provence; Right: St-Tropez (p279), Provence

dozen-and-one **Cézanne landscapes** (p255), poke around the **Musée Granet** (p253) and book a table for dinner at **La Chimère Café** (p256).

❹ CARCASSONNE

A three-hour scenic drive along the Mediterranean brings you to this **fairytale medieval city** (p260) in Languedoc. Admire its witches'-hat turrets from afar before joining the inner-wall crowd. Feasting on a local *cassoulet* (casserole dish) at L'Ecu d'Or is part of the experience.

❺ LOURDES

This **pilgrimage town** (p316), three hours west in the rugged Pyrenees mountains, is another people-busy spot and a place that has to be seen at least once in a lifetime.

❻ ST-JEAN-PIED-DE-PORT & BIARRITZ

Spain is just 8km from this **walled town** (p313) deep in the heart of French Basque country. **Market day** (p315) is fabulous, as is the final leg of this 10-day trip: the northbound D918 to Cambo-les-Bains and beyond to glitzy **Biarritz** (p311) on the Atlantic Coast meanders through rocky hills, forests and lush meadows dotted with white farmhouses selling local cheese. Take your foot off the pedal and enjoy.

UNESCO TREASURE TROVE

TWO WEEKS PARIS TO LYON

This lavish fortnight tours France's biggest and best, oldest and most precious: every stop is a Unesco World Heritage site, making the trip particularly tantalising for culture vultures and history buffs.

❶ PARIS & ITS DAY TRIPS

One of this city's sweetest attractions is the **River Seine** (p77), a Unesco World Heritage treasure. Walk or cycle its banks, stopping to savour the striking **Musée du Quai Branly** (p76), scale the **Eiffel Tower** (p76) and so on. Day two, day-trip it to France's most breathtaking castle, **Château de Versailles** (p95). Third day, pick from chivalrous **Fontainebleau** (p96) or blue **Chartres** (p98).

❷ REIMS

As a day trip or overnight flit from the capital, this elegant city sits on thousands of bottles of Champagne ripening in cellars. Park up and drink your way around, breaking for afternoon tea at **Waïda** (p117) and ending at the **Grand Hôtel des Templiers** (p117); make **Le Continental** (p117) your dinner date.

❸ MONT ST-MICHEL

Hit the road early for the five-hour drive to this sea-splashed tidal island in **Normandy** (p155) and its priceless bay. **Walking barefoot across the sand** (p164) is an atmospheric way of visiting its **abbey** (p166). Later explore the coast: Breton oysters in **Cancale** (p153) is a culinary must.

JOHN ELK III

Château de Chambord (p182), Loire Valley

❹ CHAMBORD

Potter southeast into the **Loire Valley** (p178), stretching your legs along medieval lanes woven with waterways in Breton capital **Rennes** (p140). Arrive in **Amboise** (p187) for lunch amid neoclassical furnishings at **L'Épicerie** (p188) and an afternoon of château-exploring at **Chambord** (p182). Come dusk be wooed by the *son et lumière* (sound and light) dramatically projected on its stone walls.

❺ BORDEAUX & ST-ÉMILION

The next World Heritage site is port city **Bordeaux** (p298) where exceedingly **fine dining** (p300) in the company of prestigious reds is a winner. Basking in the city's surrounds are the listed vineyards of **St-Émilion** (p302), reason itself to linger a couple of days in this tasty part of southwest France.

❻ VEZÈRE VALLEY

Peer at prehistory close-up in this extraordinary **Dordogne valley** (p198), littered with caves decorated by Cro-Magnan man. The drive east from Bordeaux is an easy two hours and takes you past the must-stop hilltop village of **Périgueux** (p196). Book a tour at the world-famous **Grotte de Lascaux** (p201) in advance.

❼ CARCASSONNE & THE CANAL DU MIDI

Four million annual visitors cannot be wrong: the 19th-century resurrection of **Carcassonne's walled city** (p260), vines in foreground, snow-capped Pyreneen peaks in background, *is* spectacular. Lunch on **cassoulet** then flee the crowds and freewheel along the banks of the pea-green **Canal du Midi** on its serene journey across gentle Languedoc plains.

❽ PONT DU GARD & ARLES

Check what the Romans got up to in Languedoc at this gargantuan **aqueduct** (p261). Paddle under it in a canoe, walk in scented scrubland and nip into **Arles** (p256) for dinner at **Le Cilantro** (p258).

❾ AVIGNON

This beautiful walled city in Provence is the belle of the ball with its **papal castle** (p263), summertime festivals and vibrant café life. Dance on its fabled bridge, sail the Rhône and don't miss **Christian Etienne's** (p264) refined Provençal cuisine.

❿ LYON

The perfect stop for last-minute shopping on your return north, this big city with gorgeous medieval and Renaissance **old town** (p216) is France's gastronomic capital. **Cook your own lunch** (p220), dine local *bouchon*-style or splurge on one of the country's most exciting chefs, **Nicolas Le Bec** (p221).

RIGHT: GLENN BEANLAND; LEFT: JOHN ELK III.

Left: La Cité, Carcassonne (p260); Right: Pont St-Bénezet (p261), Avignon

↘ PLANNING YOUR TRIP

FRANCE'S BEST...

⇘ SHOPPING

- **Paris** (p91) Flea markets or haute couture fashion, it has it all.
- **Champagne** (p112) Taste and buy French fizz in the wine cellars of Épernay and Reims, a quick skip from the capital.
- **Troyes** (p120) French designer fashion at a snip of the original price.
- **St-Tropez** (p279) Fabulous twice-weekly Provençal outdoor market on mythical place des Lices.
- **Quimper** (p144) Buy colourful Breton *faïence* (earthenware) in Quimper's half-timbered medieval old town.

⇘ CHATEÂUX

- **Versailles** (p95) France's most famous, grandest, busiest.
- **Fontainebleau** (p96) Renaissance gem southeast of Paris.

- **Chambord** (p182) King of the awe-inspiring Renaissance collection littering the Loire Valley.
- **Chenonceau** (p186) Supreme grace on the banks of the Cher.
- **Guédelon** (p198) Watch a 13th-century château being built using medieval technology.

⇘ MEDIEVAL VILLAGES

- **Sarlat-la-Canéda** (p198) Among France's best-preserved medieval architecture.
- **St-Paul de Vence** (p275) Hilltop village packed with beautiful people and art galleries on the French Riviera.
- **Èze** (p283) The hair-raising coastal drive here is as dramatic as the village itself.
- **Carcassonne** (p260) Be bewitched by the witches'-hat turrets of Languedoc's medieval icon.

BETHUNE CARMICHAEL

Château de Versailles (p95)

- St-Émilion (p302) Combine wine with medieval enchantment in this Unesco-listed village amid Bordeaux vines.

ARTIST PILGRIMAGE

- Maison et Jardins de Claude Monet, Giverny (p159) Monet's home for his last 43 years, with lily pond and beautiful gardens.
- Musée Matisse, Nice (p270) & Chapelle du Rosaire, Vence (p275) Essential stops on any Matisse tour in and around Nice.
- Atelier de Cézanne, Aix-en-Provence (p255) One of a trio of Cézanne sights in bourgeois Aix.
- Musée de Picasso, Antibes (p274) Striking seafront 12th-century château, turned Picasso studio.

CELEBRITY BEACHES

- Plage de l'Écluse, Dinard (p152) Join hip Parisians lounging on the sand in old-fashioned blue-and-white striped bathing tents.
- Promenade des Planches, Deauville (p161) Strut beachside with the rich and beautiful along this 643m-long boardwalk, lined with cabins named after American film stars.
- Bd de la Croisette, Cannes (p276) Beach after beach full of rich and famous guests stud this cinematic seafront.
- Plage de Pampelonne, St-Tropez (p280) Play Brigitte Bardot on the French Riviera.

- Grande Plage & Plage Mirimar, Biarritz (p312) The sand to be seen on in this cool-dude surf resort on the Atlantic.

ISLAND DAY-TRIPS

- Île de la Cité (p70) In the heart of Paris, no French island has two more famous churches than this.
- Île de Ré (p305) The island chic Parisians flock to at weekends.
- Belle Île (p146) Brittany's largest island, as beautifully *belle* as its name.
- Îles de Lérins (p276) The secret to escaping Cannes' madness.
- Îles d'Hyères (p282) Mediterranean–island trio offshore from the Riviera.

NATURAL WONDERS

- Mont Blanc (p221) Europe's mightiest peak, best viewed from ski-mad Chamonix.
- Massif de l'Estérel (p279) Burnt-red mountain range snug against the blue Med.
- Fontaine de Vaucluse (p265) The world's fifth most powerful spring, most dazzling after heavy rain.
- Gorges du Verdon (p266) Europe's largest canyon with emerald green waters, swooping eagles and dramatic driving.
- Dune du Pilat (p308) Romp like a sand bunny on Europe's largest sand dune.

THINGS YOU NEED TO KNOW

AT A GLANCE

- **ATMs** At every airport, most train stations and every other city street corner.
- **Credit Cards** Visa and MasterCard widely accepted.
- **Currency** Euro (€)
- **Language** French; some English spoken in tourist areas.
- **Plugs** Have two round pins, so bring an adaptor.
- **Smoking** No go in public places; yes go on alfresco café terraces.
- **Tipping** 10% for good service.
- **Visas** Not required for most nationalities.

ACCOMMODATION

- **Hotels** Wide range of budget, midrange and top-end choices in towns and cities; see p373.
- **Chambres d'Hôtes** What the French call a B&B, particularly popular in rural France; see p372.
- **Châteaux** The quintessential French, dreamy way to stay; generally upmarket hotels or chambres d'hôtes; see p373.

ADVANCE PLANNING

- **Three months before** Book flight (p384) and accommodation (p372); book tickets for 'gold-dust' festivals and sporting events.
- **One month before** Arrange car hire (p390) or ongoing train travel (p392); book festival tickets.
- **One week before** Take your pick of guided walks and tours, and snag a spot on the most popular. Ditto for Loire Vallley son et lumière (sound and light) shows and admission tickets to the Louvre, Versailles and other big sights.

BE FOREWARNED

- **Shops** Are all but shut on Sunday and public holidays; shops generally close for lunch too.
- **Restaurants** Few serve all day; orders are generally taken between noon and 2pm and 7pm to 10.30pm six days a week. Sunday evening and all day Monday are popular days to close.
- **Motorists in France** Drive on the right-hand side of the road. Pay tolls to use motorways (autoroutes).

COSTS

- **€60 per day** The minimum a budget traveller staying in hostels or cheap hotels and living on cheese and baguette can survive on.
- **€120 to €200** The price you pay for midrange hotels, restaurants and choice of museums.
- **More than €200** France is your oyster: top-end hotels, Michelin three-star dining, fancy nightclubs and cabarets, theatre tickets and so on.

EMERGENCY NUMBERS

- Fire ☎ 18
- Police ☎ 17
- Ambulance ☎ 15
- EU-wide central emergency ☎ 112 (English spoken)

GETTING AROUND

- Train Regular rail links between main towns and cities.
- Car Buys immediate freedom, flexibility and a ticket to the secret corners of rural France.
- Bicycle A hip way of navigating Paris, Lyon and other big cities. Particularly lovely trails link sights in the Loire Valley, Provence and Brittany.

GETTING THERE & AWAY

- Air Paris is where most land; for the southbound, aim for Nice or Marseille.
- Eurostar Puts Paris a mere 2½ hours from London.
- Ferries Plough the Channel from the UK to northern France.

TECH STUFF

- Wi-fi Is free in more and more hotels, train stations and airports.
- Wireless hotspots Track them down countrywide at www.wifinder.com.
- Internet cafes At least one in most towns (tourist offices have lists); pay €2 to €6 an hour to surf.
- Hotels Flagged in this guide with a computer icon (💻) tout a computer guests can use to get online.

TGV trains at Gare de Lyon (p392)

JEAN-BERNARD CARILLET

↘ WHAT TO BRING

- **Sunglasses, sunscreen, hat** and mosquito repellent for southern France
- **A brolly** for wet 'n' soggy Brittany, neighbouring northern climes and Paris
- **An adventurous appetite**, a pleasure-seeking palate, a thirst for good wine and a corkscrew for gourmet picnics
- **French phrasebook**
- **Valid travel insurance** (p378)
- **ID and passport** and a visa if required (p383)
- **Driving licence, car documents** and car insurance (p390)

↘ WHEN TO GO

- **Beat the crowds** April, May, June, September and October.
- **Worship the sun** June to early September in southern France.
- **Play snowballs and ski bunnies** Late December to late March or early April in the Alps.
- **Sizzle in traffic jams** July and August in the south of France.

KEVIN CLOGSTOUN

Buskers performing on street corner, Latin Quarter (p72), Paris

➤ GET INSPIRED

➤ BOOKS

- **A Motor Flight through France** (Edith Wharton) A pioneering automobile trip through belle époque France.
- **Another Long Day on the Piste** (Will Randal) Refreshingly different from the 'renovate-a-farmhouse' genre, this comedy details a season spent in a ski resort.
- **In the Merde for Love & Talk to the Snail** (Stephen Clarke) Dog poo on pavements, unnecessary bureaucracy, how to get served… Stephen Clarke spouts on about it.
- **Everybody Was So Young** (Amanda Vaill) Beautiful account of an American couple and their glam mates (Hemingway, Picasso etc) on the French Riviera in the 1920s.

➤ FILMS

- **La Môme** (La Vie en Rose; 2007) Portrayal of French singer Édith Piaf.
- **La Fabuleux Destin d'Amélie Poulain** (Amélie; 2001) This feel-good story takes viewers on a colourful tour of Montmartre with Parisian Amélie.
- **Subway** (1985), **Le Grand Bleu** (Big Blue; 1988), **Nikita** (1990) and **Jeanne d'Arc** (Joan of Arc; 1999) Pick from a list of Luc Besson box-office hits.
- **Bienvenue Les Ch'tis** (2008) The highest grossing film in French cinematic history looks at the regional differences between France's hot south and soggy north.

➤ MUSIC

- **Histoire de Melody Nelson** (Serge Gainsbourg; 1971) The best and most influential album of 1950s Parisian French *chansonnier* Gainsbourg.
- **Moon Safari** (AIR) Chill to this 1998 electronic classic by French duo AIR ('Amour, Imagination, Rêve').
- **Made in Medina** (Rachid Taha) Franco-Algerian singer.
- **L'Absente** (Yann Tielsen) Raw emotion by the multitalented Breton musician, a particular dab hand at film soundtracks.
- **Gibraltar** and **Dante** (Abd al Malik) No artist has cemented France's reputation in world music more than this Paris-born, Franco-Congolese rapper and slam poet.

➤ WEBSITES

- **France Guide** (http://us.franceguide.com) French government tourist office website.
- **French Word a Day** (http://french-word-a-day.typepad.com) Fun language learning.
- **Meg Zimbeck** (http://megzimbeck.com) On-the-ball snapshots of Parisian life.
- **SNCF** (www.sncf.com) France's national railways.
- **Motorist Information** (www.bison-fute-equipement.gouv.fr, in French) Road and traffic conditions, key motoring info.

↘ CALENDAR

| JAN | FEB | MAR | APR |

DAN HERRICK

Soldiers assembled for Bastille Day parade

↘ JANUARY

PARIS FASHION WEEK
Prêt-à-Porter, the ready-to-wear fashion salon held twice a year (in late January and again in September) is a must for fashion buffs. Find it in Paris' Parc des Expositions at Porte de Versailles in the 15th arrondissment (Ⓜ Porte de Versailles).

↘ FEBRUARY

CARNIVAL DE NICE
Merrymaking spills across the streets of Nice on the French Riviera during France's largest street carnival (p270), celebrated with gusto for two weeks. The brightly coloured float parade and firework displays are sights to behold indeed.

↘ MARCH–APRIL

FERIA PASCALE
In the ancient Roman amphitheatre of Arles (p256) in the Camargue, the annual bullfighting season kicks off with much cavorting and merriment during this vibrant Easter-time *feria*. As per local tradition, no blood is spilled.

↘ MAY–JUNE

MAY DAY 1 MAY
Across France, workers' day is celebrated with trade-union parades and diverse protests. People give each other *muguets* (lilies of the valley) for good luck. No one works – except waiters and *muguet* sellers.

CANNES FILM FESTIVAL
Stars and celebrities of world cinema walk the red carpet at Cannes, the

PLANNING YOUR TRIP

CALENDAR

biggest of Europe's see-and-be-seen cinema extravaganzas, during this two-week international film fest. Fans note, unless you're Angelina or Brad, the event is something of a closed shop.

PÉLERINAGE DES GITANS
24-25 MAY

Twice a year *gitans* (Roma Gitano people) from all over Europe make their way to Les-Stes-Maries-de-la-Mer in the Camargue, south of France, for a flamboyant street fiesta of music, dancing and dipping their toes in the sea. A second pilgrimage fills the same seaside town on the Sunday nearest 22 October.

FÊTE DE LA MUSIQUE   21 JUNE

Bands, orchestras, crooners, buskers and spectators take to the streets for this brilliant countrywide celebration (www.fetedelamusique.culture.fr, in

Paris Fashion Week
© TRINITY MIRROR / MIRRORPIX / ALAMY

French) of music that really does spill into the tiniest of hamlets and the biggest of towns.

◥ JULY

FESTIVAL D'AIX-EN-PROVENCE

This month-long festival (www.festival-aix.com) of international renown attracts some of the world's best classical music, opera, ballet and buskers. It takes to the stage late June to mid-July.

BASTILLE DAY   14 JULY

Fireworks, balls, processions (including a military and fire-brigade parade down Paris' Champs-Élysées) and all-round hoo-ha mark France's National Day, on the anniversary of the storming of the Bastille in 1789. Celebrations are countrywide.

FESTIVAL DE CANNES

Cannes Film Festival
RICHARD CUMMINS

CALENDAR

JAN   FEB   MAR   APR

FESTIVAL D'AVIGNON & FESTIVAL OFF

Actors, dancers and musicians from all over Europe flock to the papal city of Avignon in Provence to perform in this prestigious theatre festival (p263), held every year from early July to early August. Funky, fun and eclectic is its fringe fest, Festival Off.

NICE JAZZ FESTIVAL

See jazz cats and other pop, rock and world artists take over public spaces, parks, gardens and ancient olive groves in Nice during this sky-topped summer fest (p271) in mid-July.

PARIS PLAGES

For four weeks, mid-July to mid-August, three Seine-side waterfronts are decked out with sand or pebbles, sun beds, parasols and palm trees for Parisians to sun themselves in style on the beach. Beaches open 8am to midnight.

FÊTES DE BAYONNE

Bullfighting, cow-chasing and Basque music are the order of the day at Bayonne's biggest event (www.fetes -de-bayonne.com) held from late July to early August.

TOUR DE FRANCE

Since 1975 the last stage of the world's most prestigious cycling event (www .letour.fr) has ended with a sprint along av des Champs-Élysées on the third or fourth Sunday in July. Crowds galore gather to meet the cyclists.

AUGUST–SEPTEMBER

FÊTES D'ARVOR

Revel in street parades, concerts and numerous *festoù-noz* (night festivals) during this passionate celebration of local Breton culture that takes over Vannes in mid-August.

GREG ELMS

Mussel feast at Braderie de Lille

Tour de France

BRADERIE DE LILLE
Three days of mussel-munching as this colossal flea market (p125) engulfs the city with antiques, handicrafts and bric-a-brac during the first weekend in September.

FESTIVAL DU CINEMA AMÉRICAIN
The silver screen flickers next to the sea at this celebration of American cinema (www.festival-deauville.com) in trendy Deauville, the place where all cinematically hip Parisians flock in early September.

JOURNÉES DU PATRIMOINE
Each year on the third weekend in September, a treasure trove of historical buildings, gardens and other sights otherwise closed to the public open their doors during France's 'Days of Patrimony'.

☑ OCTOBER

NUIT BLANCHE
'White Night' is when Paris 'does' New York and becomes the city that doesn't sleep. The cultural fest lasts two days from sunrise until sundown on the first Saturday and Sunday of October, with museums joining bars and clubs in staying open until dawn.

☑ DECEMBER

ALSACE CHRISTMAS MARKETS
Colourful, traditional pre-Christmas markets and celebrations (last weekend in November through Christmas or New Year).

FÊTE DES LUMIÈRES
8 DECEMBER
France's biggest and best light show (www.lumieres.lyon.fr) transforms its second largest city, Lyon, into a beautiful mirage of twinkling candles on windowsills and public buildings illuminated a rainbow of colours.

PLANNING YOUR TRIP

CALENDAR

⬂ PARIS & ITS DAY TRIPS

GREATER PARIS

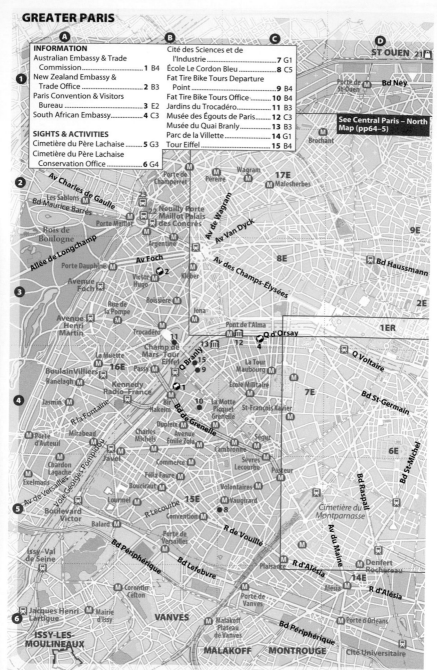

INFORMATION

Australian Embassy & Trade
 Commission **1** B4
New Zealand Embassy &
 Trade Office **2** B3
Paris Convention & Visitors
 Bureau **3** E2
South African Embassy **4** C3

SIGHTS & ACTIVITIES

Cimetière du Père Lachaise **5** G3
Cimetière du Père Lachaise
 Conservation Office **6** G4

Cité des Sciences et de
 l'Industrie **7** G1
École Le Cordon Bleu **8** C5
Fat Tire Bike Tours Departure
 Point **9** B4
Fat Tire Bike Tours Office **10** B4
Jardins du Trocadéro **11** B3
Musée des Égouts de Paris **12** C3
Musée du Quai Branly **13** B3
Parc de la Villette **14** G1
Tour Eiffel **15** B4

See Central Paris – North
Map (pp64–5)

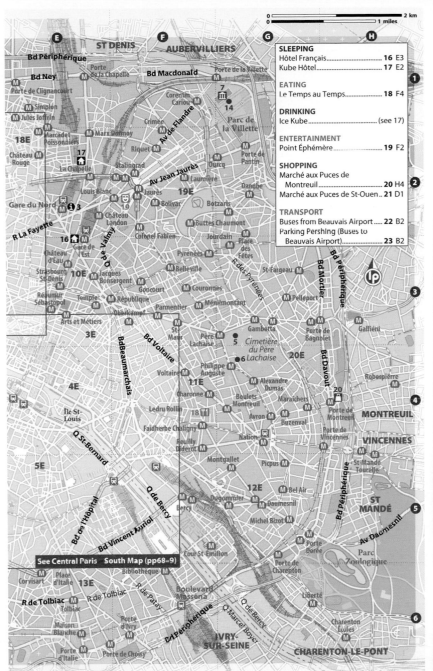

SLEEPING
Hôtel Français.............................. **16** E3
Kube Hôtel................................... **17** E2

EATING
Le Temps au Temps...................... **18** F4

DRINKING
Ice Kube......................................(see **17**)

ENTERTAINMENT
Point Éphémère............................ **19** F2

SHOPPING
Marché aux Puces de
  Montreuil.................................. **20** H4
Marché aux Puces de St-Ouen.. **21** D1

TRANSPORT
Buses from Beauvais Airport..... **22** B2
Parking Pershing (Buses to
  Beauvais Airport)...................... **23** B2

See Central Paris   South Map (pp68–9)

HIGHLIGHTS

1 THE LOUVRE

BY NIKO SALVATORE MELISSANO, MUSÉE DU LOUVRE

I've worked at the Louvre for 10 years and each day I still experience many emotions: we're in the heart of Paris; it is a magical place, charged with history and very intimate... The Louvre was a 12th-century fortress, then a royal palace, today one of the most famous art museums in the world, an unforgettable place with magnificent gardens.

↘ NIKO SALVATORE MELISSANO'S DON'T MISS LIST

❶ WINGED VICTORY OF SAMOTHRACE

It's impossible to reduce the collections of the Louvre to a hit parade... A definite highlight is the *Winged Victory of Samothrace* atop the Daru Staircase (1st floor, Denon Wing). I adore her wings. I just cannot stop contemplating her from all angles. She is, moreover, very photogenic.

❷ THE SEATED SCRIBE & MONA LISA

I could admire this statuette (room 22, 1st floor, Sully Wing) from the ancient Egyptian empire for hours. The face of the scribe (probably that of Saqqara), like his posture and his deep stare, say many things to me: serenity, strength of character, eternal wisdom.

Then there is *La Joconde* (Mona Lisa; Room 6, 1st floor, Salle de la Joconde, Denon Wing) and that amazing fascination of why and how she intrigues spirits with her mysteries.

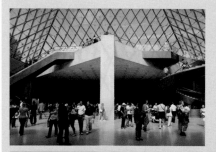

Clockwise from top: Pyramide Inversée by IM Pei (p66); Marble sculpture; Outside café tables; Galerie d'Apollon; Interior of IM Pei's glass Pyramide du Louvre (p66)

❸ COUR KHORSABAD

With its enormous human-headed winged bulls, this courtyard on the ground floor of the Richelieu Wing is a jump in time into the cradle of one of the oldest cultures in the world: Mesopotamia. During the region of King Sargon II in the 8th century, these bulls carved from alabaster guarded the Assyrian city and palace of Khorsabad (northern Iraq). Their beaded faces with bull ears and a heavy tiara of horns wore a benevolent smile. A mix of force and serenity, perfectly balanced despite their colossal size, these protective monsters with four or five paws were a measure of the power of the Assyrian Empire in its heyday.

❹ GRANDE GALERIE

It's a real highlight this gallery (1st floor, Denon Wing), with masterpieces from the great masters of the Italian Renaissance. For more on all these works of art, borrow the Louvre's multimedia guide (http://monguide.louvre .fr; adult/under 18yr €6/2) which makes for a fun visit at your own pace.

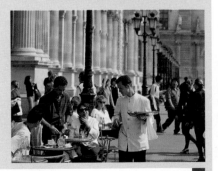

↘ THINGS YOU NEED TO KNOW

Hard facts 40 sq hectares, 5000 art works, 8 million annual visitors **The brutal truth** One visit can not cover all the collections and the Louvre's extraordinary cultural richness **Forward plan** Take time to prepare your visit; study www.louvre .fr to optimize your time accordingly **See our author's review on p63.**

HIGHLIGHTS

2 | VERSAILLES

BY SYLVAIN POSTOLLE, OFFICIAL GUIDE, CHÂTEAU DE VERSAILLES

Versailles, as official residence of the kings of France, is magnificent – the only place where the daily life of the monarchy before the French Revolution can really be felt. My favourite moment is the evening, after the crowds have gone, when I quietly walk from room to room lecturing to just a small group...extraordinary.

↘ SYLVAIN POSTOLLE'S DON'T MISS LIST

❶ KING'S PRIVATE APARTMENT

This is the most fascinating part of the palace as it shows the king as a man and very much reflects his daily life in the 18th century. Of the 10 or so rooms, the most famous is his bedroom where he not only slept but also held cere-monies. He had lunch here each day at 1pm and also supper, which up to 150 courtiers and people invited from outside the court would watch! By the 1780s, the king's life had become more private – he had an official supper just once a week on Sunday.

❷ KING LOUIS VXI'S LIBRARY

This is a lovely room – full of books, a place where you can really imagine the king coming to read for hours and hours. Louis XVI loved geography and his copy of *The Travels of James Cook* – in English – is still here.

❸ HERCULES SALON

I love one particular perspective inside the palace: from the Hercules Salon you can see all the rooms comprising the King's State Apartment, and to the right, through the gallery leading to

Clockwise from top: Parterre d'Eau sculpture in front of Château de Versailles; Grand Appartement; Geometric patterns in surrounding gardens; Galerie des Glaces (Hall of Mirrors); The palace overlooking manicured hedges

CLOCKWISE FROM TOP: DENNIS JOHNSON; JOHN ELK III; RUSSELL MOUNTFORD; GLENN BEANLAND; JOHN ELK III

the opera house. The salon served as a passageway in fact for the king to go from his state apartment to the chapel to celebrate daily mass.

❹ THE ROYAL CHAPEL

This is an exquisite example of the work of a very important architect of the time, Jules Hardouin-Mansart (1646–1708). The paintings, very representative of art fashions at the end of the reign of Louis XIV, are also stunning: they evoke the idea that the French king was chosen by God and as such was his lieutenant on earth. This is the chapel where, in 1770, the future king Louis XVI wed Marie Antoinette in 1770 – the beginning of the French Revolution.

❺ ENCELADE GROVE

Versailles' gardens are extraordinary but my favourite spot is this grove by André Le Nôtre. A gallery of trellises surround a pool with a statue of Enceladus, chief of the Titans who was punished for his pride by the gods from Mount Olympus. When the fountains are on, it's impressive.

⭷ THINGS YOU NEED TO KNOW

Long queues Avoid by arriving early morning or after 4pm **Day to avoid** Tuesday when many Paris museums are closed, making Versailles queues *even worse* **Absolute must** Buy tickets in advance on www.chateauversailles.fr, from a branch of Fnac or an SNCF train station **See our author's review on p95.**

HIGHLIGHTS

3

⬊ NOTRE DAME

This magnificent **cathedral** (p71) is Paris' most visited site. Not just a masterpiece of French Gothic architecture, it has been the focus of Catholic Paris for seven centuries. Best up is its sublime balance: meander to Square Jean XXIII, the lovely little park behind the cathedral, and let your soul fly with an extraordinary mirage of flying buttresses encircling the cathedral's chancel, walls and roof.

4

⬊ CENTRE POMPIDOU

Not only can you admire fabulous modern art and spectacular rooftop views at this **architectural stunner** (p66), the talk of the town for years after it opened. The surrounding streets and squares buzz with cafés; buskers, musicians, jugglers and mime artists (place Georges Pompidou); and fanciful mechanical fountains of skeletons, hearts, treble clefs and a big pair of ruby-red lips (place Igor Stravinsky).

↘ EIFFEL TOWER

It was only the fact that it was a perfect platform for the transmitting antennas needed for the new science of radiotelegraphy that saved the 'metal asparagus', as many Parisians in 1909 snidely called it, from being ripped down. A century on, 7 million visitors a year make their way to the top of this **iconic landmark** (p76), more Parisian than Paris itself.

↘ THE SEINE

There are 101 different ways to woo **France's most timeless river**, a Unesco World Heritage Site. Walk, bike or sail along it (p77); revel in its riverbanks' richest museum, the architecturally stunning **Musée du Quai Branly** (p76); brunch on the quays at La Baba Bourgeois (p85); frolic in **Jardin des Tuileries** (p75); or flop on the sand during **Paris Plages** (p48).

↘ STE-CHAPELLE & CHARTRES

Be stunned and inspired by the veritable wall of sublime stained glass in Paris' **Ste-Chapelle** (p72), one of Christendom's most beautiful places of worship. Then head out of town to Chartres where you can't get bluer than the awesome stained-glass windows of **Cathédrale Notre Dame de Chartres** (p98).

3 & 6 JOHN ELK III; 4 JEAN-BERNARD CARILLET; 5 KEVIN CLOGSTOUN; 7 GLENN BEANLAND

3 Cathédrale de Notre Dame de Paris (p71); 4 Jean Tinguely sculpture, Centre National d'Art et de Culture Georges Pompidou (p66); 5 Gilded figures gaze towards the Eiffel Tower (p76); 6 River Seine; 7 Ste-Chapelle (p72)

THE BEST...

↘ PARISIAN CAFÉ LIFE

- **Les Deux Magots** (p88) Too famous, but a must-visit-once address in literary St-German des Près.
- **Le Bistrot du Peintre** (p88) A favourite since the belle époque.
- **Le Café qui Parle** (p87) Best for breakfast and brunch.

↘ CAPITAL VIEWS

- **Cathédrale de Notre Dame de Paris** (p71) Scale 422 steps inside the cathedral's north tower for a view of Paris you'll never forget.
- **Arc de Triomphe** (p//) Little-known fact: you can climb to the top of the arch.
- **Eiffel Tower** (p76) Has to be done at least once by lift or on foot.
- **Tour Montparnasse** (p74) Spectacular views of the capital atop an eyesore 1970s skyscraper.
- **Basilique du Sacré Cœur** (p77) Spiral 234 steps up into the dome of this iconic basilica in Montmartre.

↘ TRADITIONAL BISTROS

- **Le Trumilou** (p83) A century-old with same-era dishes to match.
- **Bofinger** (p83) Paris' oldest, born 1864.
- **Bouillon Racine** (p85) An art nouveau 'soup kitchen' from 1906; end with an old-fashioned sherbet.
- **Le Roi du Pot au Feu** (p86) The address for authentic *pot au feu*.
- **Polidor** (p85) The most famous *tarte tatin* in Paris.

↘ PARISIAN QUIRK

- **Catacombes** (p74) Skulls are everywhere.
- **Musée des Égouts de Paris** (p76) Immerse yourself in Paris' sewage system.
- **Paris Walks** (p79) Explore from a different perspective: fashion, chocolate, French Revolution…

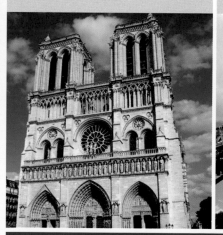

Left: Cathédrale de Notre Dame de Paris (p71); Right: Eiffel Tower (p76)

THINGS YOU NEED TO KNOW

⤷ VITAL STATISTICS

- **Population** 2.177 million
- **Best time to visit** April to June, September and December

⤷ ADVANCE PLANNING

- **As early as possible** Book accommodation (p79).
- **One week before** Cut queues in situ by buying admission tickets online for Château de Versailles (p95) and the Louvre (p63); book city tour (p77).

⤷ RESOURCES

- **Paris Convention & Visitors Bureau** (www.parisinfo.com) City tourist office.
- **Espace du Tourisme d'Île de France** (☎ 01 44 50 19 98; www .new-paris-ile-de-france.co.uk; Galerie du Carrousel du Louvre, 99 rue de Rivoli, 1er; Ⓜ Palais Royal-Musée du Louvre; ⏱ 10am-6pm) Tourist office for surrounding Île de France area.
- **Go Go** (www.gogoparis.com) 'Fashion, food, arts, gigs, gossip.'
- **Paris.fr** (www.paris.fr) Paris city information.

⤷ EMERGENCY

- **Ambulance** ☎ 15
- **Fire** ☎ 18
- **Police** ☎ 17
- **SOS Helpline** (☎ 01 47 23 80 80, in English; ⏱ 3-11pm daily)
- **Urgences Médicales de Paris** (Medical Emergencies; ☎ 01 53 94 94 94; www.ump.fr)

⤷ GETTING AROUND

- **Metro & RER** (pp94-5) Get around underground between 5.30am and midnight.
- **Bicycle** The capital's self-service bike rental scheme Vélib' (p94) makes freewheeling a breeze (and a joy).
- **Boats** cruise along the Seine (p77).

⤷ BE FOREWARNED

- **Museums** Closed Monday or Tuesday (days to avoid Versailles); *all* Paris museums and monuments shut their doors 30 minutes to one hour before listed closing times.
- **Bars & Cafés** A drink costs more sitting at a table than standing, more on a fancy square than a backstreet.
- **Shopaholics** Note: sales start mid-January and second week of June.
- **Metro stations** Worth skipping late at night: Châtelet–Les Halles and its seemingly endless corridors, Château Rouge (Montmartre), Gare du Nord, Strasbourg St-Denis, Réaumur Sébastopol and Montparnasse Bienvenüe.

DISCOVER PARIS & ITS DAY TRIPS

Claiming more famous landmarks than any other city in the world, the French capital evokes all sorts of expectations for first-time visitors: of grand vistas, of intellectuals discussing weighty matters in cafés, of romance along the Seine, of naughty nightclub revues, of rude people who won't speak English. If you look hard enough, you can probably find all of those. But another approach is to set aside the preconceptions of Paris that are so much a part of English-speaking culture, and to explore the city's avenues and backstreets as though the tip of the Eiffel Tower or the spire of Notre Dame Cathedral weren't about to pop into view at any moment. You will soon discover that Paris is enchanting almost everywhere, at any time.

ORIENTATION

Paris is divided into 20 arrondissements (districts). In this chapter, the respective arrondissement numbers are given after a street address using the usual French notation: 1er for *premier* (1st), 2e for *deuxième* (2nd), 3e for *troisième* (3rd) and so on.

PARIS IN...

Two Days

If you only have a couple of days in Paris (bad decision, that one) you should join a morning **tour** (p78) and then concentrate on the most Parisian of sights and attractions: **Notre Dame** (p71), the **Louvre** (p63), the **Eiffel Tower** (p76) and the **Arc de Triomphe** (p77). In the late afternoon have a coffee or a pastis (aniseed-flavoured aperitif) on the **av des Champs-Élysées** (p77) and then make your way to **Montmartre** (p77) for dinner. The following day take in such sights as the **Musée d'Orsay** (p74), **Ste-Chapelle** (p72), **Conciergerie** (p72), **Musée National du Moyen Âge** (p73) and/or the **Musée Rodin** (p76). Have brunch on the **place des Vosges** (p67) and enjoy a night of mirth and gaiety in the **Marais** (p67).

Four Days

With another couple of days to look around the city, you should consider a **cruise** (p77-8) along the Seine or Canal St-Martin and visit some place further afield – the **Cimetière du Père Lachaise** (p78), say, or **Parc de la Villette** (p75). On one of the two nights take in a concert, opera or ballet at the **Palais Garnier** (p91) or **Opéra Bastille** (p90). The **Bastille area** (p67) is another option for a night out.

A Week

If you have one week in the French capital, you can see a good many of the major sights listed in this chapter, visit places around Paris such **Fontainebleau** (p96), and, if you travel hard and fast, **Chartres** (p98) with **Versailles** (p95).

INFORMATION
TOURIST INFORMATION

The main branch of the **Paris Convention & Visitors Bureau** (Office de Tourisme et de Congrès de Paris; Map pp68-9; ☎ 08 92 68 30 00; www.parisinfo.com; 25-27 rue des Pyramides, 1er; Ⓜ Pyramides; ⊙ 9am-7pm Jun-Oct, 10am-7pm Mon-Sat & 11am-7pm Sun Nov-May, closed 1 May) is 500m northwest of the Louvre. The bureau also maintains centres elsewhere in Paris (telephone numbers and websites are the same as for the main office).

Gare de Lyon (Map pp68-9; Hall d'Arrivée, 20 bd Diderot, 12e; Ⓜ Gare de Lyon; ⊙ 8am-6pm Mon-Sat, closed Sun & 1 May) In the mainline trains arrivals hall.

Gare du Nord (Map pp52-3; 18 rue de Dunkerque, 10e; Ⓜ Gare du Nord; ⊙ 8am-6pm, closed Christmas Day, New Year's Day & 1 May) Beneath the glass roof of the Île de France departures and arrivals area at the eastern end of the train station.

Syndicat d'Initiative de Montmartre (Map pp64-5; ☎ 01 42 62 21 21; 21 place du Tertre, 18e; Ⓜ Abbesses; ⊙ 10am-7pm) This locally run tourist office and shop is in Montmartre's most picturesque square and is open year-round.

SIGHTS
LOUVRE & LES HALLES
MUSÉE DU LOUVRE

The Palais du Louvre was constructed as a fortress in the early 13th century and rebuilt in the mid-16th century for use as a royal residence. In 1793 the Revolutionary Convention transformed the building into

CLOCKWISE FROM TOP: BRUCE BI; WILL SALTER; JOHN ELK III; KARL BLACKWELL

Clockwise from top: Musée du Louvre; mural at Bastille metro station; Arc de Triomphe (p77); Musée d'Orsay (p74)

CENTRAL PARIS – NORTH

INFORMATION
Bienvenue à la Ferme	**1** B6
Canadian Embassy	**2** B6
Espace IGN	**3** B5
Fédération Nationale des Gîtes de France	**4** F4
Japanese Consulate	**5** B3
Pharmacie des Champs	**6** B5
Syndicat d'Initiative de Montmartre	**7** G2
UK Consulate	**8** D5
UK Embassy & Trade Office	**9** D5
US Consulate	**10** E6
US Embassy & Trade Office	**11** D5

SIGHTS & ACTIVITIES
Arc de Triomphe	**12** A4
Basilique du Sacré Cœur	**13** G2
Basilique du Sacré Cœur Dome Entrance	**14** G2
Bateau Lavoir	**15** G2
Bateaux Mouches	**16** B6
Cimetière de Montmartre Entrance & Conservation Office	**17** F2

Cours de Cuisine Olivier Berté	**18** G5
École Ritz Escoffier	**19** E5
Flamme de la Liberté	**20** B6
Galeries du Panthéon Bouddhique du Japon et de la Chine	**21** A6
Jardin des Tuileries	**22** E6
Jardin du Palais Royal	**23** G6
L'Open Tour	**24** E4
Musée de l'Orangerie	**25** E6
Palais de Tokyo	**26** A6
Place de la Concorde Obelisk	**27** D6

SLEEPING
Hôtel Bonséjour Montmartre	**28** F2
Hôtel des Arts	**29** F2
Hôtel Favart	**30** G5
Hôtel Résidence des 3 Poussins	**31** G3
Hôtel Utrillo	**32** F2
Hôtel Vivienne	**33** G5

EATING
Bistrot du Sommelier	**34** D4
Chartier	**35** G5

Chez Toinette	**36** G2
Fromagerie Alléosse	**37** A3
La Mascotte	**38** F2
L'Ardoise	**39** E6
Le Café Qui Parle	**40** F2
Le Grand Colbert	**41** G6
Le Roi du Pot au Feu	**42** E4
L'Étoile Verte	**43** A4

DRINKING
Harry's New York Bar	**44** F5

ENTERTAINMENT
Fnac Champs-Élysées	**45** B5
Kiosque Théâtre Madeleine	**46** E5
Le Lido de Paris	**47** B4
Le Limonaire	**48** H5
Moulin Rouge	**49** F2
Palais Garnier	**50** F5
Palais Garnier Box Office	(see 50)
Salle Pleyel	**51** B4
Social Club	**52** G5
Virgin Megastore Barbès	**53** H2
Virgin Megastore Champs-Élysées	**54** B5

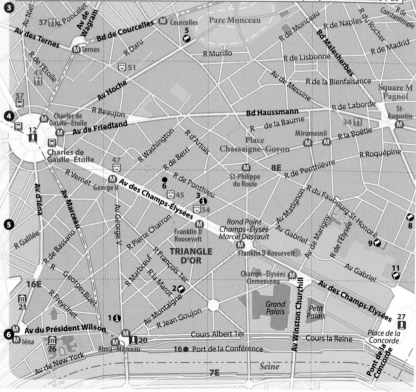

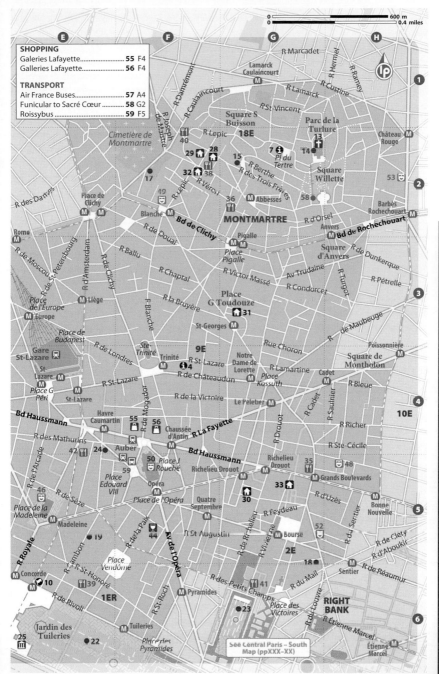

SHOPPING

TRANSPORT

See Central Paris – South
Map (ppXXX–XX)

the **Musée du Louvre** (Louvre Museum; Map pp68-9; ☎ 01 40 20 53 17; www.louvre.fr; Ⓜ Palais Royal-Musée du Louvre; permanent collections/permanent collections & temporary exhibitions €9/13, after 6pm Wed & Fri €6/11, permanent collections free for under 18yr & after 6pm Fri for under 26yr, admission free 1st Sun of month; ☽ 9am-6pm Mon, Thu, Sat & Sun, 9am-10pm Wed & Fri), the nation's first national museum.

The paintings, sculptures and artefacts on display in the Louvre Museum have been assembled by French governments over the past five centuries. Among them are works of art and artisanship from all over Europe and important collections of Assyrian, Etruscan, Greek, Coptic and Islamic art and antiquities. Traditionally the Louvre's raison d'être is to present Western art from the Middle Ages to about the year 1848 (at which point the Musée d'Orsay takes over), as well as the works of ancient civilisations that informed Western art.

The Louvre may be the most actively avoided museum in the world. Most people do their duty and come, but many leave overwhelmed, unfulfilled, exhausted and frustrated at having got lost on their way to da Vinci's *La Joconde,* better known as *Mona Lisa* (room 6, 1st floor, Salle de la Joconde, Denon Wing).

The most famous works from antiquity include the *Code of Hammurabi* (room 3, ground floor, Richelieu Wing) and that armless duo, the *Venus de Milo* (room 7, ground floor, Denon Wing) and the *Winged Victory of Samothrace* (opposite room 1, 1st floor, Denon Wing). From the Renaissance, don't miss Michelangelo's *The Dying Slave* (ground floor, Michelangelo Gallery, Denon Wing) and works by Raphael, Botticelli and Titian (1st floor, Denon Wing). French masterpieces of the 19th century include Ingres' *The Turkish Bath* (room 60, 2nd floor, Sully Wing), Géricault's *The Raft of the Medusa* (room 77, 1st floor, Denon Wing) and works by Corot, Delacroix and Fragonard (2nd floor, Denon Wing).

The main entrance and ticket windows in the Cour Napoléon are covered by the 21m-high **Pyramide du Louvre**, a glass pyramid designed by the Chinese-born American architect IM Pei. You can avoid the queues outside the pyramid or at the Porte des Lions entrance by entering the complex via the Carrousel du Louvre shopping centre entrance at 99 rue de Rivoli, or by following the 'Musée du Louvre' exit from the Palais Royal-Musée du Louvre metro station. Buy in advance from the ticket machines in the Carrousel du Louvre or, for an extra €1.10, online, from Fnac (see p88) or by telephone (☎ 08 92 68 36 22 or ☎ 08 25 34 63 46), and walk straight in without queuing. Tickets are valid for the whole day, so you can come and go as you please.

The centrepiece of the **Carrousel du Louvre** (Map pp68-9; ☎ 01 43 16 47 10; www.carrouseldulouvre.com; 99 rue de Rivoli; ☽ 8am-11pm), the shopping centre that runs underground from the pyramid to the **Arc de Triomphe du Carrousel** (Map pp68–9) in the Jardin du Carrousel, is the glass **Pyramide Inversée** (Inverted Pyramid), also created by Pei.

English-language guided tours (☎ 01 40 20 52 63) lasting 1½ hours depart from the area under the Grande Pyramide, marked 'Acceuil des Groupes' (Reception for Groups). Tickets cost €5 in addition to the cost of admission. Sign up at least 30 minutes before departure time.

CENTRE POMPIDOU

The **Centre National d'Art et de Culture Georges Pompidou** (Georges Pompidou National Centre of Art & Culture; Map pp68-9; ☎ 01 44 78 12 33; www.centrepompidou.fr; place Georges Pompidou, 4e; Ⓜ Rambuteau) has amazed and delighted visitors since it was inaugurated in 1977, not just for its outstanding collection of modern art, but also for its radical architectural statement.

The **Forum du Centre Pompidou** (admission free; 🕙 11am-10pm Wed-Mon), the open space at ground level, has temporary exhibitions and information desks. The 4th and 5th floors of the centre house the **Musée National d'Art Moderne** (MNAM, National Museum of Modern Art; Map pp68-9; adult €10-12, senior & 18-25yr €8-10, admission free under 18yr, 6-9pm Wed for 18-25yr, 1st Sun of month for all; 🕙 11am-9pm Wed-Mon), France's national collection of art dating from 1905 onwards.

ÉGLISE ST-EUSTACHE
One of the most beautiful churches in Paris, the majestic **Église St-Eustache** (Map pp68-9; ☎ 01 42 36 31 05; www.st-eustache.org, in French; 2 impasse St-Eustache, 1er; Ⓜ Les Halles; 🕙 9.30am-7pm Mon-Fri, 10am-7pm Sat, 9am-7.15pm Sun), constructed between 1532 and 1637, is primarily Gothic. Inside, there are some exceptional Flamboyant Gothic arches holding up the ceiling of the chancel. The gargantuan organ above the west entrance, with 101 stops and 8000 pipes, is used for concerts (long a tradition here) and during High Mass on Sunday (11am and 6.30pm).

MARAIS & BASTILLE
The Marais, the area of the Right Bank north of Île St-Louis in the 3e and 4e, was exactly what its name implies – 'marsh' or 'swamp' – until the 13th century, when it was converted to farmland. In the early 17th century, Henri IV built the place Royale (today's place des Vosges), turning the area into Paris' most fashionable residential district. The Marais has become a much desired address in recent years, while remaining the centre of Paris' gay life and home to a long-established Jewish neighbourhood called the Pletzl.

Place des Vosges (Map pp68-9; Ⓜ St-Paul or Bastille) is an ensemble of three dozen symmetrical houses with ground-floor arcades, steep slate roofs and large dormer windows arranged around a large square. The author Victor Hugo lived at the **Maison de Victor Hugo** (Victor Hugo House; Map pp68-9; ☎ 01 42 72 10 16; www.musee-hugo.paris.fr, in French; permanent collections admission free, temporary exhibitions adult/14-26yr/senior & student/under 14yr €7.50/5.50/3.50/free; 🕙 10am-6pm Tue-Sun), now devoted to the life and times of the celebrated novelist and poet.

One of Paris' best-loved art museums, the **Musée Picasso** (Picasso Museum; Map pp68-9; ☎ 01 42 71 25 21; www .musee-picasso .fr, in French; 5 rue de Thorigny, 3e; Ⓜ St-Paul or Chemin Vert; adult/18-25yr/under 18yr €7.70/5.70/ free, admission free 1st Sun of month; 🕙 9.30am-

WILL SALTER
Henri de Miller sculpture, Église St-Eustache

CENTRAL PARIS – SOUTH

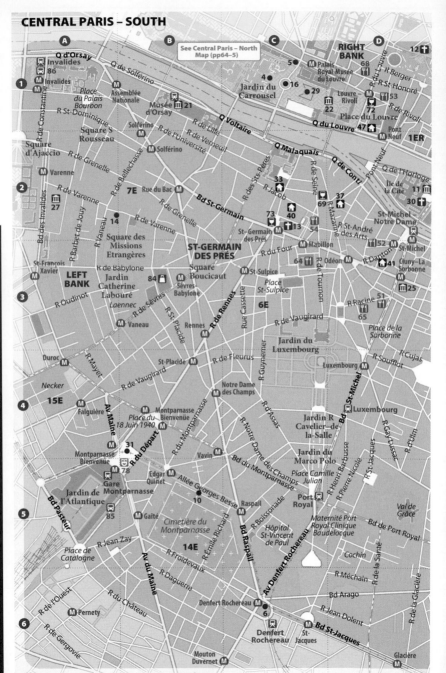

See Central Paris – North Map (pp64–5)

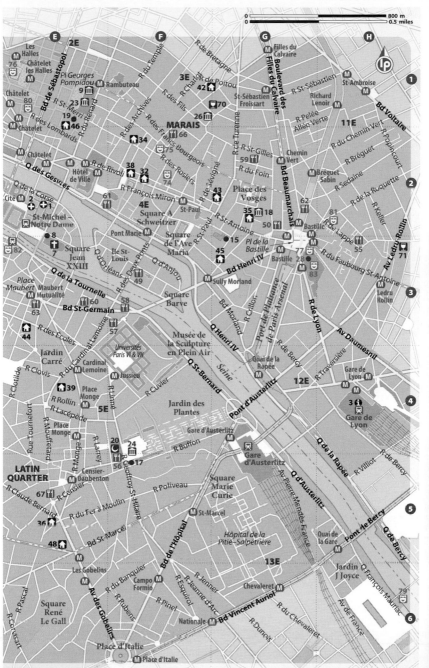

6pm Wed-Mon Apr-Sep, 9.30am-5.30pm Wed-Mon Oct-Mar) includes more than 3500 of the *grand maître's* engravings, paintings, ceramic works, drawings and sculptures.

The Bastille, built during the 14th century as a fortified royal residence, is probably the most famous monument in Paris that no longer exists; the notorious prison was demolished by a Revolutionary mob on 14 July 1789. **Place de la Bastille (Map pp68-9; Ⓜ Bastille),** where the prison once stood, is now a very busy traffic roundabout.

THE ISLANDS

Paris' twin set of islands could not be more different. Île de la Cité (Map pp68–9) is bigger, full of sights and very touristed (though very few people actually live here). Île St-Louis (Map pp68–9) is residential and much quieter, with just enough boutiques and restaurants – and a legendary ice-cream maker (p84) – to attract visitors.

ÎLE DE LA CITÉ

The site of the first settlement in Paris, around the 3rd century BC, and later the Roman town of Lutèce (Lutetia), the Île de la Cité remained the centre of royal and ecclesiastical power even after the city spread to both banks of the Seine during the Middle Ages. The buildings on the middle part of the island were demolished and rebuilt during Baron Haussmann's great urban renewal scheme of the late 19th century.

NOTRE DAME CATHEDRAL

The **Cathédrale de Notre Dame de Paris** (Cathedral of Our Lady of Paris; Map pp68-9; ☎ 01 42 34 56 10; www.cathe draledeparis.com; place du Parvis Notre Dame, 4e; Ⓜ Cité; audioguide €5; ⊗ 7.45am-6.45pm) is the true heart of Paris. Constructed on a site occupied by earlier churches – and, a millennium before that, a Gallo-Roman temple – it was begun in 1163. The interior alone is 130m long, 48m wide and 35m high and can accommodate more than 6000 worshippers.

Inside, exceptional features include three spectacular **rose windows**. The central choir, with its carved wooden stalls and statues representing the Passion of the Christ, is also noteworthy. There are free 1½-hour guided tours of the cathedral in English at noon on Wednesday and Thursday and at 2.30pm on Saturday.

The **trésor** (treasury; adult/3-12yr/student €3/1/2; ⊗ 9.30am-6pm Mon-Sat, 1-6pm Sun) contains artwork, liturgical objects, church plate and first-class relics – some of them of questionable origin. Among these is the Ste-Couronne, the 'Holy Crown' – purportedly the wreath of thorns placed on Jesus' head before he was crucified – which was brought here in the mid-13th century. It is exhibited between 3pm and 4pm on the first Friday of each month, 3pm to 4pm every Friday during Lent and 10am to 5pm on Good Friday.

The entrance to the **tours de Notre Dame** (Notre Dame towers; ☎ 01 53 10 07 02; www

DIANA MAYFIELD

Central portal, Cathédrale de Notre Dame de Paris

.monuments-nation aux.fr; rue du Cloître Notre Dame; adult/18-25yr/under 18yr €7.50/4.80/free, admission free 1st Sun of the month Oct-Mar; ⊗ 10am-6.30pm daily Apr-Jun & Sep, 9am-7.30pm Mon-Fri, 9am-11pm Sat & Sun Jul & Aug, 10am-5.30pm daily Oct-Mar), which can be climbed, is from the **North Tower**, to the right and around the corner as you walk out of the cathedral's main doorway. The 422 spiralling steps bring you

PARIS & ITS DAY TRIPS

SIGHTS

VIEWINGS AT A DISCOUNT

The **Paris Museum Pass** (www.parismuseumpass.fr; 2/4/6 days €30/45/60) is valid for entry to some 38 venues in Paris, including the Louvre, Centre Pompidou, Musée d'Orsay and Musée du Quai Branly. Outside the city limits, it will get you into another 22 places, including parts of Versailles (p95) and Fontainebleau (p96). The pass is available online as well as from branches of the Paris Convention & Visitors Bureau (p63) and major metro stations.

PARIS & ITS DAY TRIPS

SIGHTS

Palais du Luxembourg at Jardin du Luxembourg

to the top of the west facade, where you'll find yourself face to face with many of the cathedral's most frightening gargoyles, the 13-tonne bell Emmanuel (all the cathedral's bells are named) in the **South Tower**, and a spectacular view of Paris.

STE-CHAPELLE

The most exquisite of Paris' Gothic monuments, **Ste-Chapelle** (Holy Chapel; Map pp68-9; ☎ 01 53 40 60 97; www.monuments-nationaux.fr; 4 bd du Palais, 1er; Ⓜ Cité; adult/18-25yr/under 18yr €6.50/4.50/free, admission free 1st Sun of month Oct-Mar; ⓧ 9.30am-6pm Mar-Oct, 9am-5pm Nov-Feb) is tucked away within the walls of the **Palais de Justice** (Law Courts). The 'walls' of the **upper chapel** are sheer curtains of richly coloured and finely detailed **stained glass**, which bathe the chapel in extraordinary coloured light on a sunny day. Built in just under three years (compared with nearly 200 years for Notre Dame), Ste-Chapelle was consecrated in 1248. The chapel was conceived by Louis IX to house his personal collection of holy relics (now kept in the treasury of Notre Dame).

CONCIERGERIE

Built as a royal palace in the 14th century for the concierge of the Palais de la Cité, the **Conciergerie** (Map pp68-9; ☎ 01 53 40 60 97; www.monu ments-nationaux.fr; 2 bd du Palais, 1er; Ⓜ Cité; adult/18-25yr/under 18yr €8/6/free, admission free 1st Sun of month Oct-Mar; ⓧ 9.30am-6pm Mar-Oct, 9am-5pm Nov-Feb) was the main prison during the Reign of Terror (1793–94). Among the 2700 prisoners held in the *cachots* (dungeons) here before being sent to the guillotine were Queen Marie-Antoinette (see a reproduction of her cell).

A joint ticket with Ste-Chapelle costs adult/18 to 25 years €11.50/9.

LATIN QUARTER & JARDIN DES PLANTES

The centre of Parisian higher education since the Middle Ages, the Latin Quarter is so called because conversation between students and professors until the Revolution was in Latin. To the southeast, the Jardin des Plantes, with its tropical greenhouses, offers a bucolic alternative to the chalkboards and cobblestones.

MUSÉE NATIONAL DU MOYEN ÂGE

The **Musée National du Moyen Âge** (National Museum of the Middle Ages; Map pp68-9; ☎ 01 53 73 78 00; www .musee-moyenage.fr; 6 place Paul Painlevé, 5e; Ⓜ Cluny-La Sorbonne or St-Michel; adult/18-25yr/under 18yr €7.50/5.50/free, admission free 1st Sun of month; ☽ 9.15am-5.45pm Wed-Mon) is housed in two structures: the **frigidarium** (cooling room) and other remains of Gallo-Roman baths dating from around AD 200, and the late-15th-century **Hôtel de Cluny**, considered the finest example of medieval civil architecture in Paris.

The spectacular displays at the museum include statuary, illuminated manuscripts, weapons, furnishings, and objets d'art made of gold, ivory and enamel. But nothing compares with *La Dame à la Licorne* (The Lady with the Unicorn), a sublime series of late-15th-century tapestries from the southern Netherlands now hung in circular room 13 on the 1st floor.

JARDIN DES PLANTES

Paris' 24-hectare **Jardin des Plantes** (Botanical Garden; Map pp68-9; ☎ 01 40 79 56 01, 01 40 79 54 79; 57 rue Cuvier & 3 quai St-Bernard, 5e; Ⓜ Gare d'Austerlitz, Censier Daubenton or Jussieu; ☽ 8am-5.30pm, to 8pm in summer) was founded in 1626 as a medicinal herb garden for Louis XIII.

Created by a decree of the Revolutionary Convention in 1793, the **Musée National d'Histoire Naturelle** (National Museum of Natural History; Map pp68-9; ☎ 01 40 79 30 00; www.mnhn.fr, in French; 57 rue Cuvier, 5e; Ⓜ Censier Daubenton or Gare d'Austerlitz) is along the southern edge of the Jardin des Plantes. A highlight for kids, the museum's **Grande Galerie de l'Évolution** (Great Gallery of Evolution; 36 rue Geoffroy St-Hilaire, 5e; adult/4-13yr/under 4yr €8/6/free; ☽ 10am-6pm Wed-Mon) has some imaginative exhibits on evolution and humankind's effect on the global ecosystem.

MOSQUÉE DE PARIS

With its striking 26m-high minaret, the central **Mosquée de Paris** (Paris Mosque; Map pp68-9; ☎ 01 45 35 97 33; www.mosquee-de-paris .org; 2bis place du Puits de l'Ermite, 5e; Ⓜ Censier Daubenton or Place Monge; adult/senior & 7-25yr/under 7yr €3/2/free; ☽ 9am-noon & 2-6pm Sat-Thu) was built in 1926 in the ornate Moorish style. Visitors must be modestly dressed and remove their shoes at the entrance to the prayer hall. The complex includes a North African–style *salon de thé* (tearoom) and restaurant (p85) and a **hammam** (☎ 01 43 31 38 20; admission €15; ☽ men 2-9pm Tue & 10am-9pm Sun, women 10am-9pm Mon, Wed, Thu & Sat, 2-9pm Fri), a traditional Turkish-style bathhouse.

ST-GERMAIN, ODÉON & LUXEMBOURG

Centuries ago the Église St-Germain des Prés and its affiliated abbey owned most of today's 6e and 7e. The neighbourhood around the church began to develop in the late 17th century, and these days it is celebrated for its heterogeneity. Cafés such as Les Deux Magots (p88) were favourite hang-outs of postwar Left Bank intellectuals and the birthplaces of existentialism.

Paris' oldest church, the Romanesque **Église St-Germain des Prés** (Church of St Germanus of the Fields; Map pp68-9; ☎ 01 55 42 81 33; 3 place St-Germain des Prés, 6e; Ⓜ St-Germain des Prés; ☽ 8am-7pm Mon-Sat, 9am-8pm Sun) was built in the 11th century on the site of a 6th-century abbey.

When the weather is fine, Parisians of all ages come flocking to the formal terraces and chestnut groves of the 23-hectare **Jardin du Luxembourg** (Luxembourg Garden; Map pp68-9; Ⓜ Luxembourg; ☽ 7.30am to 8.15am–5pm to 10pm according to the season) to read, relax and sunbathe.

MONTPARNASSE

After WWI, writers, poets and artists of the avant-garde abandoned Montmartre on the Right Bank and crossed the Seine, shifting the centre of artistic ferment to the area around bd du Montparnasse.

A steel-and-smoked-glass eyesore that was built in 1974, the 210m-high **Tour Montparnasse** (Montparnasse Tower; Map pp68-9; ☎ 01 45 38 52 56; www.tourmontparnasse56.com; rue de l'Arrivée, 15e; Ⓜ Montparnasse Bienvenüe; adult/student & 16-20yr/7-15yr/under 7yr €9.50/6.80/4/free; Ⓨ 9.30am-11.30pm daily Apr-Sep, 9.30am-10.30pm Sun-Thu, 9.30am-11pm Fri & Sat Oct-Mar) affords spectacular views over the city – a view, we might add, that does not take in this ghastly oversized lipstick tube.

The **Cimetière du Montparnasse** (Montparnasse Cemetery; Map pp68-9; bd Edgar Quinet & rue Froidevaux, 14e; Ⓜ Edgar Quinet or Raspail; Ⓨ 8am-6pm Mon-Fri, 8.30am-6pm Sat, 9am-6pm Sun mid-Mar–early Nov, 8am-5.30pm Mon-Fri, 8.30am-5.30pm Sat, 9am-5.30pm Sun early Nov–mid-Mar) contains the tombs of such illustrious personages as writer Guy de Maupassant, playwright Samuel Beckett, sculptor Constantin Brancusi, photographer Man Ray, industrialist André Citroën, philosopher Jean-Paul Sartre, writer Simone de Beauvoir and the crooner Serge Gainsbourg.

In 1785 it was decided to solve the hygiene and aesthetic problems posed by Paris' overflowing cemeteries by exhuming the bones and storing them in the tunnels of three disused quarries. One ossuary created in 1810 is the **Catacombes** (☎ 01 43 22 47 63; Map pp68-9; www.catacombes.paris.fr, in French; 1 av Colonel Henri Roi-Tanguy, 14e; Ⓜ Denfert Rochereau; adult/14-26yr/under 14yr €7/3.50/free; Ⓨ 10am-5pm Tue-Sun). Visitors follow 1.7km of underground corridors in which the bones and skulls of millions of former Parisians are neatly stacked along the walls.

FAUBOURG ST-GERMAIN & INVALIDES

Paris' most fashionable neighbourhood during the 18th century was Faubourg St-Germain in the 7e. **Hôtel Matignon** (Map pp68-9; 57 rue de Varenne, 7e) has been the official residence of the French prime minister since the start of the Fifth Republic in 1958.

MUSÉE D'ORSAY

The **Musée d'Orsay** (Orsay Museum; Map pp68-9; ☎ 01 40 49 48 14; www.musee-orsay.fr; 62 rue de Lille, 7e; Ⓜ Musée d'Orsay or Solférino; adult/18-30yr/under 18yr €8/5.50/free, admission free 1st Sun of the month; Ⓨ 9.30am-6pm Tue, Wed & Fri-Sun, 9.30am-9.45pm Thu) is housed in a former train station (1900). It displays France's national collection of paintings, sculptures, objets d'art and other works produced between the 1840s and 1914.

Many visitors to the museum go straight to the upper level (lit by a skylight) to see the famous **Impressionist paintings** by Monet, Pissarro, Renoir, Sisley, Degas and Manet and the **post-Impressionist works** by Cézanne, van Gogh, Seurat and Matisse, but there's also lots to see on the ground floor, including some early works by Manet, Monet, Renoir and Pissarro. The middle level has some superb **art-nouveau rooms**.

English-language tours (☎ information 01 40 49 48 48; admission fee plus €7.50/5.70), lasting 1½ hours, include the 'Masterpieces of the Musée d'Orsay' tour, departing at 11.30am Tuesday to Saturday. The 1½-hour **audioguide tour** (€5), available in six languages, points out around 80 major works. Tickets are valid all day, so you can leave and re-enter the museum as you please. Those visiting the Musée Rodin the same day save €2 with a combined ticket (€12).

WILL SALTER

Jardin des Tuileries

❧ IF YOU LIKE...

If you love ambling through **Jardin du Luxembourg** (p73), signature sage-green chairs et al, you'll like these other Parisian parks and gardens:

- **Galeries du Panthéon Bouddhique du Japon et de la Chine** (Map pp64-5; Buddhist Pantheon Galleries of Japan & China; ☎ 01 47 23 61 65; 19 av d'Iéna; Ⓜ Iéna; admission free; ⊙ 10am-6pm Wed-Mon) Leave the rest of Paris behind with a serene stroll through the wonderful **Japanese garden** (⊙ 1-5pm Wed-Mon) framing this Asian art gallery, itself housed in the sumptuous Hôtel Heidelbach.
- **Jardin du Palais Royal** (Map pp64-5; ☎ 01 47 03 92 16; 6 rue de Montpensier, 1er) Lovely park surrounded by elegant 19th-century shopping arcades, just north of the neoclassical Palais Royal (Royal Palace).
- **Jardin des Tuileries** (Map pp64-5; ☎ 01 40 20 90 43; Ⓜ Tuileries or Concorde) These formal gardens were laid out in the mid-17th century and almost immediately became the most fashionable spot in Paris to parade about in one's finery; today joggers love it. Several Monets hang in the **Musée de l'Orangerie** (Orangery Museum; www.musee-orangerie.fr), in the garden's southwestern corner.
- **Jardins du Trocadéro** (Map pp52-3; Ⓜ Trocadéro) Fronting the Eiffel Tower, the fountains and statues of these gardens are grandly illuminated at night.
- **Parc de la Villette** (Map pp52-3; ☎ 01 04 03 75 75; www.villette .com; Ⓜ Porte de la Villette or Porte de Pantin) Split into two sections by the Canal de l'Ourcq, this whimsical 35-hectare park is central Paris' largest open green space. Enlivened by shaded walkways, imaginative street furniture, a series of themed gardens for kids and fanciful, bright-red pavilions known as *folies*, it has been called 'the prototype urban park of the 21st century'. At its northern end is **Cité des Sciences et de l'Industrie** (www.cite-sciences.fr), a must for families with its interactive and explorative children's spaces.

MUSÉE RODIN

One of our favourite cultural attractions in Paris, the **Musée Rodin** (Rodin Museum; Map pp68-9; ☎ 01 44 18 61 10; www.musee-rodin.fr; 79 rue de Varenne, 7e; Ⓜ Varenne; adult/18-25yr permanent collections or temporary exhibitions plus garden €6/4, both exhibitions plus garden €9/7, garden only €1, admission free under 18yr & 1st Sun of month; ☺ 9.30am-5.45pm Tue-Sun Apr-Sep, 9.30am-4.45pm Tue-Sun Oct-Mar) is both a sublime museum and one of the most relaxing spots in the city, with a lovely **garden**, full of sculptures and shade trees, in which to rest. Rooms on two floors of this 18th-century residence display extraordinarily vital bronze and marble sculptures by Rodin, including the incomparable *The Kiss* (Le Baiser).

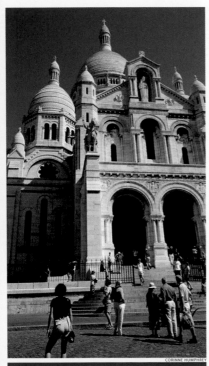

CORINNE HUMPHREY

Basilique du Sacré Cœur

EIFFEL TOWER AREA

The symbol of Paris is surrounded by open areas on both banks of the Seine, which take in both the 7e and 16e, the most chichi (and snobby) part of the capital.

TOUR EIFFEL

When it was built for the 1889 Exposition Universelle (World Fair), the **Tour Eiffel** (Eiffel Tower; Map pp52-3; ☎ 01 44 11 23 23; www.tour-eiffel.fr; Ⓜ Champ de Mars-Tour Eiffel or Bir Hakeim; ☺ lifts 9am-midnight mid-Jun–Aug, 9.30am-11pm Sep–mid-Jun, stairs 9am-midnight mid-Jun–Aug, 9.30am-6pm Sep–mid-Jun) faced massive opposition from Paris' artistic and literary elite.

Three levels are open to the public. The lifts cost €4.80 to the 1st platform (57m above the ground), €7.80 to the 2nd (115m) and €12 to the 3rd (276m). If you are strong of thigh and lung you can avoid the lift queues by taking the stairs (€4/3.10 over/under 25 years) in the south pillar to the 1st and 2nd platforms.

MUSÉE DU QUAI BRANLY

Housed in architect Jean Nouvel's impressive new structure of glass, wood and turf along the Seine, the long-awaited **Musée du Quai Branly** (Quai Branly Museum; Map pp52-3; ☎ 01 56 61 70 00; www.quaibranly.fr; 37 quai Branly, 7e; Ⓜ Pont de l'Alma or Alma-Marceau; adult/student & 18-25yr/under 18yr €8.50/6/free, admission free after 6pm Sat for 18-25yr, 1st Sun of month for all; ☺ 11am-7pm Tue, Wed & Sun, to 9pm Thu-Sat) introduces the art and cultures of Africa, Oceania, Asia and the Americas through innovative displays, film and musical recordings. The anthropological explanations are kept to a minimum; what is displayed here is meant to be viewed as art.

MUSÉE DES ÉGOUTS DE PARIS

The **Musée des Égouts de Paris** (Paris Sewers Museum; Map pp52-3; ☎ 01 53 68 27

81; place de la Résistance, 7e; Ⓜ Pont de l'Alma; adult/student & 6-16yr/under 6yr €4.20/3.40/free; ☺ 11am-5pm Sat-Wed May-Sep, 11am-4pm Sat-Wed Oct-Dec & Feb-Apr) is a working museum whose entrance – a rectangular maintenance hole topped with a kiosk – is across the street from 93 quai d'Orsay, 7e. Raw sewage flows beneath your feet as you walk through 480m of odoriferous tunnels, passing artefacts illustrating the development of Paris' waste-water disposal system.

ÉTOILE & CHAMPS-ÉLYSÉES

A dozen large avenues radiate out from the place de l'Étoile, and first among them is the av des Champs-Élysées. Symbolising the style and joie de vivre of Paris since the mid-19th century, the avenue is scuzzy in parts but remains a popular tourist destination.

The **Arc de Triomphe** (Triumphal Arch; Map pp64-5; ☎ 01 55 37 73 77; www.monuments-nationaux.fr; Ⓜ Charles de Gaulle-Étoile; viewing platform adult/18-25yr/under 18yr €9/6.50/free, admission free 1st Sun of month Nov-Mar; ☺ 10am-11pm Apr-Sep, to 10.30pm Oct-Mar) is the world's largest traffic roundabout. It was commissioned by Napoléon in 1806 to commemorate his imperial victories. Since 1920, the body of an **Unknown Soldier** from WWI has lain beneath the arch; his fate and that of countless others is commemorated by a **memorial flame** that is rekindled each evening around 6.30pm.

From the **viewing platform** on top of the arch (50m up via 284 steps and well worth the climb) you can see the dozen broad avenues radiating towards every part of the city. Tickets are sold in the underground passageway that surfaces on the even-numbered side of av des Champs-Élysées. It is the only sane way to get to the base of the arch and is not linked to nearby metro tunnels.

MONTMARTRE

During the late 19th and early 20th centuries the bohemian lifestyle of Montmartre in the 18e attracted a number of important writers and artists, including Picasso, who lived at the studio called **Bateau Lavoir** (Map pp64-5; 11bis Émile Goudeau; Ⓜ Abbesses) from 1908 to 1912.

The easiest way to reach the top of the Butte de Montmartre (Montmartre Hill) is via the RATP's sleek funicular. Perched at the very top, the **Basilique du Sacré Cœur** (Basilica of the Sacred Heart; Map pp64-5; ☎ 01 53 41 89 00; www.sacre-coeur-montmartre.com; place du Parvis du Sacré Cœur, 18e; Ⓜ Anvers; ☺ 6am-10.30pm) was built from contributions pledged by Parisian Catholics as an act of contrition after the humiliating Franco-Prussian War of 1870–71. Some 234 spiralling steps lead you to the basilica's **dome** (admission €5; ☺ 9am-7pm Apr-Sep, 9am-6pm Oct-Mar), which affords one of the most spectacular panoramas you'll find in Paris.

The most famous cemetery in Paris after Père Lachaise, **Cimetière de Montmartre** (Montmartre Cemetery; Map pp64-5; Ⓜ Place de Clichy; ☺ 8am-6pm Mon-Fri, 8.30am-6pm Sat, 9am-6pm Sun mid-Mar–early Nov, 8am-5.30pm Mon-Fri, 8.30am-5.30pm Sat, 9am-5.30pm Sun early Nov–mid-Mar) contains the graves of writers Émile Zola, Alexandre Dumas and Stendhal among others.

TOURS

Fat Tire Bike Tours (Map pp52-3; ☎ 01 56 58 10 54; www.fattirebiketoursparis.com; 24 rue Edgar Faure, 15e; Ⓜ La Motte Picquet Grenelle; ☺ office 9am-6pm) offers four-hour English-language tours of the city (adult/student €24/22) year-round. Costs include the bicycle and rain gear. **Bateaux Mouches** (Map pp64-5; ☎ 01 42 25 96 10; www.bateauxmouches.com, in French; Port de la Conférence, 8e; Ⓜ Alma Marceau;

JOHN ELK III

Cimetière du Père Lachaise

◥ CIMETIÈRE DU PÈRE LACHAISE

The world's most visited graveyard, **Cimetière du Père Lachaise** opened its one-way doors in 1804. Its 69,000 ornate, even ostentatious, tombs form a verdant, 44-hectare open-air sculpture garden.

Among the 800,000 people buried here are the composer Chopin, the playwright Molière, the poet Apollinaire; the writers Balzac, Proust, Gertrude Stein and Colette; the actors Simone Signoret, Sarah Bernhardt and Yves Montand; the painters Pissarro, Seurat, Modigliani and Delacroix; the chanteuse Édith Piaf; the dancer Isadora Duncan; and even those immortal 12th-century lovers, Abélard and Héloïse, whose remains were disinterred and reburied here together in 1817.

Particularly frequented graves are those of **Oscar Wilde**, interred in division 89 in 1900, and 1960s rock star **Jim Morrison**, who died in an apartment at 17–19 rue Beautreillis, 4e, in the Marais in 1971 and is buried in division 6.

Père Lachaise has five entrances, two of which are on bd de Ménilmontant. Maps indicating the location of noteworthy graves are available free from the **conservation office** in the southwestern corner of the cemetery.

Things you need to know: Cimetière du Père Lachaise (Père Lachaise Cemetery; Map pp52-3; www.pere-lachaise.com; Ⓜ Philippe Auguste, Gambetta or Père Lachaise; ☺ 8am-6pm Mon-Fri, 8.30am-6pm Sat, 9am-6pm Sun mid-Mar–early Nov, 8am-5.30pm Mon-Fri, 8.30am-5.30pm Sat, 9am-5.30pm Sun early Nov–mid-Mar); conservation office (Map pp52-3; ☎ 01 55 25 82 10; 16 rue du Repos, 20e)

adult/senior & 4-12yr/under 4yr €9/4/free; ☺ mid-Mar–mid-Nov), the most famous riverboat company in Paris, runs 1000-seat tour boats which are the biggest on the Seine.

L'Open Tour (Map pp64-5; ☎ 01 42 66 56 56; www.pariscityrama.com; 13 rue Auber, 9e; Ⓜ Havre Caumartin or Opéra; 1 day adult/4-11yr/under 4yr €26/13/free, 2 consecutive days €29/13/free) runs open-deck buses along four circuits. You can jump on and off at more than 50 stops.

Paris Walks (☎ 01 48 09 21 40; www.paris-walks.com; adult/student under 21/under 15yr from €10/8/5) has English-language tours focusing on people and themes, such as Hemingway, medieval Paris, the Latin Quarter, fashion, the French Revolution and even chocolate.

SLEEPING

The Paris Convention & Visitors Bureau (p63), notably the Gare du Nord branch, can find you a place to stay for the night of the day you stop by. Queues can be very long in the high season.

Bed-and-breakfast accommodation in Paris: **Alcôve & Agapes** (☎ 01 44 85 06 05; www.bed-and-breakfast-in-paris.com) and **Good Morning Paris** (☎ 01 47 07 44 45; www.goodmorningparis.fr).

LOUVRE & LES HALLES

The very central area encompassing the Musée du Louvre is more disposed to welcoming top-end travellers, but there are some decent midrange places to choose from.

Le Relais du Louvre (Map pp68-9; ☎ 01 40 41 96 42; www.relaisdulouvre.com; 19 rue des Prêtres St-Germain l'Auxerrois, 1er; Ⓜ Pont Neuf; s €108, d & tw €165-198, tr €212, ste €237-430; ⌗ 💻) If you are someone who likes style but in a traditional sense, choose this lovely 21-room hotel just west of the Louvre. If you are looking for something spacious, ask for one of the five rooms ending in a '2' and looking out onto the garden/patio.

MARAIS & BASTILLE

There are quite a few top-end hotels in the heart of the lively Marais as well as in the vicinity of the elegant place des Vosges.

Hôtel Jeanne d'Arc (Map pp68-9; ☎ 01 48 87 62 11; www.hoteljeannedarc.com; 3 rue de Jarente, 4e; Ⓜ St-Paul; s €60-97, d €84-97, tr/q €116/146; 💻) This cosy, 36-room hotel near lovely place du Marché Ste-Catherine has almost a country feel to it. But everyone knows about it, so book well in advance.

Hôtel de Nice (Map pp68-9; ☎ 01 42 78 55 29; www.hoteldenice.com; 42bis rue de Rivoli, 4e; Ⓜ Hôtel de Ville; s/d/tr €80/110/135) This is an especially warm, family-run place with 23 comfortable rooms. Every square inch of wall space is used to display old prints, and public areas and guestrooms are full of Second Empire–style furniture, Indian carpets and lamps with fringed shades.

Hôtel de la Place des Vosges (Map pp68-9; ☎ 01 42 72 60 46; www.hotelplacedesvosges.com; 12 rue de Birague, 4e; Ⓜ Bastille; r €90-95, ste €150; 💻) This superbly situated 17-room hotel is an oasis of tranquillity due south of sublime place des Vosges. A suite on the top floor has choice views and can accommodate up to four people.

Hôtel St-Louis Marais (Map pp68-9; ☎ 01 48 87 87 04; www.saintlouismarais.com; 1 rue Charles V, 4e; Ⓜ Sully Morland; s €99, d & tw €115-140, tr/ste €150/160; 💻) This especially charming hotel in a converted 17th-century convent is more Bastille than Marais. Wooden beams, terracotta tiles and heavy brocade drapes tend to darken the 19 rooms but certainly add to the atmosphere.

Hôtel de la Bretonnerie (Map pp68-9; ☎ 01 48 87 77 63; www.bretonnerie.com; 22 rue Ste-Croix de la Bretonnerie, 4e; Ⓜ Hôtel de Ville; r €125-160, ste €185-210; 💻) This is a very charming upper-midrange place in the heart of the Marais nightlife area, dating from the 17th century. The decor of each of the 22 guestrooms and seven suites is unique, and some rooms have four-poster and canopy beds.

Hôtel Caron de Beaumarchais (Map pp68-9; ☎ 01 42 72 34 12; www.carondebeaumarchais.com; 12 rue Vieille du Temple, 4e; Ⓜ St-Paul; r €125-162; ⌗ 💻 ✕) Decorated like an

18th-century private house, this themed hotel has to be seen to be believed. The museumlike lobby, with its prized 18th-century pianoforte, gaming tables, gilded mirrors, and candelabras, sets the tone of the place.

ourpick **Hôtel St-Merry** (Map pp68-9; ☎ 01 42 78 14 15; www.hotelmarais.com; 78 rue de la Verrerie, 4e; Ⓜ Châtelet; d & tw €160-230, tr €205-275, ste €335-407; 💻) The 11 rooms and one suite of this hotel, by far our favourite medieval number in the Marais, are in the one-time presbytery of the attached Église St-Merry. So very close are both structures that two flying buttresses straddle the double bed of room 9.

Hôtel du Petit Moulin (Map pp68-9; ☎ 01 42 74 10 10; www.hoteldupetitmoulin.com; 29-31 rue de Poitou, 3e; Ⓜ Filles du Calvaire; r €180-280, ste €350; 💈 💻) This scrumptious boutique hotel in what was once a bakery was designed from top to bottom by Christian Lacroix. It features 17 completely different rooms – from medieval and rococo Marais, sporting exposed beams and dressed in toile de Jouy wallpaper, to a more modern quarter with contemporary murals and heart-shaped mirrors just this side of kitsch.

LATIN QUARTER & JARDIN DES PLANTES

There are dozens of attractive two- and three-star hotels very popular with visiting academics in the Latin Quarter, so rooms are hardest to find when conferences and seminars are scheduled (March to June and in October).

Port Royal Hôtel (Map pp68-9; ☎ 01 43 31 70 06; www .hotelportroyal.fr; 8 bd de Port Royal, 5e; Ⓜ Les Gobelins; s €41-89, d €52.50-89) It's hard to imagine that this 46-room hotel, owned and managed by the same family for three generations, still only bears one star.

Hôtel de l'Espérance (Map pp68-9; ☎ 01 47 07 10 99; www.hoteldelesperance.fr; 15 rue Pascal, 5e; Ⓜ Censier Daubenton; s €71-80, d €80-90; 💈 💻) Just a couple of minutes' walk south of lively rue Mouffetard, the 'Hotel of Hope' is a quiet and immaculately kept 38-room place with faux antique furnishings and a warm welcome from the charming couple who own it.

Hôtel St-Jacques (Map pp68-9; ☎ 01 44 07 45 45; www.hotel-saintjacques.com; 35 rue des Écoles, 5e; Ⓜ Maubert Mutualité; s €92, d €105-137, tr €168; 💈 💻 ✖) This very stylish 38-room hotel has balconies that overlook the Panthéon. Audrey Hepburn and Cary Grant, who filmed some scenes of *Charade* here in the 1960s, would appreciate the mod cons that now complement the original 19th-century details.

Hôtel des Grandes Écoles (Map pp68-9; ☎ 01 43 26 79 23; www.hotel-grandes-ecoles .com; 75 rue du Cardinal Lemoine, 5e; Ⓜ Cardinal Lemoine or Place Monge; d €110-135, tr €125-155; ✖) This wonderful and very welcoming hotel has one of the loveliest situations in the Latin Quarter, tucked away in a courtyard off a medieval street with its own garden.

ST-GERMAIN, ODÉON & LUXEMBOURG

The well-heeled St-Germain-des-Prés is a delightful area to stay in; there are some excellent midrange hotels in this neighbourhood.

Hôtel de Nesle (Map pp68-9; ☎ 01 43 54 62 41; www.hotel denesleparis.com; 7 rue de Nesle, 6e; Ⓜ Odéon or Mabillon; s €55-85, d €75-100) The Nesle is a relaxed, colourfully decorated hotel with 20 rooms, half of which are painted with murals taken from (mostly French) literature. What is by far its greatest asset, though, is the huge back garden accessible from the 1st floor, with pathways, trellis and small fountain.

Hôtel du Lys (Map pp68-9; ☎ 01 43 26 97 57; www.hoteldulys.com; 23 rue Serpente, 6e; Ⓜ Odéon; s/d/tr €100/120/140) This 22-room hotel situated in what was a *hôtel particulier* (private mansion) in the 17th century has been owned by the same family for six decades. We love the beamed ceiling and the chinoiserie wallpaper in the lobby.

Hôtel des Marronniers (Map pp68-9; ☎ 01 43 25 30 60; www.hotel-marronniers.com; 21 rue Jacob, 6e; Ⓜ St-Germain des Prés; s €115-181, d & tw €161-181, tr/q €216/256; 🔀 🖳) At the end of a small courtyard 30m from the main street, the 'Chestnut Trees' has 37 cosy rooms and a delightful conservatory opening onto a back garden.

Hôtel d'Angleterre (Map pp68-9; ☎ 01 42 60 34 72; www.hotel-dangleterre.com; 44 rue Jacob, 6e; Ⓜ St-Germain des Prés; s incl breakfast €100-255, d €200-265, ste €285-320; 🖳 🔀) The 'England Hotel' is a beautiful 27-room property in a quiet street. Guests breakfast in the courtyard of this former British Embassy, where the Treaty of Paris ending the American Revolution was signed and where Hemingway once lodged. Breakfast is included in room rates.

OPÉRA & GRANDS BOULEVARDS

The avenues around bd Montmartre are popular for their nightlife area and it's a lively area in which to stay. It's very convenient for shopping.

Hôtel Vivienne (Map pp64-5; ☎ 01 42 33 13 26; www .hotel-vivienne.com; 40 rue Vivienne, 2e; Ⓜ Grands Boulevards; s €60-114, d & tw €75-114; 🖳 🔀) This stylish 45-room hotel is amazingly good value for Paris. While the rooms are not huge, they have all the mod cons, some have little balconies and the public areas are bright and cheery.

Hôtel Favart (Map pp64-5; ☎ 01 42 97 59 83; www.hotel-paris-favart.com; 5 rue Marivaux, 2e; Ⓜ Richelieu Drouot; s €100-130, d €130-160, tr

JULIET COOMBE

Statue in Jardin des Plantes (p73)

€140-180, q €155-200; 🔀 🔀) With 37 rooms facing the Opéra Comique, the Favart is a stylish art-nouveau hotel that feels like it never let go of the belle époque.

GARE DU NORD, GARE DE L'EST & RÉPUBLIQUE

There are quite a few two- and three-star places around the train stations in the 10e that are convenient if you are catching an early-morning train to London or want to crash immediately upon arrival.

Hôtel Français (Map pp52-3; ☎ 01 40 35 94 14; www.hotelfrancais.com; 13 rue du 8 Mai 1945, 10e; Ⓜ Gare de l'Est; s €94-101, d €99-106, tr €134-141; 🔀 🖳 🔀) This two-star hotel facing the Gare de l'Est has 72 attractive, almost luxurious and very quiet rooms, some of which have balconies.

Kube Hôtel (Map pp52-3; ☎ 01 42 05 20 00; www.kube hotel.com; 1-5 passage Ruelle, 18e; Ⓜ La Chapelle; s €250, d €300-400, ste €500-750; ⚡ 🖳 ⊠) The theme at this boutique hotel is three-dimensional square – from the glassed-in reception box in the entrance courtyard and the cube-shaped furnishings in the 41 guestrooms to the ice in the cocktails at the celebrated Ice Kube bar.

MONTMARTRE & PIGALLE
Montmartre is one of the most charming neighbourhoods in Paris.

Hôtel Bonséjour Montmartre (Map pp64-5; ☎ 01 42 54 22 53; www.hotel-bonsejour -montmartre.fr; 11 rue Burq, 18e; Ⓜ Abbesses; s €33-40, d €44-55, tr €58-65; 🖳) At the top of a quiet street in Montmartre, the 'Good Stay' is a perennial budget favourite. It's a simple place with no lift and linoleum or parquet floors, but it's welcoming, comfortable and very clean. Hall showers cost €2.

Hôtel Utrillo (Map pp64-5; ☎ 01 42 58 13 44; www.hotel -paris-utrillo.com; 7 rue Aristide Bruant, 18e; Ⓜ Abbesses or Blanche; s €73, d & tw €83-88, tr €105; 🖳) This friendly 30-room hotel, named for the 'painter of Montmartre', Maurice Utrillo (1883–1955), and decorated in primary colours, has a few extras such as a little leafy courtyard in back and a small sauna.

Hôtel des Arts (Map pp64-5; ☎ 01 46 06 30 52; www .arts-hotel-paris.com; 5 rue Tholozé, 18e; Ⓜ Abbesses or Blanche; s €75-95, d & tw €95-105, tr €160; 🖳) The 'Arts Hotel' is a friendly and attractive 50-room place convenient to both place Pigalle and Montmartre. Towering over it is the old-style windmill Moulin de la Galette. The resident canine is very friendly.

Hôtel Résidence des 3 Poussins (Map pp64-5; ☎ 01 53 32 81 81; www.les3poussins.com; 15 rue Clauzel, 9e; Ⓜ St-Georges; s/d €137/152, 1- or 2-person studios €187, 3- or 4-person studios €222; ⚡ 🖳) The 'Hotel of the Three Chicks' is a lovely property due south of place Pigalle with 40 rooms, half of which are small studios with their own cooking facilities. This place positively exudes style, and the back patio is a delightful place in the warmer months for breakfast or a drink.

EATING
LOUVRE & LES HALLES
The area is filled with trendy restaurants, but they mostly cater to tourists. Streets lined with places to eat include rue des Lombards and pedestrians-only rue Montorgueil, a market street and probably your best bet for something quick. Those in search of Asian food flock to rue Ste-Anne in Paris' Japantown.

Scoop (Map pp68-9; ☎ 01 42 60 31 84; 154 rue St-Honoré, 1er; Ⓜ Palais Royal-Musée du Louvre; dishes €10.90-16.90; ⏰ 11am-7pm) This American-style ice-cream parlour has been making quite a splash for its excellent wraps, burgers, tarts and soups and central, very fashionable location. Sunday brunch (11.30am to 4pm) includes pancakes with maple syrup.

Le Grand Colbert (Map pp64-5; ☎ 01 42 86 87 88; 2-4 rue Vivienne, 2e; Ⓜ Pyramides; starters €10-21.50, mains €19.50-30, lunch menus €32-39, dinner menus €39; ⏰ noon-3am) This former workers' *cafétéria* transformed into a fin-de-siècle showcase is more relaxed than many similarly restored restaurants and a convenient spot for lunch if visiting the *passages couverts* or cruising the streets late at night (last orders: 1am).

Chez la Vieille (Map pp68-9; ☎ 01 42 60 15 78; 1 rue Bailleul, 1er; Ⓜ Louvre-Rivoli; starters €15-21, mains €18-25, lunch menus €23; ⏰ lunch Mon-Fri, dinner to 9.45pm Mon, Tue, Thu & Fri) Seating 'At the Old Lady's' is on two floors, but don't expect a slot on the more rustic ground floor; that's reserved for regulars. The small menu reflects the size of the place but is universally sublime.

WITOLD SKRYPCZAK

Place des Vosges (p67)

MARAIS & BASTILLE

The Marais is one of Paris' premier neighbourhoods for eating out. If you're looking for authentic Chinese food, check rue Au Maire, 3e (Ⓜ Arts et Métiers). The kosher and kosher-style restaurants along rue des Rosiers, 4e (Ⓜ St-Paul), the so-called Pletzl, serve specialities from North Africa, Central Europe and Israel. Bastille is another area chock-a-block with restaurants.

Le Trumilou (Map pp68-9; ☎ 01 42 77 63 98; 84 quai de l'Hôtel de Ville, 4e; Ⓜ Hôtel de Ville; starters €4.50-13, mains €15-22, menus €16.50 & €19.50; ☽ lunch & dinner) This no-frills bistro is a Parisian institution in situ for over a century. If you're looking for an authentic menu from the early 20th century and prices (well, almost) to match, you won't do better than this. The *confit aux pruneaux* (duck with prunes) and the *ris de veau grand-mère* (veal sweetbreads in mushroom cream sauce) are particularly good.

Robert et Louise (Map pp68-9; 01 42 78 55 89; 64 rue Vieille du Temple, 3e; Ⓜ St-Sébastien Froissart; starters €6-13, mains €12-18, lunch menus €12; ☽ lunch & dinner Tue-Sat) This 'country inn', complete with its red gingham curtains, offers delightful, simple and inexpensive French food, including *côte de bœuf* (side of beef, €40 for two), which is cooked on an open fire. It's a jolly, truly Rabelaisian evening.

Le Petit Marché (Map pp68-9; ☎ 01 42 72 06 67; 9 rue de Béarn, 3e; Ⓜ Chemin Vert; starters €8-11, mains €15-25, lunch menus €14; ☽ lunch & dinner) This great little bistro just up from the place des Vosges attracts a mixed crowd with its hearty cooking and friendly service. The salad starters are popular, as is the *brochette d'agneau aux épices doux* (spicy lamb brochette).

Bofinger (Map pp68-9; ☎ 01 42 72 87 82; 5-7 rue de la Bastille, 4e; Ⓜ Bastille; starters €8 18.50, mains €15.50-31.50, lunch menus €24-31.50, dinner menus €31.50; ☽ lunch & dinner to 12.30am) Founded in 1864, Bofinger is reputedly the oldest brasserie in Paris and specialities include Alsatian-inspired dishes such as *choucroute* (sauerkraut with assorted meats; €18 to €20) and seafood dishes. Its polished art-nouveau brass, glass and mirrors are all stunning.

Le Temps au Temps (Map pp68-9; ☎ 01 43 79 63 40; 3 rue Paul Bert, 11e; Ⓜ Faidherbe Chaligny; menus €30; Ⓨ lunch & dinner Tue-Sat) This place with about 10 tables has an exciting three-course menu that changes daily; some of the dishes have been inspired by the *cuisine récréative* (entertaining cuisine) of the great Catalan chef Ferran Adria. You're much more likely to get a seat at lunch.

QUICK EATS

Crêpes Show (Map pp68-9; ☎ 01 47 00 36 46; 51 rue de Lappe, 11e; Ⓜ Ledru Rollin; crêpes & galettes €3-9.80, lunch menus €8.90; Ⓨ lunch Mon-Fri, dinner to 1am Sun-Thu, to 2am Fri & Sat) Head for this unpretentious little restaurant for sweet crêpes and *galettes* (savoury buckwheat crêpes). There are lots of vegetarian choices, including great salads from around €5.

SELF-CATERING

Markets in the Marais and Bastille area include the incomparable (and open-air) **Marché Bastille** (Map pp68-9; bd Richard Lenoir, 11e; Ⓨ 7am-2.30pm Tue & Sun; Ⓜ Bastille or Richard Lenoir).

THE ISLANDS

Famed more for its ice cream than dining options, Île St-Louis is a pricey place to eat, although there are a couple of fine places worth a brunch or lunchtime munch. As for Île de la Cité, forget it.

Berthillon (Map pp68-9; ☎ 01 43 54 31 61; 31 rue St-Louis en l'Île, 4e; Ⓜ Pont Marie; ice cream €2-5.40; Ⓨ 10am-8pm Wed-Sun) While the fruit flavours (eg cassis) produced by this celebrated *glacier* (ice-cream maker) are justifiably renowned, the chocolate, coffee, *marrons glacés* (candied chestnuts), *Agenaise* (Armagnac and prunes), *noisette* (hazelnut) and *nougat au miel* (honey nougat) are even richer. Choose from among 70 flavours.

LATIN QUARTER & JARDIN DES PLANTES

From cheap student haunts to chandelier-lit palaces loaded with history, the 5e has something to suit every budget and culinary taste. Rue Mouffetard is famed for its food market and food shops.

Ice-cream shop, Île de la Cité

ANNE DOWIE

Le Petit Pontoise (Map pp68-9; ☎ 01 43 29 25 20; 9 rue de Pontoise, 5e; Ⓜ Maubert Mutualité; starters €8-13.50, mains €15-25; ☯ lunch & dinner) This charming bistro offers a blackboard menu of seasonal delights. Regular dishes to look out for include old-fashioned classics like *rognons de veau à l'ancienne* (calf's kidneys) or roast quail with dates.

L'AOC (Map pp68-9; ☎ 01 43 54 22 52; 14 rue des Fossés St-Bernard, 5e; Ⓜ Cardinal Lemoine; meals around €35; ☯ lunch & dinner Tue-Sat) The concept here is AOC (Appellation d'Origine Contrôlée), meaning everything has been reared or made according to strict guidelines designed to protect a product unique to a particular village, town or area. The result? Only the best! Rare is the chance to taste *porc noir de Bigorre,* a type of black piggie bred in the Pyrénées.

La Mosquée de Paris (Map pp68-9; ☎ 01 43 31 38 20; 39 rue Geoffroy St-Hilaire, 5e; Ⓜ Censier Daubenton or Place Monge; mains €13.50-25; ☯ lunch & dinner) The central Mosque of Paris (p73) has an authentic restaurant serving 11 types of couscous (€13 to €25) and 10 tajines (€15.50 to €17). There's also a North African–style **tearoom** (☯ 9am-11.30pm) where you can enjoy peppermint tea (€2) and *pâtisseries orientales* (oriental pastries; €2).

QUICK EATS

Le Baba Bourgeois (Map pp68-9; ☎ 01 44 07 46 75; 5 quai de la Tournelle, 5e; Ⓜ Cardinal Lemoine or Pont Marie; mains €15-20; ☯ lunch & dinner Wed-Sat, 11.30am-5pm Sun) This contemporary eating and drinking space slap bang on the Seine, with a pavement terrace facing Notre Dame, is a former architect's studio. Its imaginative *tartines* (open-face sandwiches), terrines, *tartes salées* (savoury tarts) and salads make for a simple, stylish bite any time of day. Sunday offers a splendid all-day buffet brunch, *à volonté* (as much as you can eat).

SELF-CATERING

Place Maubert, 5e, becomes the lively food market **Marché Maubert** (Map pp68-9) on Tuesday, Thursday and Saturday mornings. There's a particularly lively food market set out along **rue Mouffetard** (Map pp68-9; rue Mouffetard; ☯ 8am-7.30pm Tue-Sat, 8am-noon Sun; Ⓜ Censier Daubenton).

ST-GERMAIN, ODÉON & LUXEMBOURG

Place St-Germain des Prés is home to celebrated cafés such as Les Deux Magots (p88).

Polidor (Map pp68-9Marais; ☎ 01 43 26 95 34; 41 rue Monsieur le Prince, 6e; Ⓜ Odéon; starters €4.50-17, mains €11-22, menus €22-32; ☯ lunch & dinner to 12.30am Mon-Sat, to 11pm Sun) A meal at this quintessentially Parisian *crémerie restaurant* (dairy shop) is like taking a trip back to Victor Hugo's Paris – the restaurant and its decor date from 1845. Specialities include *bœuf bourguignon* (€11), *blanquette de veau* (veal in white sauce; €15) and the most famous *tarte tatin* (€8) in Paris.

Bouillon Racine (Map pp68-9; ☎ 01 44 32 15 60; 3 rue Racine, 6e; Ⓜ Cluny-La Sorbonne; starters €7.50-14.50, mains €15.50-28, lunch menus €14.90-29, dinner menus €29; ☯ lunch & dinner) This 'soup kitchen' built in 1906 to feed city workers is an art-nouveau palace. Oh, and the food? Wholly classic, inspired by age-old recipes such as roast snails, *caille confite* (preserved quail) and lamb shank with liquorice. Finish off your foray into gastronomic history with an old-fashioned sherbet.

Chez Allard (Map pp68-9; ☎ 01 43 26 48 23; 41 rue St-André des Arts; Ⓜ St-Michel; starters €8-20, mains €25, menus €25-34; ☯ lunch & dinner Mon-Sat) One of our favourite places on the Left Bank is this positively charming bistro where the staff couldn't be kinder and more professional – even during its enormously busy lunchtime – and the food is superb. Try 12 snails, some *cuisses de grenouilles* (frogs' legs) or *un poulet de Bresse* (France's most legendary chicken, from Burgundy) for two. Enter from 1 rue de l'Éperon.

QUICK EATS

Cosi (Map pp68-9; ☎ 01 46 33 35 36; 54 rue de Seine, 6e; Ⓜ Odéon; sandwich menus €9-11; ☽ noon-11pm) With sandwich names like Stonker, Tom Dooley and Naked Willi, Cosi (which, incidentally, is of New Zealand origin) could easily run for Paris' most imaginative sandwich maker. Classical music playing in the background and homemade Italian bread, still warm from the oven, only adds to Cosi's natural sex appeal.

SELF-CATERING

With the Jardin du Luxembourg nearby, this is the perfect area for putting together a picnic lunch. The covered **Marché St-Germain** (Map pp68-9; 4-8 rue Lobineau, 6e; Ⓜ Mabillon; ☽ 8.30am-1pm & 4-7.30pm Tue-Sat, 8.30am-1pm Sun) has a huge array of produce and prepared food.

ÉTOILE & CHAMPS-ÉLYSÉES

Eateries lining the touristy 'Avenue of the Elysian Fields' offer little value for money. However, restaurants in the surrounding areas can be excellent.

L'Étoile Verte (Map pp64-5; ☎ 01 43 80 69 34; 13 rue Brey, 17e; Ⓜ Charles de Gaulle-Étoile; starters €9-13, mains €13-22, lunch menus €14-18, dinner menus €18, menus with wine €25; ☽ lunch Mon-Fri, dinner daily) When one of us was a student in Paris (back when the glaziers were still installing the stained glass at Ste-Chapelle), this was the place for both Esperanto speakers and students in search of old French classics: onion soup, snails, rabbit. That may have changed a bit, but the lunch *menu* is still a great deal for this neighbourhood.

L'Ardoise (Map pp64-5; ☎ 01 42 96 28 18; 28 rue du Mont Thabor, 1er; Ⓜ Concorde or Tuileries; menus €33; ☽ lunch Tue-Sat, dinner Tue-Sun) This is a little bistro with no menu as such – *ardoise* means 'blackboard', which is all there is. The food, such as hare in black pepper and beef fillet with morels, is superb, and the three-course set menu offers excellent value.

SELF-CATERING

Place de la Madeleine (Map pp64-5; Ⓜ Madeleine) is the luxury food centre of one of the world's food capitals. Rue Poncelet and rue Bayen have some excellent food shops, including the incomparable **Fromagerie Alléosse** (Map pp64-5; 13 rue Poncelet, 17e; ☽ 9.30am-1pm & 4-7pm Tue-Thu, 9am-1pm & 3.30pm-7pm Fri & Sat, 9am-1pm Sun; Ⓜ Ternes).

OPÉRA & GRANDS BOULEVARDS

The neon-lit bd Montmartre (Ⓜ Grands Boulevards or Richelieu Drouot) and nearby sections of rue du Faubourg Montmartre form one of the Right Bank's most animated café and dining districts. A short distance to the north there's kosher Jewish and North African restaurants on rue Richer, rue Cadet and rue Geoffroy Marie, 9e.

Chartier (Map pp64-5; ☎ 01 47 70 86 29; 7 rue du Faubourg Montmartre, 9e; Ⓜ Grands Boulevards; starters €2.20-12.40, mains €6.50-16, menus with wine €20; ☽ lunch & dinner) Chartier is justifiably famous for its 330-seat belle-époque dining room, virtually unaltered since 1896, and its excellent-value menu. Reservations are not accepted and lone diners will have to share a table.

Le Roi du Pot au Feu (Map pp64-5; ☎ 01 47 42 37 10; 34 rue Vignon, 9e; Ⓜ Havre Caumartin; starters €5-7, mains €17-20, menus €24-29; ☽ noon-10.30pm Mon-Sat) The typical Parisian bistro atmosphere adds to the charm, but what

RUSSELL MOUNTFORD

Moulin Rouge (p91)

you really want to come here for is a genuine *pot au feu*, a stockpot of beef, root vegetables and herbs stewed together, with the stock served as an entree and the meat and vegetables as the main course. No bookings.

ourpick Bistrot du Sommelier (Map pp64-5; ☎ 01 42 65 24 85; www.bistrotdusommelier.com; 97 bd Haussmann, 8e; Ⓜ St-Augustin; starters €14-25, mains €22-32, lunch menus €32 & €39, incl wine €45 & €54, dinner menus incl wine €65, €80 & €110; Ⓨ lunch & dinner Mon-Fri) This is the place in Paris to head for if you are as serious about wine as you are about food. The whole point of this attractive eatery is to match wine with food, and owner Philippe Faure-Brac, one of the world's foremost sommeliers is at hand to help. The best way to sample his wine-and-food pairings is on Friday, when a three-course tasting lunch with wine is €45 and a five-course dinner with wine is €70.

MONTMARTRE & PIGALLE

When you've got Sacré Cœur, place du Tertre and its portrait artists, and Paris

literally at your feet, who needs decent restaurants? In this well-trodden tourist area pick and choose carefully.

Chez Toinette (Map pp64-5; ☎ 01 42 54 44 36; 20 rue Germain Pilon, 18e; Ⓜ Abbesses; starters €6-9, mains €15-20; Ⓨ dinner Tue-Sat) The atmosphere of this convivial restaurant, which has somehow managed to keep alive the tradition of old Montmartre in one of the capital's most touristy neighbourhoods, is rivalled only by its fine cuisine. Game lovers in particular won't be disappointed.

Le Café Qui Parle (Map pp64-5; ☎ 01 46 06 06 88; 24 rue Caulaincourt, 18e; Ⓜ Lamarck Caulaincourt or Blanche; starters €7-14, mains €13.50-20, menus €12.50-17; Ⓨ lunch & dinner Thu-Tue) 'The Talking Café' offers inventive, reasonably priced dishes prepared by owner-chef Damian Mœuf amid comfortable surroundings. We love the art on the walls. Brunch (€15) is served from 10am on Saturday and Sunday.

La Mascotte (Map pp64-5; ☎ 01 46 06 28 15; 52 rue des Abbesses, 18e; Ⓜ Abbesses; starters €8.50-11.50, mains €19-25, lunch menus

€19.50-35, dinner menus €35; ☺ lunch & dinner) The 'Mascot' is a small, unassuming spot much frequented by regulars who can't get enough of its seafood and regional cuisine. The big terrace is a delight in the warmer months.

DRINKING

Le Fumoir (Map pp68-9; ☎ 01 42 92 00 24; 6 rue de l'Amiral Coligny, 1er; Ⓜ Louvre-Rivoli; ☺ 11am-2am) The 'Smoking Room' is a stylish colonial-style bar opposite the Louvre. It's a fine place to sip top-notch gin from quality glassware while nibbling olives.

L'Apparemment Café (Map pp68-9; ☎ 01 48 87 12 22; 18 rue des Coutures St-Gervais, 3e; Ⓜ St-Sébastien Froissart; ☺ noon-2am Mon-Sat, 12.30pm-midnight Sun) Tucked not so 'apparently' behind the Musée Picasso, this tasteful haven looks and feels like a private living room, with wood panelling, leather sofas, scattered parlour games and dog-eared books.

Le Bistrot du Peintre (Map pp68-9; ☎ 01 47 00 34 39; 116 av Ledru-Rollin, 11e; Ⓜ Bastille; ☺ 8am-2am) This lovely belle-époque bistro and wine bar, with its 1902 art-nouveau bar, elegant terrace and spot-on service, is on our apéritif A-list – and that of local artists, *bobos* and local celebs.

La Palette (Map pp68-9; ☎ 01 43 26 68 15; 43 rue de Seine, 6e; Ⓜ Mabillon; ☺ 8am-2am Mon-Sat) In the heart of 6e gallery land, this fin-de-siècle café and erstwhile stomping ground of Cézanne and Braque attracts a grown-up set of fashion people and local art dealers.

Les Deux Magots (Map pp68-9; ☎ 01 45 48 55 25; www.lesdeuxmagots.fr; 170 bd St-Germain, 6e; Ⓜ St-Germain des Prés; ☺ 7am-1am) This erstwhile literary haunt dates from 1914, although it's best known as the hang-out of Sartre, Hemingway, Picasso and André Breton. Everyone has to sit on the terrace here at least once and have a coffee or the famous hot chocolate served in porcelain jugs.

Harry's New York Bar (Map pp64-5; ☎ 01 42 61 71 14; 5 rue Daunou, 2e; Ⓜ Opéra; ☺ 10.30am-4am) One of the most popular American-style bars in the interwar years, Harry's manages to evoke a golden past without feeling like a museum piece. Lean upon the bar where F Scott Fitzgerald and Ernest Hemingway once drank and gossiped, and have the expert, white-smocked gentlemen prepare you a killer martini or the house creation: the Bloody Mary.

Ice Kube (Map pp52-3; ☎ 01 42 05 20 00; 1-5 passage Ruelle, 18e; Ⓜ La Chapelle; ☺ 7pm-1.30am Wed-Sat, 2-11pm Sun) This *temple de glace* (ice temple) on the first floor of the *très boutique* Kube Hotel (p82) is the French capital's first. The temperature is set at -20°C, there are down jackets on loan and the bar is a shimmering block of carved ice.

ENTERTAINMENT

It's impossible to sample the richness of Paris' entertainment scene without first studying *Pariscope* (€0.40) or *Officiel des Spectacles* (€0.35); both are in French, come out on Wednesday and are available at newsstands.

Buy tickets in **Fnac** (Map pp68-9; ☎ 08 92 68 36 22; www.fnacspectacles.com, in French) or **Virgin Megastores** (Map pp68-9; ☎ 08 25 12 91 39; www.virginmega.fr, in French). Both accept reservations by phone and internet.

On the day of a performance, **Kiosque Théâtre Madeleine** (Map pp64-5; opposite 15 place de la Madeleine, 8e; Ⓜ Madeleine; ☺ 12.30-8pm Tue-Sat, 12.30-4pm Sun) sells tickets at half price plus a commission of about €3. There's also **Kiosque Théâtre Montparnasse** (Map pp68-9; parvis Montparnasse, 15e; Ⓜ Montparnasse Bienvenüe) in Montparnasse, open the same hours.

The French-language websites www.billetreduc.com, www.ticketac.com and www.webguichet.com all offer online discounts.

LIVE MUSIC

Salle Pleyel (Map pp64–5; ☎ 01 42 56 13 13; www.salle pleyel.fr; 252 rue du Faubourg St-Honoré, 8e; Ⓜ Ternes; concert tickets €10–85; ☯ box office noon-7pm Mon-Sat, to 8pm on day of performance) Dating from the 1920s, this highly regarded hall hosts many of Paris' finest classical music recitals and concerts, including those by the celebrated Orchestre de Paris (www.orchestredeparis.com, in French).

Le Baiser Salé (Map pp68–9; ☎ 01 42 33 37 /1; www.le baisersale.com, in French; 58 rue des Lombards, 1er; Ⓜ Châtelet; admission free–€20) 'The Salty Kiss' is one of several jazz clubs on the same street. Combining big names and unknown artists, it is known for its relaxed vibe and its gift for discovering new talents. Music starts at 7pm and again at 10pm.

Le Caveau de la Huchette (Map pp68–9; ☎ 01 43 26 65 05; www.caveaudelahuchette.fr; 5 rue de la Huchette, 5e; Ⓜ St-Michel; Sun-Thu/Fri & Sat €11/13; ☯ 9.30pm-2.30am Sun-Wed, to 4am Thu-Sat) Housed in a medieval *caveau* (cellar) that was used as a courtroom and torture chamber during the Revolution, this club is where virtually all the jazz greats have played since the end of WWII. It's touristy, but the atmosphere can often be more electric than at the more serious jazz clubs. Sessions start at 10pm.

Le Limonaire (Map pp64–5; ☎ 01 45 23 33 33; http://limonaire.free.fr; 18 cité Bergère, 9e; Ⓜ Grands Boulevards; admission free; ☯ 7pm-midnight Mon, 6pm-midnight Tue-Sun) This little wine bar is one of the best places to listen to French *chansons* and other traditional French bistro music. Simple meals (€8.50 to €11) are served.

CLUBS

Paris does not have a mainstream club scene such as that found in London or New York; the music, theme and crowd

Drinks on the terrace at Les Deux Magots
WILL SALTER

changes regularly according to the whims of the moment, and the scene is extremely mobile.

La Dame de Canton (Map pp68–9; ☎ 01 53 61 08 49, 06 10 41 02 29; www.damedecanton.com, in French; opposite 11 quai François Mauriac, 13e; Ⓜ Quai de la Gare or Bibliothèque; admission €10; ☯ 7pm-2am Tue-Thu, 7pm-dawn Fri & Sat) This floating *boîte* (club) aboard a three-masted Chinese junk hosts concerts (8.30pm) that range from pop and indie to electro, hip-hop, reggae and rock.

Le Balajo (Map pp68–9; ☎ 01 47 00 07 87; www.balajo.fr, in French; 9 rue de Lappe, 11e; Ⓜ Bastille; admission €12–18; ☯ 10pm-2am Tue & Thu, 9pm-2am Wed, 11pm-5am Fri & Sat, 3-7.30pm Sun) A mainstay of Parisian nightlife since 1936, this ancient ballroom scores a mention for its historical value and its old-fashioned *musette* gigs on Sundays: waltz, tango and cha-cha for aficionados of retro tea-dancing.

Point Éphémère (Map pp52-3; ☎ 01 40 34 02 48; www .pointephemere.org; 200 quai de Valmy, 10e; Ⓜ Louis Blanc; admission free-€14; ☯ 10am-2pm) A relatively new arrival by the Canal St-Martin with some of the best electronic music nights in town.

Social Club (Map pp64-5; ☎ 01 40 28 05 55; www.myspace.com/parissocialclub; 142 rue Montmartre, 2e; Ⓜ Grands Boulevards; admission free-€20; ☯ 11pm-3am Wed & Sun, to 6am Thu-Sat) Once known as Triptyque, this vast and very popular club is set up in three underground rooms and fills something of a gap in inner-city clubbing. Musically they're onto it, with a serious sound system spanning electro, hip-hop and funk, as well as jazz and live acts.

GAY & LESBIAN VENUES

The Marais has been Paris' main centre of gay and lesbian nightlife for two decades.

3W Kafé (Map pp68-9; ☎ 01 48 87 39 26; www.3w-kafe.com, in French; 8 rue des Écouffes, 4e; Ⓜ St-Paul; ☯ 5.30pm-2am) This glossy lesbian cocktail bar is the flagship venue on a street with several dyke bars. It's relaxed and elegant and there's no ban on men.

Amnésia (Map pp68-9; ☎ 01 42 72 16 94; www.amnesia-café.com; 42 rue Vieille du Temple, 4e; Ⓜ Hôtel de Ville; ☯ 11am-2am) In the heart of the Marais, cosy Amnésia remains resolutely popular with gay guys but is more mixed than many of its counterparts. There's an attractive lounge area upstairs and a tiny dance floor in the *cave* (wine cellar) downstairs with DJ music from the 1980s and 1990s.

OPERA

Opéra Bastille (Map pp68-9; 2-6 place de la Bastille, 12e; Ⓜ Bastille; opera €7-150, ballet €5-80, concert tickets €10-65; ☯ box office 10.30am-6.30pm Mon-Sat) Tickets are available from the box office at 130 rue de Lyon, 11e, some 14 days before the date of the performance. The cheapest opera seats are €7 and are only sold from the box office. Note, on

Galeries Lafayette

the first day they are released, box office tickets can only be bought from the opera house at which the performance is to be held. At Bastille, standing-only tickets for €5 are available 1½ hours before performances begin. Just 15 minutes before the curtain goes up, last-minute seats at reduced rates (usually €20 for opera and ballet performances) are released to people who are aged under 28 or over 60.

Palais Garnier (Map pp64-5; ☎ 08 92 89 90 90; place de l'Opéra, 9e; Ⓜ Opéra; ☯ box office 11am-6.30pm Mon-Sat) Ticket prices and conditions (including last-minute discounts) at the city's original opera house are almost exactly the same as those at the Opéra Bastille.

CABARET

Paris' risqué cabaret revues – those dazzling, pseudo-bohemian productions where the women wear two beads and a feather (or was it two feathers and a bead?) – are another one of those things that everyone sees in Paris except the Parisians themselves. But they draw in the crowds and can be a lot of fun. Tickets cost anything from €65 to €120 per person (€140 to €400 with swish dinner and Champagne). Venues sell tickets online.

Le Lido de Paris (Map pp64-5; ☎ 01 40 76 56 10; www.lido.fr; 116bis av des Champs-Élysées, 8e; Ⓜ George V) Founded at the close of WWII, the Lido gets top marks for its ambitious sets and the lavish costumes of its 70 *artistes*, including the famed Bluebell Girls and now the Lido Boy Dancers.

Moulin Rouge (Map pp64-5; ☎ 01 53 09 82 82; www.moulinrouge.fr; 82 bd de Clichy, 18e; Ⓜ Blanche) This legendary cabaret founded in 1889, whose dancers appeared in Toulouse-Lautrec's celebrated posters, sits under its trademark red windmill (actually a 1925 copy of the 19th-century original)

and attracts viewers and voyeurs by the busload.

SHOPPING
CLOTHING & FASHION

The Right Bank, especially the so-called **Triangle d'Or** (Map pp64-5; Ⓜ Franklin D Roosevelt or Alma Marceau, 1er & 8e) formed by av Montaigne and av Georges V, **rue du Faubourg St-Honoré** (Ⓜ Madeleine or Concorde, 8e) and its eastern extension, **rue St-Honoré** (Ⓜ Tuileries), **place des Victoires** (Ⓜ Bourse or Sentier, 1er & 2e) and the Marais' **rue des Rosiers** (Ⓜ St-Paul, 4e), is traditionally the epicentre of Parisian fashion, though **St-Germain** (Map pp68-9; Ⓜ St-Sulpice or St-Germain des Prés) on the Left Bank can also claim a share of boutiques.

Grands magasins (department stores):

Galeries Lafayette (Map pp64-5; ☎ 01 42 82 34 56; 40 bd Haussmann, 9e; Ⓜ Auber or Chaussée d'Antin; ☯ 9.30am-7.30pm Mon-Wed, Fri & Sat, 9.30am-9pm Thu) Features a wide selection of fashion and accessories and the world's largest lingerie department. A fashion show (☎ bookings 01 42 82 30 25) takes place at 3pm on Friday.

Le Bon Marché (Map pp68-9; ☎ 01 44 39 80 00; 24 rue de Sèvres, 7e; Ⓜ Sèvres Babylone; ☯ 9.30am-7pm Mon-Wed & Fri, 10am-9pm Thu, 9.30am-8pm Sat) Opened by Gustave Eiffel as Paris' first department store in 1852.

FLEA MARKETS

Marché aux Puces de Montreuil (Map pp52-3; av du Professeur André Lemière, 20e; Ⓜ Porte de Montreuil; ☯ 8am-7.30pm Sat-Mon) Established in the 19th century, this flea market is renowned for its quality second-hand clothing and designer seconds. The 500 stalls also sell engravings, jewellery, linen, crockery, old furniture and appliances.

Marché aux Puces de St-Ouen (Map pp52-3; rue des Rosiers, av Michelet, rue Voltaire, rue Paul Bert & rue Jean-Henri Fabre, 18e; Ⓜ Porte de Clignancourt; ☉ 9am-6pm Sat, 10am-6pm Sun, 11am-5pm Mon) This vast flea market was founded in the late 19th century and is said to be Europe's largest. It has some 2500 stalls grouped into 10 marchés (market areas), each with its own speciality.

GETTING THERE & AWAY
AIR

Paris is served by **Aéroport d'Orly** (ORY; Map p97; ☎ 39 50, 01 70 36 39 50; www .aero portsdeparis.fr), 18km south of the city, and **Aéroport Roissy Charles de Gaulle** (CDG; Map p97; ☎ 39 50, 01 70 36 39 50; www .aeroportsdeparis.fr), 30km northeast of Paris, both well linked by public transport to central Paris. **Aéroport Paris-Beauvais** (BVA; off Map p97; ☎ 08 92 68 20 66, 03 44 11 46 86; www.aeroportbeauvais.com), 80km north of Paris, handles some budget carriers.

TRAIN

Gare d'Austerlitz (Map pp68-9; bd de l'Hôpital, 13e; Ⓜ Gare d'Austerlitz) Loire Valley and non-TGV trains to southwestern France.

Gare de l'Est (Map pp68-9; bd de Strasbourg, 10e; Ⓜ Gare de l'Est) TGV Est trains to areas of France east of Paris (Champagne).

Gare de Lyon (Map pp68-9; bd Diderot, 12e; Ⓜ Gare de Lyon) Regular and TGV Sud-Est and TGV Midi-Méditerranée trains to areas southeast of Paris, including Lyon, Provence, the Côte d'Azur and the Alps.

Gare Montparnasse (Map pp68-9; av du Maine & bd de Vaugirard, 15e; Ⓜ Montparnasse Bienvenüe) Brittany and places en route from Paris (eg Chartres, Angers, Nantes); TGV Atlantique Ouest and TGV Atlantique Sud-Ouest trains to Tours, Nantes, Bordeaux and other destinations in southwestern France.

Gare du Nord (Map pp52-3; rue de Dunkerque, 10e; Ⓜ Gare du Nord) UK; trains to the northern suburbs of Paris and northern France, including TGV Nord trains to Lille and Calais.

Gare St-Lazare (Map pp64-5; rue St-Lazare & rue d'Amsterdam, 8e; Ⓜ St-Lazare) Normandy.

GETTING AROUND
TO/FROM THE AIRPORTS
AÉROPORT D'ORLY

There is a surfeit of public-transport options to get to and from Orly airport. Services call at both terminals. Tickets for the bus services are sold on board.

Air France bus 1 (☎ 08 92 35 08 20; www .cars-airfrance.com; one-way/return €9/14; 30-45min; every 15min; ☉ 6am-11.30pm from Orly, 5.45am-11pm from Invalides) This navette (shuttle bus) runs to/from the eastern side of Gare Montparnasse (Map pp68–9; rue du Commandant René Mouchotte, 15e; Ⓜ Montparnasse Bienvenüe).

Orlyval (☎ 08 92 68 77 14; adult/4-10yr €9.30/4.65; 35-40min; every 4-12min ☉ 6am-11pm) This RATP service links Orly with the city centre via a shuttle train and the RER (p94). An automated shuttle train runs between the airport and Antony RER station (eight minutes) on RER line B, from where it's an easy journey into the city; to get to Antony from the city (26 minutes), take line B4 towards St-Rémy-lès-Chevreuse. Orlyval tickets are valid for travel on the RER and for metro travel within the city.

RER C (☎ 08 90 36 10 10; adult/4-10yr €6/4.25; 50min; every 15-30min ☉ 5.30am-11.50pm) An Aéroports de Paris (ADP) shuttle bus links the airport with RER line C at Pont de Rungis-Aéroport d'Orly RER station. From the city, take a C2 train towards Pont de Rungis or Massy-Palaiseau. Tickets are valid for onward travel on the metro.

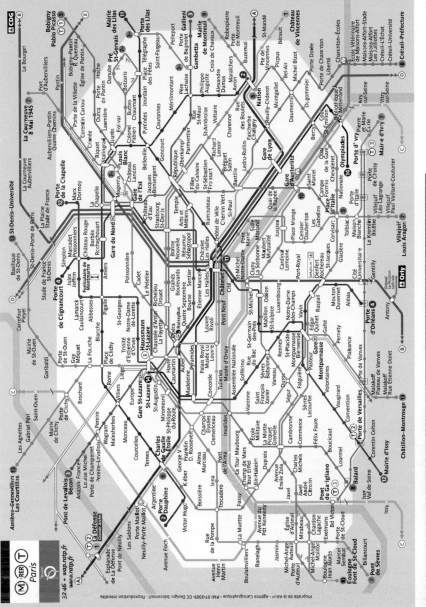

AÉROPORT ROISSY CHARLES DE GAULLE

Roissy Charles de Gaulle has two train stations: Aéroport Charles de Gaulle 1 (CDG1) and the sleek Aéroport Charles de Gaulle 2 (CDG2). Both are served by commuter trains on RER line B3. A free shuttle bus links all of the terminals with the train stations.

There is public transport between Aéroport Roissy Charles de Gaulle and Paris. Tickets for the bus are sold on board.

Air France bus 2 (☎ 08 92 35 08 20; www .cars-airfrance.com; one-way/return €13/18; 35-50min; every 15min 🕓 5.45am-11pm) Air France bus 2 links the airport with two locations on the Right Bank: near the Arc de Triomphe just outside 2 av Carnot, 17e (Map pp68–9; Ⓜ Charles de

Metro station, Galeries Lafayette (p91)

Gaulle-Étoile) and the Palais des Congrès de Paris (Map pp68–9; bd Gouvion St-Cyr, 17e; Ⓜ Porte Maillot).

Air France bus 4 (☎ 08 92 35 08 20; www .cars-airfrance.com; one-way/return €14/22; 45-55min; every 30min; 🕓 7am-9pm from Roissy Charles de Gaulle, 6.30am-9.30pm from Paris) Air France bus 4 links the airport with Gare de Lyon (Map pp68–9; 20bis bd Diderot, 12e; Ⓜ Gare de Lyon) and with Gare Montparnasse (Map pp68–9; rue du Commandant René Mouchotte, 15e; Ⓜ Montparnasse Bienvenüe).

RER B (☎ 08 90 36 10 10; adult/4-11yr €8.20/5.80; 30min; every 10-15min 🕓 5am-midnight) RER line B3 links CDG1 and CDG2 with the city. To get to the airport, take any RER line B train whose four-letter destination code begins with E (eg EIRE), and a shuttle bus (every five to eight minutes) will ferry you to the appropriate terminal. Regular metro ticket windows can't always sell RER tickets as far as the airport so you may have to buy one at the RER station where you board.

Roissybus (Map pp64-5; ☎ 08 92 68 77 14; €8.60; 45-60min; every 15min; 🕓 5.45am-11pm) This direct public bus links both terminals with rue Scribe behind the Palais Garnier in the 9e.

BICYCLE

A runaway success since its launch in 2007, **Vélib'** (☎ 01 30 79 79 30; www.velib .paris.fr; day/week/year subscription €1/5/29, bike hire per 1st/2nd/additional 30min free/€2/4) has revolutionised how Parisians get around. Its more than 1500 *stations* across the city – one every 300m – sport 20-odd bike stands a head (at the last count there were 20,600 bicycles in all flitting around Paris) and are accessible around-the-clock.

One- and seven-day subscriptions can be done on the spot at any station with any major credit card, which must have a chip. Bikes are geared to cyclists aged 14 and over, and are fitted with gears, anti-theft lock with key, reflective strips and front/rear lights. Bring your own helmet!

PUBLIC TRANSPORT

Paris' underground network consists of the metro, with 14 lines, and the RER, a network of suburban lines, designated A to E and then numbered, that pass through the city centre. Each metro train is known by the name of its terminus. The last metro train on each line begins its run sometime between 12.35am and 1.04am. The metro starts up again around 5.30am.

The same **RATP (Régie Autonome des Transports Parisians; ☎ 32 46, 08 92 69 32 46; www.ratp.fr; ⊙ 7am-9pm Mon-Fri, 9am-5pm Sat & Sun)** tickets are valid on the metro, the RER (for travel within the city limits), buses, the Montmartre funicular and Paris' three tram lines. A single ticket costs €1.50; a carnet (book) of 10 is €11.10 (€5.55 for children aged four to 11 years). One metro/bus ticket lets you travel between any two metro stations – no return journeys – for a period of 1½ hours.

TOURIST PASSES

The Mobilis card coupon allows unlimited travel for one day in two to six zones (€5.60 to €15.90; €4.55 to €13.70 for children aged four to 11 years). Depending on how many times you plan to hop on/off the metro in a day, a carnet might work out to be cheaper.

The Paris Visite pass allows the holder unlimited travel (including to/from airports) as well as discounted entry to certain museums and activities. They are valid for one, two, three or five consecutive days of travel in three, five or eight zones. The version covering one to three zones costs €8.50/14/19/27.50 for one/two/three/five days. Children aged four to 11 years pay €4.25/7/9.50/13.75.

Weekly tickets (coupon hebdomadaire) cost €16.30 for zones 1 and 2. Even if you're in Paris for three or four days, it may work out to be cheaper than buying carnets and will certainly cost less than buying a daily Mobilis or Paris Visite pass.

TAXI

Prise en charge (flag fall) in a Parisian taxi is €2.10. Within city limits, it costs €0.82 per kilometre and €1.10 per kilometre from 5pm to 10am, Sunday and public holidays.

To order a taxi:

Central taxi switchboard (☎ 01 45 30 30 30)

Alpha Taxis (☎ 01 45 85 85 85; www.alpha taxis.com)

Taxis Bleus (☎ 01 49 36 29 48, 08 91 70 10 10; www.taxis-bleus.com)

DAY TRIPS
VERSAILLES
pop 87,100

The prosperous, leafy and very bourgeois suburb of Versailles, 21km southwest of Paris, is the site of the grandest and most famous château in France.

Office de Tourisme de Versailles (☎ 01 39 24 88 88; www.versailles-tourisme.com; 2bis av de Paris; ⊙ 10am-6pm Mon, 9am-7pm Tue-Sun Apr-Sep, 9am-6pm Tue-Sat, 9am-6pm Sun Oct-Mar) Sells the Passeport to Château de Versailles.

CHÂTEAU DE VERSAILLES

The splendid and enormous **Château de Versailles** (Versailles Palace; ☎ 08 10 81 16 14; www.chateauversailles.fr; adult/under 18yr €13.50/free, from 3pm €10/free; ⊙ 9am-6.30pm Tue-Sun Apr-Oct, to 5.30pm Tue-Sun Nov-Mar) was

Château de Fontainebleau

JOHN ELK III

⬎ IF YOU LIKE...

If you fell in love with **Château de Versailles** (p95), you'll enjoy exploring these other châteaux around Paris.

- **Château de Fontainebleau** (☎ 01 60 71 50 70; www.musee-chateau-fontainebleau .fr, in French, www.chateaudefontainebleau.net; adult/18-25yr/under 18yr €8/6/free, admission free 1st Sun of month; ◷ 9.30am-6pm Wed-Mon Jun-Sep, to 5pm Wed-Mon Oct-May) This 1900-room palace, which is located 67km southeast of Paris, is one of France's most beautifully furnished châteaux. Every centimetre of wall and ceiling space is richly adorned with wood panelling, gilded carvings, frescos, tapestries and paintings. The parquet floors are of the finest woods, the fireplaces are ornamented with exceptional carvings, and many pieces of the furniture date to the Renaissance. Beyond its extraordinary formal gardens slumbers the beautiful **Forêt de Fontainebleau**, a favourite hunting ground of many French kings. SNCF trains link Paris' Gare de Lyon hourly with Fontainebleau-Avon station (€7.60, 40 to 60 minutes).

- **Château de Chantilly** (☎ 03 44 27 31 80; www.chateaudechantilly.com; adult/under 18yr €10/free; ◷ 10am-6pm Wed-Mon Mar-Oct, 10.30am-5pm Wed-Mon Nov-Feb) Left in a shambles after the Revolution, Chantilly, situated 48km north of Paris is of interest mainly because of several superb paintings it contains; its gardens, which are among France's most spectacular; and its lavish stables built between 1719 and 1740 to house 240 horses and more than 400 hounds. The daily 30-minute dressage demonstrations performed here are enthralling but it is the equestrian shows it hosts that are truly magical; reserve tickets (like gold dust) online. RER and SNCF commuter trains link Paris' Gare du Nord and Chantilly-Gouvieux train station (€7, 30 to 45 minutes).

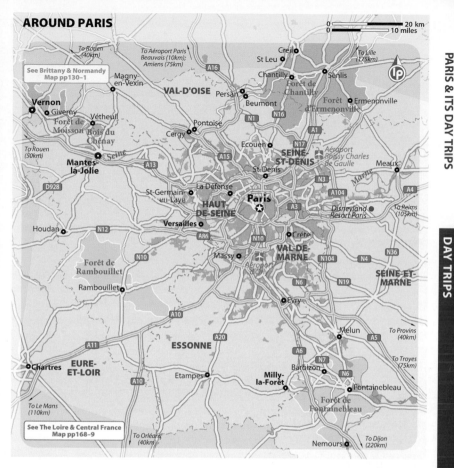

AROUND PARIS

0 — 20 km
0 — 10 miles

To Rouen (40km)

To Aéroport Paris Beauvais (10km); Amiens (75km)

A16

Creil

St Leu

Chantilly

Forêt de Chantilly

Senlis

To Lille (175km)

See Brittany & Normandy Map pp130–1

Magny-en-Vexin

VAL-D'OISE

Persan

Beumont

Forêt d'Ermenonville

Ermenonville

Vernon

Giverny

Vétheuil

Forêt de Moisson

Bois du Chénay

Pontoise

Cergy

N1

N16

A1

To Rouen (50km)

Seine

Mantes-la-Jolie

A13

Ecouen

St-Germain-en-Laye

A15

SEINE-ST-DENIS

N17

Aéroport Roissy Charles de Gaulle

Meaux

Marne

St-Denis

N3

Houdan

D928

N12

La Défense

HAUT-DE-SEINE

Paris

A3

A104

Disneyland Resort Paris

A4

To Reims (105km)

Versailles

A86

Créteil

N10

VAL-DE-MARNE

N104

N4

N36

Forêt de Rambouillet

N10

Massy

Aéroport d'Orly

N6

N19

SEINE-ET-MARNE

Rambouillet

Evry

A10

Melun

To Provins (40km)

A11

A20

ESSONNE

A6

A5

Chartres

EURE-ET-LOIR

A10

Etampes

Milly-la-Forêt

Barbizon

N7

N6

Fontainebleau

To Troyes (75km)

To Le Mans (110km)

See The Loire & Central France Map pp168–9

To Orléans (40km)

Forêt de Fontainebleau

Nemours

To Dijon (220km)

built in the mid-17th century during the reign of Louis XIV. The château has undergone relatively few alterations since its construction, though almost all the interior furnishings disappeared during the Revolution and many of the rooms were rebuilt by Louis-Philippe (r 1830–48). The current €370 million restoration program is the most ambitious yet and until it's completed in 2020 at least a part of the palace is likely to be clad in scaffolding when you visit.

The château complex comprises four main sections: the palace building, a 580m-long structure with multiple wings, grand halls and sumptuous bedchambers and the Grands Appartements du Roi et de la Reine; the vast gardens, canals and pools to the west of the palace; two much smaller palaces (outbuildings almost!), the **Grand Trianon** and, a few hundred metres to the east, the **Petit Trianon**; and the **Hameau de la Reine** (Queen's Hamlet).

The basic palace ticket includes an English-language audioguide and allows visitors to freely visit the palace's state apartments, the chapel, the **Appartements du Dauphin et de la Dauphine** (Dauphin's

PARIS & ITS DAY TRIPS

DAY TRIPS

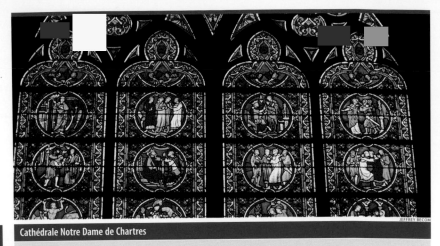

JEFFREY BECOM

Cathédrale Notre Dame de Chartres

⬋ CATHÉDRALE NOTRE DAME DE CHARTRES

With its astonishing blue stained glass and other treasures, the **Cathédrale Notre Dame de Chartres**, France's best-preserved medieval basilica, is a must-see for any visitor.

It was built in the Gothic style during the first quarter of the 13th century to replace a Romanesque cathedral that had been devastated by fire on the night of 10 June 1194. The cathedral's west entrance, **Portail Royal**, is the only one that pre-dates the 12th-century fire. The structure's other main Romanesque feature is the 112m-high **Clocher Vieux**, the tallest Romanesque steeple still standing anywhere.

A visit to the 112m-high **Clocher Neuf** is well worth the climb up the long spiral stairway. A 70m-high platform on the lacy Flamboyant Gothic spire affords superb views of the three-tiered flying buttresses and the 19th-century copper roof turned green.

The cathedral's 172 extraordinary **stained-glass windows** are renowned for the depth and intensity of their blue tones, famously called 'Chartres blue'. The cathedral's 110m **crypt**, a tombless Romanesque structure built in 1024 around a 9th-century predecessor, is the largest in France.

More than 30 trains a day link Paris' Gare Montparnasse (€12.90, 70 minutes) with Chartres, all of which pass through Versailles-Chantiers (€10.90, 45 minutes to one hour).

Things you need to know: Cathédrale Notre Dame de Chartres (Cathedral of Our Lady of Chartres; ☎ 02 37 21 22 07; www.diocese-chartres.com, in French; place de la Cathédrale; ⊗ 8.30am-7.30pm); Clocher Neuf (New Bell Tower; adult/18-25yr/under 18yr €6.50/4.50/free; ⊗ 9.30am-noon & 2-5.30pm Mon-Sat, 2-5.30pm Sun May-Aug, 9.30am-noon & 2-4.30pm Mon-Sat, 2-4.30pm Sun Sep-Apr); crypt (adult/7-18yr €2.70/2.10)

and Dauphine's Apartments) and various galleries. The so-called **Passeport (adult/ under 18yr €20/free Tue-Fri, €25/free Sat & Sun Apr-Oct, €16/free Tue-Sun Nov-Mar)** includes the same as well as the Grand Trianon and, in high season, the Grandes Eaux Musicales fountain displays (see below). Enter the palace through Entrée A with a palace ticket; Entrée C with a Passeport.

The section of the vast **château gardens** (8.30am-8.30pm Apr-Oct, 8am-6pm Nov-Mar) nearest the palace, laid out between 1661 and 1700 in the formal French style, is famed for its geometrically aligned terraces, flowerbeds, tree-lined paths, ponds and fountains. Admission to the gardens is free, except on weekends during the Grandes Eaux Musicales, between April and October.

The **Grand Canal** is oriented to reflect the setting sun. It is traversed by the 1km-long **Petit Canal**, creating a cross-shaped body of water with a perimeter of more than 5.5km. Louis XIV used to hold boating parties here. In season, you too can paddle around the Grand Canal in four-person **rowing boats**.

Try to time your visit for the **Grandes Eaux Musicales (adult/student & 11-18yr/under 11yr €7/5.50/free, admission free after 4.50pm;** 11am-noon & 3.30-5pm Sat & Sun Apr-Sep) or the after-dark **Grandes Eaux Nocturnes (adult/11-18yr/under 10yr €7/5.50/free;** 9.30-11.30pm Sat & Sun Jul & Aug), truly magical 'dancing water' displays set to music composed by baroque- and classical-era composers throughout the grounds in summer.

Tickets to **guided tours** (08 10 81 16 14; adult with/without palace ticket, Passeport or ticket to the Domaine de Marie-Antoinette €7.50/14.50, under 18yr €5.50; 9.45am-3.45pm Tue-Sun) addressing different themes are sold at the main ticket office. Some are conducted in English.

GETTING THERE & AWAY

RATP bus 171 (€1.50 or one metro/bus ticket, 35 minutes) links Pont de Sèvres (15e) in Paris with the place d'Armes every six to nine minutes.

RER line C5 (€2.80) goes from Paris' Left Bank RER stations to Versailles-Rive Gauche station, 700m southeast of the château and close to the tourist office. Trains run every 15 minutes until shortly before midnight.

SNCF operates up to 70 trains a day from Paris' Gare St-Lazare (€2.80) to Versailles-Rive Droite, 1.2km from the château. An SNCF package *(forfait loisir)* covering the Paris metro, return train journey to/from Versailles and château admission costs €19.20.

DISNEYLAND RESORT PARIS

Disneyland Resort Paris, 32km east of Paris, consists of three main areas: **Disney Village**, with its hotels, shops, restaurants and clubs; **Disneyland Park**, with its five theme parks; and **Walt Disney Studios Park**, which brings film, animation and TV production to life. The first two are separated by the RER and TGV train stations; the studios neighbour Disneyland Park. Moving walkways whisk visitors to the sights from the far-flung car park.

One-day admission fees at **Disneyland Resort Paris** (01 60 30 60 30; www.disney landparis.com; adult/3-11yr/under 3yr €46/38/free) include unlimited access to all rides and activities in *either* Walt Disney Studios Park or Disneyland Park. Multiple-day passes are available, including a **Passe-Partout (adult/3-11yr/under 3yr €56/48/free)**, which allows entry to both parks for one day, and the two-/three-day **Hopper Ticket (adult €103/128, 3-11yr €84/105)** with which you can enter and leave both parks

LEFT: OLIVIER CIRENDINI; RIGHT: DENNIS JOHNSON

Left: Disneyland Resort Paris (p99); Right: Château de Versailles (p95)

as often as you like over nonconsecutive days used within one year. Admission fees change from season to season, and a multitude of special offers and accommodation/transport packages are always available.

You are not allowed to picnic on resort grounds but there's an ample number of themed restaurants to choose from. To avoid another queue, pick your place online and reserve a table in advance (☎ 01 60 30 40 50).

GETTING THERE & AWAY

Marne-la-Vallée/Chessy, Disneyland's RER station, is served by line A4; trains run every 15 minutes or so from central Paris (€7.50, 35 to 40 minutes).

D 23

MAREUIL
LE PORT

EPERNAY

CHÂTILLON ˢ/ M.
VILLE ᴇɴ Tᴺᴼᴵˢ

ROUTE
TOURISTIQUE DU
CHAMPAGNE

CHAMPAGNE & THE NORTHEAST

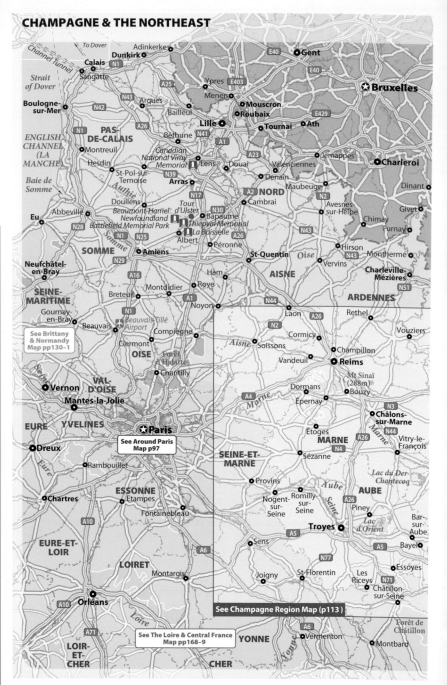

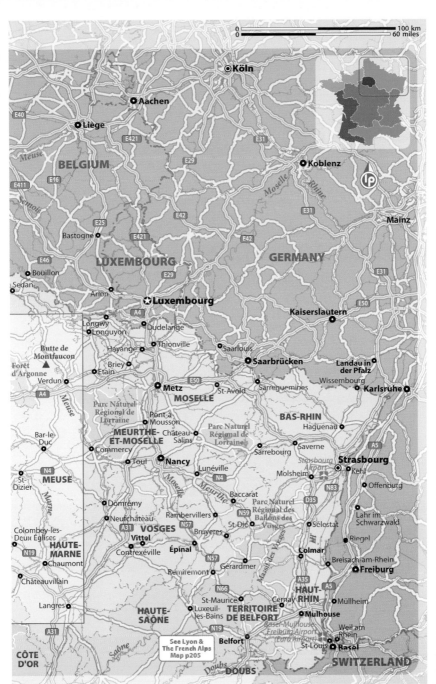

HIGHLIGHTS

1 WINE TASTING IN CHAMPAGNE

BY MICHAEL EDWARDS, GASTRONOMIC WRITER, RESTAURANT CRITIC & CHAMPAGNE CONNOISSEUR

At first sight, Champagne is a cold misty land, the most northerly of France's great wine regions. Look again and savour the subtle beauty of huge skies, rolling hills and attractive villages. Oh, and the wine, the finest sparkler in the world, with an exceptional aptitude to age well and mellow.

⬈ MICHAEL EDWARDS' DON'T MISS LIST

❶ REIMS

This great city is now just 45 minutes from Paris by TGV train. Walk on foot from the station to the splendid cathedral (p113) where the kings of France were crowned for 600 years, and then to the even more beautiful, Romanesque Basilique St-Rémi (p115). Reims has a fine range of places to eat and, for me, one of France's best fish restaurants: Le Foch (☎ 03 26 47 48 22; www.lefoch.com; 37 blvd Foch), close to central place d'Erlon in the city's heart.

❷ LE MESNIL-SUR-OGER

Head for the village of Le Mesnil in the Côte des Blancs, the greatest Chardonnay commune in Champagne. Taste with rising star, Christophe Constant, at Champagne JL Vergnon (☎ 03 26 57 53 86; www.champagne-jl-vergnon .com; 1 Grand Rue) in the village centre and lunch afterwards at Le Mesnil (☎ 03 26 57 95 57; www.restaurantlemesnil.com; 2 rue Pasteur), five minutes' walk away, where Cedric the chef cooks monkfish beautifully – perfect with one of the fine, fairly priced Champagnes on the list.

Clockwise from top: Cathédrale Notre Dame (p113), Reims; Decorative wine barrel; Entry to Mumm Champagne house (p115); Mercier Champagne (p118); Bottles in their second fermentation

CLOCKWISE FROM TOP: OLIVER STREWE; ELLIOT DANIEL; ELLIOT DANIEL; ELLIOT DANIEL; OLIVER STREWE

❸ CHAMPAGNE PRODUCER

My favourite right now is **Veuve Fourny & Fils** (☎ **03 26 52 16 30; www .champagne-veuve-fourny.com; rue du Mesnil, Vertus**). They are masters of the bone-dry, non-dosed Champagne; theirs is called Brut Nature and is a wonderful partner for all sorts of shellfish and those great cheese pastry balls called *gougères au fromage.*

❹ THE CHAMPENOIS

I love the region so much, mainly be-cause of the people. Reserved but with great inner warmth and a deliciously dry sense of humour, the Champenois are resilient and hard working. But they also know how to play: go to any dance hall and you'll see what I mean.

↘ THINGS YOU NEED TO KNOW

Best panorama From the high ridge in Cramant to fully appreciate Cham-pagne's austere beauty **Catch the harvest** in September when grapes must be hand picked **Bedtime reading** *Michael's Wine Diary* (http://edwards-onwine .skynetblogs.be) and his latest book, *The Finest Wine of Champagne* (2009)

HIGHLIGHTS

2

⤡ CHAMPAGNE ROUTE

This scenic driving route (p116) wends its way through Champagne's vineyards. A handful of name-brand *maisons* (literally 'houses', meaning Champagne producers) are known the world over, but much of Champagne's best liquid gold is made by almost 5000 small-scale *vignerons* (wine makers) in around 320 villages. Dozens welcome visitors for a taste, tipple and shop at producer prices.

3

⤡ REIMS

This regal Champagne-producing city (p112) also boasts two Unesco-protected sacred spaces: scale Cathédrale Notre Dame's tower for 360-degree views and be dazzled by the same rose window that bathed Charles VII in blue as he was crowned in 1429 (Joan of Arc at his side). Nearby stands Basilique St-Rémi with its perfectly sculpted Romanesque nave and graceful Gothic, candle-lit choir.

4

↘ TROYES

Meander through the back streets and alleys of this picturesque old city (p120), home to a clutch of exceptional museums and entire streets lined with some of Europe's best-preserved half-timbered houses that were built during the Renaissance. Atmospheric mooching aside, Troyes' other selling point is its factory-outlet jackpot of designer goods at bargain prices.

5

↘ BATTLE OF THE SOMME MEMORIALS

It is all rather grizzly but pondering the sacrifices and horror of WWI at these moonscape battlefields (p124) around Arras in northeastern France is a moving experience. Of the dozens of evocative memorials and cemeteries, the Thiepval Memorial honouring 'the missing' is the most visited.

6

↘ AMIENS & METZ CATHEDRALS

This twinset of Gothic cathedrals is among France's most visited. Connoisseurs rave about the soaring arches of Amiens's Cathédrale Notre Dame (p126) with tower to climb, John the Baptist's skull encased in gold, and summer light show. At Metz's Cathédrale St-Étienne (p127), France's finest stained glass stuns.

2 NEIL SETCHFIELD; 3 OLIVER STREWE; 4 ELLIOT DANIEL; 5 GLENN HARPER/ALAMY; 6 CHRIS MELLOR

2 Vineyards, Vallée de la Marne (p116); 3 Cathédrale Notre Dame (p113), Reims; 4 Half-timbered houses, Troyes (p120); 5 WWI military cemetery; 6 Cathédrale St-Étienne (p127), Metz

THE BEST...

⬎ CULINARY TEMPTATIONS

- **Biscuits rosés** Pink sweet bites traditionally nibbled with Champagne; sample at Waïda (p117).
- **Andouillette de Troyes** (p121) We dare you to bite into a juicy Troyes tripe sausage.
- **Otée à la Champenoise** (p118) Try this Champenois speciality at Épernay's La Cave à Champagne.
- **Moules frites** (p125) Feast on mounds of mussels and fries in Lille and other northern cities.

⬎ CAFÉ LOUNGING

- **L'Apostrophe & Le Continental** (p117) The pick of Reims' Champagne-fuelled café life.
- **Marrott Street** (p126) Eiffel-designed and *the* space in Amiens to sip Champagne.
- **Café Jeanne d'Arc** (p127) Drink in Metz beneath 16th-century wood beams.

⬎ SHOPPING

- **Troyes' factory outlets** (p123) Designer fashion at rock-bottom prices.
- **Braderie de Lille** (p125) The world's largest flea market.
- **Vins CPH** (p117) Where local Reimois buy wine.

⬎ STUNNING CITY SQUARES

- **Place des Héros & Grand' Place, Arras** (p123) A Flemish-baroque feast for the eyes; stunning at night.
- **Place Notre-Dame, Amiens** (p126) Best viewed in summer when a light show illuminates the cathedral.
- **Place Stanislas, Nancy** (p122) Among Europe's most dazzling public spaces, this neoclassical square is a World Heritage site.

MICHAEL GEBICKI

Champagne vineyards south of Reims

THINGS YOU NEED TO KNOW

⇘ VITAL STATISTICS

- **Population** 1.3 million (Champagne), 5.9 million (far northern France), 4 million (Alsace & Lorraine)
- **Best time to visit** Spring and summer
- **Points of entry** Reims, Troyes and Lille (all from Paris)

⇘ ADVANCE PLANNING

- **A month before** or earlier, book accommodation; the most sought-after boutique addresses such as seven-room Le Clos Raymi (p118) fill fast.
- **Two weeks before** Plan which Reims and Épernay Champagne cellars you want to visit and reserve a guided tour; ditto for Champagne Domi Moreau's fabulous guided bike rides between vines (p118).
- **One week before** Gen up on money-saving city passes; the Reims City Card (p112) is a particular deal.

⇘ RESOURCES

- **Tourism in Champagne-Ardenne** (www.tourisme-champagne -ardenne.com) Walks, gardens, nature, history, outdoor action etc in the Champagne region.
- **Northern France Tourist Office** (www.cdt-nord.fr) Particularly excellent audio downloads.

- **Tourism in Nord-Pas de Calais** (www.northernfrance-tourism.com) Regional tourist office.
- **Somme Battlefields** (www.somme -battlefields.co.uk) The practical guide.

⇘ GETTING AROUND

- **Car** is perfect for uncovering Champagne, although it does restrict bubbly-tasting.
- **Train** to/from Paris (Reims, Épernay, Troyes and Metz are easy day trips); excellent Reims–Épernay rail connections.
- **Eurostar** (www.eurostar.com) puts London a hop, skip and jump away (80 minutes to Lille).
- **Bus** is the best for getting between Reims and Troyes.

⇘ BE FOREWARNED

- **Champagne producers** along Champagne routes around Reims and Épernay close their doors to visitors during the *vendange* (grape harvest) in September and October.
- **Épernay hotels** are often full weekends Easter to September and weekdays May, June and September.
- **Battle of Verdun** site interiors are closed in January.

ITINERARIES

Champagne and the northeast of France offer bubbly delights, gorgeous villages surrounded by vineyards and stunning architectural highlights.

CHAMPAGNE TASTER Three Days

Spend a day getting to know Pommery, Mumm and other big-name Champagne houses in **(1) Reims** (p112). Lunch brasserie-style at **(2) L'Apostrophe** (p117) or in more modern surrounds at **(3) Côté Cuisine** (p117) and clear your head afterwards with a 250-step hike up the **(4) cathedral tower** (p113). Later indulge in a spot of wine and Champagne shopping, breaking for 'afternoon tea' (aka Champagne and local *biscuits rosés*) at **(5) Waïda** (p117).

Next day move onto wealthy **(6) Épernay** (p117) and its wealth of subterranean cellars – 110km in all – where 200 million-plus bottles of Champers, just waiting to be popped open for a sparkling occasion, are being aged. Take your pick of **(7) Champagne house** (p118), lunch on regional cuisine at **(8) La Cave à Champagne** (p118) and spend the afternoon pedalling between vines on a two-hour **(9) guided bike ride** (p118).

Final day hop in the car and motor west along the Vallée de la Marne **(10) Champagne Route** (p116) or south through scenic **Côte des Blancs** (p116) vineyards for a beautiful drive between pea-green vineyards, flowery villages and medieval churches.

CHAMPAGNE CONNOISSEUR Five Days

Immerse yourself into France's most sparkling viticulture region: devote the first three days to a **Champagne Taster** (see above) in the cellars and vineyards of Champagne towns **(1) Reims** (p112) and **(2) Épernay** (p117); overnight at **(3) Le Clos Raymi** (p118), the 19th-century town house of Monsieur Chandon of Champagne fame. Motor south on day three to **(4) Mutigny** (p116) for a walk through vines, then continue through the pretty villages of **(5) Cuis** (p116), **(6) Le Mesnil-sur-Oger** (p116), **(7) Vertus** (p116) and Renoir's **(8) Sézanne** (p116) to Troyes.

On the fourth day explore **(9) Troyes** (p120), indulging that penchant for the finer things in life with outstanding modern art at the **(10) Musée d'Art Moderne** (p121), 180 stained-glass windows in the **(11) cathedral** (p120), lunch in a **(12) hybrid art-gallery-wine-bar** (p123) and an afternoon shop for a designer cocktail dress (to sip Champagne in, darling) in nearby **(13) St-Julien-les-Villas** (p123) and **(14) Pont Ste-Marie** (p123).

End on a Champagne-fuelled high with a quintessential French day trip southeast of Troyes, through Côte des Bar vineyards, along the region's other **(15) Champagne Route** (p116).

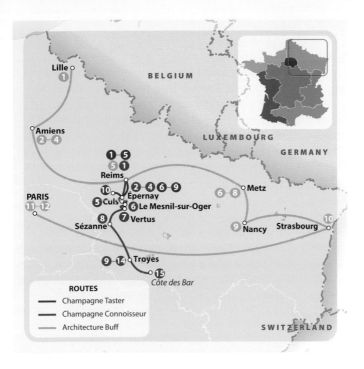

ARCHITECTURE BUFF One Week

(1) Lille (p122), with its Flemish Renaissance old town and art museum strikingly ensconced in a 1920s art-deco swimming pool, is a grand place to start architectural explorations, especially if you're arriving fresh off the *Eurostar* from London.

On the second day train it to (2) Amiens (p125) to admire France's largest Gothic cathedral. Lunch at the Eiffel-designed (3) Marrot Street (p126), lingering until dark to see (4) Cathédrale Notre-Dame (p126) bathed in a pageant of rich medieval colours. On day three zip into Paris, cross the city, and catch an eastward-bound TGV to (5) Reims (p112) to be seduced by its Romanesque basilica (a Unesco World Heritage site). From here it's an easy 40-minute trip by TGV to elegant (6) Metz (p127) in Alsace. Another night-time beauty, its (7) cathedral (p127) is famed for its stained glass while the (8) Centre Pompidou-Metz (p127) delights the least dedicated of architecture buffs.

Next up is a lesson in neoclassical architecture in (9) Nancy (p122) and a taste of Germanic culture, and a very different France east again in (10) Strasbourg (p122); devote a trio of days to this cosmopolitan twinset to avoid museum fatigue.

End the week back in (11) Paris (p50) with a day exploring the city's original (12) Centre Pompidou (p67) and other architectural icons.

DISCOVER CHAMPAGNE & THE NORTHEAST

No French region's name better evokes its essence than Champagne, a wine producing part of northern France that has been famed for its bubbly ever since a 17th-century monk called Dom Pierre Pérignon perfected the process of using a second fermentation to inject sparkle into ho-hum still wine. Sauntering, tasting hat on, from prestigious bottle-crammed cellar to cellar in Reims and Épernay is a unique experience. Later, meander on foot or by bike through vines, from one medieval gold-stone village to another, and pinch yourself: life *can* be this good!

Looking north, cities such as Lille – a mere hop from the UK for *Eurostar* travellers – and Arras ooze regional flavour with their Flemish architecture, cuisine and beer. Francophiles flock here in October to suck mussels at the world's biggest flea market; while art and architecture lovers know this part of France as the 'insider' address, with the new Centre Pompidou opening in Metz in late 2009, followed by a branch of the Louvre in Lens in 2010.

CHAMPAGNE

Known in Roman times as Campania, meaning 'plain', Champagne is a largely agricultural region and is celebrated around the world for the sparkling wines that have been produced here for more than three centuries. According to French law, only bubbly originating from this region – grown in designated areas (now being expanded to meet growing demand), then aged and bottled according to the strictest of rules – can be labelled as Champagne.

The town of Épernay, 30km to the south of Reims, is the de facto capital of Champagne (the drink, that is) and is the best place to head for *dégustation* (tasting session).

REIMS

pop 202,600

Over the course of a millennium (816 to 1825), some 34 sovereigns, among them two dozen kings, began their reigns as rulers in Reims' famed cathedral. The city, whose name is pronounced something like 'rance' and is often anglicised as Rheims, is neat and orderly, with wide avenues and well-tended parks. Along with Épernay, it is the most important centre of Champagne production.

INFORMATION

Tourist Office (☎ 03 26 77 45 00, 08 92 70 13 51; www.reims-tourisme.com; 2 rue Guillaume de Machault; ☼ 9am-7pm Mon-Sat, 10am-6pm Sun & holidays mid-Apr–mid-Oct, 10am-6pm Mon-Sat, 11am-4pm Sun & holidays mid-Oct–mid-Apr) The Reims City Card (€14) gets you a Champagne-house tour, an all-day bus ticket, entry to all four municipal museums and a guided tour of the cathedral.

SIGHTS

Imagine the extravagance, the over-the-top costumes and the egos writ large of a French royal coronation… The focal point of such pompous occasions was **Cathédrale Notre Dame** (www.cathedrale -reims.com, in French; place du Cardinal Luçon; ☽ 7.30am-7.30pm, closed Sun morning), a Gothic edifice begun in 1211.

Very badly damaged by artillery and fire during WWI, the 138m-long cathedral, now a Unesco World Heritage site, is more interesting for its dramatic history than its heavily restored architectural features. The finest stained-glass windows are the western facade's 12-petalled great rose window, its almost cobalt-blue

neighbour below, and the rose window in the north transept (to the left), above the Flamboyant Gothic organ case (15th and 18th centuries) topped with a figure. Nearby you will find a 15th-century wooden **astronomical clock**.

Those who have strong thighs may want to climb the 250 steps of the **cathedral tower** (adult/12-25yr €6.50/4.50; ☽ Tue-Sat & Sun afternoon early May–early Sep, Sat & Sun afternoon mid-Mar–early May & early Sep-Oct) on a one-hour tour. Book next door at the **Palais du Tau** (☎ 03 26 47 81 79; www .palais-du-tau.fr, in French; 2 place du Cardinal

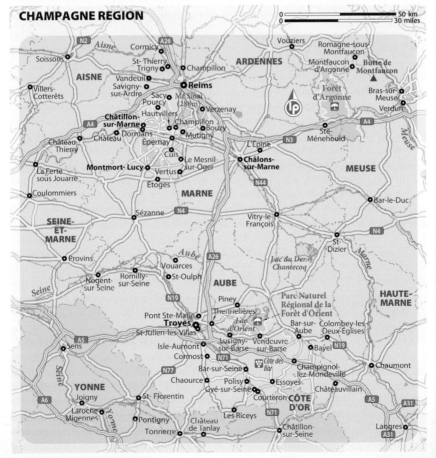

CHAMPAGNE REGION

REIMS

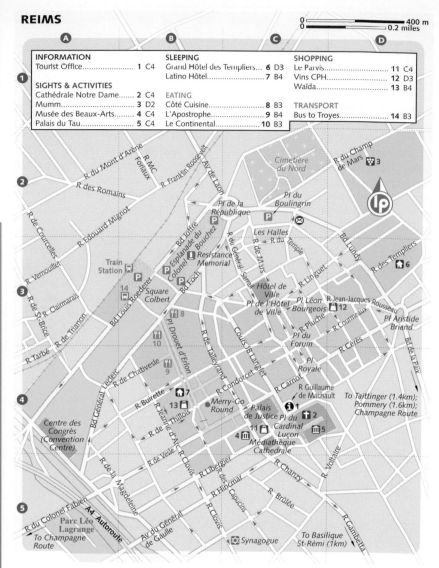

INFORMATION	
Tourist Office.....................	**1** C4

SIGHTS & ACTIVITIES	
Cathédrale Notre Dame.......	**2** C4
Mumm................................	**3** D2
Musée des Beaux-Arts.........	**4** C4
Palais du Tau......................	**5** C4

SLEEPING	
Grand Hôtel des Templiers...	**6** D3
Latino Hôtel.......................	**7** B4

EATING	
Côté Cuisine......................	**8** B3
L'Apostrophe.....................	**9** B4
Le Continental..................	**10** B3

SHOPPING	
Le Parvis...........................	**11** C4
Vins CPH...........................	**12** D3
Waïda...............................	**13** B4

TRANSPORT	
Bus to Troyes.....................	**14** B3

Luçon; adult/student/under 18yr €6.50/4.50/free; 9.30am-6.30pm Tue-Sun early May–early Sep, 9.30am-12.30pm & 2-5.30pm Tue-Sun early Sep–early May), a former archbishop's residence constructed in 1690. Now a museum, it displays truly exceptional statuary, liturgi-cal objects and tapestries from the cathe-dral, some in the impressive Gothic Salle de Tau (Great Hall).

The rich collections of the **Musée des Beaux-Arts** (☎ 03 26 47 28 44; 8 rue Chanzy; 10am-noon & 2-6pm Wed-Sun) include one of only four versions of Jacques-Louis David's world-famous *The Death of Marat* (yes, the bloody corpse in the bathtub) and 27 works by Camille Corot (only the Louvre has more).

The 121m-long **Basilique St-Rémi** (place du Chanoine Ladame; ⏳ 8am-7pm) is named in honour of Bishop Remigius, who baptised Clovis and 3000 Frankish warriors in 498. Once a Benedictine abbey church and now a Unesco World Heritage Site, its Romanesque nave and transept – worn but stunning – date mainly from the mid-11th century. The choir (constructed between 1162 and 1190) is in the early Gothic style, with a large triforium and, way up top, tiny clerestory windows. The 12th-century-style chandelier has 96 candles, one for each year of the life of St Rémi, whose tomb (in the choir) is marked by a mausoleum from the mid-1600s.

CHAMPAGNE HOUSES

The musty *caves* (cellars) and dusty bottles of eight Reims Champagne houses can be visited on guided tours. The following places all have fancy websites, cellar temperatures of 8°C to 10°C, and frequent English-language tours that end, *naturellement,* with a tasting session.

Mumm (☎ 03 26 49 59 70; www.mumm.com; 34 rue du Champ de Mars; tours adult/under 12yr €8/free; ⏳ tours 9am-11am & 2-5pm Mar-Oct, Sat Nov-Feb) Mumm (pronounced 'moom'), the only *maison* in the centre of Reims, was founded in 1827 and is now the world's third-largest producer (eight million bottles a year), offering edifying one-hour cellar tours in cellars containing 25 million bottles. Phone ahead for weekday tours from November to February. A tasting session with oenological commentary is available for €14/19.50 for two/three Champagnes.

Pommery (☎ 03 26 61 62 55; www.pommery .fr; 5 place du Général Gouraud; tours adult /student & 12-17yr/under 12yr €10/7/free; ⏳ tours 9.30am-7pm Apr–mid-Nov, 10am-6pm Sat & Sun mid-Nov–Mar) Pommery occupies an Elizabethan-style hilltop campus (built 1868–78) 1.8km southeast of the cathedral. The year-round cellar tours take you 30m underground to Gallo-Roman quarries and 25 million bottles of bubbly. Telephoning ahead for reservations is recommended.

Taittinger (☎ 03 26 85 84 33; www.taittinger .com; 9 place St-Niçaise; tours adult/under 12yr €10/free; ⏳ tours 9.30am-noon & 2-4.30pm, closed Sat & Sun mid-Nov–mid-Mar) The headquarters of Taittinger, 1.5km southeast of the cathedral, is an excellent place to come for a clear presentation on how

OLIVER STREWE

Vineyard picnic lunch

NEIL SETCHFIELD

Champagne vineyards, Vallée de la Marne

↘ THE CHAMPAGNE ROUTE

The Route du Champagne weaves its way among neatly tended vines covering the slopes between small villages. All along the route, beautiful panoramas abound and small-scale *producteurs* (Champagne producers) welcome travellers in search of bubbly, though you should phone ahead before stopping by.

The route's signposted tertiary roads pass through the Marne's four most important wine-growing areas. The first two start in Reims, the last two in Épernay.

- **Massif de St-Thierry** (70km) – northwest of Reims, through such villages as Cormicy (WWI national cemetery), St-Thierry (Benedictine monastery with 12th-century chapel), Trigny (where French kings-to-be began their journey to Reims and coronation), flower-bedecked Vandeuil and Savigny-sur-Ardre (where Charles de Gaulle first broadcast his appeal for French resistance).

- **Montagne de Reims** (70km) – between Reims and Épernay, through Sacy (the church has an elegant spire), Verzenay (identifiable from afar by the lighthouse), Bouzy (famed for its nonsparkling reds) and Mutigny (has a 2km *sentier de vignoble* – 'vineyard walking path').

- **Vallée de la Marne** (90km) – west of Épernay towards Dormans, through Champillon (panoramic views), Hautvillers, Damery (medieval church), Châtillon-sur-Marne (huge statue of Pope Urban II, initiator of the First Crusade) and Dormans (château and park).

- **Côte des Blancs** (100km) – south of Épernay towards Sézanne, through Cuis (Romanesque church), Le-Mesnil-sur-Oger (flowers), Vertus (fountains and a church), Étoges (17th-century château) and medieval Sézanne.

Champagne is made. On the one-hour tours visitors are shown everything from *remuage* (bottle turning) to *dégorgement* (sediment removal at -25°C) to the corking machines. Parts of the cellars occupy 4th-century Roman stone quarries; other bits were made by 13th-century Benedictine monks.

SLEEPING

Latino Hôtel (☎ 03 26 47 48 89; www.latino cafe.fr, in French; 33 place Drouet d'Erlon; s & d €54-74, apt €130; 🔀 🖳 🗶) This almost boutique hotel above a buzzy musical café has a dozen gaily painted guestrooms (think cherry, pumpkin and aubergine) over five floors but no lift. The furnishings are fun, the welcome exceptionally warm and we love the quotes from the great and the good (Gandhi, Boris Vian) sgraffitoed on the hall walls.

our pick **Grand Hôtel des Templiers** (☎ 03 26 88 55 08; http://pagesperso-orange.fr/hotel.templiers; 22 rue des Templiers; r €190-280, ste €350; 🔀 🖳 🗶 🐾) Built in the 1800s as the home of a rich Champagne merchant, this luxurious four-star neo-Gothic extravaganza retains its original ceilings, stained glass and furnishings. The sweeping wooden staircase imparts a certain retro theatricality but the 17 rooms and suites come with luscious fabrics and modern marble bathrooms.

EATING

Côté Cuisine (☎ 03 26 83 93 68; 43 bd Foch; starters €6-21, mains €11.80-22.50, weekday lunch menus €13.50-16.90, dinner menus €32.50; 😊 lunch & dinner Mon-Sat) A spacious, modern place with well-regarded traditional French cuisine.

L'Apostrophe (☎ 03 26 79 19 89; 59 place Drouet d'Erlon; starters €6.50-15.10, mains €14.50-25, weekday lunch menu €14; 😊 lunch & dinner) This stylish (and sprawling) café-brasserie is a perennial favourite thanks to its chic atmosphere, summertime terrace and good value. Open as a café straight through from 9am to 1am.

Le Continental (☎ 03 26 47 01 47; 95 place Drouet d'Erlon; starters €15.90-27, mains €16.90-39, menus, some incl wine, €18.90-55; 😊 lunch daily, dinner Mon-Sat) Built in the early 20th century, this classy, marble-floored place with an extravagant golden 'tree' holding up the ceiling serves up panoramic views and classic French dishes such as *magret de canard au miel d'acacia* (duck breast fillet with acacia honey; €15.90). It's open for drinks all afternoon and is a great spot for a tea-time glass/bottle of Champagne (€8/44).

SHOPPING

Le Parvis (☎ 03 26 47 44 44; place du Cardinal Luçon) Enormous range of Champagnes and regularly scheduled tastings (€7 to €10).

Vins CPH (☎ 03 26 40 12 12; www.vinscph.com; 3 place Léon Bourgeois;) Where locals buy good-value wines.

our pick **Waïda** (☎ 03 26 47 44 49; 5 place Drouet d'Erlon; 😊 7.30am-7.30pm Wed-Sun) An old-fashioned *salon de thé* (tearoom) and confectioner with mirrors, mosaics and marble, Waïda is the place to buy a box of *biscuits rosés* (€3.30), traditionally nibbled with Champagne.

GETTING THERE & AWAY

The best way to get to Troyes (€21.80, 1¾ to 2¼ hours) is to take a bus. The stop is in front of the train station.

Direct services link Reims with Épernay (€5.70, 22 to 38 minutes) and Paris' Gare de l'Est (€22.70, 1¾ hours), half of which are TGVs (€28, 45 minutes).

ÉPERNAY

pop 24,500

Prosperous Épernay, the self-proclaimed *capitale du champagne* and home to many of the world's most celebrated Champagne houses, is the best place in Champagne for touring cellars and sampling bubbly. The town also makes a good base for exploring the Champagne Route.

INFORMATION

Tourist Office (☎ 03 26 53 33 00; www.ot-epernay.fr; 7 av de Champagne; 😊 9.30am-

12.30pm & 1.30-7pm Mon-Sat, 11am-4pm Sun & holidays mid-Apr–mid-Oct, 9.30am-12.30pm & 1.30-5.30pm Mon-Sat mid-Oct–mid-Apr)

TOURS
CHAMPAGNE HOUSES
Many of the *maisons* on or near av de Champagne offer interesting, informative cellar tours, followed by tasting and a visit to the factory-outlet bubbly shop.

Moët & Chandon (☎ 03 26 51 20 20; www .moet.com; 1/2 glasses adult €11/18, 10-18yr €6.70, under 10yr free; 20 av de Champagne; ☺ tours 9.30-11.30am & 2-4.30pm, closed Sat & Sun mid-Nov–Mar) This prestigious *maison* offers frequent one-hour tours that are among the region's most impressive.

De Castellane (☎ 03 26 51 19 11; www.cas tellane.com, in French; 64 av de Champagne; 1/2/3 glasses adult €7/12/18, under 10yr free; ☺ tours 10.30-11.15am & 2.30-5.15pm mid-Mar–Dec, Sat & Sun Jan–mid-Mar) The 45-minute tours take in the *maison*'s informative bubbly museum. The reward for climbing the 237 steps up the 66m-high tower is a panoramic view.

Mercier (☎ 03 26 51 22 22; www.champagne mercier.com; 68-70 av de Champagne; adult/12-17yr €7/3; ☺ tours 9.30-11.30am & 2-4.30pm mid-Mar-late Nov, closed Tue & Wed late Nov–mid-Mar) The most popular brand in France (and No 2 in overall production). Everything here is flashy, including the lift that transports you 30m underground and the laser-guided touring train.

VINEYARDS
Champagne Domi Moreau (☎ 06 30 35 51 07, after 7pm 03 26 59 45 85; www.champagne -domimoreau.com; tours €20; ☺ tours 9.30am & 2.30pm except Wed, no tours 2nd half of Aug, Christmas period & Feb school holidays) Runs three-hour minibus tours (in French and English) to nearby vineyards. Pick-up is across the street from the tourist office

on av de Champagne. It also organises two-hour bicycle tours of the vineyards for €10. Call ahead for reservations.

SLEEPING
La Villa St-Pierre (☎ 03 26 54 40 80; www.vil lasaint pierre.fr, in French; 1 rue Jeanne d'Arc; d €33-50, with washbasin €23; ☐ ☒) In an early-20th-century mansion that has hardly changed in half a century, this homey one-star place has 15 simple rooms that retain the charm and atmosphere of yesteryear.

Le Clos Raymi (☎ 03 26 51 00 58; www.clos raymi-hotel.com; 3 rue Joseph de Venoge; d from €100, ste €160; ☐ ☒) Staying at this delightful three-star place away from the centre is like being a personal guest of Monsieur Chandon of Champagne fame, who occupied this luxurious home over a century ago. The seven romantic rooms have giant beds, 3.7m-high ceilings, ornate mouldings and parquet floors.

EATING
L'Ancêtre (☎ 03 26 55 57 56; 20 rue de la Fauvette; starters €8.30-12, mains €13-22, menus €15.50-29; ☺ closed Mon & lunch Wed) A rustic eatery with a grape-patterned stained-glass door, traditional French cuisine and a mere half-dozen tables. Call ahead for reservations.

La Cave à Champagne (☎ 03 26 55 50 70; 16 rue Gambetta; starters €9-15, mains €12-16, menus €16.50 & €32; ☺ closed Tue & Wed) 'The Champagne Cellar' is well regarded by locals for its Champenois cuisine, including *potée à la champenoise* (poultry and pork oven-baked with cabbage; €14).

SELF-CATERING
Open-air market (place Auban Moët; ☺ Sun morning)

Charcutier-Traiteur (9 place Hugues Plomb; ☺ 8am-12.45pm & 3-7.30pm, closed Sun & Wed) Sells scrumptious prepared dishes.

G P BOWATER/ALAMY

Côte des Bar vineyards

⤵ IF YOU LIKE...

If you like the Champagne Route (p116), you'll salivate over the lesser-known Champagne- and wine-making villages framed by Côte des Bar vineyards, southeast of Troyes:

- **Bar-sur-Aube (tourist office ☎ 03 25 27 24 25; www.barsuraube.net, in French; place de l'Hôtel de Ville)**, a 30-minute train trip from Troyes (€8.80), is graced by a medieval quarter and two churches, notably 13th-century Église St-Pierre **(rue St-Pierre).**

- **Bayel (tourist office ☎ 03 25 92 42 68; www.bayel-cristal.com; 2 rue Belle Verrière)** is known for crystal; tour the Cristallerie Royale de Champagne **(Royal Champagne Glassworks; ☎ 03 25 92 37 60; place de l'Église)** next to the tourist office.

- **Colombey-les-Deux-Églises** is home to Charles de Gaulle, buried in the village-centre churchyard. La Boisserie **(☎ 03 25 01 50 50; adult/under 12yrs €4/ free, incl memorial €7/free; ۞ 10am-12.30pm & 2-6.15pm daily mid-Apr–mid-Oct, to 5.15pm Wed-Mon mid-Oct–Nov & Feb–mid-Apr)**, the general's home from 1934 to 1970, is now a museum.

- **Essoyes (tourist office ☎ 03 25 29 64 64; place de la Mairie)** is the village where Renoir chose to spend his last 25 summers and be buried; the Atelier Renoir **(☎ 03 25 38 56 28; adult/under 12yrs €2/free; ۞ 2.30-6.30 daily Easter-Oct)** in the centre is where the great Impressionist worked. Nearby Les Riceys **(tourist office ☎ 03 25 29 15 38; place des Héros de la Résistance)** is noted for its trio of churches, three different AOCs and exceptional rosé wines.

La Cloche à Fromage **(19 rue St-Thibault; ۞ 9am-12.15pm & 3.15-7pm Tue-Sat)** Head to this establishment to select from wonderful cheeses as well as other fine food products.

GETTING THERE & AROUND

From the train station **(place Mendès France)** there are direct services to Reims (€5.70, 23 to 32 minutes) and Paris' Gare de l'Est (€19.40, 1¼ hours).

ELLIOT DANIEL

Street artist, Troyes

TROYES

pop 60,500

Troyes – like Reims – has a lively old centre that's graced with one of France's finest ensembles of Gothic churches and medieval and Renaissance half-timbered civic buildings.

Troyes does not have any Champagne cellars. However, you can shop till you drop in its scores of outlet stores that carry brand-name clothing and accessories.

INFORMATION

Tourist Office (www.tourisme-troyes.com) Train Station (☎ 03 25 82 62 70; 16 bd Carnot; ◷ 9am-12.30pm & 2-6.30pm Mon-Sat year-round except holidays, 10am-1pm Sun & holidays Nov-Mar); City Centre (☎ 03 25 73 36 88; rue Mignard; ◷ 10am-7pm daily Jul–mid-Sep, 9am-12.30pm & 2-6.30pm Mon-Sat, 10am-noon & 2-5pm Sun & holidays Apr-Jun & mid-Sep–Oct, closed Nov-Mar)

SIGHTS

Half-timbered houses line the streets of Troyes' old centre, rebuilt after a devastat-ing fire in 1524. Off rue Champeaux (between No 30 and 32), a stroll along tiny **ruelle des Chats** (Alley of the Cats), as dark and narrow as it was four centuries ago, is like stepping back into the Middle Ages.

Known as *la ville aux 10 églises* (the town with 10 churches), Troyes sees its most im-portant house of worship in **Cathédrale St-Pierre et St-Paul** (place St-Pierre; ◷ 10am-7pm daily Jul & Aug, 10am-1pm & 2-6pm Mon-Sat, to 5pm Sun & holidays Sep-Jun, closed Mon Nov-Mar), a 114m-long hybrid that incorporates ele-ments from every period of *champenois* Gothic architecture. The interior is illu-minated by a spectacular series of about 180 **stained-glass windows** (dating from the 13th to the 17th centuries) that, on a sunny day, shine like jewels.

Église Ste-Madeleine (rue Général de Gaulle; ◷ 9.30am-12.30pm & 2-5.30pm, closed Sun morning), Troyes' oldest and most in-teresting church has an early-Gothic nave and transept from the mid-12th century; the choir and tower weren't built until the Renaissance. The main attractions are the splendid Flamboyant Gothic **rood**

screen, which dates from the early 1500s, and the 16th-century stained glass in the presbytery portraying scenes from Genesis.

Some 10,000 centuries-old hand tools bring to life a world of manual skills made obsolete by the Industrial Revolution at Maison de l'Outil et de la Pensée Ouvrière (Museum of Tools & Crafts; ☎ 03 25 73 28 26; www.maison-de-l-outil.com; 7 rue de la Trinité; adult/student & 12-18yr/under 18yr €6.50/3/free, admission free 1st Sun of month; ☺ 10am-6pm). Definitely worth a visit.

Musée d'Art Moderne (☎ 03 25 76 26 80; place St-Pierre; adult/student under 25yr, under 18yr €5/free, admission free 1st Sun of month; ☺ 10am-1pm & 2-6pm Tue-Sun) owes its existence to all those alligator shirts, whose global success allowed the museum's benefactors, Lacoste entrepreneurs Pierre and Denise Lévy, to amass this outstanding collection. Housed in an erstwhile bishop's palace (from the 16th to 18th centuries), the museum focuses on glass (especially the work of local glassmaker Maurice Marinot), ceramics and French painting (including lots of fauvist works) created between 1850 and 1950. Featured artists include Derain, Dufy, Matisse, Modigliani, Picasso and Soutine

If you happen to come down with an old-fashioned malady – scurvy, perhaps, or unbalanced humours – the place to go is the Apothicaire de l'Hôtel-Dieu-le-Comte (☎ 03 25 80 98 97; quai des Comtes de Champagne; adult/student under 25yr, under 18yr €2/free, admission free 1st Sun of month; ☺ 9am-noon & 1-5pm Tue-Sun), a fully outfitted, wood-panelled pharmacy from 1721.

SLEEPING
our pick Hôtel Arlequin (☎ 03 25 83 12 70; www.hotelarlequin.com; 50 rue de Turenne; d with shower/shower & toilet from €41/58; ☺ reception 8am-12.30pm & 2-10pm Mon-Sat, 7am-12.30pm &

6.30-10pm Sun & holidays; ☒ ☐) The 22 cheerful rooms at this charming and very yellow two-star hostelry come with antique furnishings, high ceilings and commedia dell'arte playfulness.

Hôtel Les Comtes de Champagne (☎ 03 25 73 11 70; www.comtesdechampagne.com; 56 rue de la Monnaie; d/q from €50/70, d with washbasin €33; ☐ ☒) For centuries, the same massive wooden ceiling beams have kept this superwelcoming place from collapsing into a pile of toothpicks. Bicycles (see below) are available for rent.

EATING
The people of Troyes are enormously proud of the local speciality, andouillette de Troyes (pork or veal tripe sausage).

Au Jardin Gourmand (☎ 03 25 73 36 13; 31 rue Paillot de Montabert; starters €9-14, mains €17-25, weekday lunch menu €17; ☺ closed Sun

WAY TO GO
A 42km-long bike path called Vélovoie (☎ 03 25 42 50 00; www.aube-champagne.com) links the southeastern Troyes suburb of St-Julien-les-Villas with Lac d'Orient and two adjacent lakes (Lac du Temple and Lac Amance) further north. The lakes are known for their birdlife (cranes, kingfishers), and there's a hide on a narrow isthmus between Lac d'Orient and Lac du Temple for budding birders. At least 15 daily trains a day from Paris' Gare de l'Est (up to a dozen at the weekend) allow passengers to transport their bicycles. Ask the tourist office in Troyes for the brochure-map Vélovoie Troyes > Les Lacs or download it from the Aube-Champagne website.

ROCCO FASANO

Lille

⬎ IF YOU LIKE...

If the magnificent architecture of Troyes (p120) inspires you, so will these northern towns:

- **Lille** (tourist office ☎ from abroad 03 59 57 94 00, in France 08 91 56 20 04; www.lilletourism .com; place Rihour) An 80-minute train trip from London, Lille is overtly Flemish. Explore its attractive old town, shop, dine fine and revel in great art at its trio of renowned art museums (one in a 1920s art-deco swimming pool).

- **Nancy** (tourist office ☎ 03 83 35 22 41; www.ot-nancy.fr; place Stanislas) With its magnificent neoclassical central square (among Europe's most dazzling), fine museums and sparkling shop windows, this former capital of the dukes of Lorraine feels as opulent today as it did in the 16th to 18th centuries. Look for art nouveau stained-glass windows and sinuous grillwork gracing building entrances.

- **Strasbourg** (tourist office ☎ 03 88 52 28 28; www.otstrasbourg.fr; 17 place de la Cathédrale) This metropolis of northeastern France is the intellectual and cultural capital of the Alsace region, as well as the seat of the European Parliament and the Council of Europe. Think lively old city abuzz with *winstubs* (traditional Alsatian eateries); a medieval cathedral that is sculpted in pink sandstone; and one of the finest ensembles of museums that you will find in France.

- **Colmar** (tourist office ☎ 03 89 20 68 92; www.ot-colmar.fr; 4 rue d'Unterlinden) This city is a harmonious maze of cobbled alleys and historic Alsatian-style buildings painted blue, orange, red or green. The Musée d'Unterlinden (www.musee-unterlinden.com) is famed worldwide for the profoundly moving *Issenheim Altarpiece,* set around a Gothic-style Dominican cloister shaded by hazelnut trees. Later explore the Alsatian wine-road (www.alsace-route -des-vins.com).

& lunch Mon) This intimate restaurant uses only the freshest ingredients for its French and *champenois* dishes, including no fewer than 13 kinds of *andouillette*. Enjoy the terrace in summer.

ourpick **La Mignardise** (☎ 03 25 73 15 30; 1 ruelle des Chats; starters €18-28.50, mains €27.50-32, menus €26-53; ☯ closed dinner Sun & Mon) An elegant restaurant whose traditional French cuisine is served beneath ancient wooden beams, 19th-century mouldings and ultramodern halogen lamps. The chef is a particular fan of fish, with more than half of the 15 mains on offer from the briny deep.

Le Bougnat des Pouilles (☎ 03 25 73 59 85; www.bougnatdespouilles.com, in French; 29 rue Paillot de Montabert; ☯ noon-3am Mon-Sat) A funky wine bar that doubles as an art gallery. Attacks of the munchies can be overcome with plates of cold cuts and cheese (€7.50) or *tartines* (open sandwiches; €3.80 to €4.20).

SHOPPING

Troyes is well known across France for its **magasins d'usine** (factory outlets; ☯ generally 10am-7pm Mon-Fri, from 9.30am Sat, closed Sun), a legacy of the local knitwear industry.

Most stores are situated in two main zones: **St-Julien-les-Villas**, about 3km south of the city centre on bd de Dijon (the N71 to Dijon) and **Pont Ste-Marie**, located about 3km northeast of Troyes' city centre along rue Marc Verdier, which links av Jean Jaurès (the N77 to Châlons-en-Champagne) with av Jules Guesde (the D960 to Nancy).

GETTING THERE & AWAY

Troyes is on the rather isolated train line linking Basel (Bâle; €40.20, four hours) in Switzerland with Paris' Gare de l'Est (€22.20, 1½ hours, 12 to 15 daily).

NORTHEASTERN FRANCE

When it comes to culture, cuisine, shopping and dramatic views of land and sea – not to mention good old-fashioned friendliness – the Ch'tis (residents of the far north) and their region compete with the best France has to offer.

Regional flavour is on offer in Arras, whose Flemish-style squares are unique in France. Amiens, not far from the battlefields of the Somme and a number of moving WWI memorials, boasts a magnificent Gothic cathedral.

ARRAS

pop 41,400

Arras is worth seeing mainly for its harmonious ensemble of Flemish-style arcaded buildings. The city makes a good base for visits to the Battle of the Somme Memorials (p124).

Tourist office (☎ 03 21 51 26 95; www .ot-arras.fr, in French; place des Héros; ☯ 9am or 10am-noon & 2-6pm or 6.30pm Mon-Sat, no midday closure Apr-Sep, 10am-12.30pm or 1pm & 2.30-6.30pm Sun & holidays).

Arras' two market squares, **place des Héros** and the **Grand' Place**, are surrounded by 17th- and 18th-century Flemish-baroque houses, especially handsome at night. Their 345 sandstone columns form a common arcade unique in France.

The Flemish-Gothic **hôtel de ville** (place des Héros) dates from the 16th century but was completely rebuilt after WWI. If you're in the mood for a panoramic view, this is the place to hop on the lift to the top of the 75m **belfry** (adult/student €2.30/1.60; ☯ same as tourist office). But for a truly unique perspective on Arras, head into the slimy **souterrains** (tunnels). They run under place des Héros and were turned into British

ELLIOT DANIEL
Children's war memorial, Vimy

Arras is on the main line linking Lille–Flandres (€9.40, 24 to 45 minutes) with Paris' Gare du Nord (€28.70 or €38.90 by TGV, 50 minutes). Other destinations include Amiens (€10.50, 50 minutes).

BATTLE OF THE SOMME MEMORIALS

The First Battle of the Somme, a WWI Allied offensive waged northeast of Amiens, was designed to relieve pressure on the beleaguered French troops at Verdun. On 1 July 1916, British, Commonwealth and French troops 'went over the top' in a massive assault along a 34km front. On the first day of the battle an astounding 21,392 British troops were killed and another 35,492 were wounded.

By the time the offensive was called off in mid-November, a total of 1.2 million lives had been lost on both sides. The British had advanced 12km, the French 8km.

The tourist offices in Amiens and Arras can provide details on minibus tours.

NORTH OF ARRAS

The best place to get some sense of the unimaginable hell known as the Western Front is at the chilling, eerie moonscape of **Vimy Ridge**. Visitors can also visit **tunnels** (admission free; ☯ with a guide early May-Nov) and reconstructed **trenches** (☯ 10am-6pm early May-Oct, 9am-5pm Nov-early May).

Of the 66,655 Canadians who died in WWI, 3589 lost their lives in April 1917 taking this ridge, a German defensive line. Its highest point was later chosen as the site of Canada's **WWI memorial**. The **Historical Interpretive Centre** (☎ 03 21 50 68 68; www.vac-acc.gc.ca; admission free; ☯ 10am-6pm early May-Oct, 9am-5pm Nov-early May), at the entrance to the trenches, is staffed by Canadian students, who also serve as tour guides from May to November.

A taxi from Arras costs €22 to €24.

command posts, hospitals and barracks during WWI. Each spring, plants and flowers turn the tunnels into the lush, creative, life-affirming **Jardin des Boves** (Cellar Garden; ☯ mid- or late Mar–mid- or late Jun). **Tours** (adult/student €4.70/2.70) of the *souterrains* lasting 45 minutes (in English upon request).

Lots of eateries are hidden away under the arches of the Grand' Place.

Café Georget (☎ 03 21 71 13 07; 42 place des Héros; plat du jour €8; ☯ lunch Mon-Sat) Madame Delforge has been serving hearty, home-style French dishes to people who work in the neighbourhood since 1985.

GETTING THERE & AWAY

Alliance Arras Taxis-GT (☎ 03 21 23 69 69; ☯ 24hr) can take you to Somme battlefield sites, such as Vimy.

SOUTH OF ARRAS

Perhaps the best place to start a visit to the Somme battlefields is in the river port of Péronne (population 8400), at the well-designed and informative **Historial de la Grande Guerre** (Museum of the Great War; ☎ 03 22 83 14 18; www.historial.org; Château de Péronne; adult/over 60yr/children 6-18yr incl audio-guide €7.50/6/3.80; ☉ 10am-6pm, closed mid-Dec –mid-Jan). This innovative museum tells the story of the war chronologically.

THIEPVAL MEMORIAL

Dedicated to 'the Missing of the Somme', this **memorial** was built in the early 1930s. Most of the discreet, glass-walled **visitors centre** (☎ 03 22 74 60 47; admission free; ☉ 10am-6pm Mar-Oct, 9am-5pm Nov-Feb, closed two weeks around New Year) is below ground level.

BEAUMONT-HAMEL NEWFOUNDLAND BATTLEFIELD MEMORIAL PARK

Like Vimy (p124), the evocative **Beaumont-Hamel Newfoundland Battlefield Memorial Park** preserves part of the Western Front in the state it was in at fighting's end. The zigzag trench system, which still fills with mud in winter, is clearly visible, as are countless shell craters and the remains of barbed-wire barriers. Canadian students based at the **visitors centre** (☎ 03 22 76 70 87; www.vac -acc.gc.ca; admission free; ☉ 10am-6pm Apr-Oct, to 5pm Nov-Mar, closed 2 weeks around New Year) give free guided tours year-round.

THIRTY-SIXTH (ULSTER) DIVISION MEMORIAL

Built on a German frontline position assaulted by the overwhelmingly Protestant 36th (Ulster) Division on 1 July 1916, the **Tour d'Ulster** (Ulster Tower; ☎ 03 22 74 87 14; teddy.ulstertower@orange.fr; ☉ museum 10am-

5pm, to 6pm Apr-Sep, closed Dec-Feb) is an exact replica of Helen's Tower at Clanboye, County Down, where the unit did its training. A black obelisk known as the **Orange Memorial to Fallen Brethren** stands in an enclosure behind the tower.

LA GRANDE MINE

Just outside the hamlet of La Boisselle, this enormous **crater** looks like the site of a meteor impact. Some 100m across and 30m deep and officially known as the **Lochnagar Crater Memorial**, it was created on the morning of the first day of the First Battle of the Somme by about 25 tonnes of ammonal laid by British sappers in order to create a breach in the German lines.

AMIENS

pop 136,600

One of France's most awe-inspiring Gothic cathedrals is reason enough to spend time in Amiens, the comfy, if reserved, former capital of Picardy, where Jules Verne lived

---

BRADERIE DE LILLE

On the first weekend in September, Lille's entire city centre – 200km of footpaths – is transformed into the world's largest flea market. The extravaganza, with stands selling antiques, local delicacies, handicrafts and more, dates from the Middle Ages, when Lillois servants were permitted to hawk their employers' old garments for some extra cash.

The Braderie runs from 3pm on Saturday to midnight on Sunday, when street sweepers emerge to tackle the mounds of mussel shells and old *frites* (French fries) left behind by the merrymakers.

RICHARD SEMIK/ALAMY

Cathédrale Notre Dame

CATHÉDRALE NOTRE DAME

The largest Gothic cathedral in France (it's 145m long) and a Unesco World Heritage Site, the magnificent **Cathédrale Notre Dame** in Amiens was begun in 1220 to house the skull of St John the Baptist, now enclosed in gold in the northern outer wall of the ambulatory (on view from about Easter to October). Connoisseurs rave about the soaring Gothic arches (42.3m high over the transept), unity of style and immense interior.

The black-and-white, octagonal, 234m-long **labyrinth** on the floor of the nave is easy to miss as the soaring vaults draw the eye upward.

Weather permitting, it's possible to climb the **north tower** with a guide.

A free 45-minute **light show** bathes the cathedral's facade in vivid medieval colours nightly from mid-June to mid-September and December to 1 January; the photons start flying at 7pm in winter and sometime between 9.45pm (September) and 10.45pm (June) in summer.

Things you need to know: Cathédrale Notre Dame (place Notre Dame; 8.30am-6.15pm Apr-Sep, to 5.15pm Oct-Mar); north tower (☎ 03 22 80 03 41; adult/18-25yr/under 18yr €6.50/4.50/free)

for the last two decades of his life. Amiens is an excellent base for visits to the Battle of the Somme memorials.

Tourist Office (☎ 03 22 71 60 50; www.amiens.com/tourisme; 40 place Notre Dame; 9.30am-6pm or 6.30pm Mon-Sat, 10am-noon & 2-5pm Sun)

Hôtel Le Prieuré (☎ 03 22 71 16 71; www.hotelrestaurantleprieure.com, in French; 17 rue Porion; d €58-76; ⊠) A cobblestone's throw from the cathedral, 'The Priory' is a two-star, family-run hotel whose 23 rooms are imaginatively decorated.

Marott Street (☎ 03 22 91 14 93; 1 rue Marotte; 11am-1am) Designed by Gustave Eiffel's architectural firm in 1892, this one-time insurance office is now a bar where the trendy sip Champagne, suspended – on clear-glass tiles – over the wine cellar.

GETTING THERE & AWAY

The train station offers direct services to Arras (€10.50, 50 minutes), Lille-Flandres (€17.80, 1½ hours), Paris' Gare du Nord (€18.30, one to 1½ hours).

METZ

pop 323,000

Metz (pronounced 'mess') is a dignified city with stately public squares, shaded riverside parks, and a lively, pedestrians-only commercial centre. Quite a few of the city's most impressive buildings date from the 48-year period when Metz was part of the German Reich.

The **Tourist Office** (☎ 03 87 55 53 76; http://tourisme.mairie-metz.fr; 2 place d'Armes; 9am-7pm Mon-Sat, 10am-3pm Sun, to 5pm Sun Apr-Sep) has free wi-fi.

Metz' stupendous Gothic **Cathédrale St-Étienne** (place St-Étienne; 8am-7pm mid-Apr–Sep, to 6pm Oct–mid-Apr), built between 1220 and 1522, is famed for its veritable curtains of 13th- to 20th-century stained glass, among the finest in France. Try to visit on a bright day. Beautifully illuminated at night.

The **Centre Pompidou-Metz** (www.centre pompidou-metz.fr) was supposed to open its doors to aficionados of modern and contemporary art from the fall of 2009.

SLEEPING & EATING

our pick **Hôtel de la Cathédrale** (☎ 03 87 75 00 02; www.hotelcathedrale-metz.fr; 25 place de Chambre; d €58-105, ste €110) Ensconced in a gorgeous 17th-century town house, this three-star place positively oozes romance! The 30 large rooms – 10 with spectacular views of the cathedral – are tastefully furnished with antiques and rugs that complement perfectly the ancient wooden beams overhead.

Place St-Jacques is taken over by cafés in the warmer months.

our pick **L'Étude** (☎ 03 87 36 35 32; www .l-etude.com, in French; 11 av Robert Schuman; 2-/3-course lunch menus €13/15, other menus €22/27, during concerts €29/35; Mon-Sat) Hugely popular with local cognoscenti, this eatery is a quintessentially French mixture of the intellectual (the walls are lined with weighty tomes) and the gastronomic (French, of course). Live music Friday and Saturday; reservations are recommended.

Café Jeanne d'Arc (☎ 03 87 37 39 94; place Jeanne d'Arc; 11.30am-midnight Mon-Wed, 11.30am-2am Thu & Fri, 3pm-3am Sat) This bar bears its long history – the roof beams are from the 1500s, the faint frescos two or three centuries older – with good humour and mellowness.

SIMON GREENWOOD
Promenade de l'Esplanade, Metz

War cemetery, Verdun

NEIL SETCHFIELD

GETTING THERE & AWAY

Metz' **train station** (pl du Général de Gaulle) is on the line from Paris' Gare de l'Est (€50.50 to €62.70 by TGV, 80 minutes) to Luxembourg (€12.80, 50 minutes, at least 15 daily). Direct trains also go to Verdun (€6, 1½ hours).

VERDUN

pop 19,300

The horrific events that took place in and around Verdun between February 1916 and August 1917 have turned the town's name into a byword for wartime slaughter. During the last two years of WWI, more than 800,000 soldiers (some 400,000 French and almost as many Germans, along with thousands of the Americans who arrived in 1918) lost their lives in this area.

A brand-new **Tourist Office** (☎ 03 29 84 55 55; Pavillon Japiot, av du Général Mangin; 9am-7pm Mon-Sat, 9am-noon & 2-6pm Sun Jul & Aug, 9.30am-12.30pm & 1.30-6pm Mon-Sat, 10am-noon & 2-5pm Sun Sep-Jun) is run by the city.

Much of the **Battle of Verdun** was fought 5km to 8km (as the crow flies) northeast of Verdun. Today, the area – still

a jumble of trenches and artillery craters, now forested – are on and along the D913 and D112; by car follow the signs to 'Douamont', 'Vaux' or the 'Champ de Bataille 14-18'. Signposted paths lead to dozens of minor remnants of the war. Site interiors are closed in January.

The bitter fighting northwest of Verdun, in which more than 26,000 Americans died, convinced the Kaiser's government to cable US President Woodrow Wilson with a request for an armistice. The largest US military cemetery in Europe, the WWI **Meuse-Argonne American Cemetery**, is at Romagne-sous-Montfaucon, 41km northwest of Verdun along the D38 and D123.

Verdun's small train station, built by Eiffel in 1868, has direct services to Metz (€7, 1½ hours). **Hôtel Les Colombes** (☎ 03 29 86 05 46; www.hotel-a-verdun.com, in French; 9 av Garibaldi; d/q €35/45; closed Dec) rents out mountain bikes, an excellent way to tour the Verdun battlefields.

For a taxi call **Taxis de Place** (☎ 03 29 86 05 22).

BRITTANY & NORMANDY

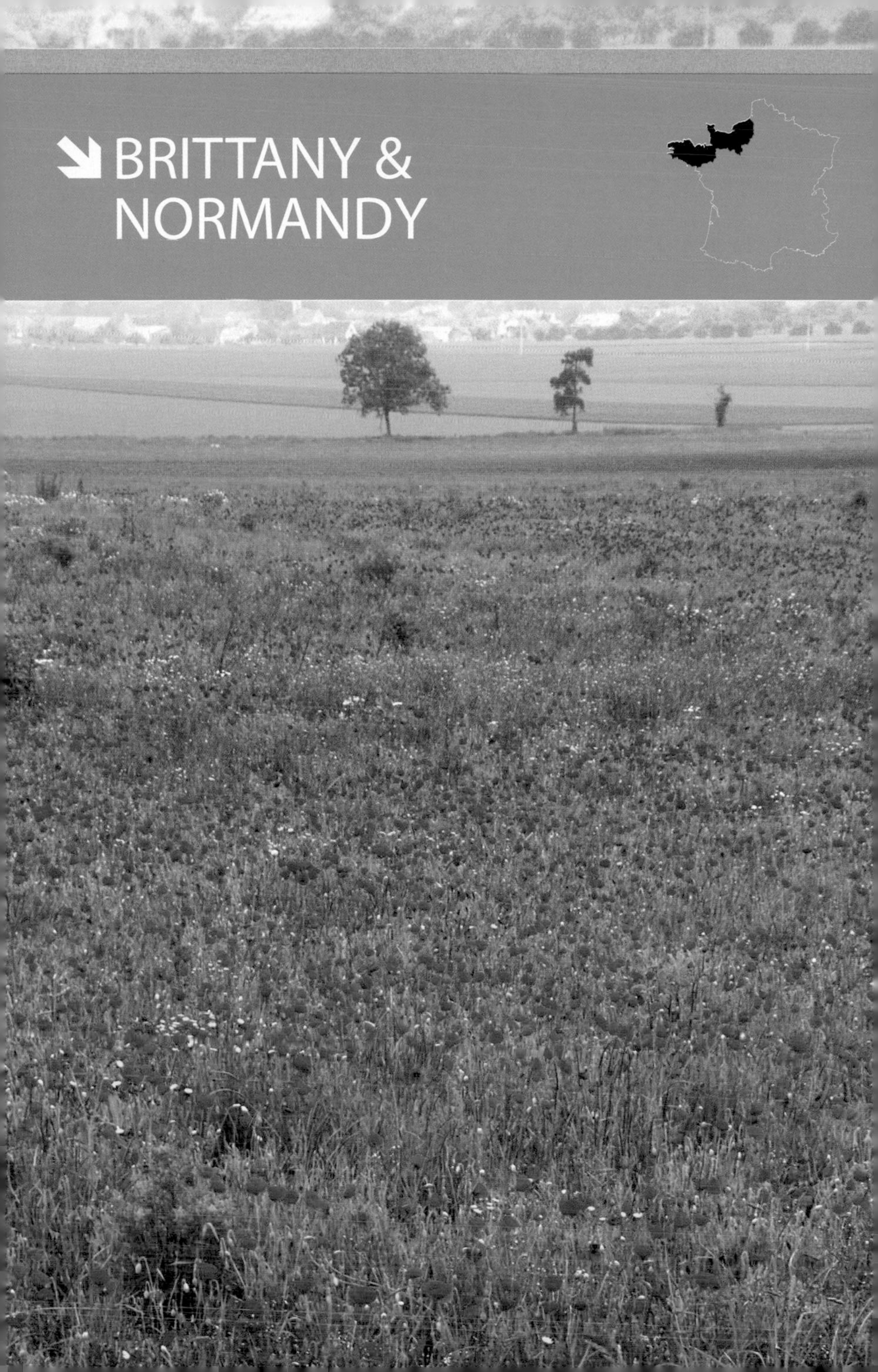

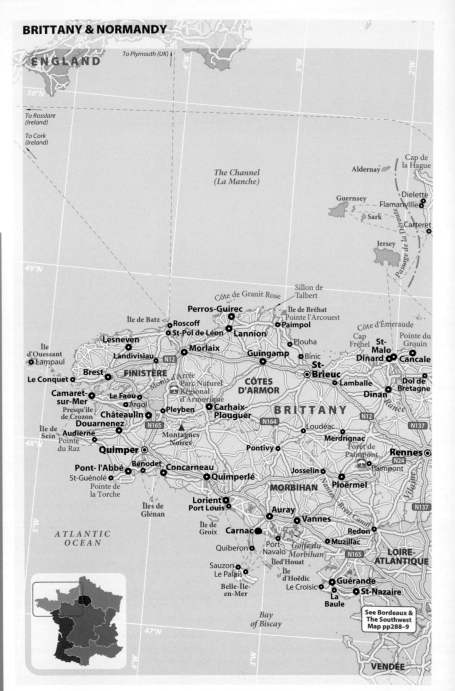

BRITTANY & NORMANDY

ENGLAND

To Plymouth (UK)

To Rosslare (Ireland)

To Cork (Ireland)

The Channel (La Manche)

Aldernay

Cap de la Hague

Guernsey

Dielette

Flamanville

Sark

Carteret

Jersey

Passage de la Déroute

Côte de Granit Rose

Sillon de Talbert

Côte d'Émeraude

Perros-Guirec

Île de Bréhat

Pointe l'Arcouest

Île de Batz

Paimpol

Cap Fréhel

Pointe du Grouin

Roscoff

Lannion

St-Malo

St-Pol-de-Léon

Dinard

Cancale

Lesneven

Plouha

Morlaix

Guingamp

Binic

Île d'Ouessant

Landivisiau

N12

FINISTÈRE

Dol de Bretagne

Lampaul

Brest

St-Brieuc

Lamballe

Le Conquet

Monts d'Arrée

CÔTES D'ARMOR

Dinan

Camaret-sur-Mer

Le Faou

Parc Naturel Régional d'Armorique

Rance

Presqu'île de Crozon

Argol

Pleyben

Carhaix-Plouguer

BRITTANY

Châteaulin

N164

N12

N137

Douarnenez

N165

Loudéac

Île de Sein

Audierne

Montagnes Noires

Merdrignac

Pointe du Raz

Quimper

Pontivy

Forêt de Paimpont

Rennes

N24

Paimpont

Pont-l'Abbé

Bénodet

Concarneau

Josselin

St-Guénolé

Quimperlé

Ploërmel

Pointe de la Torche

MORBIHAN

Vilaine

Brest Canal

Îles de Glénan

Lorient

Port Louis

Auray

N137

Île de Groix

Vannes

Redon

Carnac

Muzillac

Quiberon

Port-Navalo

Golfe du Morbihan

N165

Sauzon

Île d'Houat

LOIRE-ATLANTIQUE

Le Palais

Île d'Hoëdic

Le Croisic

Guérande

Belle-Île-en-Mer

La Baule

St-Nazaire

ATLANTIC OCEAN

Bay of Biscay

See Bordeaux & The Southwest Map pp288–9

VENDÉE

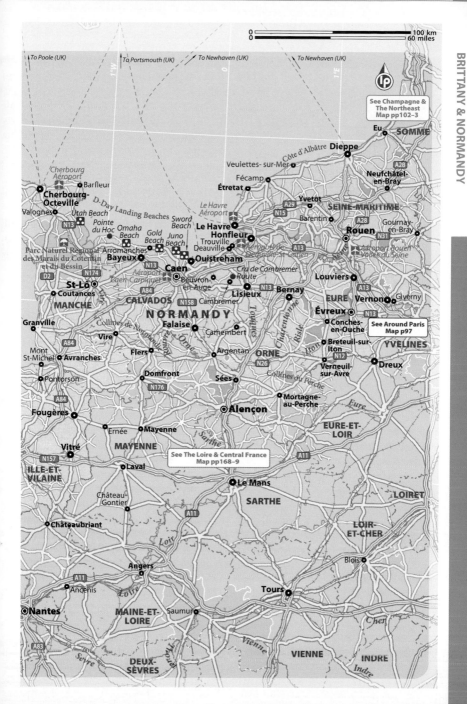

HIGHLIGHTS

1 # MONT ST-MICHEL

BY JACK LECOQ, WALKING GUIDE & STORY-TELLER EXTRAORDINAIRE

The mount's charm is the *marais* (salt marshes) and the immensity of the view – so magical, so very mysterious. It evokes the bible, the crossing of the Red Sea. Pilgrims have trekked across the sand since the 8th century and it's steeped in legend. I walk and I talk, of princesses, knights and broken hearts...

➥ JACK LECOQ'S DON'T MISS LIST

❶ THE BAREFOOT WALK

You can wear plastic shoes, but walking the 13km from Bec d'Andaine in Genêts to Mont St-Michel (p164) barefooted is wonderful. We walk across a mix of pitch sand, quicksand, sand flats and endless ripple marks made by the tides. At times we're almost knee-deep in mud.

❷ ÎLOT DE TOMBELAINE

After walking for about one hour (3km) this islet, which was occupied by the English for 35 years during the Hundred Years' War, pops up. It is a bird reserve

and from April to July, full of exceptional birdlife. November to March, once the birds have left, a tiny footpath leads to the top of the islet from where an exceptional view of Mont St-Michel unfolds – quite, quite astonishing.

❸ ABBAYE DE ST-MICHEL

We cross the River Couesnon, the medieval border between Normandy and Brittany, and there is the mount. The abbey is marvellous. It has beautiful works of art and rooms: the hall where pilgrims gathered is magnificent, as is

Clockwise from top: Cloisters surrounding courtyard; Abbaye de St-Michel; Pastures near Mont St-Michel; School children walking across the 'sea of sand'; Mont St-Michel surrounded by water

CLOCKWISE FROM TOP: IZZET KERIBAR; IZZET KERIBAR; DENNIS JOHNSON; MARK DAFFEY; GREG ELMS

the Salle des Chevaliers (Knights Hall) where monks spent hours illuminating manuscripts.

❹ AVRANCHES

I was born here. After visiting the abbey, it's worth going to Avranches' Scriptoria (Musée des Manuscrits du Mont St-Michel; ☎ 02 33 79 57 00; www.ville-avranches .fr; place d'Estouteville) where all the historical documents and manuscripts scribed at the abbey are preserved. It illuminates Mont St-Michel's many legends and stories.

❺ MEMORABLE MOUNT VIEWS

The view from Jardin des Plantes botanical gardens in Avranches is unique, as are the bay panoramas from Pointe du Grouin du Sud near the fishing vil-

lage of St-Léonard, 5km southwest, and the cliff tops in Carolles, 20km north. If you like oysters, you can even spot the mount from Cancale (p153) in Brittany, and if wildlife is your thing, being afloat on a tiny boat in the 365-island archipelago of Îles Chausey (p151) is out of this world.

⤷ THINGS YOU NEED TO KNOW

Dangerous! Navigating the swift tides and River Coueson alone; take a guide **Guided walks** Découverte de la Baie (☎ 02 33 70 83 49; www.decouvertebaie.com; Malson du Guide, 1 rue Montoise, Genêts) **When** April to October **Essential** Shorts and a wind breaker **See our author's review on p164.**

HIGHLIGHTS

2

◥ CARNAC MEGALITHS

Around Carnac cycle past fields full of mysterious megaliths (p145), strewn along a tiny wedge of Brittany's southern coast around the Golfe de Morbihan. No one really knows *how* the original constructors hewed, hauled and built these gargantuan menhirs, dolmens, cromlechs, tumuli and cairns or indeed why. A phallic fertility cult? Sun worship? Representation of a long-forgotten divinity? You decide.

3

◥ BAYEUX TAPESTRY

Travel back a thousand years with the world's oldest comic strip, the Bayeux Tapestry (p158), whose 58 scenes embroidered with wool thread onto linen cloth tell the story of the Norman invasion of England in 1066. The final showdown at the Battle of Hastings is depicted in graphic fashion, complete with severed limbs and decapitated heads.

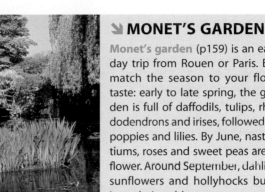

⬊ MONET'S GARDEN

Monet's garden (p159) is an easy day trip from Rouen or Paris. But match the season to your floral taste: early to late spring, the garden is full of daffodils, tulips, rhododendrons and irises, followed by poppies and lilies. By June, nasturtiums, roses and sweet peas are in flower. Around September, dahlias, sunflowers and hollyhocks burst into glorious bloom.

⬊ D-DAY BEACHES

Ponder the price of war at the D-Day beaches and WWII war cemeteries on Normandy's northern coast (p160). On 5 June 1944 six amphibious divisions stormed ashore at night, backed up by 6000 sea craft, 13,000 aeroplanes and, the following morning, 45,000 land troops. The horrific number of soldiers who died on both sides was equally unimaginable.

⬊ CANCALE

No Breton fishing port does the seafood thing better than Cancale (p153), best known for its oyster farms and rough-cut oyster morning at the lighthouse. Top off the experience with a Michelin-starred lunch exquisitely crafted from local oysters, baby squid and other marine life by top regional chef Olivier Roellinger (p153).

2 JEAN-BERNARD CARILLET; 3 ROBERT HARDING/ALAMY; 4 JOHN HAY; 5 JOHN ELK III; 6 OLIVIER CIRENDINI

2 Megaliths at Carnac (p145), Brittany; 3 Bayeux Tapestry (p158), Normandy; 4 Monet's Garden (p159), Normandy; 5 Map at Omaha Beach (p161), Normandy; 6 Oysters

THE BEST...

⬎ ISLANDS & BOAT TRIPS

- **Belle Île** (p146) Sail from Quiberon to Brittany's largest island.
- **Île de Batz** (p150) Ferries link Roscoff with this paradise.
- **Île d'Ouessant** (p148) Get windswept along its coastal footpath.
- **River Rance** Drift along this river between Dinan (p154), Dinard (p152) and St-Malo (p150).
- **Rennes' waterway** (p140) Explore Rennes' Venice-like waterways.

⬎ BRETON CRÊPES

- **Le Saint Georges, Rennes** (p143) Crêpes named for famous Georges.
- **Crêperie au Pressoir, Carnac** (p144) Crêpes between menhirs.
- **Musée du Cidre du Bretagne, Argol** (p147) Crêpes 'n' cider in a barn at Brittany's cider museum.
- **Crêperie la Krampouzerie, Quimper** (p147) Seaweed and algae crêpes in the bastion of Breton culture, Quimper.

⬎ SUPERFRESH SEAFOOD

- **L'Entrecôte, Honfleur** (p162) Packed since 1966 with one *menu* and a daily queue at noon.
- **Poissonerie, Trouville** (p162) Join chic Parisians at Trouville's fish market.
- **Marché aux Huîtres, Cancale** (p153) Oyster market in the shade of a lighthouse.

⬎ GUIDED WALKS & TOURS

- **Centre de Découverte des Algues, Roscoff** (p149) Learn about seaweed harvesting.
- **Conserverie La Belle-Iloise, Quiberon** (p144) Buy cheap fish and tour this ex-sardine cannery.
- **Maison des Johnnies, Roscoff** (p149) Meet Brittany's mythical onion farmers.
- **Ferme Marine, Canale** (p153) Tour an oyster farm.

JEAN-BERNARD CARILLET

Roscoff Bay and Île de Batz (p150), Brittany

THINGS YOU NEED TO KNOW

↘ VITAL STATISTICS

- **Population** 2.9 million (Brittany), 3.2 million (Normandy)
- **Best time to visit** spring, summer and autumn
- **Points of entry** Rennes, Roscoff, St Malo, Rouen

↘ ADVANCE PLANNING

- **Two weeks before** Book a table at tip-top dining address O Roellinger (p153) and a night-time walking tour of Honfleur (at its tourist office; p163)
- **One day before** in July/August reserve ferries to Île d'Ouessant (p148).

↘ RESOURCES

- **Brittany Tourism** (www.brittany tourism.com)
- **Normandy Tourism** (www.nor mandie-tourisme.fr)
- **Normandie Mémoire** (www.nor mandiememoire.com) and **D-Day: Operation Overlord** (www.6juin1944.com) D-Day and its context.

↘ GETTING AROUND

- **Budget flights** from the UK to Dinard, Brest and Nantes.
- **Ferries** link St-Malo with the Channel Islands and Portsmouth, Poole and Weymouth (UK); and Roscoff with Plymouth (UK) and Cork (Ireland). Normandy-bound ferries from the UK and Ireland to Cherbourg, Dieppe, Le Havre and Ouistreham (Caen); and the Channel Islands to St-Malo.
- **Trains** serve major towns and cities but the interior...forget it.
- **Car** is the best way to see the area.
- **Bicycle** is popular and rental outlets are easy to find.
- **Organised Minibus tour** is an excellent way to visit the D-Day beaches; contact Bayeux tourist office.

↘ BE FOREWARNED

- **At Mont St-Michel** there are lots of steps, some spiral. Motorists pay attention to signs warning which areas get flooded by the incoming tide. Tides above 13.10m submerge the two car parks closest to the Mont!
- **Mass** at Mont St-Michel's Abby Church is at 12.15pm Tuesday to Sunday, 11.30am Sunday.
- **St-Malo hotels** get booked up quickly in summer. For *chambres d'hôtes* (B&Bs), try Cancale, Dinan and their surrounds.

ITINERARIES

Explore the best of this region on two wheels or along the coast, then step back in time to learn about prehistoric wonders and the horrors of war.

BRITTANY BY BIKE Three Days

Clear the cobwebs and let the sea wind frisk your hair with this three-day bicycle tour. Pick up wheels and maps in **(1) Carnac** (p143) and spend a day pedalling from one prehistoric **(2) Morbihan megalith** (p145) to another. Munch traditional Breton crêpes for lunch at **(3) Creperie au Pressoir** (p144), encircled by 70 such mysterious stones, and end the day with a visit to Carnac's **(4) Musée de Préhistoire** (p145) and a flop on the sculpture-decorated beach. On the second day make your way south along the windswept **(5) Presqu'île de Quiberon** (p144) and catch a ferry to **(6) Belle Île** (p146). Spend the day exploring this 'beautiful island' by bike, sailing back to **(7) Quiberon** (p144) in time to take your **(8) pick of seafood** (p144) at the peninsula town's former fish auction house. On the final day hop in the car and motor inland to the **(9) Forêt de Paimpont** (p143), steeped in Breton legend and riddled with forested cycling trails. End the day out of the saddle in the bewitching fairytale village of **(10) Josselin** (p154).

TIME TRAVELLER Five Days

No part of France is better suited to history buffs than this: Start your travels in prehistory with the magnificent megaliths in and around **(1) Carnac** (p145). Then hop to the Middle Ages for a flash back in time around the quintessential medieval village of **(2) Vitré** (p154). Continue northeast to **(3) Bayeux** (p157) where 11th-century Normandy comes to life with extraordinary realism in the shape of a very famous tapestry. The town also makes an excellent base for a compelling history lesson in WWII along the **(4) D-Day Beaches** (p160). On the fourth day soothe harrowed souls with sweet floral scenes that inspired post-Impressionist art at Monet's house-garden museum in **(5) Giverny** (p159). Last up, stand on the spot where Joan of Arc was burnt at the stake as a heretic in cathedral-clad **(6) Rouen** (p155).

COAST CRUISER One Week

This full-on tour snakes along the Breton and Norman coastline from Brittany's **(1) Roscoff** (p149) to Honfleur in Normandy (from where Paris is an easy hop). In Roscoff rub shoulders with local tradition – clue: onions and seaweed – at **(2) Maison des Johnnies** (p149) and fascinating **(3) Centre des Découvertes des Algues** (p149). Lunch

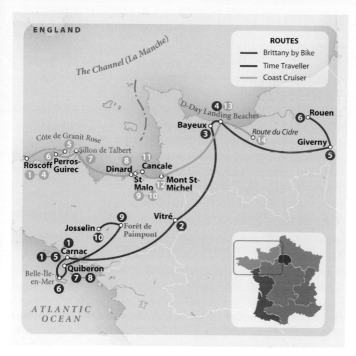

Breton farmer–style at (4) Chez Janie (p150), then make your way east of town in time to watch the pink (5) Côte de Granit Rose (p165) turn red as the sun sets. Overnight it in (6) Perros-Guirec (p165) and rise early the next morning to catch local fishermen selling their catch and see seaweed farmers at work around (7) Sillon de Talbert (p165).

Devote day two to (8) Dinard (p152); buy lunch at the market and picnic in a striped bathing tent! Day three continue east, breaking in (9) St-Malo (p150) for a brisk rampart stroll or walk, if the tide allows, to (10) Île du Grand Bé (p151). Overnight it in seafaring (11) Cancale (p153), pebble-throwing distance from Normandy's iconic (12) Mont St-Michel (p164).

On day five cruise towards the sobering (13) D-Day Beaches (p160). A couple of days later resuscitate numbed nerves and end your holiday on a high with a tasty cider-fuelled cruise along the region's (14) Route du Cidre (p164).

DISCOVER BRITTANY & NORMANDY

The sea crashing against the granite coast and a scattering of islands is what Brittany is all about – along with cider, crêpes and Muscadet wine. Enveloped by belle-époque beach resorts, fishing villages and curled headlands, this storybook region is the stuff of old-fashioned dreams: wellies and rock pooling, cliff-top walks, shucking oysters and climbing lighthouses. The Breton language and dancing needle-and-thread style to traditional music at *festoù-noz* (night festivals) are vibrant expressions of Breton culture – as interwoven with French culture as the intricate lace of women's traditional headdresses and the churches' filigreed stone steeples.

Next door is Normandy, bordered to the north and west by the English Channel (La Manche). This is a land of cows, cider and Camembert, of churned butter and soft cheeses, and where gentle fields divided by hedgerows end at chalk-white cliffs and dune-lined beaches. Inland, lovely Rouen, a favourite haunt of Monet and Simone de Beauvoir, is one of the most intriguing cities in northern France.

BRITTANY

Thrust out into the Atlantic, France's westernmost promontory might be called Finistère, meaning 'land's end', but its Breton name, Penn ar Bed, translates as 'head of the world', highlighting how Bretons have long viewed it and the rest of this spirited, independent region.

The one-time frontier between Brittany and France, fertile eastern Brittany fans out around the region's lively capital, Rennes. Central Brittany conceals the enchanting Forêt de Paimpont, sprinkled with villages and ancient Breton legends. In the crook of Brittany's southern coastline, the Golfe du Morbihan (Morbihan Coast) is a haven of islands, oyster beds and birdlife. But the area is perhaps best known for its proliferation of mystifying Celtic megaliths.

RENNES

pop 210,500

A crossroads since Roman times, Brittany's vibrant capital sits at the junction of highways linking northwestern France's major cities. Its contemporary and medieval quarters are woven with waterways, which are best explored by renting a boat.

The centre is divided by La Vilaine, a river channelled into a cement-lined canal that disappears underground just before the central square, place de la République.

INFORMATION

Tourist Office (☎ 02 99 67 11 11; www.tourisme-rennes.com; 11 rue St-Yves; ☼ 1-6pm Mon, 9am-7pm Tue-Sat, 11am-1pm & 2-6pm Sun Jul & Aug, 1-6pm Mon, 9am-6pm Tue-Sat, 11am-1pm & 2-6pm Sun Sep-Jun)

SIGHTS

Much of Rennes was gutted by the great fire of 1720, started by a drunken carpenter who accidentally set alight a pile of shavings. Half-timbered houses that survived line the old city's cobbled streets such as **rue St-Michel** and **rue St-Georges**. The

RENNES

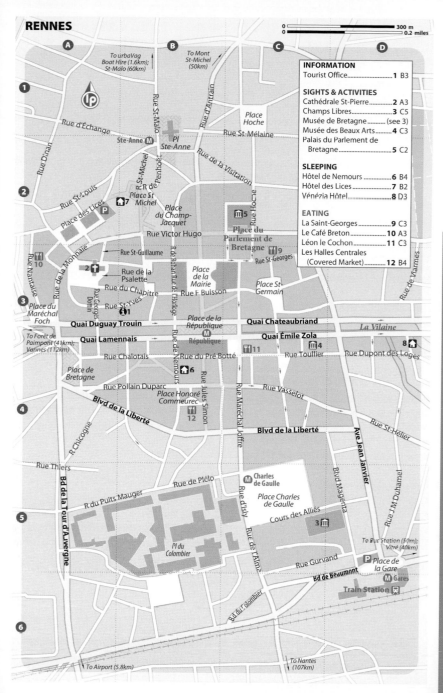

0   300 m
0   0.2 miles

INFORMATION
Tourist Office.............................**1** B3

SIGHTS & ACTIVITIES
Cathédrale St-Pierre..............**2** A3
Champs Libres.........................**3** C5
Musée de Bretagne..........(see 3)
Musée des Beaux Arts.........**4** C3
Palais du Parlement de
   Bretagne..............................**5** C2

SLEEPING
Hôtel de Nemours **6** B4
Hôtel des Lices **7** B2
Vénézia Hôtel.........................**8** D3

EATING
La Saint-Georges **9** C3
Le Café Breton **10** A3
Léon le Cochon **11** C3
Les Halles Centrales
   (Covered Market) **12** B4

To urbaVag
Boat Hire (1.6km);
St-Malo (60km)

To Mont
St-Michel
(50km)

Rue Ste-Malo

Rue d'Antrain

Place
Hoche

Rue St-Mélaine

Rue d'Échange

Ste-Anne

Pl
Ste-Anne

Rue de la Visitation

Rue Dinan

Rue St-Malo

R St-Michel

R de Penhoët

Rue St-Louis

Place St
Michel

Place des Lices

Place
du Champ-
Jacquet

Rue Victor Hugo

Place du
Parlement de
Bretagne

Rue Hoche

Rue Nantaise

Rue de la Monnaie

Rue St-Guillaume

Rue de la
Psalette

Place
de la
Mairie

Rue St-Georges

Rue du Chapitre

Rue Rohan

Rue de l'Horloge

Rue F Buisson

Place St
Germain

Rue Georges
Dottin

Rue St-Yves

Place de
Maréchal
Foch

Place de la
République

Quai Chateaubriand

La Vilaine

Quai Duguay Trouin

To Forêt de
Paimpont (41km);
Varnes (112km)

Quai Lamennais

République

Quai Émile Zola

Rue Dupont des Loges

Rue Chalotais

Rue du Pré Botté

Rue Toullier

Rue de Vannes

Place de
Bretagne

Rue de Nemours

Rue Vasselot

Rue Pollain Duparc

Rue Jules Simon

Rue Maréchal Joffre

Place Honoré
Commeurec

Blvd de la Liberté

Blvd de la Liberté

Rue St-Hélier

Rue Thiers

R du Puits Mauger

Rue de Plélo

Rue d'Isly

Charles
de Gaulle

Place Charles
de Gaulle

Cours des Alliés

Blvd Magenta

Ave Jean Janvier

Rue J M Duhamel

Bd de la Tour d'Auvergne

R Chicogne

Pl du
Colombier

Rue de l'Alma

To Bus Station ($0m);
Vitré (40km)

Place de
la Gare

Rue Gurvand

Bd de Beaumont

Gares

Train Station

Bd du Colombier

To Airport (5.8km)

To Nantes
(107km)

BRITTANY & NORMANDY

BRITTANY

DAVID TOMLINSON

Streetside cafés, Rennes

latter runs alongside the place de la Mairie and the site of the 17th-century **Palais du Parlement de Bretagne**, the former seat of the rebellious Breton parliament and, more recently, the Palais de Justice. In 1994 this building too was destroyed by fire, started by demonstrating fishermen. Now restored, it houses the Court of Appeal. In July and August, guided tours in English (adult/child €6.80/4; book at the tourist office) take you through the ostentatiously gilded rooms.

Crowning the old city is the 17th-century **Cathédrale St-Pierre** (9.30am-noon & 3-6pm), which has a stunning neoclassical interior.

BRETON CRÊPES

Crêpes are Brittany's traditional staple, and ubiquitous throughout the region. Unlike the rolled-up crêpes sold at stalls on Paris' street corners, Breton crêpes are folded envelope-style at the edges, served flat on a plate and eaten using cutlery.

Rooms devoted to the Pont-Aven school are the highlight of the **Musée des Beaux-Arts** (☎ 02 99 28 55 85; 20 quai Émile Zola; adult/student/child €4.30/2.20/free; 10am-noon & 2-6pm Tue-Sun).

Rennes' futuristic cultural centre, **Champs Libres** (☎ 02 23 40 66 00; 10 cours des Alliés), is home to the **Musée de Bretagne** (☎ 02 23 40 66 70; www.musee-bretagne.fr), with displays portraying Breton history and culture.

TOURS

urbaVag (☎ 02 99 33 16 88, 06 82 37 67 72; www.urbavag.fr, in French; rue Canal St-Martin; per hr €26-31) Cruise Rennes' waterways on a whisper-quiet electric boat rented from urbaVag.

FESTIVALS & EVENTS

Les Mercredis du Thabor Traditional Breton dancing and music take place in Rennes' beautiful Parc du Thabor on Wednesdays during June and July (usually from 4pm).

SLEEPING

Vénézia Hôtel (☎ 02 99 30 36 56; hotel .venezia@wana doo.fr; 27 rue Dupont des Loges; s €28-38, d €38-48) Named for the Venice-like canals surrounding this small 'island' in the city centre; half of this charming hotel's 16 rose-toned rooms have pretty views over the canalside garden.

Hôtel des Lices (☎ 02 99 79 14 81; www .hotel-des-lices.com; 7 place des Lices; r €48-78; ⊠ ⊠) You can peer down from the steel balconies or through the floor-to-ceiling glass doors to see the Saturday-morning market. Inside, rooms are small but sleek with pared-down contemporary furnishings and textured walls. Wi-fi's free.

Hôtel de Nemours (☎ 02 99 78 26 26; www.hotelnemours.com, in French; 5 rue de Nemours; r €54-90; ⊠ ⊠) Lined with historic black-and-white photographs of Rennes, boutique Hôtel de Nemours is an understatement in elegance, with cream-, chocolate- and caramel-coloured furnishings, high-thread-count white linens, flat-screen TVs and free wi-fi.

EATING

Rues St-Malo and St-Georges are the city's two main 'eat streets'; the latter particularly specialises in crêperies.

Le Saint-Georges (☎ 02 99 38 87 04; 31 rue St-Georges; crêpes €2.50-15; ⊙ lunch & dinner Tue-Sat) Innovative crêpes here are named after famous people called George.

Léon le Cochon (☎ 02 99 79 37 54; 1 rue Maréchal Joffre; menu €25, mains €11-24; ⊙ lunch & dinner, closed Sun Jul & Aug) Basking in the plaudits of almost every French gastronomic guidebook, but still fun and informal, 'Leon the Pig' specialises not just in pork but porcine products in all their many and varied manifestations.

Le Café Breton (☎ 02 99 30 74 95; 14 rue Nantaise; menus €13-30; ⊙ lunch & dinner Mon-Sat) Diminutive rue Nantaise has a handful of top restaurants, including this local fave for its tarts, salads and gratins.

SELF-CATERING

Fresh produce and Breton specialities are available daily at Rennes' covered markets, **Les Halles Centrales** (place Honoré Commeurec; ⊙ 7am-7pm Mon-Sat, 9.30am-12.30pm Sun); on Saturdays, a fabulous open-air market fills the surrounding streets and squares.

GETTING THERE & AWAY

Destinations include St-Malo (€12.10, one hour), Dinan (€12.70, one hour including a change), Vannes (€17.80, 1½ hours), Quimper (€30.10, 2½ hours) and Paris' Gare Montparnasse (€52.20, 2¼ hours).

FORÊT DE PAIMPONT

Also known as Brocéliande, the Paimpont Forest is about 40km southwest of Rennes, and legendary as the place where King Arthur received the Excalibur sword (forget that these stories are thought to have been brought to Brittany by Celtic settlers and hence probably took place offshore – it's a magical setting all the same).

The best base for exploring the forest is the lakeside village of **Paimpont**. The tourist office (☎ 02 99 07 84 23; syndicat -dinitiativepaimpont@wanadoo.fr; ⊙ 10am-noon & 2-6pm daily Apr-Sep, 10am-noon & 2-6pm Tue-Sun Oct-Mar), beside the 12th-century Église Abbatiale (Abbey Church), has a free brochure outlining a 62km-long driving circuit with numerous short walks that rae along the way and accessible to the public. In July and August it leads guided tours (morning/afternoon/full day €6/10/12).

CARNAC

pop 4600

Pre-dating Stonehenge by around 100 years, Carnac (Garnag in Breton) tops it too with sheer numbers. There are no fewer than 3000 of these upright stones, most around thigh-high, erected between 5000 and 3500 BC.

Tourist Office (☎ 02 97 52 13 52; www.ot -carnac.fr; 74 av des Druides, Carnac-Plage; ☺ 9am-7pm Mon-Sat & 3-7pm Sun Jul & Aug, 9am-noon or 12.30pm & 2-6pm Mon-Sat Sep-Jun) Offers helpful service.

Crêperie au Pressoir (☎ 02 97 52 01 86; village du Ménec; galettes €3-8; ☺ lunch & dinner Easter-Aug) This artisan crêperie in a traditional long Breton house is a rare opportunity to dine right in the middle of a 70-strong cromlech (circle of menhirs). From Carnac-Ville, take rue St-Cornély northwest and turn right on rue du Ménec and follow it north for about 1km.

Woman in traditional Breton costume
JEAN-BERNARD CARILLET

QUIBERON

pop 5200

Quiberon (Kiberen in Breton) sits at the southern tip of a sliver-thin, 14km-long peninsula flanked on the western side by the rocky, wave-lashed Côte Sauvage (Wild Coast). The town fans out around the port where ferries depart for Belle Île, and is wildly popular in summer.

The **tourist office** (☎ 08 25 13 56 00; www .quiberon.com; 14 rue de Verdun; ☺ 9am-1.30pm & 2-7pm Mon-Fri, to 5pm Sat, 10am-1pm & 2-5pm Sun Jul & Aug, 9am-12.30pm & 2-6pm Mon-Sat Sep-Jun) is between the train station and La Grande Plage.

Conserverie La Belle-Iloise (☎ 02 97 50 08 77; rue de Kerné; ☺ visits 10am, 11am, 3pm & 4pm daily Jul & Aug, 10-11am & 3-4pm Mon-Fri Sep-Jun) offers guided visits around its former sardine cannery, with bargain-priced sardines available from the adjacent shop.

our pick **Villa Margot** (☎ 02 97 50 33 89; 7 rue de Port Maria; lunch menus €17.50-21.50, dinner menus €21.50-36, mains €19.50-27; ☺ lunch & dinner Thu-Mon) The interior of this stunning stone restaurant looks like it'd be at home in a chic Parisian *quartier*. That is until you head out onto the timber deck, which has direct access to the beach for a post-repast stroll.

La Criée (☎ 02 97 30 53 09; 11 quai de l'Océan; mains €25-45; ☺ lunch & dinner Tue-Sun Feb-Dec) Within the former fish auction house, this long-established seaside restaurant keeps with its traditions by laying out its seafood on a table for you to take your pick.

QUIMPER

pop 64,900

Small enough to feel like a village with its slanted half-timbered houses and narrow cobbled streets, and large enough to buzz as the troubadour of Breton culture and arts, Quimper *(kam-pair)* is Finistère's thriving capital.

MORBIHAN'S MIGHTY MEGALITHS

The best way to appreciate the stones' sheer numbers is to walk or bike between the Le Ménec and Kerlescan groups, with menhirs almost continuously in view.

Because of severe erosion the sites are fenced off to allow the vegetation to regenerate. However, between 10am and 5pm from October to May you can wander freely through parts. Sign up for guided visits at the Maison des Mégalithes (☎ 02 97 52 89 99; rte des Alignements; admission free; ☺ 9am-8pm Jul & Aug, to 5.15pm Sep-Apr, to 7pm May & Jun), which also has a rolling video, topographic models and views of the menhirs from its rooftop terrace. Opposite, the largest menhir field – with no less than 1099 stones – is the Alignements du Ménec. From here, the D196 heads northeast for about 1.5km to the equally impressive Alignements de Kermario. Climb the stone observation tower midway along the site to see the alignment from above. Another 500m further on are the Alignements de Kerlescan, a smaller grouping also accessible in winter.

Tumulus St-Michel, at the end of rue du Tumulus and 400m northeast of the Carnac-Ville tourist office, dates back to at least 5000 BC and offers sweeping views.

Between Kermario and Kerlescan, 500m to the south of the D196, deposit your fee in an honour box at Tumulus de Kercado (admission €1; ☺ year-round). Dating from 3800 BC and the burial site of a neolithic chieftain, it was used during the French Revolution as a hiding place for Breton royalists. From the parking area 300m further along the D196, a 15-minute walk brings you to the Géant du Manio, the highest menhir in the complex, and the Quadrilatère, a group of minimenhirs, close-set in a rectangle.

Near Locmariaquer, 13km southeast of Carnac-Ville, the major monuments are the Table des Marchands, a 30m-long dolmen, and the Grand Menhir Brisé (adult/student/child €5/3.50/free; ☺ 10am-7pm Jul & Aug, to 6pm Apr-Jun, to 5pm Sep-Mar), the region's largest menhir, which once stood 20m high but now lies broken on its side. Both are off the D781, just before the village.

The Musée de Préhistoire (☎ 02 97 52 22 04; 10 place de la Chapelle, Carnac-Ville; adult/child €5/2.50; ☺ 10am-6pm Jul & Aug, 10am-12.30pm & 2-6pm Wed-Mon Apr, May, Jun & Sep, 10am-12.30pm & 2-5pm Wed-Mon Oct-Mar) chronicles life in and around Carnac from the Palaeolithic and neolithic eras to the Middle Ages.

INFORMATION

Tourist Office (☎ 02 98 53 04 05; www .quimper-tourisme.com, in French; place de la Résistance; ☺ 9am-7pm Mon-Sat, 10am-12.45pm & 3-5.45pm Sun Jul & Aug, 9.30am-12.30pm & 1.30-6pm or 6.30pm Mon-Sat Sep-Jun, 10am-12.45pm Sun Jun & 1-15 Sep) Offers useful local information.

SIGHTS

Quimper's cathedral (☺ 9.30am-noon & 1.30-6.30pm Mon-Sat, 1.30-6.30pm Sun May-Oct, 9am-noon & 1.30-6.30pm Mon-Sat, 1.30-6.30pm Sun Nov-Apr) has a distinctive kink built into its soaring light-filled interior – said by some to symbolise Christ's head inclined on one shoulder as he was dying on the

Rugged coastline, Belle Île

BETHUNE CARMICHAEL

↘ BELLE ÎLE

pop 5200

Accessed by ferries from Quiberon, the population of Belle Île (in full, Belle-Île-en-Mer) swells tenfold in summer thanks to its namesake beauty. But as it's Brittany's largest island (at 20km by 9km), there's room to escape the crowds.

Turn left as you leave the ferry in Le Palais to reach the main **tourist office**.

The dramatic **citadel**, strengthened by Vauban in 1682, dominates the little Le Palais port. Inside, the **Musée Historique** interprets the history of both the defensive system and the island. For all-out luxury, the **citadel** also incorporates a lavish hotel and a gastronomic restaurant, La Table du Gouverneur (*menus* from €30 to €65).

Belle Île's fretted southwestern coast has spectacular rock formations and caves including **Grotte de l'Apothicairerie** (Cave of the Apothecary's Shop), where waves roll in from two sides.

Plage de Donnant has great surf, though swimming here is dangerous. Sheltered **Port Kérel**, to the southwest, is better for children, as is the 2km-long **Plage des Grands Sables**, the busiest strand, spanning the calm waters of the island's eastern side. The tourist office sells walking and cycling guides.

The shortest crossing to Belle Île is from Quiberon. **Compagnie Océane** operates car/passenger ferries (45 minutes, year-round) and fast passenger ferries to Le Palais and to Sauzon in July and August.

Things you need to know: Tourist Office (☎ 02 97 31 81 93; www.belle-ile.com; quai Bonnelle; ☯ 8.45am-7.30pm Mon-Sat & to 1pm Sun Jul & Aug, 9am-12.30pm & 2-6pm Mon-Sat, 10am-12.30pm Sun Sep-Jun); Musée Historique (☎ 02 97 31 84 17; adult/child €6.10/3.05; ☯ 9.30am-6pm May-Oct, 9.30am-noon & 2-5pm Nov-Apr); citadel (www.citadellevauban.com); Compagnie Océane (☎ 02 97 35 02 00; www.compagnie-oceane.fr)

cross. Begun in 1239, the cathedral wasn't completed until the 1850s.

The ground-floor halls are home to some fairly morbid 16th- to 20th-century European paintings, but things lighten up on the upper levels of the **Musée des Beaux-Arts** (☎ 02 98 95 45 20; 40 place St-Corentin; adult/child €4.50/2.50; ☺ 10am-7pm daily Jul & Aug, 10am-noon & 2-6pm Wed-Mon Apr-Jun, Sep-Oct, 10am-noon & 2-6pm Wed-Sat & Mon, 2-6pm Sun Nov-Mar). A room dedicated to Quimper-born poet Max Jacob includes sketches by Picasso.

Recessed behind a magnificent stone courtyard beside the cathedral, the **Musée Départemental Breton** (☎ 02 98 95 21 60; 1 rue du Roi Gradlon; adult/child €4/2.50; ☺ 9am-6pm daily Jun-Sep, 9am-noon & 2-5pm Tue-Sat, 2-5pm Sun Oct-May) is housed in the former bishop's palace. Superb exhibits showcase Breton history, furniture, costumes, crafts and archeology.

Following the switchback path just east of the tourist office up the 72m-high **Mont Frugy** rewards with captivating city views.

SHOPPING

Several shops sell Quimper's traditional *faïance* pottery, including **Ar Bed Keltiek** (Celtic World; ☎ 02 98 95 42 82; 2 rue du Roi Gradlon) and **François Le Villec** (☎ 02 98 95 31 54, 4 rue du Roi Gradlon). Breton and Celtic music and art are available at **Keltia Musique** (☎ 02 98 95 45 82; 1 place au Beurre).

SLEEPING & EATING

Hôtel Gradlon (☎ 02 98 95 04 39; www.hotel-gradlon.com; 30 rue de Brest; r €82-160; ☺ closed mid-Dec–mid-Jan) Quimper's most charming hotel is this former 19th-century coach house. Its 22 rooms include three elegant junior suites set around a rose-garden courtyard.

ourpick **Crêperie la Krampouzerie** (☎ 02 98 95 13 08; 9 rue du Sallé; galettes €3.50-

7.70; ☺ lunch & dinner Tue-Sat) In an atmospheric space with blue-and-white tiled wooden tables, crêpes and galettes are made from organic flours and regional ingredients like *algues d'Ouessant* (seaweed from the Île d'Ouessant), Roscoff onions and homemade ginger caramel. Tables fill the square out the front in fine weather, giving it a lovely street-party atmosphere.

L'Ambroisie (☎ 02 98 95 00 02; www.ambroisie-quimper.com; 49 rue Elie Fréron; menus €23-48, mains €29; ☺ lunch & dinner Tue-Sat, lunch Sat, closed mid-Jun–mid-Jul) Quimper's most celebrated gastronomic restaurant. Regional produce provided by chef Gilbert Guyon's friends is used to create house specials like sole with new potatoes and caramelised onions. Cooking classes are available by request.

GETTING THERE & AWAY

There are frequent trains that run to Rennes (€30.10, 2½ hours, five daily) and Paris (Gare Montparnasse; €68.20, 4¾ hours).

PRESQU'ÎLE DE CROZON

The anchor-shaped Crozon Peninsula is part of the Parc Naturel Régional d'Armorique, and one of the most scenic spots in Brittany. The partly forested peninsula is criss-crossed by some 145km of signed walking trails, with crêperies in traditional stone buildings tucked in and around the hinterland.

Argol is a quaint village in its own right, but its main draw is the **Musée du Cidre du Bretagne** (Breton Cider Museum; ☎ 02 98 27 35 85; adult/child €5/free; ☺ 10am-noon & 2-7pm Apr-Sep & school holidays, 10am-1pm & 2-7pm Jul & Aug). This former dairy's old stone buildings have been transformed into a working *cidrerie* producing over 300,000 bottles annually. A visit takes you through the history of cider in Brittany and present-day production. And, of course, you get to taste it too. In July and August only, one of the barns is used as a crêperie.

At the western extremity of the Crozon Peninsula, **Camaret** is a classic little fishing village – or at least, it was until early last century, as France's then biggest crayfish port. Abandoned fishing-boat carcasses now decay in its harbour, but it remains an enchanting place that lures artists, with an ever-increasing number of **art galleries**. Camaret's **tourist office** (☎ 02 98 27 93 60; www.camaret-sur-mer.com, in French; 15 quai Kléber; ☺ 9am-7pm Mon-Sat & 10am-1pm Sun Jul & Aug, 9am-noon & 2-6pm Mon-Sat Sep-Jun) is on the waterfront.

To rent a bike, contact **Point Bleu** (☎ 02 98 27 09 04; quai Kador, Morgat) or, in summer, the open air stall located in front of Morgat's tourist office.

ÎLE D'OUESSANT

pop 950

Although it's frequented by summer visitors by the ferryload, free-roaming little black sheep and traditional houses give the windswept Île d'Ouessant (Enez Eusa in Breton, meaning 'Island of Terror'; Ushant in English) an ends-of-the-earth feel – best experienced by hiking its 45km craggy coastal path.

Île d'Ouessant's **tourist office** (☎ 02 98 48 85 83; www.ot-ouessant.fr, in French; place de l'Église, Lampaul; ☺ 10am-noon & 1.30-5pm Mon-Sat, 10am-noon Sun Jun-Sep, closed Oct-May) sells walking brochures and can hook you up with operators offering horse riding, sailing and other activities.

The black-and-white-striped **Phare de Créac'h** is the world's most powerful lighthouse. Beaming two white flashes every 10 seconds, visible for over 50km, it serves as a beacon for over 50,000 ships entering the Channel each year. Beneath is the island's main museum, the **Musée des Phares et des Balises** (Lighthouse & Beacon Museum; ☎ 02 98 48 80 70; adult/child €4.10/2.60; ☺ 10.30am-6.30pm Apr-Sep, 1.30-5pm Oct-Mar).

SLEEPING & EATING

Hôtel Roc'h Ar Mor (☎ 02 98 48 80 19; roch .armor@wanadoo.fr; Lampaul; d €55-87, tr €66.50-

Beach at Quiberon (p144)

DIANA MAYFIELD

87; ☯ mid-Feb–Dec) It's worth paying a tad extra for a panoramic sea view and a balcony at this appealing 15-room hotel with sunlit blue-and-white rooms. In a superb location next to the Baie de Lampaul, there's also a good restaurant with a terrace overlooking the ocean.

Crêperie Ti A Dreuz (☎ 02 98 48 83 01; Lampaul; crêpes around €3-8; ☯ Easter–mid-Sep) You could be forgiven for thinking you'd been at sea too long, or knocked back too much Breton cider, but 'the slanting house' is so-named for its wonky walls. This quaint island crêperie serves delicious galettes: try the *ouessantine,* with creamy potato, cheese and sausage.

GETTING THERE & AROUND

Ferries depart from Brest and the tiny town (and Brittany's most westerly point) of Le Conquet. Buses operated by **Les Cars St-Mathieu** (☎ 02 98 89 12 02) link Brest with Le Conquet (€2, 45 minutes).

Penn Ar Bed (☎ 02 98 80 80 80; www.penn arbed.fr) sails from the Port de Commerce in Brest (adult/child €33.40/19.10, 2½ hours) and from Le Conquet (€29.20/16.60, 1½ hours). Boats run between each port and the island two to five times daily from May to September and once daily between October and April.

Bike-hire operators have kiosks at the Port du Stiff ferry terminal. Cycling on the coastal footpath is forbidden.

ROSCOFF

pop 3700

Arriving across the Channel into Roscoff (Rosko in Breton) provides a captivating first glimpse of Brittany. Granite houses dating from the 16th century wreathe this pretty port, which is surrounded by emerald-green fields producing cauliflower, onions, tomatoes, new potatoes and artichokes. Roscoff farmers in distinctive horizontally

striped tops, known as 'Johnnies', loaded-up boats with plaited strings of onions, crossed the Channel to the UK, then peddled and pedalled with their onions hanging from their bikes' handlebars.

Roscoff's waters conceal beds of *goémon* (algae), harvested for foodstuffs as well as *thalassothérapie* health and beauty treatments.

INFORMATION

Tourist Office (☎ 02 98 61 12 13; www .roscoff-tourisme.com; quai d'Auxerre; ☯ 9am-12.30pm & 1.30-7pm Mon-Sat, 10am-12.30pm Sun Jul & Aug, 9am-noon & 2-6pm Mon-Sat Sep-Jun) By the time you're reading this, the tourist office will have moved to its new home next to the lighthouse.

SIGHTS & ACTIVITIES

With its Renaissance belfry rising above the flat landscape, the 16th-century Flamboyant Gothic **Église Notre Dame de Kroaz-Batz** (place Lacaze-Duthiers; ☯ 9am-noon & 2-6pm excluding religious services) is one of Brittany's most impressive churches.

Photographs trace Roscoff's roaming onion farmers from the early 19th century at the **Maison des Johnnies** (☎ 02 98 61 25 48; 48 rue Brizeux; adult/child €4/2.50; ☯ tours in English & French 10.30am Tue & 3pm Thu outside school holidays, 3pm Mon, Tue, Thu & Fri school holidays, additional tours 11am & 5pm Mon, Tue, Thu & Fri & 3pm & 5pm Sun mid-Jun–mid-Sep). Tours at 5pm on Tuesdays between mid-June and mid-September include a free hour-long meeting with Johnnies from 6pm to 7pm.

You can learn about local seaweed harvesting at the **Centre de Découverte des Algues** (☎ 02 98 69 77 05; 5 rue Victor Hugo; admission free, walks per adult/child €5/3.50; ☯ 9am-noon & 2-7pm Mon-Sat), which also organises guided walks. Then immerse yourself in the stuff at **Thalasso Roscoff** (☎ 08 25 00 20

99; www.thalasso.com, in French; rue Victor Hugo; (🕑) closed Dec).

The beaches on Île de Batz are a peaceful place to bask. Ferries (adult/child €7.50/4 return, bike €7, 20 minutes each way) between Roscoff and Île de Batz run every 30 minutes late June to mid-September; there are about eight sailings daily during the rest of the year.

SLEEPING & EATING

Hôtel Les Arcades (☎ 02 98 69 70 45; www.hotel-les-arcades-roscoff.com, in French; 15 rue Amiral Réveillère; d €46-70; 🕑 Easter-early Nov; 🖳) Perched right above the rocks on the waterfront, this cosy two-star hotel, run by the same family for nearly a century, has 24 light-filled, light-coloured rooms and

Crêpes and cider

GREG ELMS

a glass-paned restaurant (mains around €15) serving up seafood and spectacular views.

Hôtel du Centre (☎ 02 98 61 24 25; www.chezjanie.com; r €59-108; 🕑 mid-Feb-mid-Nov) Contemporary, artistic rooms at this boutique hotel look like they've been lifted out of a magazine. But it's perhaps best known for its restaurant, Chez Janie (*menu* €24), serving Breton classics like *kig ha farz* – a farmers' family meal based around the Breton cake *far,* cooked in a linen bag within a boiling bacon and vegetable stew.

GETTING THERE & AWAY

Brittany Ferries (☎ reservations 08 25 82 88 28; www.brittany-ferries.com) links Roscoff to Plymouth in England (five to nine hours) and Cork in Ireland (14 hours). Boats leave from Port de Bloscon, about 2km east of the town centre.

ST-MALO

pop 49,600

The mast-filled port of St-Malo has a cinematically changing landscape. With one of the world's highest tidal ranges, brewing storms under blackened skies see waves lash over the top of the ramparts ringing its walled city. Hours later, the blue sky merges with the deep marine-blue sea, exposing beaches as wide and flat as the clear skies above and creating land bridges to the granite outcrop islands.

Construction of the walled city's fortifications began in the 12th century. These days English arrivals are tourists, for whom St-Malo, a short ferry hop from the Channel Islands, is a summer haven.

INFORMATION

Tourist Office (☎ 08 25 13 52 00, 02 99 56 64 43; www.saint-malo-tourisme.com; esplanade

St-Vincent; ☺ 9am-7.30pm Mon-Sat, 10am-6pm Sun Jul & Aug, 9am-12.30pm & 1.30pm-6pm or 6.30pm Mon-Sat Sep-Jun, 10am-12.30pm & 2.30-6pm Sun Easter-Jun & Sep)

SIGHTS

For the best views of the walled city, stroll along the top of the ramparts, constructed at the end of the 17th century and measuring 1.8km.

Though you'd never guess it from the cobblestone streets and reconstructed monuments in 17th- and 18th-century style, during August 1944 the battle to drive German forces out of St-Malo destroyed around 80% of the old city. Damage to the town's centrepiece, Cathédrale St-Vincent (place Jean de Châtillon; ☺ 9.30am-6pm except during Mass), constructed between the 12th and 18th centuries, was severe.

The ramparts' northern stretch looks out across to the remains of the former prison, Fort National (adult/child €4/2; ☺ Jun-Sep), accessible only at low tide. Within Château de St-Malo, built by the dukes of Brittany in the 15th and 16th centuries, is the Musée du Château (☎ 02 99 40 71 57; adult/child €5.20/2.60; ☺ 10am-noon & 2-6pm daily Apr-Sep, Tue-Sun Oct-Mar).

At low tide, cross the beach to walk out via the Porte des Bés to the rocky islet of Île du Grand Bé, where the great St Malo–born 18th-century writer Chateaubriand is buried. Once the tide rushes in, the causeway remains impassable for about six hours – check tide times with the tourist office.

The pretty fishing port of St-Servan sits south of the walled city. Allow around two hours to see the excellent Grand Aquarium (☎ 02 99 21 19 00; av Général Patton; adult/child €15.50/10.50; ☎ 10am-6pm Feb-Oct & Dec, to 8pm Jul & Aug, closed Nov), about 4km south of the city centre.

Compagnie Corsaire (☎ 08 25 13 80 35; www.compagniecorsaire.com) runs ferries from just outside Porte de Dinan to Îles Chausey, Île Cézembre and along the river to Dinan.

SLEEPING

Hôtel San Pedro (☎ 02 99 40 88 57; www.sanpedro-hotel.com; 1 rue Ste-Anne; s €46-48, d €53-70; ☺ Feb-Nov; ✗) Tucked at the back of the old city, the San Pedro has cool, crisp, neutral-toned decor with subtle splashes of colour, friendly service and superb sea views.

Hôtel de l'Univers (☎ 02 99 40 89 52; www.hotel-univers-saintmalo.com, in French; place Chateaubriand; s €48-78, d €63-95) Right by the most frequently used gateway to the old city (Porte St-Vincent), this cream-coloured two-star place with 63 rooms is perfectly positioned for easy access to all of St-Malo's attractions.

EATING

Le Biniou (☎ 02 99 56 47 57; 3 place de la Croix du Fief; crêpes €2-8, menus around €10; ☺ 10am-1am in summer, closed Thu in winter) St-Malo has no shortage of crêperies but this one, with cute little illustrations of traditional Breton *biniou* (bagpipes), is a time-honoured favourite.

Côté Jardin (☎ 02 99 81 63 11; 36 rue Dauphine, St-Servan; menus €25; ☺ lunch Tue-Sun, dinner Tue & Thu-Sun) The charming, friendly Côté Jardin presents regional and traditional French cuisine, with a scenic terrace that overlooks the marina and St-Malo's walled city. Doodlers can draw on the table with the coloured pencils provided.

Restaurant Delaunay (☎ 02 99 40 92 46; 6 rue Ste-Barbe; menus €33-49; ☺ closed Sun year-round & Mon in winter) Chef Didier Delaunay creates standout gastronomic cuisine at his aubergine-painted restaurant inside the walls. The menu features succulent dishes both from the surf (Breton lobster's a speciality) and turf (tender lamb).

Cheeses and butters handmade by Jean-Yves **Bordier** (9 rue de l'Orme; ☺ Tue-Sat) are shipped to famous restaurants all over the world. Just down the street is the covered market, **Halle au Blé** (rue de la Herse; ☺ 8am-noon Tue & Fri).

GETTING THERE & AWAY
Brittany Ferries (www.brittany-ferries.com) sails between St-Malo and Portsmouth, and **Condor Ferries** (www.condorferries.co.uk) runs to/from Poole and Weymouth via Jersey or Guernsey.

April to September, **Compagnie Corsaire** (☎ 08 25 13 80 35) and **Vedettes de St-Malo** (☎ 02 23 18 41 08; www.vedettes-saint-malo.com) run a **Bus de Mer** (Sea Bus; adult/child return €6/4; ☺ hourly) shuttle service (10 minutes) between St-Malo and Dinard.

TGV trains run between St-Malo and Rennes (€12.10, one hour), Dinan (€8.30, one hour), and a direct service to Paris' Gare Montparnasse (€58, three hours).

DINARD
pop 10,700

Visiting Dinard 'in season' is a little like stepping into one of the canvases Picasso painted here in the 1920s. Belle-époque mansions built into the cliffs form a timeless backdrop to the beach dotted with blue-and-white striped bathing tents. Wintry walks along the coastal paths are spectacular.

Tourist Office (☎ 02 99 46 94 12; www.ot-dinard.com, in French; 2 bd Féart; ☺ 9.30am-7pm Jul & Aug, 9.30am-12.15pm & 2-6pm Mon-Sat Sep-Jun).

The romantically named **promenade du Clair de Lune** (moonlight promenade) has views across the Rance River estuary to St-Malo's walled city, and nightly sound-and-light spectacles in summer. Beautiful **seaside trails** extend along the coast in both directions. Framed by fashionable hotels, a casino and neo-Gothic villas, **Plage de l'Écluse** is the perfect place to shade yourself in style by renting one of Dinard's trademark blue-and-white striped **bathing tents** (☎ 02 99 46 18 12; per half-day €6.80-10.80, per day €7.45-14.15).

SLEEPING & EATING
Dinard's prices match its cachet.

Hôtel Printania (☎ 02 99 46 13 07; www.printaniahotel.com, in French; 5 av George V; s €55-60, d €54-88; ☺ mid-Mar–mid-Nov) This charming Breton-style two-star hotel, complete with mature wood-and-leather furniture, has a superb location overlooking the Baie du Prieuré.

Hôtel de la Plage (☎ 02 99 46 14 87; www.dinard-hotels-plus.com; 3 bd Féart; s €55-75, d €62-90; ☺ Dec-Oct; ✗) Refreshingly unpretentious, with warm staff and solid stone-walled rooms renovated with red-and-gold furnishings and heavy timber furniture, including sleigh beds.

Chez Ma Pomme (☎ 02 99 46 81 90; 6 rue Yves Verney; menus €12-24; ☺ lunch & dinner Jul & Aug, closed Mon, dinner Sun & dinner Thu Sep-Jun) Codfish roasted in bacon and parmesan is among the innovative twists on local ocean-caught fish, while rich Breton caramel features in the tempting array of desserts. The team in the kitchen is hip and young, and the colourful interior equally bright.

Beach-picnic supplies abound at the Dinard large **covered market** (place Rochaid; ☺ 7am-1.30pm Tue, Thu & Sat).

GETTING THERE & AWAY
Ryanair (☎ 02 99 16 00 66; www.ryanair.com) has daily flights to and from London

Stansted; a day/evening taxi from Dinard to the airport costs around €15/22.

From April to September, **Compagnie Corsaire** (☎ 08 25 13 80 35; www.compagnie corsaire.com) and **Vedettes de St-Malo** (☎ 02 23 18 41 08; www.vedettes-saint-malo.com) run the **Bus de Mer** (Sea Bus; adult/child return €6/4; ☺ hourly) shuttle service (10 minutes) between St-Malo and Dinard.

Illenoo (www.illenoo.fr, in French) buses connect Dinard and the train station in St-Malo (€2.50, 30 minutes, hourly). Several buses travel to Rennes (€3.50, two hours).

CANCALE

pop 6200

The idyllic little fishing port of Cancale, 14km east of St-Malo, is famed for its offshore *parcs à huîtres* (oyster beds). A small museum dedicated to oyster farming and shellfish, the **Ferme Marine** (Marine Farm; ☎ 02 99 89 69 99; corniche de l'Aurore; adult/child €6.70/3.50; ☺ mid-Feb–Oct) runs guided tours in English at 2pm from mid-June to mid-September.

The **tourist office** (☎ 02 99 89 63 72; www .cancale-tourisme.fr; ☺ 9am-12.30pm & 2-6pm Mon-Sat Sep-Jun, 9am-12.30pm & 2-7pm Mon-Sat, 9am-12.30pm Sun Jul & Aug) is at the top of rue du Port. In July and August only, there's a tourist office **annexe** (quai Gambetta; ☺ hours vary) in the wooden house where the fish auction takes place.

our pick **O Roellinger** (☎ 02 99 89 64 76; 1 rue Duguesclin; menus €100-172; ☺ closed mid-Dec–mid-Mar) Up the hill from the port, one of the region's (and indeed France's) most acclaimed chefs, Olivier Roellinger, has his triple-Michelin-starred restaurant. Signature dishes include the 'route of the south seas' – a knock-out combination of oysters, *iraches* (local baby squid caught only 'while the lilacs are in bloom'), and poached Easter cabbage laced with spiced curry.

Clustered by the Pointe des Crolles lighthouse, stalls at the **marché aux huîtres** (oyster market; ☺ 9am-6pm) sell oysters from €3.50 per dozen for small *huîtres creuses* to upwards of €20 for saucer-sized *plates de Cancale*.

Stone ramparts, St-Malo (p150)

JOHN ELK III

DAVID TOMLINSON

River Oust and castle, Josselin

⇘ IF YOU LIKE...

If you have a soft spot for idyllic fishing port Cancale (p153), you'll enjoy these quintessential Breton villages with equal relish:

- **Dinan** (tourist office ☎ 02 96 87 69 76; www.dinan-tourisme.com; 9 rue du Château) Set high above the River Rance, the cobblestone streets and squares lined with crooked half-timbered houses making up Dinan's old town are straight out of the Middle Ages. No less than 100,000 visitors turn up to join Dinannais townsfolk dressed in medieval garb for July's two-day Fête des Remparts, held in even-numbered years. Compagnie Corsaire (www.compagniecorsaire .com) runs river boats to/from Dinard and St-Malo.
- **Vitré** (tourist office ☎ 02 99 75 04 46; www.ot-vitre.fr; place Général de Gaulle) With its narrow cobbled streets, half-timbered houses and colossal castle topped by turrets, Vitré rivals Dinan as one of Brittany's best-preserved medieval towns – with far fewer tourists and a more laissez-faire village air. Just 40km east of Rennes, its majestic medieval castle (☎ 02 99 75 04 54; place du Château; 🕙 10am-6pm Jul-Sep, 10am-noon & 2-5.30pm Apr-Jun, 10am-noon & 2-5.30pm Wed-Fri, 2-5.30pm Sat-Mon Oct-Mar) rises on a rocky outcrop overlooking the River Vilaine.
- **Josselin** (tourist office ☎ 02 97 22 36 43; www.paysdejosselin-tourisme.com; place de la Con-grégation) In the shadow of an enormous, turreted 14th-century castle (☎ 02 97 22 36 45; adult/child €7.50/5; 🕙 guided tours 10am-6pm daily mid-Jul–Aug, 2-6pm Jun–mid-Jul & Sep, 2-6pm Sat & Sun Apr-May & Oct, closed Nov-Mar) that was the long-time seat of the counts of Rohan, this village lies on the banks of the River Oust 43km northeast of Vannes. Thousands of visitors fall under its spell.

There is a stunning walk you can take for about 35km along the coast starting in Cancale and going through to St-Malo. If you feel like jumping onto two wheels, you can hire bicycles from **Les 2 Roues de Cancale** (☎ 02 99 89 80 16; 7 rue de L'Industrie; per day from €13).

NORMANDY

Ever since the armies of William the Conqueror set sail from its shores in 1066, Normandy has played a pivotal role in European history. It was the front line for Anglo-French hostilities for much of the Hundred Years' War and later became the crucible of Impressionist art, but it was during the D-Day landings of 1944 that Normandy leaped to global importance. Although many towns were shattered during the Battle of Normandy, the landscape is still dotted with sturdy châteaux and stunning cathedrals, as well as the glorious abbey of Mont St-Michel.

ROUEN

pop 108,300

With its elegant spires, beautifully restored medieval quarter and soaring Gothic cathedral, the ancient city of Rouen is one of Normandy's highlights. It was devastated several times during the Middle Ages by fire and plague, and was occupied during the Hundred Years' War. The young French heroine Joan of Arc (Jeanne d'Arc) was tried for heresy and burned at the stake in the central square in 1431.

INFORMATION

Tourist Office (☎ 02 32 08 32 40; www .rouentourisme.com; 25 place de la Cathédrale; ☯ 9am-7pm Mon-Sat, 9.30am-12.30pm & 2-6pm Sun & holidays May-Sep, 9.30am-12.30pm & 1.30-6pm Mon-Sat, 2-6pm Sun & holidays Oct-Apr)

SIGHTS

Église Jeanne d'Arc (☯ 10am-noon & 2-6pm Apr-Oct, to 5.30pm Nov-Mar), with its fish-scale exterior, marks the spot where Joan was burned at the stake. The church's soaring modernist interior, lit by some marvellous 16th-century stained glass, is well worth a look. Rue du Gros Horloge is spanned by the impressive Gros Horloge (Big Clock; ☯ 10am-noon & 2-6pm Tue-Sun Apr-Oct, 2-5pm Tue-Sun Nov-Mar), a Gothic belfry with one-handed medieval clocks on each side.

Cathédrale Notre Dame (Notre Dame Cathedral; ☯ 7.30am-7pm Mon-Sat, 8am-6pm Sun & holidays mid-Mar–Oct, 7.30am-noon & 2-6pm Mon-Sat, 8am-6pm Sun & holidays Nov–mid-Mar) was painted repeatedly by Claude Monet. Free guided visits (☯ 2.30pm Sat & Sun year-round, daily Jul, Aug & school holidays) to the crypt, ambulatory and Chapel of the Virgin are in French but some guides add English commentary.

The truly riveting Musée Le Secq des Tournelles (☎ 02 35 88 42 92; 2 rue Jacques Villon; adult/student/under 18yr €2.30/1.55/free; ☯ 10am-1pm & 2-6pm Wed-Mon) is devoted to the blacksmith's craft.

The Musée des Beaux-Arts (Fine Arts Museum; ☎ 02 35 71 28 40; esplanade Marcel Duchamp; adult/student/under 18yr €3/2/free; ☯ 10am-6pm Wed-Mon), housed in a grand structure erected in 1870, features a captivating collection of 15th- to 20th-century paintings, including canvases by Caravaggio, Rubens, Modigliani, Pissarro, Renoir, Sisley and several works by Monet, including a study of Rouen's cathedral.

For a macabre thrill check out the courtyard of Aître St-Maclou (186 rue Martainville; admission free; ☯ 8am-8pm Apr-Oct, to 7pm Nov-Mar), a curious ensemble of half-timbered buildings built between 1526 and 1533. Decorated with lurid woodcarvings of skulls, crossbones, gravediggers' tools and hourglasses, it was used as a burial ground for plague victims as recently as 1781.

SLEEPING

Hôtel des Carmes (☎ 02 35 71 92 31; www .hoteldescarmes.com, in French; 33 place des Carmes; d €49-65, tr €67-77; ☐ ☒) This sweet little hotel, trimmed in an imaginative, though rather haphazard, fashion, has 12 rooms decked out with patchwork quilts and vibrant colours.

Hôtel Le Cardinal (☎ 02 35 70 24 42; www .cardinal-hotel.fr; 1 place de la Cathédrale; s €47-59, d €58-72, q €96; ⌧) In a supercentral spot facing the cathedral, this postwar hotel

has 18 simply furnished rooms with lots of natural light. The 4th-floor rooms have fantastic private terraces overlooking the square.

Hôtel du Vieux Marché (☎ 02 35 71 00 88; www.bestwestern.com; 33 rue du Vieux Palais; d €117-

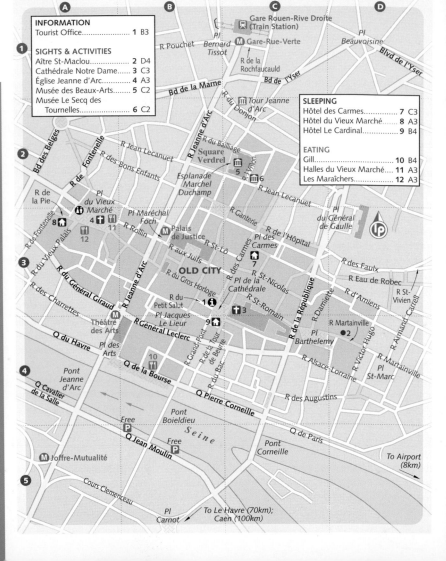

ROUEN

0 — 400 m
0 — 0.2 miles

INFORMATION
Tourist Office..................... 1 B3

SIGHTS & ACTIVITIES
Aître St-Maclou................. 2 D4
Cathédrale Notre Dame...... 3 C3
Église Jeanne d'Arc............ 4 A3
Musée des Beaux-Arts....... 5 C2
Musée Le Secq des
   Tournelles..................... 6 C2

SLEEPING
Hôtel des Carmes.............. 7 C3
Hôtel du Vieux Marché....... 8 A3
Hôtel Le Cardinal.............. 9 B4

EATING
Gill................................. 10 B4
Halles du Vieux Marché.... 11 A3
Les Maraîchers................. 12 A3

Galette (savoury buckwheat crêpe)

JEAN-BERNARD CARILLET

160) Its lobby bedecked with ship models and maritime prints, this modernist hotel has just a smidge of Zen sophistication.

EATING

Les Maraîchers (☎ 02 35 71 57 73; www.les-maraich ers.fr, in French; 37 place du Vieux Marché; menus €16-25; ⊕ lunch & dinner) All gleaming mirrors, polished wood and colourful floor tiles, this bistro, established in 1912 and classified a *café historique d'Europe*, has a genuine zinc bar and a warm and very French ambience. Specialities include Normandy-raised beef.

Gill (☎ 02 35 71 16 14; www.gill.fr; 8-9 quai de la Bourse; lunch menu Tue-Fri €35, other menus €65-92; ⊕ 12.15-1.45pm & 7.30-9.45pm Tue-Sat) *The* place to go in Rouen for *gastronomique* French cuisine served in an ultrachic, ultramodern dining room. Specialities including fresh Breton lobster, scallops with truffles, Rouen-style pigeon and, for dessert, *millefeuille à la vanille*.

Halles du Vieux Marché (place du Vieux Marché; ⊕ 7am-7pm Tue-Sat, 7am-1pm Sun) A small covered market with an excellent *fromagerie* (cheese shop).

GETTING THERE & AWAY

From **Gare Rouen-Rive Droite** (rue Jeanne d'Arc), an art-nouveau edifice built from 1912 to 1928, trains go direct to Paris' Gare St-Lazare (€19.30, 1¼ hours), Amiens (€17.10, 1¼ hours).

Cy'clic (☎ 08 00 08 78 00; http://cyclic.rouen .fr), Rouen's version of Paris' Vélib' (p94), lets you rent a city bike from 14 locations around town.

BAYEUX

pop 14,600

Bayeux has become famous throughout the English-speaking world thanks to a 68m-long piece of painstakingly embroidered cloth: the 11th-century Bayeux Tapestry.

A great place to soak up the Norman atmosphere, Bayeux's delightful city centre is crammed with 13th- to 18th-century buildings, including lots of wood-framed Norman-style houses, and a fine Gothic cathedral.

Bayeux makes an ideal launch pad for exploring the D-Day beaches.

INFORMATION

Tourist Office (☎ 02 31 51 28 28; www.bayeux -bessin-tourism.com; pont St-Jean; ☻ 9am-7pm Mon-Sat, 9am-1pm & 2-6pm Sun & holidays Jul & Aug, 9.30am-12.30pm & 2-6pm Apr-Jun, Sep & Oct, 9.30am-12.30pm & 2-5.30pm Nov-Mar)

SIGHTS

Undoubtedly the world's most celebrated embroidery, the **Bayeux Tapestry** vividly recounts the story of the Norman con- quest of England in 1066. Divided into 58 scenes briefly captioned in almost- readable Latin, the main narrative, told from an unashamedly Norman perspec- tive, fills up the centre of the canvas, while religious allegories and depictions of daily life in the 11th century unfold along the borders.

The tapestry is housed in the **Musée de la Tapisserie de Bayeux** (☎ 02 31 51 25 50; www .tapisserie-bayeux.fr; rue de Nesmond; adult/student incl audioguide €7.80/3.80; ☻ 9am-6.30pm mid-Mar– mid-Nov, to 7pm May-Aug, 9.30am-12.30pm & 2-6pm mid-Nov–mid-Mar). Upstairs is a new exhibition on the tapestry's creation, its remarkable history and its conservation.

Most of Bayeux's spectacular Norman Gothic **Cathédrale Notre Dame** (rue du Bienvenu; ☻ 8.30am-7pm Jul-Sep, 8.30am-6pm Apr-Jun & Oct, 9am-5pm Nov-Mar) dates from the 13th century.

The **Musée Mémorial de la Bataille de Normandie** (☎ 02 31 51 46 90; bd Fabien Ware; adult/student €6.50/3.80; ☻ 9.30am-6.30pm May-Sep, 10am-12.30pm & 2-6pm Oct-Apr) of- fers a first-rate introduction to WWII in Normandy.

SLEEPING

Hôtel Mogador (☎ 02 31 92 24 58; hotel.mogador @wanadoo.fr; 20 rue Alain Chartier; d €44-54; ☒)

Situated on the main market square, this friendly, family-run, two-star hotel has 14 rooms with pastel curtains and lots of old wood beams. The small patio is a lovely spot for a morning croissant. An excellent bet.

Hôtel d'Argouges (☎ 02 31 92 88 86; www .hotel-dargouges.com; 21 rue St-Patrice; d €90- 120, q €280) This graceful three-star hotel, in a stately 18th-century residence, has an elegant breakfast room overlooking a private garden, squeaky parquet floors and 28 rooms.

our pick **Château de Bellefontaine** (☎ 02 31 22 00 10; www.hotel-bellefontaine.com; 49 rue de Bellefontaine; d €125-140, ste €160; ☒) Swans and a bubbling brook welcome you to this majestic 18th-century château, which is surrounded by a 2-hectare private park. Situated 1.5km southeast of the tour- ist office (500m south of rond-point Eisenhower).

EATING

Local specialities to keep an eye out for include *cochon de Bayeux* (Bayeux-style pork).

La Table du Terroir (☎ 02 31 92 05 53; 42 rue St-Jean; lunch menus €12.50-14, dinner menus €21-28; ☻ closed dinner Sun) At this country-style restaurant, crimson chairs and white tablecloths provide an enjoy- able backdrop for specialities such as delicious grilled salmon, pork fillet and *tripes à la Caen*.

La Rapière (☎ 02 31 21 05 45; 53 rue St-Jean; lunch menu €15, dinner menus €27-33; ☻ closed Wed & Thu) Housed in a late-1400s man- sion held together by its original oak beams, this restaurant specialises in hearty home cooking – the *timbale de pêcheur* (fisherman's stew) is served up piping hot in a cast-iron pan. For dessert, *trou normand* (apple sorbet with a dash of Calvados).

BARBARA VAN ZANTEN
Monet's garden, Giverny

⌁ GIVERNY
pop 520

The tiny country village of Giverny is a place of pilgrimage for devotees of Impressionism.

Monet's home for the last 43 years of his life is now the delightful Maison et Jardins de Claude Monet. His pastel-pink house and Water Lily studio stand on the periphery of the Clos Normand, with its symmetrically laid-out gardens bursting with flowers. Monet bought the Jardin d'Eau (Water Garden) in 1895 and set about creating his trademark lily pond, as well as the famous Japanese bridge (since rebuilt) draped with purple wisteria.

Giverny is 76km northwest of Paris and 66km southeast of Rouen. From Rouen (€9.60, 40 minutes) several trains leave before noon. From Paris' Gare St-Lazare two early morning trains run to Vernon (€11.90, 50 minutes), 7km to the west of Giverny. Shuttle buses (☎ 08 25 07 60 27; www.mobiregion.net, in French) meet most trains to and from Paris.

Facing the train station, you can rent a bike at the Café de Chemin de Fer for €12 a day.

Things you need to know: Maison et Jardins de Claude Monet (☎ 02 32 51 28 21; www .fondation-monet.com; adult/student/7-12yr €5.50/4/3, gardens only €4; ☉ 9.30am 6pm Tue Sun Apr-Oct); Café de Chemin de Fer (L'Arrivée de Giverny; ☎ 02 32 21 16 01; ☉ 7am-1am)

GETTING THERE & AWAY

Destinations that are reachable via train include Caen (€5.50, 20 minutes), from where there are connections to Rouen (€24.60) and Gare St-Lazare (€32) in Paris.

A taxi (☎ 02 31 92 92 40) can take you around Bayeux or out to the D-Day sites.

Vélos Location (Le Verger de l'Aure; ☎ 02 31 92 89 16; 5 rue Larcher; per half-/full day €10/15; ☉ 8am-8pm) Offers year-round bike rental.

D-DAY BEACHES

Code-named 'Operation Overlord', the D-Day landings were the largest military operation in history. On the morning of 6 June 1944, swarms of landing craft, part of an armada of over 6000 ships and boats, hit the northern Normandy beaches and tens of thousands of soldiers from the USA, the UK, Canada and elsewhere began pouring onto French soil.

The landings on D-Day were followed by the 76-day Battle of Normandy, during which the Allies suffered 210,000 casualties, which included 37,000 troops who were killed. German casualties are believed to be around 200,000; another 200,000 German soldiers were taken prisoner. About 14,000 French civilians also died.

Caen's Mémorial and Bayeux' Musée Mémorial (p158) provide a comprehensive overview of the events of D-Day.

If you've got wheels, you can follow the D514 along the D-Day coast or several signposted circuits around the battle sites; look for signs for 'D-Day-Le Choc' in the American sectors and 'Overlord-L'Assaut' in the British and Canadian sectors. A free booklet called The D-Day Landings and the Battle of Normandy, available from tourist offices, has details on the eight major visitors' routes

ARROMANCHES

To make it possible to unload the vast quantities of cargo needed by the invasion forces, the Allies set up prefabricated marinas, code-named **Mulberry Harbours**, off two of the landing beaches. The remains of **Port Winston** can still be seen near **Arromanches**, 10km northeast of Bayeux.

Right on the beach, the **Musée du Débarquement** (Landing Museum; ☎ 02 31 22 34 31; www.normandy1944.com; place du 6 Juin; adult/student €6.50/4.50; ⊙ 9am-7pm May-Aug, 9am-6pm Sep, 9.30am-12.30pm & 1.30-5.30pm Mar, Apr & Oct, 10am-12.30pm & 1.30-5pm Feb, Nov & Dec, closed Jan), makes an informative stop before visiting the beaches.

Vieux Bassin, Honfleur (p162)

RUSSELL MOUNTFORD

OMAHA BEACH

The most brutal fighting on D-Day took place on the 7km stretch of coastline, 15km northwest of Bayeux, known as 'Bloody Omaha' to US veterans.

These days Omaha is a peaceful place, a glorious stretch of fine golden sand partly lined with sand dunes and summer homes. **Circuit de la Plage d'Omaha**, trail-marked with a yellow stripe, is a self-guided tour all along Omaha Beach.

On a bluff above the beach, the huge **Normandy American Cemetery & Memorial** (Cimetière Militaire Américain; ☎ 02 31 51 62 00; www.abmc.gov; Colleville-sur-Mer; ☺ 9am-6pm mid-Apr–mid-Sep, 9am-5pm mid-Sep–mid-Apr), 17km northwest of Bayeux at Colleville-sur-Mer, is the largest American cemetery in Europe. Featured in the opening scenes of Steven Spielberg's *Saving Private Ryan,* it contains the graves of 9387 American soldiers. White marble crosses and Stars of David stretch off in seemingly endless rows, surrounded by an immaculately tended expanse of lawn.

The **Visitor Center** (admission free) has an excellent multimedia presentation on the D-Day landings. Be prepared for airport-type security.

POINTE DU HOC RANGER MEMORIAL

At 7.10am on 6 June 1944, 225 US Army Rangers scaled the 30m cliffs at Pointe du Hoc, where the Germans had a battery of artillery guns perfectly placed to rain shells onto the beaches of Utah and Omaha.

Today the **site** (☎ 02 31 51 90 70; admission free; ☺ 24hr), which France turned over to the US government in 1979, looks much as it did half a century ago. The ground is pockmarked with bomb craters, and the German command post (no longer open to the public because it's too close to the eroding cliff) and several of the concrete

Cathédrale Notre Dame (p155), Rouen
JOHN BANAGAN

gun emplacements are still standing, scarred by bullet holes and blackened by flame-throwers.

As you face the sea, Utah Beach is 14km to the left.

UTAH BEACH

This beach is marked by memorials to the various divisions that landed here and the **Musée du Débarquement** (Landing Museum; ☎ 02 33 71 53 35; www.utah-beach.com; Ste-Marie du Mont; adult/6-14yr €5.50/2.50; ☺ 9.30am-7pm Jun-Sep, 10am-6pm Apr, May & Oct, 10am-12.30pm & 2-5.30pm 1-15 Nov, Feb & Mar, also open Sat, Sun & school holidays mid-Nov–Dec).

TROUVILLE & DEAUVILLE

The twin seaside towns of Trouville (population 5400) and Deauville (population

4400), located 15km southwest of Honfleur, are hugely popular with Parisians, who flock here year-round on weekends and all week long from April to September.

Chic Deauville has been a playground of the wealthy ever since it was founded by Napoleon III's half-brother in 1861. Exclusive, expensive and brash, it is packed with designer boutiques, deluxe hotels and public gardens of impossible neatness, and is also home to two racetracks as well as the high-profile American Film Festival (www.festival-deauville.com).

Trouville, another veteran beach resort, is also a working fishing port. The town was frequented by painters and writers during the 19th century, including Mozin and Flaubert, and many French celebrities have holiday homes here, lured by the sandy, 2km-long beach and the laid-back seaside ambience.

Visit the Deauville Tourist Office (☎ 02 31 14 40 00; www.deauville.org; place de la Mairie; ☿ 9am-7pm Mon-Sat, 10am-6pm Sun & holidays

---

CAMEMBERT COUNTRY

Some of the most enduring names in the pungent world of French *fromage* come from Normandy, including Camembert.

If you're interested in seeing how the cheese is made, you can take a guided tour of the Président Farm (☎ 02 33 36 06 60; www.fermepresident .com; adult/child €5/2; ☿ 10am-noon & 2-6pm Jun-Aug, by reservation Mar-May, Sep & Oct), an early 19th-century farm restored by Président, one of the region's largest Camembert producers. It's in the centre of the town of Camembert, which is about 60km south of Honfleur.

Jul–mid-Sep, 10am-6pm Mon-Sat, 10am-1pm & 2-5pm Sun & holidays mid-Sep–Jun).

In Trouville, Trouville Tourist Office (☎ 02 31 14 60 70; www.trouvillesurmer.org; 32 bd Fernand Moureaux; ☿ 9.30am-7pm Mon-Sat, 10am-4pm Sun Jul & Aug, 9.30am-6.30pm Mon-Sat & 10am-1pm Sun Apr-Jun, Sep & Oct, 9.30am-6pm Mon-Sat & 10am-1pm Sun Nov-Mar).

The Poissonnerie (fish market; cnr bd Fernand Moureaux & rue des Bains, Trouville; ☿ 9am-7pm) is *the* place in Trouville to head for a waterfront picnic of fresh oysters with lemon (just €6.50 to €8.50 a dozen) – or for locally caught raw fish.

HONFLEUR

pop 8200

Long a favourite with painters but now more popular with the Parisian jet set, Honfleur is arguably Normandy's most charming seaside town.

Its heart is the Vieux Bassin (Old Harbour), from where explorers once set sail for the New World. Now filled with pleasure vessels, this part of the port is surrounded by a jumble of brightly coloured buildings that evoke maritime Normandy of centuries past.

Named in honour of Eugène Boudin, an early Impressionist painter born here in 1824, the Musée Eugène Boudin (☎ 02 31 89 54 00; opposite 50 rue de l'Homme de Bois; adult/student & senior €4.70/3, Jul-Sep €5.40/3.90; ☿ 10am-noon & 2-6pm Wed-Mon mid-Mar–Sep, 2.30-5pm Mon & Wed-Fri, 10am-noon & 2.30-5pm Sat & Sun Oct–mid-Mar) features a collection of Impressionist paintings from Normandy, including works by Dubourg, Dufy and Monet.

The quirky Les Maisons Satie (☎ 02 31 89 11 11; 67 bd Charles V; adult/student & senior/ under 10yr €5.40/3.90/free; ☿ 10am-7pm Wed-Mon May-Sep, 11am-6pm Wed-Mon Oct-Apr, closed Jan) captures the spirit of the eccentric, avant-garde composer Erik Satie (1866–1925),

BARBARA VAN ZANTEN

Vieux Bassin, Honfleur

who lived and worked in Honfleur and was born in the half-timbered house that now contains the museum. Visitors wander through the museum with a headset playing Satie's music and excerpts from his writings (in French or English). Each room will be a surreal surprise for you – winged pears and self-pedalling carousels are just the beginning.

Visit the **Tourist Office** (☎ 02 31 89 23 30; www.ot-honfleur.fr; quai Lepaulmier; ☒ 9.30am-7pm Mon-Sat, 10am-5pm Sun Jul & Aug, 9.30am-12.30pm & 2pm-6pm or 6.30pm Mon-Sat, 10am-12.30pm & 2-5pm Sep-Jun, closed Sun afternoon Oct–mid-Mar).

From about March to mid-October, you can take a **boat tour** from the Avant Port out to the Seine Estuary and the Pont de Normandie.

SLEEPING

Hôtel L'Écrin (☎ 02 31 14 43 45; www.hon fleur.com/default-ecrin.htm; 19 rue Eugène Boudin; d €100-190, ste €220-250; ☒ ☒ ☒) The parlour and public spaces of this lavish Norman manor house are stuffed with porcelain, oil paintings and antique furniture, re-creating the opulence of times long past.

our pick **La Maison de Lucie** (☎ 02 31 14 40 40; www.lamaisondelucie.com; 44 rue des Capucins; d €150-220, ste €315) Former home of the novelist Lucie Delarue Mardrus (1874–1945), this marvellous little hideaway has just 10 rooms and two suites. Some of the bedrooms, panelled in oak, have Moroccan-tile bathrooms and boast fantastic views across the harbour to the Pont de Normandie. The shady terrace is a glorious place for a summer breakfast.

EATING

Quai Ste-Catherine is lined with brasseries and restaurants with warm-season terraces, chock-a-block with sharply dressed Parisians on summer weekends.

La Cidrerie (☎ 02 31 89 59 85; 26 place Hamelin; menu incl drink €10.90; ☒ closed Tue & Wed except Jul, Aug & school holidays) This tidy little crêperie, down a short alleyway, is a good find if you fancy washing your meal down with *cidre Normand*.

L'Ascot (☎ 02 31 98 87 91; 76 quai Ste-Catherine; menus €24.50-30.50; ☺ closed Tue) A great spot for fresh seafood on a summer evening, with tightly packed tables on the outside terrace and an intimate candle-lit ambience inside.

GETTING THERE & AROUND

The **bus station** (☎ 02 31 89 28 41) is two blocks east of the tourist office. Bus 20, operated by **Bus Verts** (☎ 08 10 21 42 14; www.busverts.fr, in French), goes via Deauville and Trouville (€2, 30 minutes) to Caen (€7, two hours).

CIDER HOUSE RULES

Normandy's 40km **Route du Cidre** (Cider Route), 20km east of Caen, wends its way through the **Pays d'Auge**, a rural area of orchards, pastures and stud farms, through picturesque villages. Along the way, signs reading **Cru de Cambremer** indicate the way to 20 small-scale, traditional producers who are happy to show you their facilities and sell you their home-grown cider (€3 a bottle) and Calvados.

Traditional Normandy **cider** takes about six months to make. The apples are shaken off the trees or gathered from the ground sometime between early October and early December. Alcohol levels range from about 3% for *doux* (sweet) to 4% or 5% for *brut* (dry), with *demi-sec* (semi-dry) coming in at 3% or 4%.

Making **Calvados** (apple brandy) takes longer. Another Normandy favourite is **pommeau**, an amber aperitif made by mixing unfermented apple juice with Calvados.

MONT ST-MICHEL

pop 46

This is one of the most iconic images in France – the slender towers and sky-scraping turrets of the abbey of Mont St-Michel rising from stout ramparts and battlements, the whole ensemble connected to the mainland by a narrow causeway. Fortunately, although it is visited by an incredible number of tourists, Mont St-Michel still manages to whisk you back to the Middle Ages with its fantastic architecture set against the stunning backdrop of the area's extraordinary tides.

When the tide is out, you can walk all the way around Mont St-Michel, a distance of about 1km. Straying too far from the Mont can be very risky: you might get stuck in wet sand or be overtaken by the incoming tide.

The only opening in the ramparts, Porte de l'Avancée, is located to the left at the end of the causeway. The Mont's single street, an alley deceptively called Grande Rue, is lined with restaurants, a few hotels and an exuberant array of tacky souvenir shops. **Pontorson** (population 4200), the nearest real town, is 9km to the south.

INFORMATION

Tourist Office – Mont St-Michel (☎ 02 33 60 14 30; www.ot-montsaintmichel.com; ☺ 9am-7pm Jul & Aug, 9am-12.30pm & 2-6.30pm Mon-Sat, 9am-noon & 2-6pm Sun Apr-Jun & Sep, 9am-noon & 2-6pm Mon-Sat, 10am-noon & 2-5pm Sun Oct-Mar) Just inside Porte de l'Avancée.

Tourist Office – Pontorson (☎ 02 33 60 20 65; www.mont-saint-michel-baie.com, in French; place de l'Hôtel de Ville; ☺ 9am-12.30pm & 2-6.30pm Mon-Fri, 10am-12.30pm & 3-6.30pm Sat, 10am-noon Sun Jul & Aug, 9am-noon & 2-6pm Mon-Fri, 10am-noon & 3-6pm Sat Sep-Jun)

BRITTANY & NORMANDY

NORMANDY

JEAN-BERNARD CARILLET

Côte Sauvage, Brittany

⬊ IF YOU LIKE...

If you loved watching the sun sinking into the sands around Mont St-Michel (p164), you'll be just as captivated by the majestic colours emblazing these scenic Breton coastal drives:

- **Côte de Granit Rose** This otter-inhabited coastline (literally the 'Pink Granite Coast') glows with pink granite cliffs, outcrops and boulders sculpted over the millennia by wind and waves. Their fiery colours are even more impressive when following the 5km walking path, *sentier des douaniers* (custom officers' trail), just near the area's main town, seaside resort **Perros-Guirec**. Local fishermen sell their catch here each morning on place du Marché. Offshore, sail to the **Sept-Îles** (Seven Islands; www.armor -decouverte.fr) to spot puffins, razorbills, fulmars and other marine birds.

- **Golfe du Morbihan** Most people visiting Morbihan's megaliths never make it to this part of the gulf. But swinging southwest from Vannes to Port Navalo rewards you with stupendous views over the gulf and its islands. Picnic benches perch at Port Navalo's tip; bring a hamper and a bottle of Breton cider.

- **Sillon de Talbert** Brittany's best coastal drives let you see long-standing traditions in action too. West of Paimpol on the north coast, spot local seaweed harvesters tossing strands of kelp into their carts.

- **Côte Sauvage** On the western edge of the peninsula en route to Quiberon, the aptly named 'wild coast' swoops between barren head-lands and sheer cliffs. Bonus: you avoid the choked main-road traffic here, partly because the coast road (D186a) isn't well signed. Heading south, turn off towards Kemiscob and Kervozès just before you reach St-Pierre-Quiberon.

JOHN ELK III

Mont St-Michel

SIGHTS & TOURS

The Mont's major attraction is the stunning abbey (☎ 02 33 89 80 00; www.monuments-nationaux.fr; adult/18-25yr/under 18yr incl guided tour €8.50/5/free; ☽ 9am-7pm May-Aug, 9.30am-6pm Sep-Apr, last entry 1hr before closing). In July and August, there are illuminated *nocturnes* (night-time visits) with music from 7pm to 10pm. Most rooms can be visited without a guide but it's worth taking the one-hour tour, included in the ticket price.

The Église Abbatiale (Abbey Church) was built at the rocky tip of the mountain cone. The church is famous for its mix of architectural styles: the nave and south transept (11th and 12th centuries) are solid Norman Romanesque, while the choir (late 15th century) is Flamboyant Gothic.

The buildings on the northern side of the Mont are known as La Merveille (The Marvel). The famous cloître (cloister) is surrounded by a double row of delicately carved arches resting on granite pillars. The early-13th-century, barrel-roofed réfectoire (dining hall) is illuminated by a wall of recessed windows – remarkable, given that the sheer drop precluded the use of flying buttresses. Look out for the promenoire (ambulatory), with one of the oldest ribbed vaulted ceilings in Europe.

Experienced outfits offering guided walks (€6.50) include Découverte de la Baie du Mont-Saint-Michel (☎ 02 33 70 83 33; www.decouvertebaie.com, in French) and Chemins de la Baie (☎ 02 33 89 80 88; www.cheminsdelabaie.com, in French). Tourist offices have details.

GETTING THERE & AROUND

Mont St-Michel is linked to Pontorson (€2, 13 minutes) by bus 6, operated by Manéo (☎ 08 00 15 00 50; www.mobi50.com, in French). Train destinations from Pontorson include Bayeux (€19.60, 1¾ hours) and Rennes (€11.90, 1¾ hours).

THE LOIRE & CENTRAL FRANCE

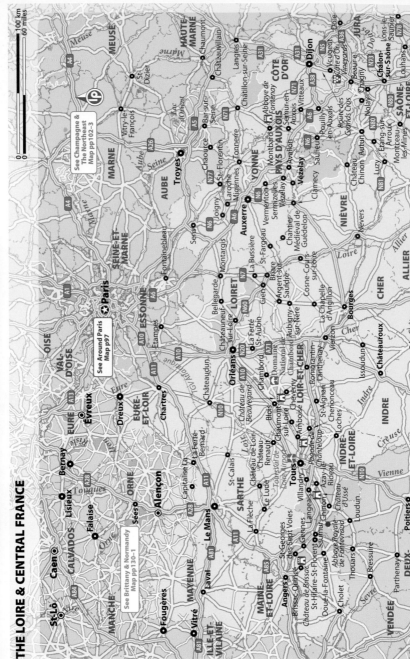

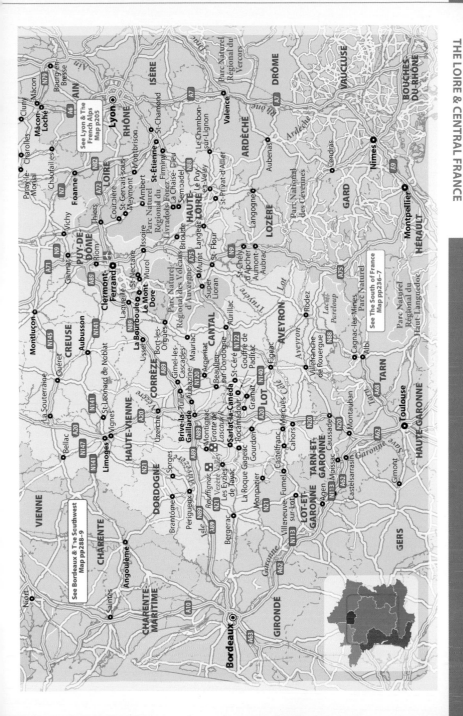

THE LOIRE & CENTRAL FRANCE

HIGHLIGHTS

HIGHLIGHTS

1 CHAMBORD

BY ELSA SAUVÉ, CHÂTEAU DE CHAMBORD

Chambord is a vast chateau of complete disproportion, a Renaissance palace that appears completely unexpectedly in the middle of a forest. It is a place of magic, an emblem of Renaissance architecture in France, a palace built purely for King François I's hunting pleasure at the height of his imperial ambition. Today, like 500 years ago, Chambord dazzles with its majesty.

➘ ELSA SAUVÉ'S DON'T MISS LIST

❶ DOUBLE-HELIX STAIRCASE & ROOFTOP

The double-helix staircase that whisks visitors from the ground floor to the rooftop keep is *the* highlight. This theatrical and majestic staircase is composed of two open parallel flights wrapped around a hollow core, the magic being that two people can see each other go up and down it without their paths ever crossing. A magnificent view of the estate unfolds from the rooftop terraces, an unforgettable place with its sculpted chimney and turrets, really a place of contemplation and daydreaming.

❷ THE 1ST FLOOR

Explore the *premier étage* (1st floor), a historical panorama of the inhabitants of Chambord from François I to Louis XIV and beyond into the 19th century. In the apartments you can really see how château lifestyle evolved over the centuries: all the furniture in Francois I was made to be dismantled and transported with him from château to château.

Clockwise from top: Château Chambord (p182) at dusk; Lantern tower; Row boats await passengers at the château; Château towers; Centre of the double-helix staircase

❸ SON ET LUMIÈRE

Every evening in July and August *Chambord, Dream off Lights* is projected on the façade of the castle. The 50-minute sound-and-light show is a voyage through time: it relives the construction of the chateau and the arrival of the court of the king, and the balls and banquets he threw. Through beautiful images, music and dance, it very much tugs at the audience's senses and emotions.

❹ THE RUTTING SEASON

Chambord is unique in that it is a monument in the middle of a vast forested park. This gives Chambord an additional magic, a place to discover the natural environment as well as culture and history. The park is a wildlife reserve with stags and wild boars. Observatories allow visitors to observe the animals during *le brame,* the rutting or mating season that falls mid-September to mid-October. The best time to see the animals in action is at sunrise or sunset – bring binoculars.

↘ THINGS YOU NEED TO KNOW

Best month to visit May to early July and end of August to September, when the weather is warm and crowds are less **Bewitching hour** Early in the morning, the light is often magical **Audioguide** Rent one for €4; the DIY tour in English lasts 1½ hours. **For more on Chambord, see p182.**

THE LOIRE & CENTRAL FRANCE

HIGHLIGHTS

HIGHLIGHTS

2

↘ THE PERFECT FAIRYTALE CASTLE

Impossible romantics in search of the perfect fairy-tale setting for the castle of their dreams need look no further than moat-ringed **Azay-le-Rideau** (p189), the fabulous kitchen gardens and formal floral displays of **Villandry** (p189), and **Beauregard** (p184), famous for its astonishing portrait gallery of medieval celebrities and its peaceful landscaped grounds.

3

↘ GROTTE DE LASCAUX

Bizarrely it was four teenage boys out searching for their lost dog who discovered this unique subterranean treasure in 1940, a vast network of chambers and galleries adorned with some of the world's most extraordinary and complex prehistoric paintings. Deep in the Dordogne, **Grotte de Lascaux** (p201) *is* the prehistoric equivalent of the Sistine Chapel.

4

↘ THE BURGUNDY WINE ROAD

Cruising lazily between vines from one old stone wine-making village to another, on foot, by car or on the back of a bicycle, is Burgundy at its best. Taste and buy prestigious world-class wines from the so-called 'Golden Hillside' in Beaune (p194) and a glorious symphony of Côte d'Or hamlets with impossibly beautiful names (p194).

5

↘ VENERATE THE SACRED

Devote part of your trip to the region's sacred twinset of abbeys, Unesco World Heritage sites to boot: conjure up medieval monastic life at Abbaye de Fontenay (p197), and lose your soul in the cloisters of one of 18th-century Europe's largest ecclesiastical complexes, the remarkable Abbaye Royale de Fontevraud (p191).

6

↘ PÉRIGUEUX

The historic, picture-perfect town of Périgueux (p196) in the Dordogne has it all: age-old Roman relics in La Cité, a cobblestoned rabbit-warren of a centre riddled with medieval houses and Renaissance mansions, a vibrant twice-weekly market and a local cuisine built from French delicacies like pig-snouted black truffles, forest-picked wild mushrooms and foie gras.

2 BARBARA VAN ZANTEN; 3 ANCIENT ART & ARCHITECTURE COLLECTION LTD/ALAMY; 4 & 6 OLIVER STREWE; 5 CHRISTOPHER WOOD.

2 Château de Villandry (p189), Loire Valley; 3 Grotte de Lascaux (p201), Dordogne; 4 Clos de Vougeot vineyard (p194), Burgundy; 5 Abbaye Royale de Fontevraud (p191), Loire Valley; 6 Périgueux (p196), Dordogne

THE LOIRE & CENTRAL FRANCE

THE BEST...

THE BEST...

⇘ HISTORY LESSONS

- **Château de Blois** (p180) A whistle-stop tour of French architecture.
- **Château Royale d'Amboise** (p187) One of the oldest and most lived in, Amboise was home to a succession of French monarchs.
- **Vezère Valley** (p198) Trace the earliest history of art in this priceless valley.
- **Orléans** (p178) A one-stop lesson in the virginal life of Joan of Arc.

⇘ VILLAGES TO GET LOST IN

- **Sarlat-la-Canéda** (p198) Think one big tangle of honey-coloured buildings, alleys, secret squares and street markets.
- **Vezelay** (p199) Spur-perched in Burgundy.
- **La Roque-Gageac** (p199) This beautiful riverside village in the Dordogne is true get-lost-in-a-second material.

⇘ PLACES TO TASTE WINE

- **Chez Bruno** (p188) If you're after Loire Valley wine tips or oenological instruction, this sleek wine bar in Amboise is the place.
- **Maison du Vin de l'Anjou** (p190) Taste and buy Anjou and Loire vintages at Agers' House of Wine.
- **Beaune** (p194) This thriving town's raison d'être and the source of its joie de vivre is wine – making it, tasting it, selling it, but most of all, drinking it.

⇘ CURIOSITIES

- **Chantier Médiéval de Guédelon** (p198) Watch a 13th century-style château being built using 13th-century technology.

LEFT: JOHN BANAGAN; RIGHT: RUSSELL MOUNTFORD.

Left: Joan of Arc statue, Orléans (p178), Loire Valley; Right: Countryside around Vézelay (p199), Burgundy

THINGS YOU NEED TO KNOW

VITAL STATISTICS

- **Population** 2,589,000 (Loire Valley), 1.6 million (Burgundy), 1,134,959 (Limousin, Dordogne & Quercy), 1,310,000 (Massif Central)
- **Best time to visit** Spring and autumn
- **Points of entry** Orléans, Blois, Tours and Angers

ADVANCE PLANNING

- **As early as possible** Book accommodation.
- **Two weeks before** Book guided tours at Saumur's École Nationale d'Équitation (p190) and the Grotte de Font de Gaume (p201).
- **One week before** Plan which châteaux to visit and consider buying a Pass'-Châteaux (p180) and/or booking an organised tour (p181).

RESOURCES

- **Chateaux Tourisme** (www.chateaux tourisme.com) Where to eat, sleep, go, in the Loire Valley.
- **Burgundy Tourism** (www.burgundy -tourism.com) Burgundy tourist board.
- **Burgundy by Bike** (www.burgundy -by-bike.com) Just that! Maps and guides.
- **Espace Tourisme Périgord** (☎ 05 53 35 50 24; www.dordogne-perigord-tourisme.fr; 25 rue du Président Wilson, Périgueux; ◷ 8.30am-5.30pm Mon-Fri) Dordogne regional tourist office.

GETTING AROUND

- **Budget flights** from the UK to/from Tours (p186) and Angers (p192) airports.
- **High-speed train** to/from Paris; regional trains between Tours and several châteaux.
- **Car** means more flexibility and freedom; vital for the Vezère Valley.
- **Organised bus tours** between châteaux from Blois (p181) and Tours (p185).
- **Bicycle** to explore the flat Loire Valley: surf **Châteaux à Vélo** (www .chateauxavelo.com) and **Loire à Vélo** (www.loireradweg.org) for routes, free maps and MP3 player guides. For bike-rental outlets contact tourist offices.

BE FOREWARNED

- **Vezère Valley** Most prehistoric sites are closed in winter.
- **Grotte de Lascaux** (p201) April to October tickets can *only* be bought next to **Montignac Tourist Office** (☎ 05 53 51 82 60; www .bienvenue-montignac.com; place Bertrand de Born).
- **Son et lumière** shows illuminate Chambord July to mid-September; visit Blois Wednesday to catch the show in English.

ITINERARIES

What a variety of experiences this part of France entails, be it Renaissance châteaux, red-hot mustard or gliding along tranquil river waters, there is a tour to suit every taste.

REGAL LIVING Three Days

Start your Loire château tour with supertanker of a castle **(1) Chambord** (p182). Tour inside with an audioguide and scale the double-helix staircase to the turret-covered rooftop for celestial views of the grounds and Tolkienesque jumble of cupolas, domes, chimneys and lightning rods. Come noon picnic and pedal or hike around the estate; at dusk trip it to **(2) Tours** (p185) for dinner at **(3) Comme Autre Fouée** (p186).

Combine **(4) Château de Cheverny** (p183) and **(5) Château de Chaumont** (p183) on day two, nipping into lesser-known **(6) Château de Beauregard** (p184) should the fancy take you. Splurge later on a killer-calorie cake in **(7) Amboise** (p188) and some good old-fashioned regional cooking at **(8) Chez Bruno** (p188).

On day three get to know original Renaissance man Leonardo da Vinci at **(9) Le Clos Lucé** (p187) and later head west to **(10) Château de Villandry** (p189) for a stroll around the Loire Valley's most remarkable château gardens. After dark watch the valley's oldest and best *son et lumière* (sound and light) projected on the salamander-sculpted stone walls of **(11) Château d'Azay-le-Rideau** (p189).

CULINARY TRIP Five Days

(1) Dijon (p192) is the starting line for tickling tastebuds: spend the morning strolling this ravishing city in Burgundy that most people have heard of thanks to its *moutarde;* sample and buy Maille mustard on tap at **(2) Moutarde Maille** (p194) then lunch medieval-style in a 13th-century cellar at **(3) La Dame d'Aquitaine** (p194). As the sun sinks saunter south through **(4) Côte d'Or vineyards** (p194) along the scenic **(5) Route des Grands Crus** (p194), overnighting in **(6) Beaune** (p194). Devote at least a day to **(7) wine-tasting** (p195) in the city ramparts: consider a two-hour introductory or blind tasting at **(8) Sensation Vin** (p196) and a dozen parsley-spiced e*scargots de Bourgogne* (Burgundy snails) for lunch at **(9) Le Bistrot Bourguignon** (p195). Day three means a **(10) vineyard tour** (p194) by bike, minibus or hot-air balloon.

Or push southwest immediately for a taste of hearty Dordogne cuisine: medieval **(11) Périgueux** (p196) with its colourful outdoor food markets and restaurants is a must, as are the seasonal duck- and goose-based products and mushrooms in **(12) Sarlat-la-Canèda** (p198) and black 'diamond' truffles in **(13) Sorges** (p200).

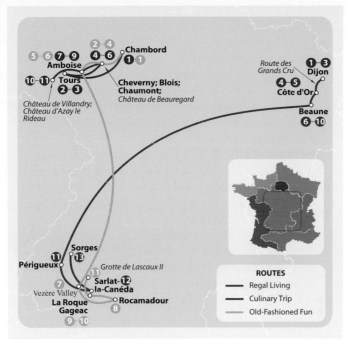

OLD-FASHIONED FUN One Week

Enjoy the Loire Valley châteaux from a different perspective with an autumnal visit to (1) Château de Chambord (p182). Rise early to watch stag caper during the rutting season and spend the day exploring the regal hunting estate by pedal-power. On day two visit (2) Château de Cheverny (p183), then feast on game dishes at a restaurant in (3) Blois (p181), returning to Cheverny at 5pm to catch the (4) Soupe des Chiens (p183). Next day hit (5) Amboise (p188) for a picnic lunch and a spin at skittles and other traditional outdoor games at the curious (6) Pagode de Chanteloup (p187).

Devote the latter part of the week to the ultimate in old-fashioned art: Stone Age art in the (7) Vezère Valley (p198). In between follow pilgrims to (8) Rocamadour (p199); float in a canoe along the River Dordogne in (9) La Roque-Gageac (p199); sail along the underground river at the (10) Gouffre de Padirac (p199); and save Europe's finest prehistoric cave paintings at the (11) Grotte de Lascaux II (p201) until last.

DISCOVER THE LOIRE & CENTRAL FRANCE

Flowing for over 1000km into the Atlantic Ocean, the Loire is one of France's last *fleuves sauvages* (wild rivers). From glittering turrets and ballrooms to lavish cupolas and chapels, the fairy-tale châteaux dotting this valley form a 1000-year snapshot of French high society. If it's aristocratic pomp and architectural splendour you're after, the regal Loire Valley is the place to linger.

Meander southeast towards the River Loire's trickling source in the Massif Central and a luxuriant patchwork of Côte d'Or pea-green vineyards, cycling trails and canals glides into view: this is Burgundy (Bourgogne in French), a paradise for outdoor enthusiasts and lovers of fine red wine. Continue journeying south through central France and you arrive in the Dordogne (Périgord in French), a land of dense oak forests, green fields and rich country cooking where sturdy *bastides* (medieval settlement) and cobblestone villages line river banks while spectacular prehistoric art dances across cave walls. Sleepy and unchanged for centuries, this is the country's heart and soul.

THE LOIRE VALLEY

In centuries past, the Loire River was a key strategic area, one step removed from the French capital and poised on the crucial frontier between northern and southern France. Throughout the centuries kings, queens, dukes and nobles established their feudal strongholds and country seats along the Loire, and the valley is littered with some of the most extravagant architecture this side of Versailles.

ORLÉANS

pop 113,000

There's a definite big-city buzz around the boulevards, flashy boutiques and elegant buildings of Orléans, 100km to the south of Paris. Orléans sealed its place in history in 1429, when a young peasant girl by the name of Jeanne d'Arc (Joan of Arc) rallied the armies of Charles VII and staged a spectacular rout against the besieging English forces, a key turning point in the Hundred Years' War.

INFORMATION

Tourist Office (☎ 02 38 24 05 05; www .tourisme-orleans.com; 2 place de l'Étape; ☯ 9am-7pm Mon-Sat, 10am-1pm Sun Jul & Aug, 9am-1pm & 2-7pm Mon-Sat Jun & Sep, 9.30am-1pm & 2-6.30pm Mon-Sat Apr-May, 10am-1pm & 2-6pm Mon-Sat Oct-Mar)

SIGHTS

Orléans' **Musée des Beaux-Arts** (Fine Arts Museum; ☎ 02 38 79 21 55; 1 rue Fernand Rabier; adult/student €3/1.50; ☯ 10am-6pm Tue-Sun) is a treat.

Orléans' Flamboyant Gothic **cathedral** (place Ste-Croix; ☯ 10am-noon & 2-5.30pm, till 6pm or later in summer) is the result of collective tinkering by successive monarchs. Inside, a series of vividly coloured stained-glass

THE LOIRE & CENTRAL FRANCE

ORLÉANS

ORLÉANS

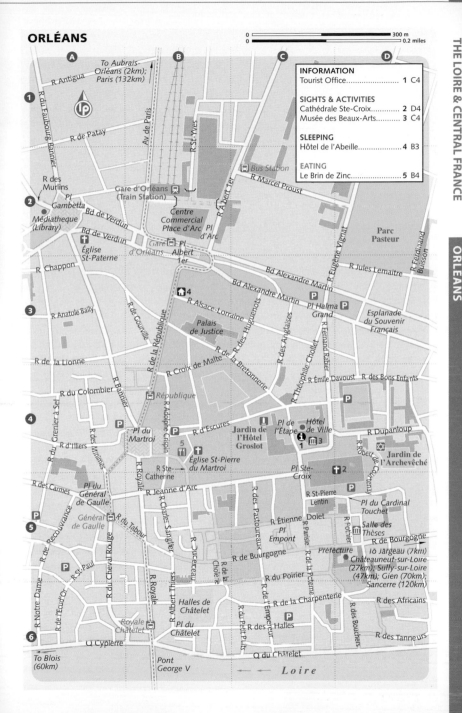

INFORMATION	
Tourist Office........................	1 C4

SIGHTS & ACTIVITIES	
Cathédrale Ste-Croix............	2 D4
Musée des Beaux-Arts..........	3 C4

SLEEPING	
Hôtel de l'Abeille...................	4 B3

EATING	
Le Brin de Zinc......................	5 B4

windows relate the life of St Joan, canonised in 1920.

Since 1430 the Orléanais have celebrated the annual **Fêtes de Jeanne d'Arc** in early May.

SLEEPING & EATING

Hôtel de l'Abeille (☎ 02 38 53 54 87; www
.hoteldelabeille.com; 64 rue Alsace-Lorraine; s €42-51, d €45-89) Bees buzz, floorboards creak and vintage Orléans posters adorn the walls at this gorgeous turn-of-the-century pile off rue de la République.

Le Brin de Zinc (☎ 02 38 53 38 77; 62 Rue St-Catherine; mains €9-18) Battered signs, old telephones and even a vintage scooter decorate this old-world bistro, serving up lashings of mussels and oysters at lunchtime and platters of rich bistro food till late. The daily blackboard *plat du jour* at €7.60 is about the best value in the city.

GETTING THERE & AWAY

Most Loire Valley destinations stop at Gare d'Orléans and Gare des Aubrais-Orléans

---

LE PASS'-CHÂTEAUX

Many of the châteaux in the Blésois are covered by the **Pass'-Châteaux**, which offers savings of between €1.20 and €5.30 depending on which châteaux you visit; contact the tourist offices in Blois, Cheverny and Chambord.

- **Chambord-Cheverny-Blois** €19
- **Chambord-Cheverny-Beauregard** €19
- **Chambord-Blois-Chaumont** €18.70
- **Blois-Chambord-Cheverny-Beauregard** €24.80
- **Blois-Cheverny-Chaumont-Chambord** €25.20

(2km north), but trains to/from Paris' Gare d'Austerlitz (€17.10, one hour 10 minutes) use Gare des Aubrais-Orléans. Orléans has frequent services to Blois (€9.40, 40 minutes) and Tours (€16.80, one to 1½ hours).

BLOIS

pop 49,200

Looming on a rocky escarpment, Blois' historic château (formerly the feudal seat of the powerful counts of Blois) has been repeatedly redeveloped over the last seven centuries.

Inland from the river the twisting streets of the old town give you some idea of how Blois might have looked to its medieval inhabitants.

INFORMATION

Tourist Office (☎ 02 54 90 41 41; www
.bloispaysdechambord.com; 23 place du Château; ◷ 9am-7pm Mon-Sat, 10am-7pm Sun Apr-Sep, 9.30am-12.30pm & 2-6pm Mon-Sat, 10am-4pm Sun Oct-Mar)

SIGHTS & ACTIVITIES

Blois' **château** (☎ 02 54 90 33 32; place du Château; adult/student/6-17yr €7.50/5/3; ◷ 9am-7pm Jul & Aug, 9am-6.30pm Apr-Jun & Sep, 9am-12.30pm & 1.30-5.30pm Oct-Mar) was intended more as an architectural showpiece than a military stronghold. From the château's huge **central courtyard** you can view four distinct periods of French architecture: the Gothic Salle des États and original medieval castle; François I's Renaissance north wing (1515–24) with its spiral loggia staircase; the classical west wing (1635–38); and the Flamboyant Gothic east wing (1498–1503), constructed in the Italianate style by Louis XII using red brick and creamy stone.

In summer the château courtyard hosts a 45-minute **son et lumière** (sound-and-

THE LOIRE & CENTRAL FRANCE

THE LOIRE VALLEY

Château de Chenonceau (p186)

GREG GAWLOWSKI

light show; ☎ 02 54 55 26 31; adult/student/child €7.50/5/3, incl château €11.50/8.50/5.50; ☺ mid-Apr–late Sep) featuring huge projections on the castle walls. There's an English version on Wednesdays.

MAISON DE LA MAGIE

Opposite the château is the former home of watchmaker, inventor and conjurer Jean Eugène Robert-Houdin (1805–71), after whom the great Houdini named himself. This town house now forms the **Maison de la Magie** (House of Magic; ☎ 02 54 55 26 26; www.maisondelamagie.fr, in French; 1 place du Château; adult/student/6-17yr €7.50/6.50/5, incl château €12.50/8.50/5.50; ☺ 10am-12.30pm & 2-6.30pm Mar-late Sep & late Oct-early Nov), with daily magic shows and optical trickery ranging from a hall of mirrors to a mysterious 'Hallucinoscope'.

MUSÉE DE L'OBJET

This brilliant (and very French) **modern arts museum** (☎ 02 54 55 37 45; www.museedelobjet.org; 6 rue Franciade; adult/student €4/2; ☺ 1.30-6.30pm Wed-Sun late Jun-Aug, 1.30-6.30pm Fri-Sun late Feb-late Jun & Sep-Dec) is based on the collection of the artist Eric Fabre, and concentrates on artworks made using everyday materials.

CHÂTEAU TOURS

The *départemental* bus company **TLC** (☎ 02 54 58 55 44; www.tlcinfo.net; adult/child excl admission fees €11.20/8.96; ☺ departures at 9.10am & 1.45pm mid-May–early Sep) runs châteaux tours from Blois to Chambord and Cheverny; tickets can be bought on the bus, or preferably in advance at the Blois tourist office.

Transport Touristique de Voyageurs (☎ 06 08 14 71 41; deveaux.pierre@wanadoo.fr; Chissay-en-Touraine; per bus up to 6 people per day €230) offers tailored trips to local châteaux in air-conditioned minibuses.

SLEEPING & EATING

Hôtel Anne de Bretagne (☎ 02 54 78 05 38; http://annedebretagne.free.fr; 31 av du Dr Jean Laigret; d €54-58) At the top of town overlooking a crescent, this creeper-covered hotel is a more traditional option, with

JOHN ELK III

Château de Chaumont

a bar full of polished wood, soft lighting and vintage pictures, and modern rooms finished in flowery wallpaper and stripy bedspreads.

Le Castelet (☎ 02 54 74 66 09; 40 rue St-Lubin; menus €17-28.20; ☒ closed Wed & Sun) Rusticana and rural frescoes cover the walls of this country restaurant, while piped medieval music fills the air: the perfect setting for more filling Touraine food, with a heavy emphasis on seasonal ingredients.

ourpick L'Orangerie (☎ 02 54 78 05 36; 1 av du Dr Jean Laigret; menus €32-74) Polish up those pumps and dust off that evening dress – the Orangery is Blois' most respected table. On summer nights, opt for a courtyard table and prepare to be pampered.

GETTING THERE & AWAY

TLC (☎ 02 54 58 55 44; www.tlcinfo.net) handles buses to and from Blois, with destinations including Chambord (€3.99, 40 minutes), Beaugency (€10.55, 55 minutes) and Cheverny (€1.10, 45 minutes).

There are trains to Amboise (€6, 20 minutes), Orléans (€9.30, 45 minutes) and Tours (€9.10, 40 minutes), plus Paris' Gare d'Austerlitz (€23.30, two hours).

CHÂTEAU DE CHAMBORD

For full-blown château splendour, you can't top **Chambord** (☎ 02 54 50 50 20; www.chambord.org; adult/18-25yr/under 18yr €9.50/7.50/free, €1 reduction Jan-Mar & Oct-Dec; ☒ 9am-7.30pm mid-Jul–mid-Aug, 9am-6.15pm mid-Mar–mid-Jul & mid-Aug–Sep, 9am-5.15pm, Jan–mid-Mar & Oct-Dec).

Begun in 1519 as a weekend hunting lodge by François I, it quickly snowballed into one of the most ambitious (and expensive) architectural projects ever attempted by any French monarch. By the time Chambord was finally finished 30-odd years later, the castle boasted some 440 rooms, 365 fireplaces, and 84 staircases, not to mention a cityscape of turrets, chimneys and lanterns crowning its rooftop, and a famous **double-helix staircase**, supposedly designed by the king's chum, Leonardo da Vinci. Ironically,

François only stayed here for 42 days during his entire reign from 1515 to 1547.

Despite its apparent complexity, Chambord is laid out according to simple mathematical rules. Each section is arranged on a system of symmetrical grid squares around a Maltese cross. At the centre stands the rectangular keep. Through the centre of the keep winds the great staircase, with two intertwining flights of stairs leading up to the great **lantern tower** and the castle's **rooftop.**

It's worth picking up the multilingual audioguide (€4) to explore the rest of the château, if only to avoid getting lost around the endless rooms and corridors. Several times daily there are 1½-hour **guided tours** (€4) in English, and during school holidays there are **costumed tours** to entertain the kids. Free *son et lumière* shows, known as **Les Clairs de Lune**, are projected onto the château's facade nightly from July to mid-September, and there are outdoor concerts held throughout summer, including a daily **spectacle équestre** (dressage show; adult/child €8.50/6.50; ☺ Tue-Sun May, Jun & Sep).

DOMAINE NATIONAL DE CHAMBORD

This huge hunting reserve (the largest in Europe) stretches for 54 sq km around the château, and is reserved solely for the use of high-ranking French government personalities (though somehow it's difficult to imagine Sarkozy astride a galloping stallion). About 10 sq km of the park is publicly accessible, with trails open to walkers, mountain bikers and horse riders.

It's great for wildlife-spotting, especially in September and October during the stag mating season. There are **aires de vision** (observation towers) around the park; set out at dawn or dusk to spot stags, boars and red deer.

Bikes can be hired from a **rental kiosk** (☎ 02 54 33 37 54; per half-/full day €10/13; ☺ Apr-early Nov) near the *embarcadère* (jetty) on the River Cosson, where you can also rent boats. There are guided **evasions à vélo** (bike trips; adult/child €10/6 plus bike hire) from mid-August to September, and half-day horse rides (€70) in July and August.

CHÂTEAU DE CHEVERNY

Thought by many to be the most perfectly proportioned château of all, **Cheverny** (☎ 02 54 79 96 29; www.chateau-cheverny.fr; adult/7-14yr €7/3.40; ☺ 9.15am-6.45pm Jul & Aug, 9.15am-6.15pm Apr-Jun & Sep, 9.45am-5.30pm Oct, 9.45am-5pm Nov-Mar) represents the zenith of French classical architecture, the perfect blend of symmetry, geometry and aesthetic order.

Since its construction between 1625 and 1634, the castle has hardly been altered, and its interior decoration includes some of the most sumptuous furnishings, tapestries and objets d'art anywhere in the Loire Valley. Behind the main château is the 18th-century **Orangerie**, where many priceless artworks (including the *Mona Lisa)* were stashed during WWII.

Near the château's gateway are the **kennels**, home to the pedigree hunting dogs still used by the owners of Cheverny: feeding time, known as the **Soupe des Chiens**, takes place daily at 5pm from April to September.

Cheverny is 16km southeast of Blois and 17km southwest of Chambord. For information on the bus from Blois see p182.

CHÂTEAU DE CHAUMONT

Set on a defensible bluff behind the Loire, **Chaumont-sur-Loire** (☎ 02 54 51 26 26; adult/12-18yr/6-12yr €7.50/5/free; ☺ 10am-6pm

THE LOIRE & CENTRAL FRANCE

THE LOIRE VALLEY

Grand Salon, Château de Brissac

⤵ IF YOU LIKE...

If you like Chambord (p182), Cheverny (p183) and Chenonceau (p186), you'll fall head-over-heels in love with these relatively crowd-free châteaux:

- **Château de Beauregard** (☎ 02 54 70 40 05; adult/8-18yr €6.50/4.50; ◷ 9.30am-6.30pm Jul & Aug, 9.30am-noon & 2-6.30pm Apr-Jun, Sep & Oct, 9.30am-noon & 2-5pm Nov, Feb & Mar, closed Dec & Jan & Wed Oct-Mar) Built as yet another hunting lodge by François I, the highlight is a portrait gallery depicting 327 notables of European aristocratic society.

- **Château d'Ussé** (☎ 02 47 95 54 05; www.chateaudusse.fr; adult/8-16yr/under 8yr €12/4/free; ◷ 9.30am-7pm daily Jul & Aug, 10am-7pm daily Apr-Jun, 10am-6pm daily Sep–mid-Nov & mid-Feb–mid-Mar) This was the inspiration for Charles Perrault's classic fairy tale, *La Belle au Bois Dormant* (Sleeping Beauty). Its most notable features are the wonderful formal gardens designed by Versailles architect Le Nôtre. Ussé is 14km north of Chinon.

- **Château de Brissac** (☎ 02 41 91 22 21; www.chateau-brissac.fr; adult/15-18yr/7-14yr incl tour €8.50/7.50/4.50, grounds only €3.50; ◷ 10am-6.30pm daily Jul & Aug, 10.15am-12.15pm & 2-6pm Wed-Mon Apr-Jun, Sep & Oct) Spread over seven storeys and 204 rooms, this chocolate-box mansion 15km south of Angers dates to 1502, and is one of the valley's most luxuriously furnished. Kip B&B-style in four of the ridiculously extravagant **château bedrooms** (d €390, dinner €90; 🍴).

mid-May–mid-Sep, 10.30am-5.30pm Apr–mid-May & mid-Sep–end Sep, 10am-5pm Oct-Mar) presents a resolutely medieval face, with its cylindrical corner turrets and sturdy drawbridge. Originally a strictly defensive fortress, the castle became a short-lived residence for Catherine de Médicis following the death

of Henry II in 1560, and later passed into the hands of Diane de Poitiers (Henry II's mistress).

The château's finest architecture is arguably reserved for the **Écuries** (stables), built in 1877. Chaumont's English-style park hosts the annual **Festival**

International des Jardins (International Garden Festival; ☎ 02 54 20 99 22; www.chaumont-jardins.com; adult/12-18yr/6-12yr €9/6.50/3; ⏱ 9.30am-nightfall) between April and October.

GETTING THERE & AWAY

Chaumont-sur-Loire is 17km southwest of Blois and 20km northeast of Amboise. Onzain, an easy walk from Chaumont across the Loire, has trains to Blois (€3, 10 minutes) and Tours (€7.20, 35 minutes).

TOURS

pop 298,000

Tours has long been considered one of the principal cities of the Loire Valley. It's a smart, solidly bourgeois kind of place, filled with wide 18th-century boulevards, parks and imposing public buildings, as well as a busy university of some 25,000 students.

INFORMATION

Tourist Office (☎ 02 47 70 37 37; www.ligeris.com; 78-82 rue Bernard Palissy; ⏱ 8.30am-7pm Mon-Sat, 10am-12.30pm & 2.30-5pm Sun mid-Apr–mid-Oct; 9am-12.30pm & 1.30-6pm Mon-Sat, 10am-1pm Sun mid-Oct–mid-Apr)

SIGHTS

Arranged around the courtyard of the former archbishop's palace, the Musée des Beaux-Arts (☎ 02 47 05 68 73; 18 place François Sicard; adult/student/under 13yr €4/2/free; ⏱ 9am-12.45pm & 2-6pm Wed-Mon) is a fine example of a French provincial arts museum – look out for works by Delacroix, Degas and Monet, as well as a rare Rembrandt miniature and a Rubens portrait of the Virgin Mary.

In a country of jaw-dropping churches, the Cathédrale St Gatien (place de la Cathédrale; ⏱ 9am-7pm) still raises a gasp. With its twin west towers, stretching skyward through a latticework of Gothic decorations, arches, flying buttresses and gargoyles, it's a show-stopper.

Tours was once an important pilgrimage city thanks to the soldier-turned-evangelist St Martin (c 317–97), bishop of Tours in the 4th century. After his death a Romanesque basilica was constructed above his tomb, but today only the north tower, the Tour Charlemagne, remains (the rest was torn down during the Wars of Religion and the French Revolution).

SLEEPING

ourpick L'Adresse (☎ 02 47 20 85 76; www.hotel-ladresse.com; 12 rue de la Rôtisserie; s €50, d €70-90) 'The Address' is a boutique bonanza, with rooms finished in sleek slates, creams and ochres, topped off with

---

CHÂTEAU TOURS

Most companies offer a choice of well-organised itineraries, taking in various combinations of Azayle-Rideau, Villandry, Cheverny, Chambord and Chenonceau (plus wine-tasting tours): entry to the châteaux isn't included, although you'll get a discount on the standard price. Half-day trips cost between €18 and €33; full-day trips range from €40 to €50 including lunch. You can reserve places via the Tours tourist office.

Acco-Dispo (☎ 06 82 00 64 51; www.accodispo-tours.com)

Alienor (☎ 02 47 61 22 23, 06 10 85 35 39; www.locationdevelos.com)

Quart de Tours (☎ 06 85 72 16 22; www.quartdetours.com)

St-Eloi Excursions (☎ 02 47 37 08 04; www.saint-eloi.com)

Abbaye Royale de Fontevraud (p191)

wi-fi, flat-screen TVs, designer sinks, wicker bathchairs and reclaimed rafters.

Hôtel de l'Univers (☎ 02 47 05 37 12; www.hotel -univers.fr; 5 bd Heurteloup; d €137-272; ✕ 🖴 ✕) Everyone from Ernest Hemingway to Édith Piaf has kipped at the Universe over its 150-year history, and it's still a prestigious address.

EATING

Place Plum is crammed with cheap eats, but the quality can be variable.

Comme Autre Fouée (☎ 02 47 05 94 78; 11 rue de la Monnaie; lunch menu €10, other menus €16-19.50; ✪ lunch Sat & Sun, dinner Tue-Sat, also lunch Tue-Thu mid-May–mid-Sep) For local flavour, you can't top this place, which churns out the house speciality of *fouées*, a pitta-like disc of dough stuffed with pork

rillettes, *haricots blancs* (white beans) or goat's cheese.

L'Atelier Gourmand (☎ 02 47 38 59 87; 37 rue Étienne Marcel; menu €20; ✪ closed Mon) Another one for the foodies, but you'll need your dark glasses – the puce-and-silver colour scheme is straight out of a Brett Easton Ellis novel. But there's no quibbling with the food – hunks of roast lamb, green-pepper duck and authentic bouillabaisse, delivered with a modern spin.

GETTING THERE & AWAY

Tours-Val de Loire Airport (☎ 02 47 49 37 00; www.tours-aeroport.com) is 5km northeast.

Touraine Fil Vert (☎ 02 47 47 17 18; www. touraine-filvert.com, in French) serves Amboise (35 minutes) and onward to Chenonceaux (1¼ hours, two daily). There is an information desk at the **bus station** (☎ 02 47 05 30 49; place du Général Leclerc; ✪ 7am-7pm Mon-Sat).

Tours is the Loire Valley's main rail hub. The train station is linked to St-Pierre-des-Corps, Tours' TGV train station, by frequent shuttle trains. Trains run at least hourly between Tours and Amboise (€4.60, 20 minutes) and Blois (€9.10, 40 minutes). SNCF lines go west to Saumur (€10, 35 minutes) and Angers (€15.30, one hour), and east to Chenonceaux (€5.70, 30 minutes).

High-speed TGVs rocket to Paris-Gare Montparnasse (€39.10 to €55.10, 1¼ hours, around 15 daily).

CHÂTEAU DE CHENONCEAU

Spanning the languid Cher River via a series of supremely graceful arches, and encircled by formal gardens and landscaped parkland, **Chenonceau** (☎ 02 47 23 90 07; www.chenonceau.com; adult/student &

7-18yr €10/7.50, with audioguide €14/11.50; ☉ 9am-8pm Jul & Aug, 9am-7.30pm Jun & Sep, 9am-7pm Apr & May, 9.30am-5pm or 6pm rest of year), not to be confused with the village spelled Chenonceaux, is one of the most elegant and unusual of the Loire Valley châteaux.

So it's perhaps unsurprising to find that this architectural fantasy land is largely the work of several remarkable women. The initial phase of construction started in 1515 on the orders of a court minister of King Charles VIII, although much of the work and design was actually overseen by his wife. The château's distinctive arches and one of the formal gardens were added by Diane de Poitiers, mistress of King Henri II. Following Henri's death, Diane was forced to exchange Chenonceau for the rather less grand château of Chaumont by the king's scheming widow, Catherine de Médicis. But Chenonceau's heyday was under the aristocratic Madame Dupin, who made the château a centre of fashionable 18th-century society and attracted guests including Voltaire and Rousseau.

The château is 34km east of Tours, 10km southeast of Amboise and 40km southwest of Blois.

AMBOISE

pop 11,500

The childhood home of Charles VIII and the final resting place of the great Leonardo da Vinci, upmarket Amboise is an elegant provincial town. With some seriously posh hotels and a wonderful weekend market, Amboise makes a less hectic base for exploring the nearby châteaux than Blois or Tours.

INFORMATION

Tourist Office (☎ 02 47 57 09 28; www .amboise-valdeloire.com; ☉ 9am-8pm Mon-Sat & 10am-6pm Sun Jul & Aug, 10am-1pm & 2-6pm Mon-Sat, 10am-1pm Sun Apr-Jun & Sep, 10am-1pm & 2-6pm Mon-Sat Oct-Mar)

SIGHTS

Château Royal d'Amboise (☎ 02 47 57 00 98; place Michel Debré; adult/15-25yr/7-14yr €9/7.50/5.30; ☉ 9am-7pm Jul & Aug, 9am-6.30pm Apr-Jun, 9am-6pm Sep & Oct, 9am-5.30pm Mar & early Nov, 9am-12.30pm Jan, Feb & mid-Nov–Dec) uses the natural terrain to maximise its defensive potential. Sprawling across a rocky escarpment with panoramic views of the river and surrounding countryside, it was used as a weekend getaway from the official royal seat at nearby Blois.

Today, just a few of the original 15th- and 16th-century structures survive, notably the **Flamboyant Gothic wing** and the **Chapelle St-Hubert**, a small chapel dedicated to the patron saint of hunting (note the carved stag horns and hunting friezes outside) and believed to be the final resting place of da Vinci.

Leonardo da Vinci installed himself in the grand manor house at **Le Clos Lucé** (☎ 02 47 57 00 73; www.vinci-closluce.com; 2 rue du Clos Lucé; adult/student/6-15yr Mar–mid-Nov €12.50/9.50/7, mid-Nov–Mar €9.50/7/6; ☉ 9am-8pm Jul & Aug, 9am-7pm Feb-Jun, Sep & Oct, 9am-6pm Nov-Jan) in 1516 on the invitation of François I: the house and landscaped grounds house scale models of many of his inventions, including a protoautomobile, tank, parachute, hydraulic turbine and even a primitive helicopter.

Two kilometres south of Amboise is the curious **Pagode de Chanteloup** (☎ 02 47 57 20 97; www.pagode-chanteloup.com; adult/7-15yr/student €7/6/5; ☉ 9.30am-7.30pm Jul & Aug, 10am-7pm Jun, 10am-6.30pm May & Sep, 10am-6pm Mar & Apr, 2-4.30pm Mon-Fri Feb, plus 10am-noon & 2-5pm Sat & Sun Feb, Oct & Nov bank holidays & school holidays), the only remains of a demolished château; clamber to the top and you'll be rewarded with glorious views.

Gourmet picnic hampers (€11 to €25) are on sale in summer.

SLEEPING

Villa Mary (☎ 02 47 23 03 31; www.villa-mary .fr; 14 rue de la Concorde; d €60-120; ✕) Four tip-top rooms in an impeccably furnished 18th-century town house, crammed with beeswaxed antiques, glittering chandeliers and antique rugs. Choose from Red, Violet, Pink and Blue, all with period pieces and patterned wallpaper.

Le Vieux Manoir (☎ 02 47 30 41 27; 13 rue Rabelais; r €140-190, ste €275-305; ✕) Run by expat Americans, this shuttered mansion is stuffed floor to ceiling with period charm. Rooms are named after French notables – our choice is Madame de Lafayette with its burnished 19th-century dresser and cupboard bathroom.

EATING

Bigot (☎ 02 47 57 59 32; 2 rue Nationale; ◷ 9am-7.30pm Tue-Fri, 8.30am-7.30pm Sat & Sun) Since 1913 this award-winning chocolatier and pâtisserie has been whipping up some of the Loire's creamiest cakes and gooiest treats.

Chez Bruno (☎ 02 47 57 73 49; place Michel Debré; 2-/3-course menu €11/15; ◷ lunch Wed-Sun, dinner Fri & Sat) Amboise's new boy uncorks a host of local vintages in a coolly contemporary setting (white tablecloths, big gleaming glasses, snazzy artwork), accompanied by honest, inexpensive regional cooking.

L'Épicerie (☎ 02 47 57 08 94; 46 place Michel Debré; menus €20.90, €25.60 & €30.90; ◷ Wed-Sun) For a more time-honoured atmosphere head along the street from Chez Bruno to the Grocery, where rich wood and neo-Renaissance decor is matched by filling fare such as *cuisse de lapin* (rabbit leg) and *tournedos de canard* (duck fillet).

For self-catering supplies, Amboise's excellent outdoor **food market** (◷ 8am-1pm Fri & Sun) fills the river-bank car parks west of the tourist office.

GETTING THERE & AROUND

Amboise is 34km downstream from Blois and 23km upstream from Tours.

CHRISTOPHER WOOD

Ornamental garden, Château de Villandry

Touraine Fil Vert's (p186) links Amboise's post office with Tours' bus terminal (€1.50, 45 minutes). One bus daily continues on to Chenonceaux (15 minutes).

The **train station** (bd Gambetta), located across the river from the centre of town, is served by trains from Paris' Gare d'Austerlitz (€24.20, 2¼ to three hours), Blois (€5.60, 20 minutes) and Tours (€4.50, 15 minutes).

CHÂTEAU DE VILLANDRY

Completed in 1756 and one of the last major Renaissance châteaux to be built in the Loire Valley, **Villandry** (☎ 02 47 50 02 09; www.chateauvillandry.com; château & gardens adult/8-18yr & student €9/5, gardens only €6/3.50; ☼ château 9am-6.30pm Jul & Aug, 9am-6pm Apr-Jun, Sep & Oct, 9am-5.30pm Mar, 9am-5pm Feb & early Nov, gardens 9am-btwn 5pm & 7.30pm year-round) is more famous for what lies outside the château's walls than what lies within. Sheltered with enclosing walls, the château's glorious landscaped gardens are some of the finest in France, occupying over 6 hectares filled with impeccably manicured lime trees, tinkling fountains, ornamental vines and razor-sharp box hedges.

Make sure you time your visit for when the gardens are in bloom between April and October – midsummer is the most spectacular season.

GETTING THERE & AWAY

Villandry is 17km southwest of Tours, 31km northeast of Chinon and 11km northeast of Azay-le-Rideau.

Touraine Fil Vert's (p186) travels between Tours and Azay-le-Rideau (€1.50, 50 minutes), stopping at Villandry (30 minutes from Tours), twice daily in July and August.

The nearest trains stop in Savonnières, 4km northeast of Villandry. Destinations include Tours (€2.90, 10 minutes) and Saumur (€8.20, 35 minutes).

CHÂTEAU D'AZAY-LE-RIDEAU

Conjure up a classic French château and chances are it will be close to **Azay-le-Rideau** (☎ 02 47 45 42 04; adult/18-25yr €7.50/4.80; ☼ 9.30am-7pm Jul & Aug, 9.30am-6pm Apr-Jun & Sep, 10am-12.30pm & 2-5.30pm Oct-Mar), a wonderful moat-ringed mansion decorated with geometric windows, ordered turrets and decorative stonework, wrapped up within a shady landscaped park. Built in the 1500s on a natural island in the River Indre, the château is one of the Loire's loveliest – Honoré de Balzac called it a 'multifaceted diamond set in the River Indre'. The most famous feature is its open loggia staircase, overlooking the central courtyard and decorated with the salamanders and ermines of François I and Queen Claude. In summer, a *son et lumière* is projected onto the castle walls every evening.

GETTING THERE & AWAY

Château d'Azay-le-Rideau is 26km southwest of Tours. Touraine Fil Vert's (p186) travels from Tours to Azay-le-Rideau (€1.50, 50 minutes) twice daily from July to August. The train station is 2.5km from the château: connections include Tours (€4.80, 20 to 50 minutes, six to eight daily).

SAUMUR

pop 30,000

Like many of the Loire's riverside towns, there's an air of Parisian sophistication around Saumur: stately, solidly bourgeois, and just a touch snooty, the town is renowned for its École Nationale d'Équitation, a national cavalry school that's been home to the crack horsemen of the Cadre Noir since 1828.

Europe's highest concentration of troglodyte dwellings dot the banks of the Loire around Saumur.

Saumur Tourist Office (☎ 02 41 40 20 60; www.saumur-tourisme.com; ☺ 9.15am-12.30pm & 2-6pm Mon-Sat, 10am-noon Sun) Offers helpful service.

Lording above the town's rooftops, Saumur's fairy-tale **château** (☎ 02 41 40 24 40; adult/under 11yr €3/free; ☺ gardens 10am-1pm & 2-5.30pm Wed-Mon Apr-Sep) was largely built during the 13th century by Louis XI, and has variously served as a dungeon, fortress and country residence. While the interior remains closed, you can still wander around the outside grounds and take a guided tour exploring the castle's history (ask at the tourist office).

Three kilometres west of the town in St-Hilaire-St-Florent, the **École Nationale d'Équitation** (National Equestrian School; ☎ 02 41 53 50 60; www.cadrenoir.fr; rte de Marson; adult/3-12yr €7.50/4.50; ☺ 9am-6pm Tue-Fri, 9am-12.30pm Sat, 2-6pm Mon Apr–mid-Oct) is one of France's foremost riding academies, responsible for training the country's Olympic teams and members of the elite Cadre Noir display team. There are guided tours every half-hour during opening hours until 4pm; morning tours usually include a Cadre Noir training session. Advance reservations are essential.

ourpick **Château de Verrières** (☎ 02 41 38 05 15; http://chateau-verrieres.com; 53 rue d'Alsace; r €120-290; 🖭) Despite its stonking size, there are actually only 10 rooms at this wonderful 1890 château, which is ensconced within the woods and ponds of a 1.6-hectare English park (parking is available).

GETTING THERE & AROUND

Trains from Saumur travel to Tours (€10 to €13.10, 35 to 55 minutes) and Angers (€7.40, 20 minutes).

ANGERS

pop 151,000

Often dubbed 'Black Angers' due to the murky stone and dark slate used in its buildings, the riverside city is the eastern gateway to the Loire Valley. It's best known for the 14th-century *Tenture de l'Apocalypse* housed in the city's old château.

INFORMATION

Tourist Office (☎ 02 41 23 50 00; www.angersloiretourisme.com; 7 place du Président Kennedy; ☺ 10am-7pm Mon, 9am-7pm Tue-Sat, 10am-6pm Sun May-Sep, 2-6pm Mon, 9am-6pm Tue-Sat, 10am-1pm Sun Oct-Apr)

SIGHTS

Angers' brooding black-stone **château** (☎ 02 41 86 48 77; 2 promenade du Bout du Monde; adult/under 18yr €7.50/free; ☺ 9.30am-6.30pm May-Aug, 10am-5.30pm Sep-Apr) looms behind quai de Ligny, ringed by battlements and 17 watchtowers. Formerly the seat of power for the counts of Anjou, the principal reason to pay a visit these days is the **Tenture de l'Apocalypse** (Apocalypse tapestry), a 101m-long series of tapestries commissioned by Louis I, duke of Anjou around 1375 to illustrate the Book of Revelation. It recounts the story of the Day of Judgment from start to finish.

Angers' most famous son is the sculptor Pierre-Jean David (1788–1856), often just known as David d'Angers. His work forms the cornerstone of the **Galerie David d'Angers** (☎ 02 41 05 38 90; 33bis rue Toussaint; adult/student/under 18yr €4/3/free; ☺ 10am-7pm daily mid-Jun–mid-Sep, 10am-noon & 2-6pm Tue-Sun mid-Sep–mid-Jun), housed in the converted 12th-century Toussaint Abbey, flooded with light through a striking glass-and-girder roof.

Head for the **Maison du Vin de l'Anjou** (☎ 02 41 88 81 13; mdesvins-angers@vinsvaldeloire

DIANA MAYFIELD

Cloisters, Abbaye Royale de Fontevraud

ABBAYE ROYALE DE FONTEVRAUD

The most interesting attraction east of Saumur is the Abbaye Royale de Fontevraud, 4km south of Montsoreau.

Until its closure in 1793, this huge complex was one of the largest ecclesiastical centres in Europe; unusually, both nuns and monks were governed by an abbess (generally a lady of noble birth retiring from public life). Around the enormous complex you can visit the former dormitories, workrooms and prayer halls, as well as the spooky underground sewer system and a wonderful barrel-vaulted refectory, where the monks and nuns would eat in silence while being read to from the scriptures.

Look out too for the space-rocket-shaped kitchens, built entirely from stone to make them fireproof.

The highlight is undoubtedly the massive, movingly simple abbey church, notable for its soaring pillars, Romanesque domes, and the polychrome tombs of four illustrious Plantagenets: Henry II, king of England from 1154 to 1189; his wife Eleanor of Aquitaine (who retired to Fontevraud following Henry's death); their son Richard the Lion-Heart; and his wife Isabelle of Angoulême.

Things you need to know: ☎ 02 41 51 71 41; www.abbaye-fontevraud.com; adult/18-25yr/under 18yr €7.90/5.90/free, €1.40 discount Nov-Apr; ☺ 9am-6.30pm Jun-Sep, 10am-6pm Oct, Apr & May, 10am-5.30pm Nov-Mar

.fr; 5bis place du Président Kennedy; ☺ 9am-1pm & 3-6.30pm Tue-Sun Apr-Sep, 9.30am-1pm & 3-6.30pm Tue-Sat Oct-Mar) for the lowdown on local vintages and tips on where to buy Anjou and Loire wines.

SLEEPING & EATING

Hôtel Bleu-Marine (☎ 02 41 87 37 20; www.marinehotel-angers.com; bd du Maréchal Foch; ☒) Clean lines, minimalist decor, businesslike styling and wall-mounted LCD TVs conjure up Angers' sharpest rooms, though the look occasionally borders on the Spartan.

Castel-Boeuf (☎ 02 41 87 11 44; 14 rue Montault; menus €12.50 & €18.50; ✆ closed Sun, dinner Mon & Tue) Homely little restaurant near the cathedral specialising in unpretentious country food – it's especially popular for its *carpaccio* beef (with Roquefort, shallots or Italian dressing).

GETTING THERE & AWAY

Angers-Marcé Airport (☎ 02 41 33 50 00; www.angers.aeroport.fr) is northeast in Marcé.

Buses travel to Saumur (€7.30, 1½ hours) and Brissac-Quincé (€1.50, 25 minutes).

Angers' train station has connections to Saumur (€7.40, 20 minutes) and Tours (€16). TGVs travel to Paris' Gare Montparnasse (€46.10 to €61.60, 1½ hours).

BURGUNDY

Amid some of the country's most gorgeous countryside, two great French passions, wine and food, come together here in a particularly enticing and hearty form.

DIJON

pop 237,000

Dijon is one of France's most appealing provincial cities. Filled with elegant medieval and Renaissance buildings, the lively centre is wonderful for strolling.

Tourist Office (☎ 08 92 70 05 58; www.dijon-tourism.com; 11 rue des Forges; ✆ 9am-7pm Mon-Sat, 9am-12.30pm & 2.30-5pm Sun & holidays May-Oct, 10am-noon & 2-6pm Mon-Sat, 2.30-5.30pm Sun & holidays Nov-Apr).

SIGHTS

Once home to the region's powerful dukes, the **Palais des Ducs et des États de Bourgogne** is right in the heart of old Dijon. The eastern wing houses the outstanding **Musée des Beaux-Arts** (☎ 03 80 74 52 09; audioguide €3.90; ✆ 9.30am-6pm Wed-Mon May-Oct, 10am-5pm Wed-Mon Nov-Apr).

Just off the **Cour d'Honneur** (the courtyard inside the wrought-iron grille), the 46m-high, mid-15th-century **Tour Philippe le Bon** (Tower of Philip the Good; ☎ 03 80 74 52 71; adult/student & over 65yr/under 12yr €2.30/1.20/free; ✆ accompanied climbs every

Vineyard, Loire Valley

OLIVER STREWE

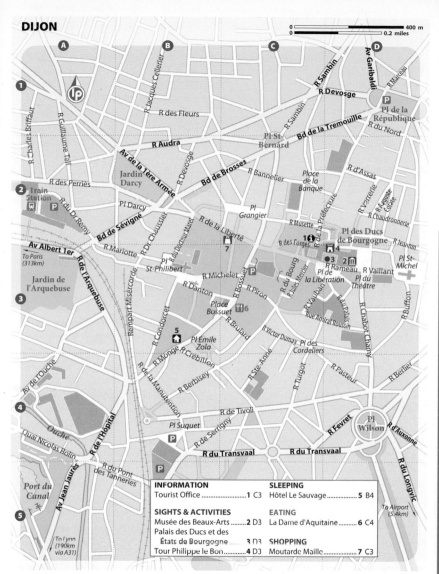

DIJON

INFORMATION	**SLEEPING**
Tourist Office 1 C3	Hôtel Le Sauvage 5 B4
SIGHTS & ACTIVITIES	**EATING**
Musée des Beaux-Arts 2 D3	La Dame d'Aquitaine 6 C4
Palais des Ducs et des	
États de Bourgogne 3 D3	**SHOPPING**
Tour Philippe le Bon 4 D3	Moutarde Maille 7 C3

45min 9am-noon & 1.45-5.30pm Easter-late Nov,
9-11am & 1.30-3.30pm Wed afternoon, Sat & Sun
late Nov-Easter) affords fantastic views over
the city. On a clear day you can see all the
way to Mont Blanc.

SLEEPING & EATING

Hôtel Le Sauvage (Hostellerie du Sauvage;
☎ 03 80 41 31 21; www.hotellesauvage.com; 64
rue Monge; d €48-58, tr €58-80) In a 15th-cen-
tury *relais de poste* (relay post house) set
around a cobbled, vine-shaded courtyard,

this good-value two-star hotel is just off lively rue Monge.

La Dame d'Aquitaine (☎ 03 80 30 45 65; 23 place Bossuet; lunch menu €22, other menus €29-45; ☼ closed Sun & lunch Mon) Excellent Burgundian and southwestern French cuisine served under the sumptuously lit bays of a 13th-century cellar. The Middle Ages at their most civilised.

SHOPPING

Moutarde Maille (☎ 03 80 30 41 02; 32 rue de la Liberté; ☼ 9am-7pm Mon-Sat) Tangy odours assault the nostrils, as they well should in a place with 36 different kinds of mustard, including three on tap that you can sample (from €76 per kilogram).

GETTING THERE & AWAY

The **train station** (rue du Dr Remy) is linked with Paris' Gare de Lyon (€43.40 to €54.10 by TGV, 1¾ hours), Lyon-Part Dieu (€25.10, two hours) and Nice (€79.10 to €91.30 by TGV, 6¼ hours).

CÔTE D'OR VINEYARDS

Burgundy's most renowned vintages come from the vine-covered Côte d'Or (Golden Hillside), the narrow, eastern slopes of a range of hills made of limestone, flint and clay that runs south from Dijon for about 60km.

Burgundy's most famous wine route, the **Route des Grands Crus** (www.road-of -the-fine-burgundy-wines.com) and its often-narrow variants wend their way between the region's stone-built villages.

If you're coming from Dijon, the Côte de Nuits begins in earnest just south of **Marsannay-la-Côte**. Most of the area's *grand cru* vineyards are between **Gevrey-Chambertin** and **Vosne-Romanée**, famed for its Romanée Conti wines, among Burgundy's most prestigious – and

priciest. **Clos de Vougeot** is known for its imposing château.

Lots of excellent restaurants are tucked away in the villages of the Côte d'Or.

ourpick **Le Charlemagne** (☎ 03 80 21 51 45; www.lecharlemagne.fr, in French; Pernand-Vergelesses; lunch menus Mon-Fri €27-33, other menus €43-82; ☼ 12.15-1.30pm & 7.15-9.30pm, closed Tue & lunch Wed, also closed dinner Wed Sep-May) has vineyard views as mouthwatering as the imaginatively prepared *escargots de Bourgogne:* the serene, Japanese-inspired dining room is the perfect spot to experience delicious dishes melding venerable French traditions with techniques and products from Japan.

BEAUNE

pop 21,300

Beaune (pronounced bone), 44km south of Dijon, is the unofficial capital of the Côte d'Or and is one of the best places in France for wine tasting.

The jewel of Beaune's old city is the magnificent **Hôtel-Dieu** (☎ 03 80 24 45 00; rue de l'Hôtel-Dieu; adult/student/under 18yr €6/4.80/2.80; ☼ tickets sold 9am-6.30pm Easter–mid-Nov, 9am-11.30am & 2-5.30pm mid-Nov–Easter, interior closes 1hr later), France's most splendiferous medieval charity hospital.

Beaune's thick stone **ramparts**, which shelter wine cellars and are surrounded by overgrown gardens, are ringed by a pathway that makes for a lovely stroll.

The **tourist office** (☎ 03 80 26 21 30; www .beaune-burgundy.com; 6 bd Perpreuil; ☼ 9am-7pm Mon-Sat, 9am-6pm Sun Easter–mid-Nov, 9am-12.30pm & 1.30-6pm Mon-Sat, 10am-12.30pm & 1.30-5pm Sun mid-Nov–Easter) handles reservations for **minibus tours** (per person €34-43) of the vineyards and for **hot-air-balloon rides**.

ACTIVITIES

WINE TASTING

Underneath Beaune's buildings, streets and ramparts, millions of dusty bottles of wine are being aged to perfection in cool, dark, cobweb-lined cellars.

Cellier de la Vieille Grange (☎ 03 80 22 40 06; 27 bd Georges Clemenceau; ☼ 9am-noon & 2-7pm Tue-Sat, by appointment Sun & Mon) This is where locals come to buy Burgundy wines for as little as €1.25 per litre.

Marché aux Vins (☎ 03 80 25 08 20; www .marcheauxvins.com, in French; 2 rue Nicolas Rolin; admission €10; ☼ 9.30-11.30am & 2-5.30pm, no midday closure mid-Jun–Aug) Using a *tastevin* (flat silvery cup whose shiny surfaces help you admire the wine's colour) you can sample an impressive 15 wines (including three whites) in the candle-lit former Église des Cordeliers and its cellars.

Patriarche Père et Fils (☎ 03 80 24 53 78; www.patriarche.com; 5 rue du Collège; audioguide tour €10; ☼ 9.30-11.30am & 2-5.30pm) The largest cellars in Burgundy, lined with three to five million bottles of wine.

SLEEPING & EATING

Hôtel des Remparts (☎ 03 80 24 94 94; www .hotel-remparts-beaune.com; 48 rue Thiers; d €92-108, low season €79-95, ste €116-150; 🔀 🖳 ✕) Set around two delightful courtyards, this three-star place, in a 17th-century town house, has 22 rooms with red tile floors, antique furniture and luxurious bathrooms.

Le Bistrot Bourguignon (☎ 03 80 22 23 24; www.restaurant-lebistrotbourguignon.com; 8 rue Monge; lunch menu €12.90; ☼ Tue-Sat) A cosy bistro-style restaurant and wine bar that serves good-value cuisine billed as *régionale et originale* and 17 Burgundy wines by the glass (€2.60 to €7). Hosts live jazz at least once a month.

Ma Cuisine (☎ 03 80 22 30 22; passage Ste-Hélène; menu €22; ☼ 12.15-1.30pm & 7.30-9pm Mon, Tue, Thu & Fri, closed Aug) A low-key, 13-table place hidden down an alley. The traditional French and Burgundian dishes, all excellent, include *pigeon de Bresse entier rôti au jus* (whole Bresse pigeon roasted in its juices; €32). The award-winning wine

ANDREW BAIN

Cycling through vineyards near Beaune

WANT TO KNOW MORE?

The **École des Vins de Bourgogne** (☎ 03 80 26 35 10; www.ecoledesvins -bourgogne.com; 6 rue du 16e Chasseurs, Beaune) offers a variety of courses to refine your vinicultural vocabulary as well as your palate.

Another Beaune-based outfit, **Sensation Vin** (☎ 03 80 22 17 57; www .sensation-vin.com; 1 rue d'Enfer, Beaune; ☽ 10am-7pm), offers introductory tasting sessions (half-/one-/two hours €8/18/33; no appointment needed) as well as tailor-made courses.

For more information, a useful website is www.bourgogne-wines .com.

list includes 850 vintages listed by colour, region and ascending price (€18 to €830).

GETTING THERE & AWAY

Beaune has frequent rail connections to Dijon (€6.50, 25 minutes) via the Côte d'Or village of Nuits-St-Georges (€3, 10 minutes), Paris' Gare de Lyon (€50.50 to €62.40) and Lyon-Part Dieu (€21.60, 1¾ hours).

THE DORDOGNE

Rich food, heady history and rolling countryside sum up the delightful Dordogne, sometimes known as the 'Land of 1001 Châteaux' thanks to its abundance of historic castles. But Cro-Magnon man was here long before, and the Vézère Valley has the most spectacular series of prehistoric cave paintings anywhere in Europe.

PÉRIGUEUX

pop 29,600

Initially occupied by Gallic tribes, and later developed by the Romans into the city of Vesunna, Périgueux is still the biggest (and busiest) city of the Dordogne.

Tourist Office (☎ 05 53 53 10 63; www .tourisme-perigueux.fr; 26 place Francheville; ☽ 9am-6pm Mon-Sat, 10am-1pm & 2-6pm Sun Jun-Sep, 9am-1pm & 2-6pm Mon-Sat mid-Sep– mid-Jun)

SIGHTS

Périgueux' most distinctive landmark is the **Cathédrale St-Front** (place de la Clautre; admission free; ☽ 8am-12.30pm & 2.30-7.30pm), notable for its five Byzantine bump-studded domes (inspired by either St Mark's Basilica in Venice or the church of the Holy Apostles of Constantinople).

Périgueux (or Vesunna, to give it its Roman name) was among the most important cities in Roman Gaul. The **Tour de Vésone** is the last remaining section of a massive Gallo-Roman temple dedicated to the Gaulish goddess Vesunna. To the north are the ruins of the city's **Roman amphitheatre**. Just west is the **Musée Gallo-Romain Vesunna** (☎ 05 53 53 00 92; www.semitour.com; rue Claude Bernard; adult/6-12yr €5.70/3.70; ☽ 10am-7pm Jul & Aug, 10am-12.30pm & 2-6pm Tue-Sun Apr-Jun & Sep-Nov, 10am-12.30pm & 2-5.30pm Tue-Sun Dec-Mar), constructed by French architect Jean Nouvel above a 1st-century Roman villa uncovered in 1959.

EATING

Au Bien Bon (☎ 05 53 09 69 91; 15 rue des Places; lunch menus €10-14, dinner menus €22; ☽ lunch Mon-Fri, dinner Fri & Sat) Chequered tablecloths, blackboard menus and chipped floor tiles set the down-home tone at this rustic place, which makes a fine spot for traditional Périgord cooking – *confit de canard* (duck leg, cured and poached in its own fat), *omelette aux cèpes* (omelette with porcini mushrooms) or full-blown *tête de veau* (vealer's head).

Abbaye de Fontenay, Burgundy

CHRISTOPHER WOOD

➘ ABBAYE DE FONTENAY

Founded in 1118 and restored to its stone-built medieval glory a century ago, **Abbaye de Fontenay** offers a fascinating glimpse of the austere, serene surroundings in which Cistercian monks lived lives of contemplation, prayer and manual labour. Set in a bucolic wooded valley along a stream called Ru de Fontenay, the abbey – a Unesco World Heritage site – includes an exquisitely unadorned Romanesque church, a barrel-vaulted monks' dormitory, landscaped gardens and the 'first metallurgical factory in Europe'. Guided **tours** (⌚ **departures hourly 10am-5pm except 1pm Apr-11 Nov)** are in French (printed information is available in six languages).

The abbey is 25km north of Semur-en-Auxois. A **taxi** from the Montbard train station, served from Dijon (€11, 40 minutes) and Paris' Gare de Lyon (one hour by TGV), costs €11 (€15 on Sunday and holidays).

Things you need to know: Abbaye de Fontenay (Fontenay Abbey; ☎ 03 80 92 15 00; www. abbayedefontenay.com; adult/student under 26yr €8.90/4.20; ⌚ 10am-6pm Apr-11 Nov, 10am-noon & 2-5pm 12 Nov-Mar); taxi (☎ 03 80 92 31 49, 03 80 92 04 79)

---

ourpick Le Clos St-Front (☎ 05 53 46 78 58; 12 rue St-Front; mains €15-25; ⌚ lunch & dinner Tue-Sat) Set around a lime-shaded garden beside a 16th-century *hôtel particulier* (private mansion), this ravishing restaurant is rightly touted as the city's *grande table*. The buzzy courtyard patio is *the* place to eat out in summer.

Périgueux' chaotic **street markets** explode on Wednesday and Saturday.

Liveliest are the **Marchés de Gras**, when local delicacies such as truffles, wild mushrooms and foie gras are sold on place St-Louis from mid-November to mid-March.

GETTING THERE & AWAY

From the **train station** (rue Denis Papin) direct services run to Bordeaux (€18, one hour 20 minutes).

SARLAT-LA-CANÉDA

pop 10,000

Ringed by forested hilltops and boasting some of the best-preserved medieval architecture in France, Sarlat makes a charming launch pad for exploring the Périgord and Vézère Valley.

Tourist Office (☎ 05 53 31 45 45; www.ot-sarlat-perigord.fr; rue Tourny; ☺ 9am-7pm Mon-Sat, 10am-noon Sun Apr-Oct, 9am-noon & 2-7pm Mon-Sat Nov-Mar)

Hôtel Les Récollets (☎ 05 53 31 36 00; www.hotel-recollets-sarlat.com; 4 rue Jean-Jacques Rousseau; d €43-69) Lost in the medieval maze of the old town, the Récollets is a budget beauty. Nineteen topsy-turvy rooms and a charming vaulted breakfast room are rammed in around the medieval *maison*.

ourpick Le Présidial (☎ 05 53 28 92 47; 6 rue Landry; menus from €29; ☺ lunch Tue-Sat, dinner Mon-Sat) Housed in a 17th-century courthouse, the superswish Présidial is one of the Dordogne's top tables. Stout gates swing back to reveal the city's loveliest terrace, filled with summer flowers and climbing ivy. But it's the romantic courtyard setting that steals the show.

For the full-blown French market experience, you absolutely mustn't miss Sarlat's chaotic **Saturday market** (place de la Liberté & rue de la République). Depending on the season, delicacies on offer include foie gras, mushrooms, duck- and goose-based products, and even the holy *truffe noir* (black truffle).

GETTING THERE & AWAY

Sarlat's **train station** (☎ 05 53 59 00 21) is 1.3km south of the old city. Destinations include Périgueux (€13.20, 1¾ hours), Les Eyzies (€8.20, 50 minutes to 2½ hours).

PREHISTORIC SITES & THE VÉZÈRE VALLEY

Flanked by limestone cliffs, subterranean caverns and ancient woodland, the Vézère Valley is world famous for its incredible collection of prehistoric paintings – the highest concentration of Stone Age art found in Europe.

LES EYZIES-DE-TAYAC-SIREUIL

pop 850

Touristy and a little tatty, the town caters for the massive influx of tourists who descend on the valley every summer.

Tourist Office (☎ 05 53 06 97 05; www.leseyzies.com; ☺ 9am-7pm Mon-Sat, 10am-noon & 2-6pm Sun Jul & Aug, 9am-noon & 2-6pm Mon-Sat, 10am-noon & 2-5pm Sun Sep-Jun, closed Sun Oct-Apr)

THEY DON'T BUILD 'EM LIKE THEY USED TO

In the year 1228 (better known to most of us as 1997), an imaginary nobleman of modest rank but great ambition began constructing a fortified château. A team of skilled artisans, using the latest 13th-century technologies, has been hard at work ever since and is right on schedule to finish the project, as planned, in 25 years.

Welcome to the fantastic **Chantier Médiéval de Guédelon** (☎ 03 86 45 66 66; www.guedelon.fr; adult/5-17yr €9/7; ☺ 10am-7pm daily Jul & Aug, 10am-5.30pm or 6pm Thu-Tue mid-Mar–Jun & Sep-2 Nov, to 7pm Sun & holidays Apr-Jun, closed 3 Nov–mid-Mar), 45km southwest of Auxerre.

A very worthwhile guided tour, sometimes in English, costs €2 per person. Kids-oriented activities include stone carving (using especially soft stone).

BARBARA VAN ZANTEN

Rocamadour

⬎ IF YOU LIKE...

If **Périgueux** (p196) tickled your fancy, you'll explore these other drop-dead gorgeous villages with equal zest:

- **Vézelay** (tourist office ☎ 03 86 33 23 69; www.vezelaytourisme.com; 12 rue St-Étienne) Perched on a spur crowned by a medieval basilica and a patchwork of vineyards, sunflower fields and sheep below, this hilltop village (population 490) in Burgundy is an architectural gem and Unesco World Heritage site.
- **Brantôme** (tourist office ☎ 05 53 05 80 63; ot.brantome@wanadoo.fr) Dubbed the 'Venice of the Périgord' thanks to its five medieval bridges and elegant riverfront architecture, Brantome (population 2122) is a glorious spot to meander its 8th-century abbey and embark on a pleasure cruise along the River Dronne.
- **Rocamadour** The dramatic silhouette of this pilgrimage spot (population 630), 51km east of Sarlat, stuns with its chapel steeples and medieval stone houses clamped to a vertical cliff beneath 14th-century château ramparts. The miraculous powers of its Black Madonna are famed, as are the sparkling subterranean caverns of **Gouffre de Padirac** (☎ 05 65 33 64 56; www.gouffre-de -padirac.com; adult/4-12yr €8.70/5.50; ⏱ 9.30am-6pm Jul, 8.30am-6.30pm Aug, 10am-5pm Sep–mid-Nov, 9.30am-5.30pm mid-Mar–Jun), 15km northeast, where boatmen ferry visitors along a navigable river.
- **Monpazier** (tourist office ☎ 05 53 22 68 59; www.pays-des-bastides.com, in French; place des Cornières) Poised on a hill 45km from Sarlat, Monpazier (population 560) is southwest France's best-preserved *bastide* town. Thursday has been market day since the Middle Ages.
- **La Roque Gageac** A jumble of amber buildings crammed into a cliff above a hairpin curve in the River Dordogne make this *beau village*, 15km south of Sarlat, enchanting. A warren of lanes lead up to an exotic garden, church and cave fort. Afterwards, canoe the river.

ALAN BENSON

Black truffles

⬎ LES DIAMANTS NOIRS

From walnuts to strawberries, *cèpe* (porcini) mushrooms, foie gras and *chanterelles,* the Dordogne is famous for its gourmet goodies. But for true culinary connoisseurs there's only one ingredient that matters, and that's the *diamant noir* – otherwise known as the black truffle.

A subterranean fungi that grows naturally in chalky soils (often around the roots of oak and hazelnut trees), this mysterious little mushroom is notoriously capricious. The art of truffle-hunting is a closely guarded secret and serious truffle hunters often employ specially trained dogs (and sometimes even pigs) to help them in the search. But it's not simply a matter of culinary perfection – truffles are seriously big business, with a vintage crop fetching as much as €850 a kilogram.

The height of truffle season is between December and March, when special truffle markets are held around the Dordogne, including Périgueux (p196), Sarlat (p198) and most notably Sorges (locally championed as France's truffle capital). For more background on this flavoursome fungi, the **Ecomusée de la Truffe** in Sorges has lots of truffle-themed exhibits and might even be able to help you hook up with a truffle hunt in season...

Things you need to know: Ecomusée de la Truffe (☎ 05 53 05 90 11; www.truffe-sorges .org; Le Bourg, Sorges; 🕑 9.30am-12.30pm & 2.30-6.30pm Jul & Aug, 10am-noon & 2-5pm Tue-Sun Sep-Jun)

The **Musée National de Préhistoire** (National Museum of Prehistory; ☎ 05 53 06 45 45; adult/18-25yr/under 18yr €5/3.50/free, 1st Sun of month free; 🕑 9.30am-6.30pm Jul & Aug, 9.30am-6pm Wed-Mon Jun & Sep, 9.30am-noon & 2-5.30pm Wed-Mon Oct-May) inside a marvellous modern building underneath the cliffs houses the most comprehensive collection of prehistoric finds in France.

The **train station** (☎ 05 53 06 97 22; ⏰ 7am-6pm Mon-Fri, noon-6pm Sat & Sun) is 700m north of town, with connections to Périgueux (€6.90, 30 minutes) and Sarlat (€8.20).

GROTTE DE FONT DE GAUME

This fascinating **cave** (☎ 05 53 06 86 00; www .leseyzies.com/grottes-ornees; adult/18-25yr/under 18yr €6.50/4.50/free; ⏰ 9.30am-5.30pm mid-May–mid-Sep, 9.30am-12.30pm & 2-5.30pm mid-Sep–mid-May), 1km northeast of Les Eyzies on the D47, contains the only original 'polychrome' (as opposed to single-colour) paintings still open to the public.

Font de Gaume is such a rare and valuable site that there is talk of the cave being closed for its own protection. Visitor numbers are already limited to 200 per day. Reservations can be made by phone or online.

GROTTE DE ROUFFIGNAC

Rouffignac (☎ 05 53 05 41 71; www.grottede rouffignac.fr; adult/child €6.20/3.90; tours in French ⏰ 9-11.30am & 2-6pm Jul & Aug, 10-11.30am & 2-5pm Mar-Jun & Sep-Oct) is one of the most complex and rewarding caves to see in the Dordogne. Hidden in woodland 15km north of Les Eyzies, this massive cavern plunges 10km into the earth through a mind-boggling maze of tunnels and sub-shafts – luckily, you'll visit aboard a somewhat ramshackle electric train, so there's no chance of getting lost. At the end of the tour the train grinds to a halt and you stumble out into a hidden gallery where the entire ceiling is covered in mammoths, ibex, enormous horses, and even a few rhinoceros.

GROTTE DE LASCAUX

France's most famous prehistoric cave paintings are to be found at the **Grotte de Lascaux**, 2km southeast of Montignac.

Lascaux' paintings are renowned for their astonishing artistry: the 600-strong menagerie of animal figures are depicted in Technicolor shades of red, black, yellow and brown, and range from reindeer, aurochs, mammoths and horses to a monumental 5.5m-long bull, the largest cave

SALLY DILLON

Vézère Valley

Montignac, near Grotte de Lascaux, Dordogne

SALLY DILLON

drawing ever found. Carbon dating has shown that the paintings are between 15,000 and 17,000 years old.

The original cave was opened to visitors in 1948. But within a few years it became apparent that human breath and body heat was causing irreparable damage to the paintings, and they were closed. In response to public demand, a replica of the most famous sections of the original cave was meticulously recreated a few hundred metres away: Lascaux II (☎ 05 53 51 95 03; www.semitour.com; adult/6-12yr €8.30/5.30; ☺ 9am-8pm Jul & Aug, 9.30am-6.30pm Sep & Apr-Jun, 10am-12.30pm & 2-6pm Oct–mid-Nov, 10am-12.30pm & 2-5.30pm mid-Nov–Mar) was opened in 1983, and although the idea sounds rather contrived, the reproductions are enormously moving.

As one of France's most famous sites, the caves can get extremely busy in the height of summer, so it's definitely worth visiting outside July and August if you can. There are several guided tours every hour.

Reservations aren't strictly necessary, but it's worth booking ahead just in case. From April to October, tickets are sold only in Montignac, next to the tourist office (☎ 05 53 51 82 60; place Bertrand de Born).

LYON & THE FRENCH ALPS

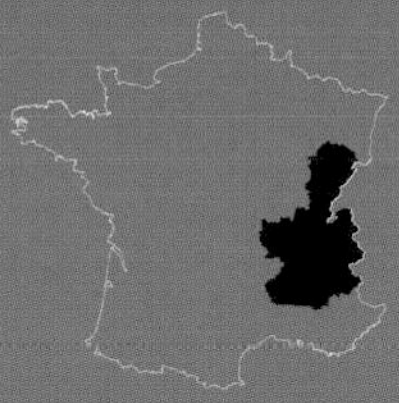

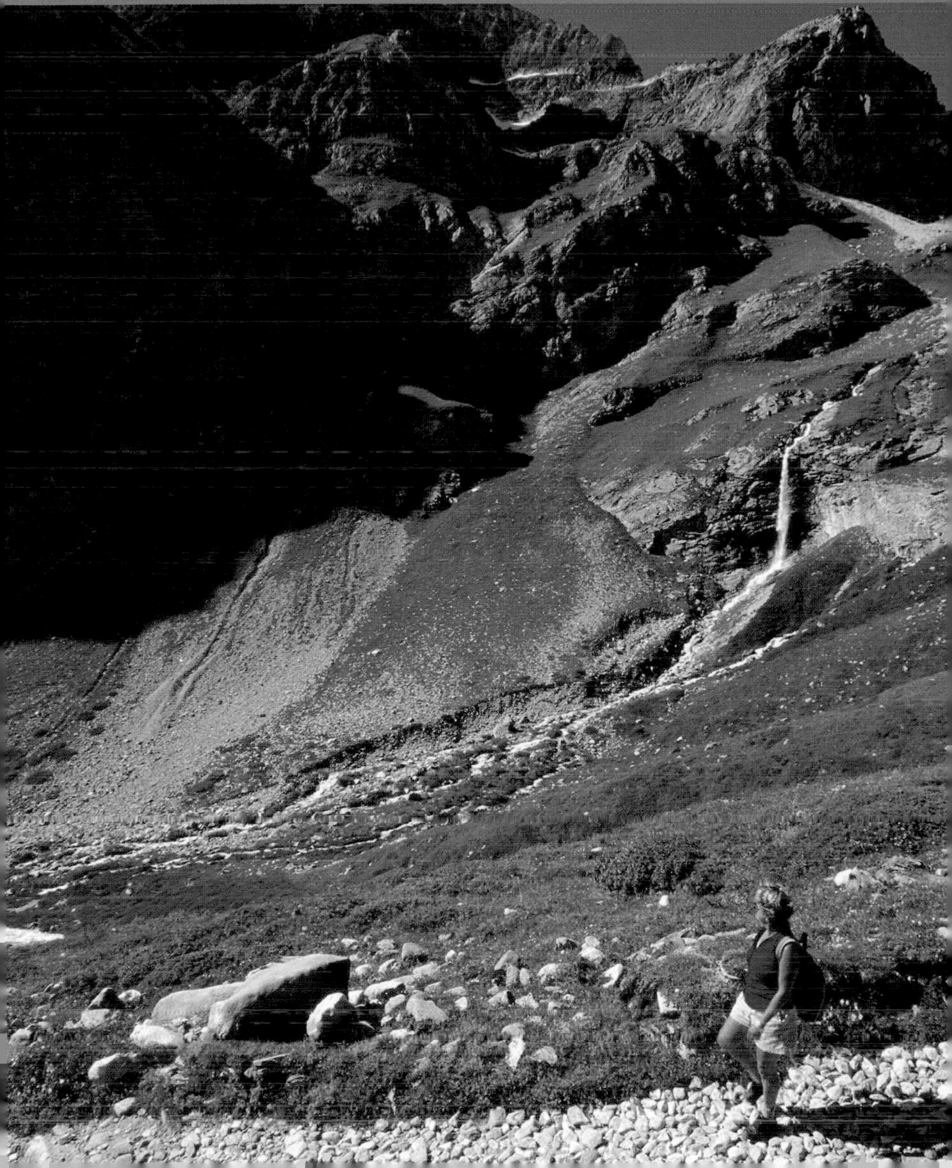

CHRISTIAN ASLUND

Mountain restaurant on Aiguille du Midi (p222), French Alps

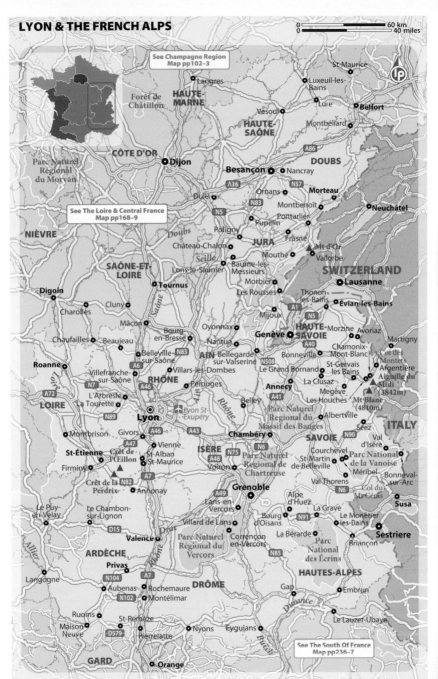

LYON & THE FRENCH ALPS

0   60 km
0   40 miles

See Champagne Region Map pp102–3

Forêt de Châtillon

HAUTE-MARNE

Langres

St-Maurice

Luxeuil-les-Bains

Vesoul

Lure

Belfort

HAUTE-SAÔNE

Montbéliard

CÔTE D'OR

Parc Naturel Régional du Morvan

Dijon

A86

DOUBS

Besançon

Nancray

A36

N57

Dole

Ornans

Morteau

See The Loire & Central France Map pp168–9

N83

Montbenoît

Neuchâtel

N5

Pontarlier

NIÈVRE

Doubs

Poligny

Pupillin

Château-Chalon

JURA

Frasne

Mt d'Or

Seille

Mouthe

Vallorbe

Lons-le-Saunier

Baume-les-Messieurs

SAÔNE-ET-LOIRE

Digoin

Charolles

Cluny

Tournus

Morbier

Les Rousses

SWITZERLAND

Lausanne

Mâcon

Mijoux

A1

N5

Thonon-les-Bains

Évian-les-Bains

Chaufailles

Beaujeau

Bourg-en-Bresse

Oyonnax

Nantua

Genève

HAUTE-SAVOIE

Morzine

Avoriaz

Martigny

Roanne

Belleville-sur-Saône

N83

AIN

Bellegarde-sur-Valserine

N508

Bonneville

Chamonix-Mont-Blanc

Col des Montets

A6

Villars-les-Dombes

Le Grand Bornand

St-Gervais-les-Bains

Argentière

Villefranche-sur-Saône

RHÔNE

Pérouges

A46

La Clusaz

Aiguille du Midi (3842m)

LOIRE

L'Arbresle

La Tourette

Annecy

Megève

Mt Blanc (4810m)

N89

Belley

A41

Les Houches

Lyon

Lyon St-Exupéry

Parc Naturel Régional du Massif des Bauges

Albertville

ITALY

Montbrison

Givors

A46

Séez

St-Étienne

Crêt de l'Œillon

Vienne

St-Alban

St-Maurice

A43

Chambéry

SAVOIE

N90

Val d'Isère

ISÈRE

N75

Courchevel

Firminy

A48

Voiron

Parc Naturel Régional de Chartreuse

St-Martin-de-Belleville

Parc National de la Vanoise

Crêt de la Perdrix

N82

Annonay

A7

Méribel

Bonneval-sur-Arc

Val Thorens

N6

Col du Mt Cénis

Grenoble

A49

Lans-en-Vercors

Alpe d'Huez

La Grave

Susa

Le Puy-en-Velay

Le Chambon-sur-Lignon

Villard de Lans

Bourg d'Oisans

N91

Le Monêtier-les-Bains

D15

La Bérarde

Sestriere

Valence

Drac

Parc Naturel Régional du Vercors

Corrençon-en-Vercors

La Grave

Parc National des Écrins

Briançon

N85

ARDÈCHE

Privas

HAUTES-ALPES

N104

A7

DRÔME

Gap

Langogne

Aubenas

Rochemaure

Embrun

N102

Montélimar

Durance

Ruoms

St-Remèze

Le Lauzet-Ubaye

Maison Neuve

D579

Pierrelatte

Nyons

Eyguians

See The South Of France Map pp236–7

GARD

Orange

HIGHLIGHTS

1 CROIX ROUSSE

BY LISE PEDERSEN, FRENCH TV JOURNALIST

I simply love its village feel, its windy roads and cosy shops, its daily market and its beautiful setting, perched on top of the hill overlooking downtown Lyon. Croix Rousse is also a living museum, which tells the story at every step of the former silk-weavers and social revolutions that happened here.

⤵ LISE PEDERSEN'S DON'T MISS LIST

❶ MARCHÉ DE LA CROIX

This market (p218) fills bd de la Croix Rousse daily (except Mondays) and brims with fresh produce, including fruit and veg from local farms. There's an organic market every Saturday morning at the boulevard's far end.

❷ CAFÉ TERRACES

Two that stand out for their remarkable view are the terrace at **Le Montana** (http://restaurantlemontana.fr) which towers over Lyon, offering a splendid panorama of **Fourvière** (p218) and the city's two rivers. The other is **Le Gros Caillou** (180 bd de la Croix Rousse), right by the eponymous Gros Caillou (literally 'large rock'). On a clear day, there's an absolutely spectacular view of Mont Blanc, creating the illusion that the Alps are but a few miles away.

❸ LE CRIEUR

On Sunday morning around 11am you can't miss *le crieur* (the town crier), Croix Roussien actor Gerald. Centre stage is place de la Croix Rousse where he reads out messages, poems and pamphlets

Clockwise from top: Croix Rousse rooftops; Street scene fresco; Rhône riverbank at Croix Rousse; Silk scarves, Maison des Canuts (p218); Croix Rousse café terrace

people have left in post boxes at bars and cafés around town during the week. He encourages people to loosen up, shake each other's hands; it's unique, entertaining and heart-warming.

❹ LYONNAIS CUISINE

Croix Rousse has become very 'bo-bo' in recent years with lots of expensive, molecular cuisine places and so on. But you really can't go wrong at **Le Comptoir du Vin** (☎ **04 78 39 89 95; 2 rue Belfort**) if you fancy tucking into decently priced, excellent Lyonnais food in a genuine Croix Rousse atmosphere. If you like your meat raw, order the steak tartare, but be warned – it's not for the faint-hearted!

❺ TRABOULES

On your way up to Croix Rousse or on your way down, follow the *traboules* path. A trip back in time, it takes you through the famous secret passageways built through the city's buildings by local 19th-century silk-weavers to avoid the long windy roads when transporting their silk.

⬎ THINGS YOU NEED TO KNOW

Hot tip Wear sturdy shoes to combat Croix Rousse's endless steps and stairs **Traboules** Pick up a free map from the tourist office **What to do Sunday** Shop at the market then indulge in oysters and white wine at one of the boulevard's many pavement cafés. **For more on Croix Rousse see p218**

HIGHLIGHTS

2 | ACTION CHAMONIX!

BY ERIC FAVRET, MOUNTAIN GUIDE, COMPAGNIE DES GUIDES DE CHAMONIX

Ever since Mont Blanc, the highest peak in the Alps, was first climbed in 1786, Chamonix has attracted travellers worldwide. And there *is* something really special about it: Not only does it sit amid extremely condensed mountaineering potential; it is also a perfectly balanced combination of pure landscape alignment and dramatic mountain views.

⬊ ERIC FAVRET'S DON'T MISS LIST

❶ SKIING IN GRANDS MONTETS

Chamonix has six main ski areas (p223). Grands Montets is particularly heavenly, with long off-piste glacial runs, easily accessible from lifts and offering over 6000ft of vertical drop! Its north-facing aspect combined with altitude moreover keeps the snow really good all winter long.

❷ AIGUILLE DU MIDI

The Aiguille du Midi (p222), with one of the highest cable cars in the world, cannot be missed. Beyond the summit ridge is a world of snow and ice offering some of the greatest intermediate off-piste terrain in the Alps.

❸ OFF-PISTE THRILLS

The **Vallée Blanche** (p225) has to be seen. But the Aiguille du Midi also has amazing off-piste runs, such as **Envers du Plan**, a slightly steeper and more advanced version of Vallée Blanche, offering dramatic views in the heart of the Mont Blanc range. There is also the less frequented run of the **'Virgin'** or **'Black Needle'**; a striking glacial run,

Clockwise from top: Evening light on Mont Blanc; Peak of Aiguille du Midi (p222); Skier, Aiguille du Midi (p222); Descending Grands Montets by rope; Chamonix (p221)

offering different views and a close-up look at the Giant's seracs.

❹ SUMMER HIKES ON MONT BUET

Mont Buet is a favourite. It is a summit in itself andoffers outstanding 360-degree panoramas over the Mont Blanc massif and its surrounding range. It requires a good level of fitness to do in a day, but there is a hut to split the trip into two days, which also takes you into a wildlife sanctuary.

❺ BEST-EVER MONT BLANC VIEW

No hesitation: the Traverse from **Col des Montets to Lac Blanc** (p225). It's as popular as the Eiffel Tower for hikers in summer. I love swimming in

mountain lakes, so I like to stop at **Lac des Chéserys**, just below, where it is quieter: what's better than a swim in pure mountain water, looking at Mont Blanc, the Grandes Jorasses and Aiguille Verte? This is what I call mountain landscape perfection!

⬊ THINGS YOU NEED TO KNOW

Off-piste Hire a local certified mountain guide for a safe experience **Essential stop** Maison de la Montagne (p231), one-stop shop for the weather office, ski school and the world's oldest mountain-guide company (1821), the Compagnie des Guides de Chamonix. **For more on Chamonix, see p221.**

HIGHLIGHTS

⬊ AIGUILLE DU MIDI

Be blown away by staggering views of Mont Blanc atop the **Aiguille du Midi** (p222). A jagged pinnacle of rock rising above glaciers, snowfields and rocky crags, 8km from the domed summit of Europe's highest mountain, this 3842m-high peak is Chamonix's iconic landmark. The subsequent journey in a bubble over brilliant-white glaciers, spurs and seracs to the French–Italian border is unforgettable.

⬊ CHEESE FEST

Savour the finest of Alpine traditions with **Raclette** (half a Raclette cheese melted and scraped on potatoes, cold meats and gherkins), oven-baked **tartiflette** (sliced Reblochon cheese baked with potatoes, cream, onions and bacon) or a bubbling pot of **fondue Savoyarde** (melted Emmental, Beaufort and Comté cheese into which stale bread is dipped). See p232 for more on cheese.

5

⬆ VALLÉE BLANCHE DESCENT

Equip yourself with a mountain guide, don your ski legs, and set out on the adventure of a lifetime down Chamonix's mythical **Vallée Blanche** (p225) – a lifelong dream for serious skiers. Snowboarders require an even better level than skiers to get down the 20km off-piste descent and guided mixed skier/boarder groups are a no-go.

6

⬆ MEDIEVAL & RENAISSANCE LYON

Stroll the Unesco World Heritage treasure of **Vieux Lyon** (p216). Gorge on medieval and Renaissance architecture under the beady eyes of gargoyles and other cheeky stone characters of the quaint old town's centuries-old, cobbled streets. Cool down afterwards in Daniel Buren's polka-dot fountains on the **Presqu'île** (p216)

7

⬆ COOK WITH A CHEF

There is no better way to get to the heart of authentic French cuisine than by having a stab at it yourself, under the guidance, *bien sûr*, of a Real McCoy French chef. The innovative cookery workshops – some themed, several over lunch – at Lyon's **L'Atelier des Chefs** (p220) allow you to do just that.

3 Skier, Aiguille du Midi (p222), French Alps; 4 Fondue Savoyarde; 5 Vallée Blanche (p225), French Alps; 6 Rooftops of Vieux Lyon (p216); 7 Cookery classes (p220), Lyon

THE BEST...

⇲ LYON CITY VIEWS

- **Funiculaire de Fourvière** (p218) Ride the funicular up Lyon's 'hill of prayer' to a sweeping panorama of France's second-largest city.
- **Opera House** (p218) End the day with an aperitif between stone-sculpted muse in the opera-house restaurant.
- **Basilique Notre Dame de Fourvière** (p218) Take a roof-top tour of Lyon's 19th-century basilica.

⇲ ADRENELIN KICKS

- **Les Grands Montets** (p223) Ski fast, ski furious in Chamonix's most exceptional downhill skiing area.
- **Morzine bike descent** (p228) Tear down this 3300m-long downhill plummet on a mountain bike.
- **Cham' Aventure** (p225) Racy white-water sports in Chamonix and neighbouring Italy.

⇲ SHORT SUMMER HIKES

- **Le Brévent** (p222) A multitude of trails with Mont Blanc view ensnare this 2525m peak.
- **Lac Blanc** (p225) This two-hour trail from the top of Chamonix's Les Praz l'Index cable car to this turquoise Alpine lake is irresistible.
- **Annecy** (p229) Strolling the sparkling shores of Lac d'Annecy is a pretty, laid-back affair.

⇲ HIGH-ALTITUDE LUNCHES

- **Grand Hôtel du Montenvers** (p225) Dramatic glacial dining.
- **La Crèmerie du Glacier** (p226) Seductive Chamonix piste dining.
- **L'Igloo** (p227) Gawp-worthy Mont Blanc frontals over lunch at 1833m.
- **La Fruitière** (p233) 'Dairy chic' on the slopes of Val d'Isère.

JOHN ELK III

Lac d'Annecy (p229), French Alps

THINGS YOU NEED TO KNOW

VITAL STATISTICS

- **Population** 8,959,000
- **Best time to visit** year-round (Lyon), Christmas to early April (skiing), June to September (hiking)
- **Points of entry** Lyon, Grenoble, Geneva (Switzerland)

ADVANCE PLANNING

- **As early as possible** Book accommodation (p218 & p225).
- **One month before** Snag tickets for Lyon's open-air Les Nuits de Fourvière (www.nuits.defourviere.fr).
- **Two weeks before** Contact mountain guides to arrange your own guided adrenalin fuelled adventure; check your insurance includes mountain rescue.
- **One week before** Buy ski passes online, get weather forecasts and snow conditions and download piste maps with www.compagnie dumontblanc.com.

RESOURCES

- **Rhône-Alpes Tourisme** (www.rho nealpes-tourisme.com) Regional tourist information.
- **Compagnie des Guides** (www .chamonix-guides.com) The crème de la crème of mountain guides founded in Chamonix in 1821: skiing, mountaineering, snowshoeing, ice climbing, hiking, mountain biking etc.
- **Henry's Avalanche Talk** (www.hen rysavalanchetalk.com) Daily avalanche forecast in English and links to other useful avalanche-related sites.

EMERGENCY NUMBERS

- **Police/Any Emergency** (☎ 17)
- **Weather Forecast** (☎ Lyon 08 36 68 02 69, Chamonix 08 36 68 02 73, Annecy 08 36 68 02 74; www.meteofrance.com)
- **Snow & Avalanche Report** (☎ 08 92 68 10 20)
- **PGHM** (☎ 04 50 53 16 89) Mountain rescue.

GETTING AROUND

- **Budget flights** from the UK to/ from Lyon (p221).
- **Walk** around Lyon, rent a **bike** for a song or ride the **metro** (p221).
- **Car & motorcycle** is the no-pain way to get around the region; sport winter tyres in winter.
- **Train** to Lyon to/from anywhere in France.
- **Satobus Alpes** (http://satobus-alpes. altibus.com) shuttles between Lyon St-Expéry airport and ski resorts.

BE FOREWARNED

- **Lyonnais bouchons & restaurants** The former shut weekends, the latter on Monday usually.
- **Opera tickets** (p221) Buy in advance online.
- **High season prices** kick in over Christmas, New Year and during the French school holidays in late February/early March.

ITINERARIES

Short and slick, a mad dash downhill or slow and green through Alpine pastures strewn with wild flowers: this vibrant region in northeast France, anchored down by the country's second-largest city and Europe's highest peak, is 'absolute must' terrain.

URBAN SOULMATE Three Days

No city better begs a weekend getaway than **(1) Lyon** (p216), a place most travellers arrive in unexpectedly (for business or en route south from Paris), are pleasantly surprised by and yearn to return to. Devote a day to exploring the **(2) Presqu'île** (p216) and **(3) Vieux Lyon** (p216) on foot; allow two hours for that quintessential long French lunch in a Lyonnais *bouchon* (bistro) and work it off afterwards with a stiff hike up the **(4) Hill of Prayer** (p218). Come dusk, enjoy a drink alfresco on one of the city squares or, for wine lovers, at **(5) Le Wine Bar d'à Côté** (p220). Day two, with a feel of mainstream Lyon under your belt, delve into its insider heart, **(6) Croix Rousse** (p218), with its lush morning market, mysterious maze of *traboules* and vibrant café life.

Day three consider a two-hour trip by bus or train to **(7) Annecy** (p229), a chic lakeside town with a sparkling lake to swim and another beautiful old town to get lost in.

SNOW FEST Five Days

To get a true feel of the French Alps, consider a two-centre winter break, kicking off where the winter-sports tradition was born in **(1) Chamonix** (p221). Start on a high with a day's skiing in Argentière's **(2) Les Grands Montets** (p223); stop for lunch at **(3) La Crèmerie du Glacier** (p212). Day two explore another ski area, breaking at noon for a cable-car ride to the top of the **(4) Aiguille du Midi** (p222) – mind-blowing! Day three ride the legendary *Mont Blanc Express* train to stylish **(5) St-Gervais les Bains** (p227), meander away the morning in the chic mountain village, then hop on a bus to neighbouring **(6) Megève** (p227) for lunch atop Mont Arbois at **(7) L'Igloo** (p227).

Day four drive 2¼ hours to **(8) Val d'Isère** (p232) for a dose of contemporary Alpine culture. Scare yourself on its Olympic downhill run La Face, lunch at **(9) La Fruitière** (p233) and try your hand at cooking up your very own cheesy fondue or racelette courtesy of **(10) La Fermette de Claudine** (p232).

THE GREAT OUTDOORS One Week

(1) Chamonix (p221) is a must-stop on any summer itinerary, its hiking and mountaineering opportunities being world-class. It is also the only time of year to experience the glacial spectacle of **(2) Pointe Helbronner** (p222). Day three take the foot of the pedal with some

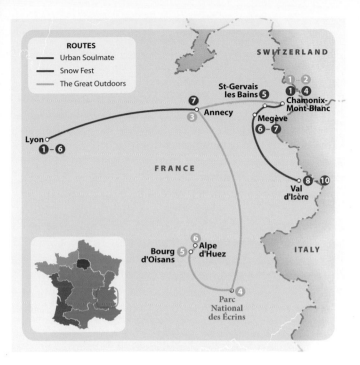

stylish lakeside strolling, cycling or rollerblading and gentle forest hikes in (3) Annecy (p229) before continuing south to the remote (4) Parc National des Écrins (p224). Stop in (5) Bourg d'Oisans (p224) to pick up information on the national park and detour 14km north along the wiggle-ridden D211 mountain road to (6) Alpe d'Huez (p234): keen cyclists won't be able to resist having a stab at its mythical 21 hairpins – a classic Tour de France stage. Finish the week with some soulful days kayaking crystal-clear water, rock climbing, hiking and soaring with the birds aboard a paraglider in the national-park outback.

DISCOVER LYON & THE FRENCH ALPS

Gourmets, eat your heart out: Lyon *is* the gastronomic capital of France, with lavish piggy-driven dishes, delicacies to savour, and a bounty of eating spaces. Be it an old-fashioned bistro with checked tablecloths and slipper-shuffling grandma or smart, minimalist space with state-of-the-art furnishings and chic city-slicker crowd, this French cuisine king thrills. Throw two mighty rivers, majestic Roman amphitheatres and elegant Renaissance architecture into the pot and the city captivates.

Turn east and the mythical mountain face of Mont Blanc, Europe's highest and mightiest, stares you smack in the face. Beneath its 4810m of raw wilderness lie the French Alps – a spectacular outdoor playground for activities ranging from skiing and snowboarding to white-water sports, paragliding and mountaineering. Throw a vast historical and architectural heritage into the fondue pot along with a unique French cuisine (cheese, more cheese!) and an invigorating summer infusion of walking, wildlife-spotting and lake swimming and you'll be kept busy for days: the Alps' pulling power has never been so strong.

LYON

pop 467,400

Commercial, industrial and banking power-house for the past 500 years, grand old Lyon (Lyons in English) is the focal point of a prosperous urban area of almost two million people. Outstanding art museums, a dynamic cultural life, a busy clubbing and drinking scene, not to mention a thriving university and fantastic shopping, lend the city a distinctly sophisticated air.

INFORMATION

Tourist Office (☎ 04 72 77 69 69; www .lyon-france.com; place Bellecour, 2e; Ⓜ Belle-cour; ◔ 9am-6pm)

SIGHTS

VIEUX LYON

Old Lyon, with its cobblestone streets and medieval and Renaissance houses below Fourvière hill, is divided into three quarters: St-Paul (north), St-Jean (middle)

and St-Georges (south). Facing the river is the grandiose **Palais de Justice** (Law Courts; quai Romain Rolland; Ⓜ Vieux Lyon).

Partly Romanesque **Cathédrale St-Jean** (place St-Jean, 5e; Ⓜ Vieux Lyon; ◔ 8am-noon & 2-7.30pm Mon-Fri, 8am-noon & 2-7pm Sat & Sun), the seat of Lyon's 133rd bishop, was built between the late 11th and early 16th centuries. Don't miss the enchanting chimes of the **astronomical clock** in the north transept at noon, 2pm, 3pm and 4pm daily.

PRESQU'ÎLE

The centrepiece of Presqu'île's beautiful **place des Terreaux** (Ⓜ Hôtel de Ville), 1er, is a 19th-century fountain made of 21 tonnes of lead and sculpted by Frédéric-Auguste Bartholdi (of Statue of Liberty fame).

Nearby, the **Musée des Beaux-Arts** (Museum of Fine Arts; ☎ 04 72 10 17 40; www.mba -lyon.fr; 20 place des Terreaux, 1er; Ⓜ Hôtel de Ville;

LYON

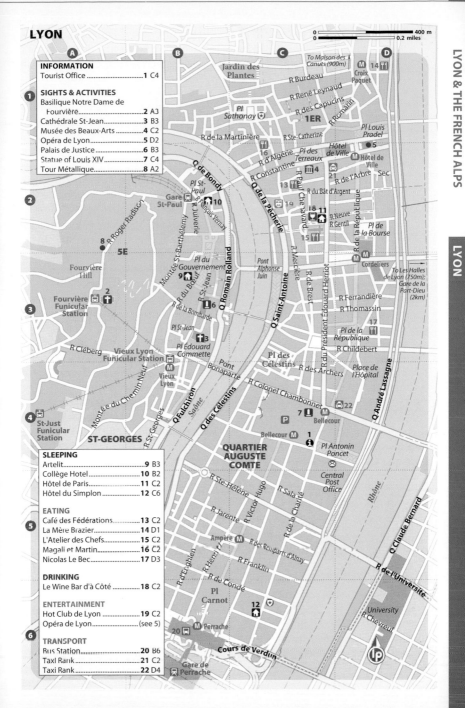

0   400 m
0   0.2 miles

INFORMATION
Tourist Office **1** C4

SIGHTS & ACTIVITIES
Basilique Notre Dame de
Fourvière.................................**2** A3
Cathédrale St-Jean.................**3** B3
Musée des Beaux-Arts **4** C2
Opéra de Lyon.........................**5** D2
Palais de Justice.....................**6** B3
Statue of Louis XIV.................**7** C4
Tour Métallique........................**8** A2

SLEEPING
Artelit..**9** B3
Collège Hotel..........................**10** B2
Hôtel de Paris........................**11** C2
Hôtel du Simplon...................**12** C6

EATING
Café des Fédérations..............**13** C2
La Mère Brazier......................**14** D1
L'Atelier des Chefs................**15** C2
Magali et Martin.....................**16** C2
Nicolas Le Bec.......................**17** D3

DRINKING
Le Wine Bar d'à Côté **18** C2

ENTERTAINMENT
Hot Club de Lyon **19** C2
Opéra de Lyon.....................(see 5)

TRANSPORT
Bus Station...............................**20** B6
Taxi Rank.................................**21** C2
Taxi Rank.................................**22** D4

GLENN VAN DER KNIJFF

Basilique Notre Dame de Fourvière

◤ FOURVIÈRE

Over two millennia ago, the Romans built the city of Lugdunum on the slopes of Fourvière. Today, Lyon's 'hill of prayer' – topped by a basilica and the Tour Métallique, an Eiffel Tower-like structure built in 1893 and used as a TV transmitter – affords spectacular views of the city and its two rivers. Footpaths wind uphill but the funicular departing from place Édouard Commette is the least taxing way up; a return ticket costs €2.20.

Crowning the hill is the 66m-long, 19m-wide and 27m-high Basilique Notre Dame de Fourvière, a superb example of the exaggerated enthusiasm for embellishment that dominated French ecclesiastical architecture in the late 19th century.

Things you need to know: ☎ 04 78 25 86 19; www.fourviere.org; ⊕ 7am-7pm

adult/under 18yr €6/free; ⊕ 10am-6pm Wed, Thu & Sat-Mon, 10.30am-6pm Fri) showcases France's finest collection of sculptures and paintings, outside Paris.

Lyon's neoclassical opera house (Opéra de Lyon; 1 place de la Comédie, 1er; Ⓜ Hôtel de Ville), built in 1832, is topped with a striking glass-domed roof by top French architect Jean Nouvel.

Laid out in the 17th century, place Bellecour (Ⓜ Bellecour), one of Europe's largest public squares, is pierced by an equestrian statue of Louis XIV.

CROIX ROUSSE

Soulful Croix Rousse quietly buzzes north up the steep *pentes* (slopes). Famed for its bohemian inhabitants and lush outdoor food market, it is historically known for its silk-weaving tradition. Following the introduction of the mechanical Jacquard loom in 1805, Lyonnais *canuts* (silk-weavers) built workshops in this quarter with large windows to let in light and hefty wood-beamed ceilings more than 4m high to accommodate the huge new machines. These workshops are chic loft apartments today.

During the bitter 1830–31 *canut* uprisings, triggered by low pay and dire working conditions, hundreds of weavers were killed. Learn about their labour-intensive life, and the evolution of Lyon's silk industry at the Maison des Canuts (☎ 04 78 28 62 04; www.maisondescanuts.com; 10-12 rue d'Ivry, 4e; Ⓜ Croix Rousse; adult/student/under 12yr €6/3/free; ⊕ 10am-6.30pm Tue-Sat, guided tours 11am & 3.30pm), a museum with a boutique selling silk; and the riveting Atelier de Passementerie (☎ 04 78 27 17 13; www .soierie-vivante.asso.fr; 21 rue Richan, 4e; adult/student €4/3; ⊕ 2-6.30pm Tue, 9am-noon & 2-6.30pm Wed-Sat, guided visits & loom demonstration 2pm & 4pm Tue-Sat), a workshop, run by the Soierie Vivante association, that functioned until 1979.

SLEEPING

The tourist office-run reservation office (☎ 04 72 77 72 50; resa@lyon-france.com) has an accommodation list; book online at www .lyon-france.com.

ourpick Hôtel de Paris (☎ 04 78 28 00 95; www.hoteldeparis-lyon.com; 16 rue de la Platière, 1er; Ⓜ Hôtel de Ville; s/d from €48/62; ⊠ 🖳) This fantastic-value hotel resides in a 19th-century bourgeois building in central Lyon's shop-packed heart. The funkiest rooms sport a retro 1970s decor with chocolate-and-turquoise or candyfloss-pink colour scheme. Check the latest best places to dine with charismatic owner and energy bomb Claude Chevanne.

Hôtel du Simplon (☎ 04 78 37 41 00; www .hoteldusimplon.com; 11 rue Duhamel, 2e; Ⓜ Perrache; s/d €71/100) With its heart-warming measure of old-fashioned charm and chivalry, the well-run house of Madame Alix Reverchon is enchanting.

ⓞⓤⓡⓟⓘⓒⓚ **Collège Hôtel** (☎ 04 72 10 05 05; www.college-hotel.com; 5 place St-Paul, 5e; Ⓜ Vieux Lyon; d €110-140; ⓧ ▯) What style this college hotel has. With reception decked out in warm, cosy ochre tones, the white minimalism of the bedrooms is quite dazzling. A roof-terrace garden tops off this refreshingly different hotel.

Artelit (☎ 04 78 42 84 83; www.dormiralyon .com; 16 rue du Bœuf, 5e; Ⓜ Vieux Lyon; d incl breakfast €150-250) A reflection of the artist who runs this three-room *chambre d'hôte*

(B&B), Artelit is a soulful place to sleep with centuries of history behind every last nook and cranny. 'Reception' is the workshop-cum-shop of Lyonnais photographer Frédéric Jean.

EATING

Cobbled **rue Mercière, rue des Marronniers** and the northern side of **place Antonin Poncet**, all in the 2nd arrondissement (metro Bellecour), are chock-a-block with eating options, pavement terraces overflowing in summer. Near the opera house, **rue Verdi**, 1er, is likewise table-filled.

Watch out for **La Mère Brazier** (rue Royale, 1er; Ⓜ Croix Paquet) to reopen near the opera house – at the time of writing, chef Mathieu Vianney was reinventing the mythical 1930s restaurant that earned Lyon its first trio of Michelin stars in 1933.

Café des Fédérations (☎ 04 78 28 26 00; www.lesfedeslyon.com, in French; 8 rue Major Martin, 1er; Ⓜ Hôtel de Ville; lunch/dinner menu €19.50/24; ✆ lunch & dinner Mon-Fri) Black-

CORINNE HUMPHREY

Place des Terreaux (p216), Presqu'île

and-white photos of old Lyon speckle the wood-panelled walls of the city's best-known *bouchon* where nothing has changed for decades. Feast on *caviar de la Croix Rousse* (lentils dressed in a creamy sauce), followed perhaps by an *andouillette* (sausage made from pig intestine) doused in a mustard sauce.

Magali et Martin (☎ 04 72 00 88 01; 11 rue Augustins, 1er; Ⓜ Hôtel de Ville; 2-/3-course menu €17/19; ☺ lunch & dinner Mon-Fri) No secrets here: peep into the third of the trio of large glass windows fronting this fantastic eating space to watch the chefs in action.

Nicolas Le Bec (☎ 04 78 42 15 00; www .nicolaslebec.com; 14 rue Grolée; menus €68 (lunch only), €118 & €158; ☺ lunch & dinner Tue-Sat, closed 3 weeks in August) Best to experience the extraordinary cuisine of Lyon's hottest chef in the company of friends who share the same tastes as you – *menus* are only served to an entire table. Given

the price tag, clientele is predominantly business.

SELF-CATERING
Les Halles de Lyon (102 cours Lafayette, 3e; Ⓜ Part-Dieu; ☺ 8am-7pm Tue-Sat, 8am-2pm Sun) The city's legendary indoor food market.

DRINKING & ENTERTAINMENT
The bounty of café terraces on place des Terreaux, 1er (metro Hôtel de Ville) buzz with drinkers all hours. English-style pubs serving €5 pints are clustered on rue Ste-Catherine, 1er, and in Vieux Lyon.

Le Wine Bar d'à Côté (☎ 04 78 28 31 46; www.cave-vin-lyon.com, in French; 7 rue Pleney, 1er; Ⓜ Cordeliers) Furnished like an English gentlemen's club with leather sofa seating, and a library of reference books including every Michelin *Guide Rouge* from 1965 to 1980, this cultured wine bar is a treat.

⤥ COOK YOUR OWN LUNCH NICOLA WILLIAMS

It might sound like a raw deal, but the cooking workshops over lunch at **L'Atelier des Chefs** are inspired – and a snip at €17.

The day I turned up at 1pm, stomach rumbling, eager beaver to don the white apron, I spent no more than 15 minutes chopping and slicing, another 15 stirring over a trendy stainless-steel stove, and a delightful half-hour or so around a shared table with new-found friends and a welcome glass of red, tucking into the result of my endeavours – a chorizo-spiced chicken filet served on a bed of baby spinach and *poivronnade* (red peppers, leeks and tomato fried with garlic, thyme and bay leaf).

Not only that, chef Stéphane Ranieri had already made dessert for us, the coffee came with a startlingly green kiwi-and-lime macaroon and I left, head reeling with the dozens of tips and tricks cleverly peppered throughout the one-hour session: adding salt to the leeks at the start of frying prevents them burning; peeled peppers cook quicker and are easier to digest; to ensure a moist chicken, pan-fry it skin-down fast until it sticks then flip it over, pour in boiling water and let it gently simmer… Food for thought indeed.

Things you need to know: ☎ 04 78 92 46 30; www.atelierdeschefs.com; 8 rue St-Nizier, 2e; Ⓜ Cordeliers; ☺ 11am-7pm Mon-Sat

Hot Club de Lyon (☎ 04 78 39 54 74; www
.hotclubjazz.com, in French; 26 rue Lanterne, 1er;
Ⓜ Hôtel de Ville; admission €9-12; ☯ 9pm-1am
Tue-Thu, 9.30pm-1am Fri, 4-7pm & 9.30pm-1am
Sat Sep-Jun) A nonprofit musical landmark since 1948, Lyon's premier jazz
club stages live jazz concerts as well
as a weekly jam session (4pm to 7pm
Saturday).

Opéra de Lyon (☎ 08 26 30 53 25; www
.opera-lyon.com, in French; place de la Comédie, 1er;
Ⓜ Hôtel de Ville; ☯ mid-Sep–early Jul) Opera,
ballet and classical concerts.

GETTING THERE & AROUND
Flights to/from European cities land at
Lyon-St-Exupéry Airport (☎ 08 26 80 08
26; www.lyon.aeroport.fr), 25km east of the
city. **Satobus** (☎ 04 72 68 72 17; www.sato
bus.com) links the airport with the centre
every 20 minutes between 5am or 6am
and midnight.

Lyon has two mainline train stations:
Gare de la Part-Dieu (Ⓜ Part-Dieu), 1.5km
east of the Rhône, and **Gare de Perrache**
(Ⓜ Perrache).

Pick up a pair of red-and-silver wheels
at one of 200-odd bike stations dotted
around the city and drop them off at another with Lyon's hugely successful **vélo'v**
(☎ 08 00 08 35 68; www.velov.grandlyon.com, in
French) bike-rental scheme.

Buses, trams, a four-line metro and the
Vieux Lyon–Fourvière funicular run from
around 5am to midnight.

THE FRENCH ALPS
Glaciers and lakes, mineral deserts and
dense Alpine forests, magnificent landscapes and everlasting snow, this is what
would qualify as proper mountains in
most people's books.

Flanked by Switzerland and Italy, Savoy
(Savoie, pronounced *sav·wa*) rises from

CHRISTIAN ASLUND

Peak of Aiguille du Midi (p222)

the southern shores of Lake Geneva,
Europe's largest Alpine lake, and culmi-
nates at the roof of Europe, Mont Blanc's
mighty 4810m. In between is a collection
of adrenalin-pumped ski resorts such as
Chamonix and party-central Val d'Isère,
as well as some lesser-known nonskiing
gems starting with the historical château
town of Annecy to the southwest.

CHAMONIX
pop 9086 / elevation 1037m
Clichéd as it sounds, Chamonix is the
mecca of mountaineering, its birthplace,
its flag-bearer, its heart and soul. Its surrounding landscapes have enthralled and
inspired countless adventurers and other
thrill-seekers.

Aiguille du Midi

RUSSELL MOUNTFORD

INFORMATION

Tourist Office (☎ 04 50 53 00 24; www
.chamonix.com; 85 place du Triangle de l'Amitié;
☯ 8.30am-7.30pm daily Dec-Apr, 9am-12.30pm
& 2-6.30pm Mon-Sat, 9am-12.30pm Sun May-Nov)
Offers helpful service.

SIGHTS

AIGUILLE DU MIDI

All year-round the **Téléphérique du
l'Aiguille du Midi** (Aiguille du Midi Cable Car;
☎ 04 50 53 30 80, advance reservations 24hr 04 50
53 22 75; 100 place de l'Aiguille du Midi; adult/4-
15yr/family return €38/30.40/114, adult/4-15yr
return to midstation Plan de l'Aiguille €21/16.80;
☯ 6.30am-6pm Jul & Aug, 8.30am-4.30pm late-Dec-
Mar, hours vary rest of year) links Chamonix with
the Aiguille du Midi. Be prepared for long
queues, especially in summer when you

need to obtain a boarding card (marked
with the number of your departing *and*
returning cable-car cabins) from the ticket
desks in addition to a ticket.

From the Aiguille du Midi, between mid-
May and mid-September, the unrepentant
can continue for a further 30 minutes (5km)
of mind-blowing scenery – think suspended
glaciers and spurs, seracs, snow plains and
shimmering ice fields – in the smaller bub-
bles of the **Télécabine Panoramic Mont
Blanc** (Panoramic Mont Blanc Cable Car ☎ 04 50
53 30 80; adult/4-15yr return from Chamonix €54/44;
☯ 8.50am-4pm mid-May–Jun & Sep, 8.15am-4.30pm
Jul & Aug) to **Pointe Helbronner** (3466m)
on the French-Italian border. From Pointe
Helbronner another cable car descends to
the Italian ski resort of Courmayeur.

LE BRÉVENT

The highest peak on the western side of
the valley, **Le Brévent** (2525m) has fabulous views of the Mont Blanc massif and
a multitude of hiking trails, ledges to para-
glide from, and a summit restaurant.

Reach it with the **Télécabine du
Brévent** (☎ 04 50 53 13 18; 29 rte Henriette
d'Angeville; Chamonix-Brévent adult/4-15yr/family
return €22/17.40/66, Chamonix-Planpraz adult/4-
15yr return €12/9.60; ☯ 8am-5.45pm Jun-Aug,
8.45am-4.45pm mid-Dec–Apr), from the end of
rue de la Mollard to midstation **Planpraz**
(2000m), then continuing on another
cable car to the top.

MER DE GLACE

The **Mer de Glace** (Sea of Ice), the second-
largest glacier in the Alps, is 14km long,
1800m wide and up to 400m deep.

Since 1946, the **Grotte de la Mer de
Glace** (☯ late Dec-Apr & mid-Jun-Sep) has been
carved every spring. The interior temperature of the ice cave is between -2°C and
-5°C. Be prepared to climb 100 or so steps
to access the cave.

There is a quaint red mountain train that links **Gare du Montenvers** (☎ 04 50 53 12 54; 35 place de la Mer de Glace; adult/4-15yr/family €21/16.80/63; ⏱ 9am-4.30pm mid-Dec–Apr, 8am-6.30pm Jul & Aug, hours vary rest of year) in Chamonix with Montenvers (1913m), from where a cable car transports tourists in summer down to the glacier and cave. The journey takes 20 minutes and admission includes entry to the caves and the cable car. Before catching the train back to Chamonix, nip into the **Grand Hôtel de Montenvers** (1880; p225) for a gander at its nine-room local-history museum and a drink on its dramatically placed terrace.

ACTIVITIES
SKIING & SNOWBOARDING
Of Chamonix' nine main skiing and snowboarding areas, the best for beginners are Le Tour, Les Planards and Les Chosalets. Brévent-Flégère, above Chamonix (connected by *téléphérique*), and Les Grands Montets, accessible from Argentière, 9km north of Chamonix, offer accomplished skiers the greatest challenges. For boarders, there is a snowpark with half-pipe,

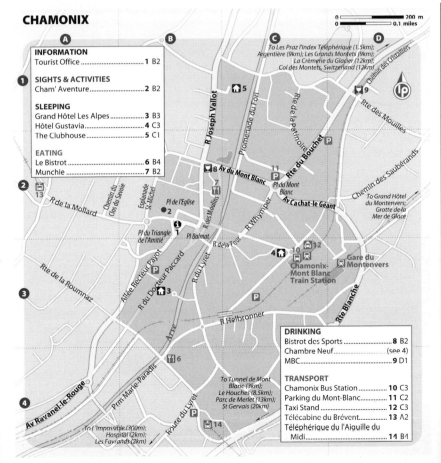

CHAMONIX

0 ——————— 200 m
0 ——————— 0.1 miles

INFORMATION
Tourist Office 1 B2

SIGHTS & ACTIVITIES
Cham' Aventure..2 B2

SLEEPING
Grand Hôtel Les Alpes...................3 B3
Hôtel Gustavia.......................................4 C3
The Clubhouse.......................................5 C1

EATING
Le Bistrot 6 B4
Munchie 7 B2

To Les Praz l'Index Téléphérique (1.5km);
Argentière (9km); Les Grands Montets (9km);
La Crèmerie du Glacier (12km);
Col des Montets, Switzerland (12km)

To Grand Hôtel
du Montenvers;
Grotte de la
Mer de Glace

Gare du
Montenvers

Chamonix-
Mont Blanc
Train Station

To Tunnel de Mont
Blanc (3km);
Le Houches (8.5km);
Parc de Merlet (13km);
St Gervais (20km)

To L'Impossible (300m);
Hospital (2km);
Les Favrands (2km)

DRINKING
Bistrot des Sports 8 B2
Chambre Neuf.............................(see 4)
MBC..9 D1

TRANSPORT
Chamonix Bus Station 10 C3
Parking du Mont-Blanc...............11 C2
Taxi Stand 12 C3
Télécabine du Brévent..................13 A2
Téléphérique de l'Aiguille du
    Midi..14 B4

BILL WASSMAN

Parc National des Ecrins

⬎ IF YOU LIKE...

If you like the magnificent landscape ensnaring **Chamonix** (p221) we know you'll love these less-visited but equally dramatic nature spots:

- **Parc National de la Vanoise** (www.vanoise.com; Maison du Val Cénis ☎ 04 79 05 23 66; www.valcenis.com; Bonneval-sur-Arc tourist office ☎ 04 79 05 95 95; www.bonneval-sur-arc.com) A wild mix of mountains, valleys and glaciers, France's first national park near Val d'Isère sports 530 sq km of spectacular scenery: snow-capped peaks mirrored in icy lakes is just the start! Marmots, chamois and France's largest colony of Alpine ibexes graze undisturbed beneath larch trees and golden eagles fly overhead. Walking trails are accessible June to September.

- **Parc Naturel Régional du Vercors** (Villard de Lans tourist office ☎ 04 76 95 10 38; www.villarddelans.com; place Mure Ravaud, Villard de Lans) Southwest of Grenoble, this park known for cross-country skiing, snowshoeing, caving and hiking, is the ideal family destination. Lans-en-Vercors, Villard de Lans and Corrençon-en-Vercors are the main villages in the 14-piste ski area – 125km of winter-wonderland downhill slopes at melting prices. See www.vercors-reservations.com for accommodation and www.accompagnateur-vercors.com for guided walks and snowshoe treks.

- **Parc National des Ecrins** (☎ 04 76 80 00 51; www.les-ecrins-parc-national.fr; rue Gambetta, Bourg d'Oisans) France's second-largest national park south of Grenoble is ensnared by steep, narrow valleys and sculpted by a trio of rivers and their erstwhile glaciers. It peaks at 4102m with the legendary Barre des Écrins, a mountaineer's dream. Footpaths used centuries ago by shepherds and smuggler make it prime hiking territory. Or dabble in kayaking turquoise river waters, rock climbing, paragliding and mountain-biking.

kicker ramps and other thrill-filled obstacles in Les Grands Montets, and a natural half-pipe in Le Tour.

The region has several marked but ungroomed trails suitable for skiers looking for off-piste thrills. The famous 20km **Vallée Blanche descent** is one of the world's most celebrated runs. It must *only* be tackled with a guide; the route crosses the crevasse-riddled glacier and passes through avalanche-prone areas.

The **Chamonix Le Pass** (1-/6-day €37/185) gives access to all Chamonix' ski domains but does not include the Aiguille du Midi (for the Vallée Blanche), nor the Montenvers train nor the higher reaches of Les Grands Montets. Cheaper passes covering single ski areas are available. View all options and buy passes online at www.compagniedumontblanc.com.

WALKING

From late spring until October, 310km of spectacular walking trails open up to hikers.

From the top of Les Praz l'Index cable car (€16) or La Flégère (€10), the line's midway point, easy 1¼- to two-hour trails lead to **Lac Blanc** (literally 'White Lake'), a turquoise-coloured lake ensnared by mountains at 2352m. Star-lovers can overnight in the **Refuge du Lac Blanc** (☎ 04 50 53 49 14; dm with half-board €47; ☺ Jun-Sep), a wooden chalet with romantic Mont Blanc views.

The **Grand Balcon Sud** trail along the western side of the valley stays at around 2000m and also affords fabulous Mont Blanc views. Reach it on foot from behind Le Brévent's *télécabine* station.

Several routes start from Plan de l'Aiguille, including the **Grand Balcon Nord**, which takes you to the Mer de Glace, from where you can walk or take the Montenvers train down to Chamonix.

For the less ambitious, **Parc de Merlet** (☎ 04 50 53 47 89; www.parcdemerlet.com, in French; adult/4-12yr €5.50/3.50; ☺ 10am-6pm May, Jun & Sep, 9.30am-7.30pm Jul & Aug) in Les Houches offers a unique opportunity to see marmots, chamois and other typical Alpine animals close up.

WHITE-WATER SPORTS

Cham' Aventure (☎ 04 50 53 55 70; www.cham-aventure.com; 190 place de l'Église), with an office inside the Maison de la Montagne, organises canyoning (half-/full day per person €64/98), rafting (€36/130 for two hours/day) and hydrospeed (€47 for two hours) on Chamonix' River Arve and the Dora Baltea in neighbouring Italy (an hour's drive).

SLEEPING

Grand Hôtel du Montenvers (☎ 04 50 53 87 70; 35 place de la Mer de Glace; half-board per person dm/d €38.50/54.40, dm/d per person incl breakfast €23.60/38.50, menus €8-10; ☺ hotel Jul & Aug, restaurant late Dec–mid-Oct) Ride the red mountain train up to Montenvers and dine in Alpine splendour at the foot of the Alps' second-largest glacier. The place dates back to 1880 and has kept many of its original features (parquet floors, enormous fireplace).

Hôtel Gustavia (☎ 04 50 53 00 31; www.hotel-gustavia.com; 272 av Michel Croz; s/d/tr from €50/80/111) Going strong since 1890, this charming manor-house hotel with bottle-green wooden shutters and wrought iron balconies oozes soul.

Grand Hôtel des Alpes (☎ 04 50 55 37 80; www.grandhoteldesalpes.com; 89 rue du Docteur Paccard; d low/high season from €140/330; ☺ mid-Dec–mid-Apr, mid-Jun–Sep; ☒ ☐ ☒) Dating from 1840, this grand old dame goes down in the chronicles of Chamonix history as one of the resort's first and finest.

Hikers at Parc National de la Vanoise (p224)

GLENN VAN DER KNIJFF

Clubhouse (☎ 04 50 90 96 56; www .clubhouse.fr; 74 promenade des Sonnailles; d 3-nights full board from €865; ☯ Dec-Sep; 🖳) Provocatively decadent, the Clubhouse lures a moneyed set into its luxurious lair – Chamonix' only remaining art-deco mansion, dating from 1927, a cross between a James Bond movie set and a retro Alpine chalet.

EATING

La Crémerie du Glacier (☎ 04 50 54 07 52; 766 chemin de la Glacière; mains €6-15) Crazy as it sounds for a piste restaurant, you might have to book to get a chance to bite into La Crémerie's world-famous *croûtes au fromage* (chunky slices of toasted bread topped with melted cheese). Ski to it with the red Pierre à Ric piste in Les Grands Montets.

Le Bistrot (☎ 04 50 53 57 64; www.lebistrot chamonix.com; 151 av de l'Aiguille du Midi; lunch menu €17, dinner menus €42 & €65; ☯ lunch & dinner) Chamonix' very own gastronomic wonder, this is a real foodie's place where chef Mickey's prowess will bowl over even the most discerning crowd.

Munchie (☎ 04 50 53 45 41; 87 rue des Moulins; mains €17-25; ☯ dinner Mon-Sun) Think fusion at this trendy hang-out with great pan-Asian food.

L'Impossible (☎ 04 50 53 20 36; 9 chemin du Cry; mains €20-30; ☯ lunch & dinner daily Dec-Apr, Jul & Aug) In a barn dating back to 1754 near the Aiguille du Midi cable car, this stunning rustic-chic eating space serves quintessential French cuisine with a modern twist.

DRINKING

Chamonix nightlife rocks. In the centre, rue des Moulins down by the quaint old riverside touts a line-up of drinking holes. Online, go to www.lepetitcanar dchx.com.

Bistrot des Sports (☎ 04 50 33 00 46; 182 rue Joseph Vallot; ☯ 11am-midnight) This inconspicuous brasserie is one that is steeped in history: as an old meeting place that muleteers and guides used on their journey up or down the mountain, it was bought by the legendary mountaineer and explorer Roger Frison-Roche in 1934. The street terrace is perfect for a mellow drink.

Chambre Neuf (☎ 04 50 55 89 81; 272 av Michel Croz; ⌚ 8pm-1am) Particularly popular with Scandinavians, this is one of the liveliest party places in Chamonix, with raucous après-ski drinking and conversations about monster jumps, epic off-pistes and, like, totally mental, man, at every table.

our pick MBC (☎ 04 50 53 61 59; www.mbchx.com; 350 rte du Bouchet; ⌚ 4pm-2am) This trendy microbrewery run by four Canadians is fab. Be it with their burger, cheesecake of the week, live music or amazing locally brewed and named beers (Blonde de Chamonix, Stout des Drus, Blanche des Guides etc), MBC really delivers.

GETTING THERE & AWAY

Chamonix bus station (☎ 04 50 53 01 15; www.altibus.com; ⌚ 6.45-10.30am & 1.25-4.45pm Mon-Fri, 6.45-11am Sat & Sun) is next to the train station.

If you are approaching Chamonix from Italy, you arrive via the 11.6km **Tunnel de Mont Blanc** (www.atmb.net; toll one-way/return €32.30/40.30).

From Chamonix-Mont Blanc **train station** (☎ 04 50 53 12 98; place de la Gare) the Mont Blanc Express narrow-gauge train trundles from the St-Gervais-Le Fayet station, 23km west of Chamonix, to Martigny, 42km northeast of Chamonix in Switzerland, stopping en route in Les Houches, Chamonix and Argentière. There are nine to 12 return trips that run between Chamonix and St-Gervais (€9.10, 40 minutes).

From St-Gervais-Le Fayet, there are trains to most major French cities.

MEGÈVE & ST-GERVAIS

A chic ski village developed in the 1920s for a French baroness disappointed with Switzerland's crowded St-Moritz, **Megève** (population 3878, elevation 1113m) looks almost too perfect to be true: horse-drawn sledges, exquisitely arranged boutique windows and carefully grown pot plants spill into medieval-style streets.

Sitting snug below Mont Blanc, 36km southwest of Chamonix, Megève's neighbour is **St-Gervais-les-Bains** (better known as simply St-Gervais, population 5400, elevation 850m), another picture-postcard winter and summer resort linked to Chamonix by the legendary Mont Blanc Express.

For staggering mountain views with no legwork, hop aboard France's highest train. The **Tramway du Mont Blanc** (☎ 04 50 47 51 83; rue de la Gare; adult/4-15yr/family return €18/14/54; ⌚ mid-Dec–mid-Apr, Jul & Aug) has laboured up to Bellevue (1800m) from St-Gervais-Le Fayet in winter and further up to the Nid d'Aigle (Eagle's Nest) at 2380m in summer since 1913.

L'Igloo (☎ 04 50 93 05 84; www.ligloo.com; 3120 rte du Crêt; mains €5-15; ⌚ lunch & dinner mid-Jun–mid-Sep & mid-Dec–mid-Apr) Feast on a fiesta of incredible Mont Blanc mountain views at this high-altitude eating joint plump on the top of Mont d'Arbois (1833m). Ski here or ride the Télécabine du Mont d'Arbois in Megève. In summer the Igloo has an open-air swimming pool.

LES PORTES DU SOLEIL

Poetically dubbed 'the Gates of the Sun' (elevation 1000m to 2466m; www.portesdusoleil.com), this gargantuan ski area – the world's largest – is formed from a chain of villages strung along the French–Swiss border. In spring and summer mountain-bike enthusiasts revel in 380km of invigorating biking trails, including the 100km-long circular Portes du Soleil tour.

GLENN VAN DER KNIJFF

La Clusaz

⤵ IF YOU LIKE...

If you like the Zen pace and quiet intimacy of **Megève** (p227), we know these other small ski resorts will make you swoon just as much:

- **Avoriaz** (www.avoriaz.com) It might be purpose-built, but this bijou chic resort clinging to a rock at 1800m in the Portes du Soleil ski area, is much-loved for its no-cars policy. Horse-drawn sleighs piled high with luggage romantically ferry wealthy guests to and from the snowy village centre where wacky 1960s mimetic architecture gets away with an 'avant-garde' tag.
- **St-Martin de Belleville** (www.st-martin-belleville.com) Ski or board with the best of them in the vast, fast Trois Vallées ski area by day; withdraw to the peace, quiet and tranquillity of this picture-postcard Savoyard village linked to Belleville come dusk.
- **La Clusaz** (www.laclusaz.com) From Annecy ski for the day at this small resort (1100m). Beginners and intermediates will have a field day on its 128km of downhill pistes, and cross-country skiers are equally well catered for.
- **Le Grand Bornand** (www.legrandbornand.com) Another day trip from Annecy, this small resort, at 1000m, is hot with locals, cheap (€26.50 for a one-day lift pass) and an ideal stomping ground for beginner and intermediate skiers given its petite size.

Morzine (population 3000, elevation 1000m), the best known of the 12 interconnected ski resorts, retains a smidgen of traditional Alpine village atmosphere. For local know-how on summer activities (hiking, biking, climbing, canyoning and paragliding) contact the **Bureau des Guides** (☎ 04 50 75 96 65; www.bureaudesguides.net),

which advises on mountain-bike hire and Morzine's 3300m-long **bike descent** (free; ☺ Jun-Sep) from the top of the Plénéy cable car (one/10 ascents €4.50/35). Book accommodation through **Morzine Réservation** (☎ 04 50 79 11 57; www.resa-morzine.com) inside the **tourist office** (☎ 04 50 74 72 72; www.morzine-avoriaz.com; place de la Crusaz).

ourpick **Farmhouse** (☎ 04 50 79 08 26; www.
thefarmhouse.fr; Morzine; d with breakfast €94-370,
dinner €40) is Morzine's oldest and loveliest building, a 1771 farmhouse run for
the past 17 years by the charming Dorrien
Ricardo. Five rooms are in the main house,
and a trio of cottages sit in the lovely
grounds. Dining – open to nonguests
too and strictly around one huge long
table – is a lavish affair and very much an
experience in itself.

ANNECY

pop 51,000 / elevation 448m

As you stroll along the shores of shimmering Lac d'Annecy, it is clear why Annecy
gets a whopping two million visitors a
year, the bulk of it in summer. Swimming
in the lake surrounded by snowy mountains really is an Alpine highlight, as is
strolling in the warren of geranium-lined
medieval streets of Vieil Annecy.

INFORMATION

Tourist Office (☎ 04 50 45 00 33; www.lac
-annecy.com; 1 rue Jean Jaurès, Centre Bonlieu;
⏰ 9am-12.30pm & 1.45-6pm Mon-Sat mid-Sep–
mid-May, 9am-6.30pm Mon-Sat mid-May–mid-
Sep, 10am-1pm Sun Mar-May)

SIGHTS & ACTIVITIES

With labyrinthine narrow streets and
colonnaded passageways, the old town
retains much of its 17th-century appear-
ance. On the central island, imposing
Palais de l'Isle (☎ 04 50 33 87 30; 3 passage de l'Île; adult/concession €3.40/1, 1st Sun
of month Oct-May free; ⏰ 10.30am-6pm daily
Jun-Sep, 10am-noon & 2-5pm Wed-Mon Oct-May)
was a prison, but now hosts local-history
displays.

In the 13th- to 16th-century castle above
town, the eclectic **Musée Château** (☎ 04
50 33 87 30; adult/concession €4.80/2; ⏰ 10.30am-
6pm Jun-Sep, 10am-noon & 2-5pm Wed-Mon Oct-

May) explores traditional Savoyard art,
crafts and Alpine natural history.

Parks and grassy areas in which to picnic and sunbathe line the **lakefront**. **Forêt
du Crêt du Maure**, south of Annecy, has
many walking trails. Biking and blading
are big, thanks to 46km of cycling tracks,
which are equally popular with roller-
bladers, around the lake.

Compagnie des Bateaux (☎ 04 50 51
08 40; www.annecy-croisieres.com; 2 place aux
Bois; 1/2hr lake cruise adult €11.40/14.60; ⏰ mid-
Mar–Oct) runs lake cruises departing from
Canal du Thiou on quai Bayreuth.

SLEEPING

Auberge du Lyonnais (☎ 04 50 51 26
10; www.auberge-du-lyonnais.com; 9 rue de la
République; s €45-70, d €50-75) Idyllically located along the canal at the heart of the
Vieil Annecy, this is a great little place.
(menus from €23).

Les Jardins du Château (☎ 04 50 45 72 28;
jardinduchateau@wanadoo.fr; 1 place du Château;
d €65-90, tr/q €100/130) If you're planning on
spending a few days in the area, this is
where you should stay: all rooms and studios at this chambre d'hôte are equipped
with kitchenettes and many have balconies and terraces where you can eat,
sunbathe and generally chill whilst taking
in the view.

Le Pré Carré (☎ 04 50 52 14 14; www.hotel
-annecy.net; 27 rue Sommeiller; s €145-195, d from
€225; 🖳) One of Annecy's chicest hotels
bears all the hallmarks of a modern four-
star place. The staff also happen to know
all the best addresses in town, so you're
in very good hands.

EATING

The quays along both sides of Canal du
Thiou in the Vieille Ville are jam-packed
with touristy cafés and restaurants.

L'Étage (☎ 04 50 51 03 28; 13 rue du Pâquier; mains €15; ☾ lunch & dinner) Glorious, glorious cheese! At L'Étage *le fromage* is given pride of place, even if you're not having a Savoyard speciality (think steak with cheese sauce, yum).

Brasserie des Européens (☎ 04 50 45 00 81; place de l'Hôtel de Ville; mains €15-25; ☾ lunch & dinner) Hang in there for the mother of all seafood platters (a cool €185 for four people) and seven different types of steak tartare (raw beef, plain, with toast, parmesan, peppercorns, Mexican spices etc) – this is the real McCoy of French brasseries.

Nature & Saveur (☎ 04 50 45 82 29; www .nature-saveur.com; place des Cordeliers; lunch €18-22, dinner with/without wine €36-42/52; ☾ lunch Tue-Sat, dinner Fri & Sat) Nature & Saveur only uses organic and wholesome ingredients from local farms. But don't be fooled: this is no tree-hugger's hut. Chef Laurence Salomon's restaurant is sophisticated and attracts a discerning boho-chic clientele.

La Ciboulette (☎ 04 50 45 74 57; cour du Pré Carré, 10 rue Vaugelas; mains €30-35; ☾ lunch & dinner Tue-Sat) In a sophisticated amber-coloured dining room, this is Annecy's affordable gastronomic gem. This being Savoy, the cheese platter here is phenomenal.

GETTING THERE & AWAY

From the **bus station** (Gare Routière Sud; rue de l'Industrie), adjoining the train station, the **Billetterie Crolard** (☎ 04 50 45 08 12; www.voyages-crolard.com; ☾ 7.15am-12.30pm & 1.30-7.15pm Mon-Sat, plus Sun high season) sells tickets for hourly buses to other lakeside destinations and for local ski resorts La Clusaz and Le Grand Bornand (single/return/return with lift pass €8/13.50/27, 50 and 60 minutes respectively). It also runs up to five buses daily to/from Lyon St-Exupéry airport (one way/return €30/45, two hours).

From Annecy's **train station** (place de la Gare), there are frequent trains to/from Chambéry (€8.60, 45 minutes), St-Gervais (€12.70, 1¾ hours), Lyon (€21.60, 2¼ hours) and Paris' Gare de Lyon (€69.80, four hours).

GLENN VAN DER KNIJFF

Château on the shore of Lac d'Annecy

LES TROIS VALLÉES

Named after its valley trio, this sought-after ski area is vast, fast and the largest in the world with 600km of pistes and 200 lifts across three ritzy resorts: **Val Thorens**, Europe's highest at a heady 2300m; wealthy old **Méribel** (elevation 1450m) created by Scotsman Colonel Peter Lindsay in 1938; and trendsetting **Courchevel** (a fave of Victoria Beckham), a series of purpose-built resorts at altitudes of 1550m, 1650m and 1850m, where fashion is as hot on as off the slopes.

INFORMATION

Courchevel 1850 Tourist Office (☎ 04 79 08 00 29; www.courchevel.com; ☺ 9am-7pm Jul-Aug & Dec-Apr, 9am-noon & 2-6pm Mon-Fri Sep-Nov, May & Jun) Sister offices at 1650m, 1550m and 1300m.
Méribel Tourist Office (☎ 04 79 08 60 01; www.meribel.net; Maison du Tourisme; ☺ 9am-7pm Dec-Apr, 9am-noon & 2-5pm Mon, Tue, Thu & Fri, 9am-noon Wed & Sat Sep-Nov, May & Jun, 9am-noon & 3-7pm Jul & Aug)
Val Thorens Tourist Office (☎ 04 79 00 08 08; www.valthorens.com; Maison de Val Thorens; ☺ 8.30am-7pm)

ACTIVITIES

The three valleys will appease the feistiest of outdoor-action appetites. A Trois Vallées pass costing €44/220 for one/six days covers the entire area, but cheaper single-valley passes are also available.

Courchevel is big on alternative snow action, the key info point being **La Croisette** (place du Forum; ☺ 7am-8pm) in Courchevel 1850, where the **ESF** (☎ 04 79 08 07 72; www.esfcourchevel.com) resides in winter, and the superfriendly **Maison de la Montagne** year-round. The latter takes bookings for guided off-piste adventures, heli-skiing, snowshoeing and ski mountaineering as well as go-karting

Tandem hang-gliding over Lac d'Annecy

JOHN ELK III

or driving on ice, snowmobile treks and snow-rafting.

In summer, rock climbing, mountain biking, hiking and paragliding are rife in all three valleys.

SLEEPING & EATING

Les Peupliers (☎ 04 79 08 41 47; www.lespeupliers.com; Le Praz; summer only d €110, half-board per person d low/high season €130/190) This hotel has managed the rare feat of combining authentic village feel with plush, stylish creature comforts such as hammam and Jacuzzi. The downstairs bar fills up every night with a jolly après-ski crowd, many of whom then move to La Table de Mon Grand-Père, the hotel's restaurant.

La Bouitte (☎ 04 79 08 96 77; www.la-bouitte.com; St-Marcel; summer d/tr from €200/250, winter €248/417; 2-/3-course menu €69/86, mains €50-100; ⊗ Jul, Aug & mid-Dec–Apr) This is a fairy-tale chalet, with everything just the way you'd imagine it to be in a perfect Alpine world. The eight exquisite rooms are an ode to centenary-old wood, and the food at the two-Michelin-star restaurant is out of this world. Find it in the hamlet of St-Marcel, 1km south of St-Martin de Belleville.

There are plenty of very expensive hang-outs in Courchevel, but normal human beings can hang out at **Prends Ta Luge et Tire-Toi** (Take Your Sledge And Piss Off; ☎ 04 79 08 78 68; www.laluge.com; Le Forum, Courchevel 1850; ⊗ 9am-2am daily), an odd combination of surf shop, Caribbean-themed bar and internet café (€8 per

---

A BOWL OF FARM AIR

Unlike many purpose-built ski resorts, Val d'Isère is a genuine village with year-round inhabitants. Claudine is one of them and she runs one of the town's most delectable shops, **La Fermette de Claudine** (☎ 04 79 06 13 89; www.la fermettedeclaudine.com; Val Village). All dairy products – fresh unpasteurised milk, the wonderful cheeses, the yoghurts – come from her dairy farm, **La Ferme de l'Adroit**, just 1km down the road in the direction of Col de l'Iseran. The farm is open to the public and you can watch cheese production (Tomme, Avalin, Beaufort) in the morning or milking in the afternoon. As well as fab cheeses, the town shop sells wondrous *saucissons* (sausages) and can lend you raclette and fondue kits.

---

hour). Extra points awarded for the most random name ever.

GETTING THERE & AWAY
Shuttle buses link all three resorts with Geneva (€70, 3½ hours) and Lyon St-Exupéry (€64, three to four hours) airports.

Moûtiers is the nearest train station, with trains to/from Chambéry (€11.70, 1¼ hours) and TGVs galore to Paris between late December and March (€76.80, 4¾ hours). **Eurostar** (www.eurostar.com) also operates direct trains to/from London during the winter season (return from €220, eight hours, overnight or day service, weekends only).

VAL D'ISÈRE
pop 1660 / elevation 1850m
It's hard to say what people come to Val d'Isère for, whether it's for the awesome skiing or the never-ending party. If you're seeking traditional Alpine atmosphere, you may have to reconsider your choice of destination, which is ironic since Val d'Isère is one of the few ski resorts to have a year-round village life. The resort is located in the upper Tarentaise Valley, 31km southeast of Bourg St-Maurice, and attracts a mostly young, foreign crowd.

INFORMATION
Tourist Office (☎ 04 79 06 06 60; www.vald isere.com; place Jacques Mouflier; ⊗ 8.30am-7.30pm Dec-Apr, Jul & Aug, 9am-noon & 2-6pm Mon-Fri rest of the year) Internet access here costs €9 per hr or €5 for wi-fi.

ACTIVITIES
Espace Killy offers fabulous skiing on 300km of marked pistes between 1550m and 3450m. In July and August you can ski on the glacier.

RICHARD NEBESKY

Courchevel (p231)

The valleys and trails that lead from Val d'Isère into the nearby Parc National de la Vanoise (p224) proffer an orgy of outdoor action. Be it walking, mountain biking, trekking or rock climbing, the **Bureau des Guides** (☎ 06 14 62 90 24; www.guide -montagne-tarentaise.com), in the Killy Sport shop next to the tourist office, can arrange it.

SLEEPING

Hôtel Bellevue (☎ 04 79 06 00 03; d with half-board per person €80, with bathroom & half-board per person €105) This central, family-run hotel on the main street screams 1960s. Rooms in the hotel, annexe and chalet are basic but good value for skiers who are in town to ski rather than self-pamper.

Relais du Ski & La Bailletta (☎ 04 79 06 02 06; http://lerelaisduski.valdisere.com; rte Fornet; s/d/tr/q incl breakfast Relais from €70/88/102/124, Bailletta from €117/136/171/196; ☼ Dec-Apr, Jul & Aug) A 500m stroll from the centre, this is effectively two hotels rolled into one. La Bailletta does comfortable midrange rooms while Relais

du Ski has nine basic rooms with shared bathrooms reminiscent of student accommodation.

EATING

La Fruitière (☎ 04 79 06 07 17; mains €20; ☼ lunch Dec-Apr) At the top of the La Daille bubble at 2400m, this piste-side oasis of fine dining is legendary. Snuggle under a rug to keep warm on the terrace and savour traditional but creative cuisine in a hip dairy setting.

Le Blizzard (☎ 04 79 06 02 07; mains €20-30; ☼ lunch & dinner) Fine dining in a refined chalet atmosphere is what one of Val d'Isère's chicest hotel-restaurants offers. Views from the dining room's bay windows are stupendous.

GETTING THERE & AWAY

Six daily buses in season link Val d'Isère with Tignes (€7.20) and Bourg St-Maurice train station (€13.10, 45 minutes). Tickets must be reserved 48 hours in advance at the **Boutique Autocars Martin** (☎ 04 79 06 00 42; ☼ 8.30-11am & 12.30-7pm Mon-Fri,

Hiker in Parc National de la Vanoise (p224)

JOHN ELK III

6.30am-7pm Sat, 6.30-11am & 12.30-7pm Sun) on the main street in the resort centre.

Eurostar (www.eurostar.com) operates direct winter weekend services between Bourg St-Maurice and London (return from €220, nine hours, overnight or day service).

ALPE D'HUEZ
elevation 1860m

Number of hairpin bends: 21. Length: 14km. Average slope gradient: 7.9%. Record time: 37 minutes 35 seconds. Portrait of a mythical *étape* (stage) of the Tour de France between Bourg d'Oisans and Alpe d'Huez, a purpose-built resort in the Massif des Grandes Rousses. Apart from legendary cycling, Alpe d'Huez has 245km of motorway pistes that range from dead-easy to deadly; at 16km La Sarenne, accessible from the Pic Blanc cable car, is the French Alps' longest black run. Experienced skiers can also ski in July and August on glaciers ranging from 2530m to 3330m. Off the slopes, speed fiends can ice-drive…in a Porsche.

Information hub **Maison de l'Alpe** (place Paganon) sells ski passes (one/six days €38.20/198.50) and houses the tip-top **tourist office** (☎ 04 76 11 44 44; www.alped huez.com; ⊗ 9am-7pm high season, 9am-12.30pm & 2.30-6pm Mon-Fri low season).

➘ THE SOUTH OF FRANCE

THE SOUTH OF FRANCE

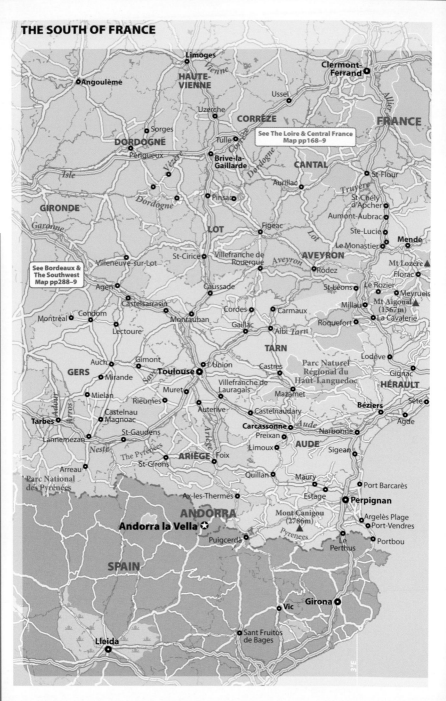

Limoges
Clermont-Ferrand
Angoulême
HAUTE-VIENNE
Ussel
Uzerche
CORRÈZE
FRANCE
Sorges
DORDOGNE
Tulle
See The Loire & Central France
Map pp168–9
Périgueux
Brive-la-Gaillarde
CANTAL
St-Flour
Aurillac
Truyère
St-Chély d'Apcher
Isle
Pinsac
Aumont-Aubrac
GIRONDE
Ste-Lucie
Mende
Garonne
LOT
Figeac
Le Monastier
Dordogne
St-Cirice
Villefranche de Rouergue
AVEYRON
Mt Lozère
Villeneuve-sur-Lot
Aveyron
Rodez
Florac
See Bordeaux &
The Southwest
Map pp288–9
Caussade
St-Léons
Le Rozier
Meyrueis
Agen
Castelsarrasin
Cordes
Carmaux
Millau
Mt Aigoual (1567m)
La Cavalerie
Montréal
Condom
Montauban
Gaillac
Albi
Roquefort
Lectoure
Tarn
TARN
Lodève
Auch
Gimont
L'Union
Castres
Parc Naturel
Régional du
Haut-Languedoc
Gignac
GERS
Mirande
Toulouse
HÉRAULT
Muret
Villefranche de
Lauragais
Mazamet
Béziers
Sète
Mielan
Rieumes
Auterive
Castelnaudary
Agde
Tarbes
Castelnau
Magnoac
Carcassonne
Aude
Narbonne
Lannemezan
St-Gaudens
Preixan
AUDE
Neste
The Pyrénées
Limoux
Sigean
Arreau
St-Girons
ARIÈGE
Foix
Quillan
Maury
Port Barcarès
Parc National
des Pyrénées
Ax-les-Thermes
Estage
Perpignan
ANDORRA
Mont Canigou
(2786m)
Argelès Plage
Port-Vendres
Andorra la Vella
Puigcerda
Pyrenees
Le Perthus
Portbou
SPAIN
Vic
Girona
Lleida
Sant Fruitós
de Bages

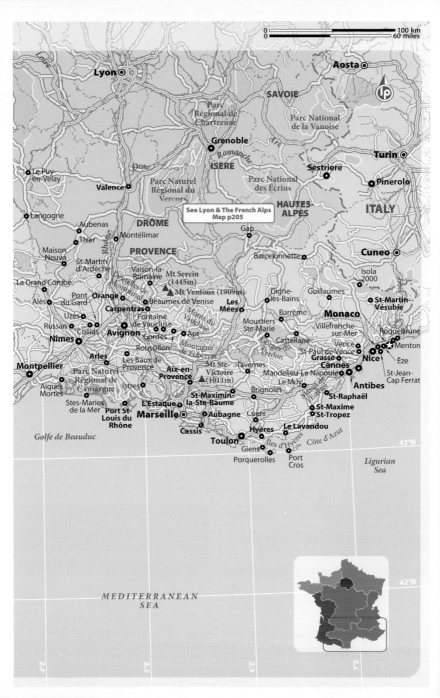

0 ___ 100 km
0 ___ 60 miles

LP

Lyon

Aosta

SAVOIE

Parc
Régional de
Chartreuse

Parc National
de la Vanoise

Grenoble

romanche

Turin

ISÈRE

Sestriere

Pinerolo

Le Puy-
en-Velay

Valence

Parc Naturel
Régional du
Vercors

Parc National
des Écrins

ITALY

Langogne

Aubenas

DRÔME

Gap

See Lyon & The French Alps
Map p205

HAUTES-
ALPES

Cuneo

Uzer

Montélimar

Maison
Neuve

St-Martin
d'Ardèche

PROVENCE

Barcelonnette

Isola
2000

La Grand'Combe

Vaison-la-
Romaine

Mt Serein
(1445m)

Guillaumes

St-Martin-
Vésubie

Pont
du Gard

Orange

▲ Mt Ventoux (1909m)

Beaumes de Venise

Les
Mées

Digne-
les-Bains

Alès

Carpentras

Monaco

Uzès

Fontaine
de Vaucluse

Barrème

Russan

Collias

Avignon

Apt

Moustiers
Ste-Marie

Villefranche-
sur-Mer

Roquebrune

Nîmes

Gordes

Castellane

Vence

Menton

Roussillon

St-Paul de Vence

Arles

Les Baux de
Provence

Montagne
de Lubéron

Grasse

Nice

Èze

Montpellier

Parc Naturel
Régional de
Camargue

Aix-en-
Provence

Mt Ste-
Victoire
(1011m)

Tavernes

Mandelieu-La Napoule

St-Jean-
Cap Ferrat

Antibes

Aigues
Mortes

Istres

Brignoles

Le Muy

Cannes

Stes-Maries
de la Mer

Port St-
Louis du
Rhône

L'Estaque

St-Maximin-
la-Ste-Baume

Aubagne

Cuers

St-Maxime

St-Raphaël

St-Tropez

Marseille

Golfe de Beauduc

Cassis

Toulon

Hyères

Le Lavandou

Côte d'Azur

43°N

Giens

Porquerolles

Port
Cros

Ligurian
Sea

42°N

MEDITERRANEAN
SEA

4°E   5°E   6°E   7°E

HIGHLIGHTS

1 PROVENÇAL MARKETS

BY PATRICIA WELLS, COOKBOOK AUTHOR & COOKING TEACHER

Provence produces so many good, fresh ingredients, from black truffles in the winter to artichokes and asparagus in spring, stunning strawberries, melons, heirloom tomatoes, baby Delicatesse potatoes, and fresh lamb, poultry and sausages. Not to mention bargain-priced wines and outstanding cheeses. What more does one need in life?

↘ PATRICIA WELLS' DON'T MISS LIST

❶ VAISON-LA-ROMAINE

The Tuesday market in Vaison-la-Romaine (p280) might be 'my' market but it is truly one of Provence's greats. It has the freshest local produce around, especially asparagus, strawberries, melons and heirloom tomatoes. Go to Lou Canesteou for cheese and Peyrerol for chocolate.

❷ ST-RÉMY DE PROVENCE

My other favourite is St-Rémy on a Wednesday: I love the town, the ambience. Perhaps it is a market to buy more trinkets than food, but whatever you are there for, you just always feel as though you are in the right place at the right time.

❸ UZÈS

The third in my top three is also on Wednesday, in Uzès west of Nîmes. The organic market on place aux Herbes, one of the prettiest little squares in all of France, is stunning – great goat's cheese, confitures (jams) from the nuns, and wonderful local olives and olive oil.

Clockwise from top: Regional olives; Bags of garlic; Ripe tomatoes; Decorated pumpkins; Lavender

CLOCKWISE FROM TOP: DIANA MAYFIELD; RUSSELL MOUNTFORD; ROCCO FASANO; GREG ELMS; JEAN-BERNARD CARILLET.

❹ RICHERENCHES

My favourite speciality market is on Saturday in Richerenches, November through February. It is a fresh black truffle market – very mysterious and you can't figure out what is going on, with lots of people selling pillow cases bulging with black truffles from the trunks of their cars. Stay until lunchtime and have a truffle omelette at one of the two cafés in the village.

❺ THE BEST PRODUCE

Tip 1 When looking for the best meat, look for a line of elderly French women. They know how to shop! **Tip 2** Look at the vendors: just as people often resemble their dogs, produce vendors resemble their produce. If the vendor is neat, trim, clean, so will his produce

be neat, trim, clean. Dirty fingernails usually mean ugly produce! **Tip 3** Take time to tour the entire market before you buy. Nothing is worse that a quick, rash purchase at the beginning of the market, only to find better, better-priced produce later on.

↘ THINGS YOU NEED TO KNOW

Get up early Markets start around 7am and end by noon **Tip 4** Bring your own basket **Read** *At Home in Provence* (Patricia Wells) for ideas on what to cook once you've shopped at the market **Truffle and Provence cooking classes** Sign up a year in advance at www.patriciawells.com.

THE SOUTH OF FRANCE

HIGHLIGHTS

HIGHLIGHTS

2 RIVIERA HIGH LIFE

BY ELIZABETH LEWIS, RADIO PRESENTER AT 106.5 RIVIERA RADIO

Monaco and the Riviera *are* glam and glitzy; it's simply impossible to tire of the exceptional beauty of the place. I wander around and I'm constantly noticing it, the architecture, the beaches... To me it is very important to live in a beautiful place, which is why I've spent the best part of 20 years here.

⬊ ELIZABETH LEWIS'S DON'T MISS LIST

❶ LIVE JAZZ

My favourite summer festival is **Nice Jazz Festival** (p271). I've seen everyone from BB King to Kool and The Gang there, dancing under olive trees as the moon rises over the outdoor stages. Then there's **La Note Bleue** (www.lanotebleue.mc), a Monaco beach club where the best jazz musicians play. Spend the afternoon on a sun lounger sipping rosé, dine on the best seafood risotto on the Riviera, and jive until the wee hours.

❷ CELEBRITY SPOTTING

So many famous people live or have second homes on the Riviera that it's hard *not* to see them! At Monte Carlo Sporting Club's **Salle des Étoiles** (www.sportingmontecarlo.com) I've chatted to Shirley Bassey (she lives next door to it) during a Liza Minelli concert; stood right behind Elton John (another celebrity resident) at a Grace Jones concert; and spotted Julian Lennon at the next table when seeing Steely Dan live.

Clockwise from top: Sunbathers, Nice (p268); Harbour, Menton; St-Tropez (p279); Port Hercule, Monaco (p284); Café de Paris (p286), Monaco

❸ ROOFTOP SPAS & BARS

Rooftops are prime Riviera real estate and many of the big hotels have rooftop spas and bars open to nonguests. Nice's **Hôtel Grand Aston** (www.hotel -aston.com) has a fabulous rooftop swimming pool where you can spend the day lounging (admission even includes a toasted open sandwich and drink!).

❹ PURE GLAMOUR

For pure glamour it has to be Monaco's **Monte Carlo Bay Hôtel** (http://fr.monte carlobay.com). It has huge colonnades everywhere, and the spa is out of this world: a big greenhouse full of lush vegetatio n with a circular pool and a bridge. There are sun loungers everywhere, poolside spas and the **Blue Gin Bar** is perfect for an aperitif.

❺ PRICELESS GEM

Cave Romagnan (http://caveromagnan .free.fr) in Nice is a tiny, unpretentious wine bar and cellar with an excellent selection of wine. On Saturdays, locals of all ages gather to dance until midnight to live jazz, blues and rock bands.

◥ THINGS YOU NEED TO KNOW

Glamour tip Most Riviera bars aren't glam; they're just full of glam people **Dress code** It's not what you pay to get in (many bars and clubs have no entrance fee); it's what you look like – dress smart **Timeless address** Monaco's Stars 'n' Bars (p286) and neighbouring terrace cafés at Monaco port

HIGHLIGHTS

↘ LAVENDER

If Provence has one defining fragrance, it's the astringent aroma of this delicate purple flower, which burns bright green in spring, blazes blue prior to harvesting between mid-June and mid-August and sits out autumn in a cropped wash of pale grey-blue. Lavender fields once seen that are never forgotten include those surrounding **Abbaye de Sénanque** (p266) and farms in the **Luberon** (p265).

↘ NICE'S THREE CORNICHES

No view is more soul-stirring than the cliff-hanging panoramas that unfurl along this trio of **coastal roads** (p283) linking Nice and Menton. No wonder Hitchcock filmed *To Catch a Thief* (1956), starring Cary Grant and Grace Kelly (who, ironically, died in car crash on same said road in 1982). Motor in style past rock tunnels and hilltop villages, epic monuments and millionaire **Monaco** (p284).

5

PONT DU GARD

The scale of this **Unesco World Heritage site** (p261) near Nîmes is gargantuan: the 35 arches astraddle the Roman aqueduct's 275m-long upper tier contain a watercourse designed to carry 20,000 cu metres of water per day. View it from afloat a canoe on the **River Gard** (p261) or pay extra to jig across its top tier.

6

FRESH PRODUCE

Shopping for herbs and olives at the market is a sensual experience. Take St-Tropez's **place des Lices** (p281), which has stalls bearing plump fruit and veg, olives, local cheeses, chestnut purée and fragrant herbs. Nice's **Cours Saleya** (p273) is the other square to find one of southern France's most vibrant local markets.

7

CARCASSONNE

That first glimpse of La Cité's stone witch's-hat turrets above **Carcassonne** (p260) in the Languedoc is enough to make your hair stand on end. To savour this fairytale walled city in its true glory, linger at dusk after the crowds have left, when the old town belongs to its 100 inhabitants and the few visitors staying at the few lovely hotels within its ramparts.

3 DAN HERRICK; 4 DAVID WALL; 5 JEAN ROBERT; 6 DIANA MAYFIELD; 7 GLENN BEANLAND

3 Butterfly on lavender blossom; 4 Èze (p283); 5 Pont du Gard (p261), Languedoc; 6 Cours Saleya market (p273), Nice; 7 La Cité, Carcassonne (p260)

THE BEST...

⬃ BEACH LOUNGING

- **Plage de Pampelonne** (p280) Play Brigitte Bardot on St-Tropez's finest golden sand.
- **Promenade des Anglais** (p270) The classic spot to lounge on Nice's mythical seaside prom.
- **St-Jean-Cap Ferrat** (p283) Dip into secluded coves between millionaire mansions.
- **Île Ste-Marguerite** (p276) Trade Cannes madness for castaway beaches, fishing and eucalyptus forest.

⬃ NATURAL BEAUTIES

- **Île de Port-Cros** (p282) Sail to France's only marine national park.
- **Marseille's Calanques** (p251) Hike between rock and scented *garrigue* to turquoise waters slipped in tiny coves.
- **Gorges du Verdon** (p266) Provence's vertigo-inducing canyon begs to be seen afloat.

⬃ SENSATIONAL ART

- **Chapelle du Rosaire** (p275) This bijou chapel was Matisse's pride and joy.
- **Fondation Maeght** (p275) World-class art in St-Paul de Vence.
- **Musée Picasso** (p274) View Picassos in Antibes' 12th-century château-turned-studio.
- **Musée de l'Annonciade** (p279) Discover St-Tropez from a pointillist perspective.

⬃ CELESTIAL SEAVIEWS

- **Musée Océanographique de Monaco** (p286) Feast on spectacular views at the rooftop restaurant of Monaco's aquarium.
- **Jardin d'Èze** (p283) Gaze as far as Corsica from this hilltop garden on the Grande Corniche.
- **Le Méditerranée** (p278) Cannes' hippest rooftop restaurant seduces with red-hot Massif de l'Estérel views.

LEFT: BETHUNE CARMICHAEL; RIGHT: DAVID TOMLINSON.

Left: Èze and St-Jean Cap Ferrat (p283); Right: Gorges du Verdon (p266)

THINGS YOU NEED TO KNOW

⇘ VITAL STATISTICS

- **Population** 2,603,500 (Provence), 2,044,000 (French Riviera & Monaco), 2,295,000 (Languedoc-Roussillon)
- **Best time to visit** April, June and September
- **Points of entry** Marseille, Nice, Toulon and Nimes airports

⇘ ADVANCE PLANNING

- **As early as possible** Book accommodation; buy tickets for May's Monaco F1 Grand Prix (p286), Avignon's theatre festival (p263) and Cannes (p276).
- **Two weeks before** Reserve a table at Marseille's Chez Fonfon, Chez Jeannet and Au Bord de l'Eau (p252) and St-Paul de Vence's La Colombe d'Or (p276).
- **One week before** Gen up on money-saving passes like the Nice Riviera Pass; contact tourist offices for details.

⇘ RESOURCES

- **Provence-Alpes-Côte d'Azur** (www.decouverte-paca.fr) Regional tourist board website.
- **Avignon & Provence** (www.avignon-et-provence.com) Online accommodation guide.
- **TER-SNCF** (www.ter-sncf.com/paca) Regional train tickets, fares and schedules.

⇘ GETTING AROUND

- **Train** is ideal for exploring the busy stretch of coast either side of Nice (to the Italian border and to Cannes and beyond).
- **Car** is essential in Provence where public transport is scant. On the coast July and August means hellish road traffic, at its worst on Saturdays, and daily approaching St-Tropez.
- **Boats** sail into St-Tropez in summer and are the loveliest way to arrive in the mythical fishing port. Dozens more tourist boats plough the Med from Marseille, Cannes and Hyères (for the glittering Îles des Hyères; p282)

⇘ BE FOREWARNED

- **Petty theft** from backpacks, pockets and bags is rife on the Riviera. Be extra vigilant at train stations and on the beach.
- **Cannes hotel prices** soar to unaffordable levels during May's film festival.
- **Monaco motorists** note, you can't take your car into Monaco Ville unless you have a Monaco or local 06 number plate.

ITINERARIES

Southern France is extraordinarily varied, enticing travellers with a 101 different ways to experience its bounty of sights, scents and gastronomic tastes.

HOW NICE! Three Days

Day one acquaint yourself with Riviera Queen **(1) Nice** (p268), not missing the vibrant **(2) Cours Saleya** street markets (p273), **(3) Vieux Nice's** (p270) enchanting maze, lunch at **(4) Acchiardo** (p273) and an aperitif over *socca* (chickpea crêpes) at **(5) Chez René Socca** (p273) or Champagne at **(6) Grand Hotel Aston** (p273). Come dark catch a train to **(7) Antibes** (p274) to dance with stars beneath the stars at the legendary **(8) La Siesta-Le Pearl** (p275).

Day two cruise the coast along the **(9) corniches** (p283): dip into the Med from secluded coves on **(10) St-Jean-Cap Ferrat** (p283); hike up the medieval village of **(11) Èze** (p283) to lunch at **(12) Château Eza** (p284); and pay homage to groundbreaking architect Le Corbusier in **(13) Roquebrune** (p284). End in **(14) Monaco** (p274) with a flutter at **(15) Casino de Monte Carlo** (p286) and dinner at **(16) Le Castelroc** (p286).

On the final day drive inland to **(17) Grasse** (p278) to tour its perfumeries and flower-filled fields; or venture west to tackle a hiking trail in the jagged, breathtakingly red crags of the extraordinary **(18) Massif de l'Estérel** (p279).

ROMAN PROVENCE Five Days

Gloriously amphitheatres, triumphal arches and other public buildings transport travellers to the period in history that gave Provence – a Roman *provincia* – its name. Devote day one to Roman giant **(1) Nîmes** (p259) with its resplendent **(2) amphitheatre** (p259), fun-fuelled **(3) férias** (bull-running festivals; p272) and **(4) Maison Carée** (p259).

Day two gawp at the world's highest aqueduct **(5) Pont du Gard** (p261), particularly awe-inspiring when skipped atop or paddled beneath in a canoe. Picnic in the scented Mediterranean scrub of **(6) Mémoires de Garrigue** (p261). Later, drive south to **(7) Arles** (p256) with its Roman-theatre twinset and, should flamingo-watching tickle your fancy, continue south into the **(8) Camargue** (p258) for a taste of southern France's wild west. Fall wildly in love with this unique wetland with an overnight at **(9) L'Auberge Cavalière** (p258).

Looking north be star-struck at **(10) Orange's** Roman amphitheatre (p272) during its magical Les Chorégies d'Orange or at Puymin's Théâtre Antique during **(11) Vaison-la-Romaine's** (p280) summer festivals.

ROUTES
— How Nice!
— Roman Provence
— Gourmet Traveller

GOURMET TRAVELLER One Week

Set tastebuds off to a brilliant start with fresh fish at (1) Au Bord de l'Eau (p252) or *bouillabaisse* at (2) Chez Fonfon (p252) in (3) Marseille (p248). Come dusk, linger over Provençal and Languedoc wines at (4) La Part des Anges (p252).

Day two titillate tastebuds at (5) Aix-en-Provence's (p253) Place Richelme food market and a *calisson* (French sweets) factory tour with (6) Roy René (p255). Next day head northwest for traditional Provençal dishes at Fontaine de Vaucluse's (7) La Figuière (p265) or northeast to (8) Moustiers Ste-Marie (p267) for a gourmet lunch beneath plane trees at Michelin-starred (9) La Bastide de Moustiers (p268).

Tastebuds blazing, hit the (10) French Riviera (p268) for a symphony of memorable dines: in (11) Nice (p268), black truffles at (12) Terres de Truffes (p273) and tripe or stockfish at (13) La Merenda (p273); in Cannes succulent shellfish at (14) Antibes' Auberge Provençal (p274) or (15) Astoux & Brun (p278); and in St-Paul de Vence fine dining between priceless art at (16) La Colombe d'Or (p276). End on a gourmet high with the lunch of a lifetime at (17) Auberge de l'Oumède (p281) in Ramatuelle near St-Tropez.

DISCOVER THE SOUTH OF FRANCE

There is no sunnier, more celebrity-rich part of France than the hot south. So get set for heart and soul seduction. Travelling here means sensual sauntering through scented lavender fields and vineyards, around vibrant morning markets groaning with fresh produce and medieval hilltop villages impossibly perched on rocky crags, along paradisiacal shores lapped by clear turquoise waters.

Roughly speaking this region splits into three: east is the iconic French Riviera, wedged between glitzy star-spangled Cannes and megalomaniacal Monte Carlo in the glamorous millionaire principality of Monaco. In the middle is Provence, hinged on the coast by the wildly contrasting fishing ports of St-Tropez and Marseille, and tethered inland by a stash of Roman vestiges, hilltop villages and exceptional natural landscapes. Languedoc lies west, an upcoming region travellers tramp to first and foremost for the walled city of Carcassonne and its bewitching witch's-hat turrets.

PROVENCE

Provence conjures up images of rolling lavender fields, blue skies, gorgeous villages, wonderful food and superb wine – most people's idea of a perfect holiday. It certainly delivers on all those fronts, but what many visitors don't expect is Provence's incredible diversity.

The Vaucluse and Luberon regions epitomise the Provençal cliché, but head south to the Alpilles with its craggy villages and olive groves and the light begins to change, a prelude to Camargue's bleached landscapes.

Further east, the spectacular Gorges du Verdon, with their 800m sheer-drop cliffs, set the scene for northeastern Provence's unspoilt wilderness.

MARSEILLE

pop 826,700

Marseille grows on you with its unique history, fusion of cultures, souklike markets, millennia-old port and corniches (coastal roads) chicaning around rocky inlets, coves and sun-baked beaches.

And then, of course, there are the Marseillais themselves, far too modest to ever admit that they are part of what makes Marseille so endearing: the accent, the warmth, the honesty, the Mediterranean flair.

INFORMATION

Tourist Office (☎ 04 91 13 89 00; www.marseille-tourisme.com; 4 La Canebière, 1er; M Vieux Port; ☽ 9am-7pm Mon-Sat, 10am-5pm Sun)

SIGHTS

Initially built as a charity shelter for the town's poor, the stunning arched pink-stone courtyard of the **Centre de la Vieille Charité** (Old Charity Cultural Centre; ☎ 04 91 14 58 80; 2 rue de la Charité, 2e; M Joliette) now houses Marseille's beautiful **Musée d'Archéologie Méditerranéenne** (Museum of Mediterranean Archeology; ☎ 04 91 14 58 59) and **Musée d'Arts Africains, Océaniens & Amérindiens** (Museum of African, Oceanic & American Indian Art; ☎ 04 91 14

CENTRAL MARSEILLE

THE SOUTH OF FRANCE

CENTRAL MARSEILLE

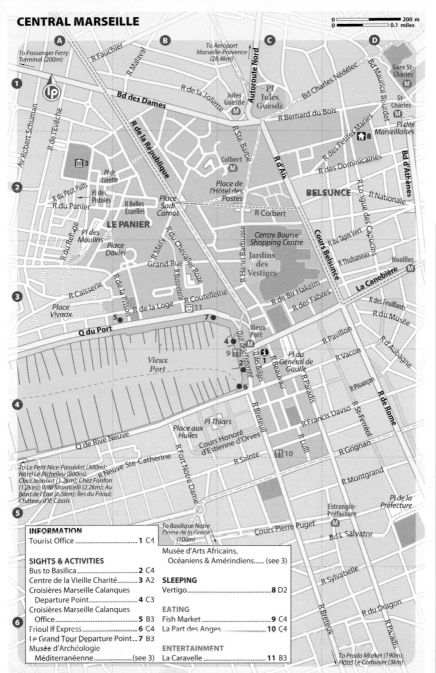

INFORMATION
Tourist Office 1 C4

SIGHTS & ACTIVITIES
Bus to Basilica 2 C4
Centre de la Vieille Charité........... 3 A2
Croisières Marseille Calanques
    Departure Point........................... 4 C3
Croisières Marseille Calanques
    Office.. 5 B3
Frioul If Express............................ 6 C4
Le Grand Tour Departure Point... 7 B3
Musée d'Archéologie
    Méditerranéenne.....................(see 3)

Musée d'Arts Africains,
    Océaniens & Amérindiens...... (see 3)

SLEEPING
Vertigo.......................................8 D2

EATING
Fish Market 9 C4
La Part des Anges 10 C4

ENTERTAINMENT
La Caravelle 11 B3

> ## MAX OUT MARSEILLE
>
> To max out your time in Marseille, the **Marseille City Pass** (1-/2-day pass €20/27) gives you access to the city's museums; guided tours of the town; and unlimited travel on all public transport (as well as the little train). It also includes the boat trip and entrance to the Château d'If, and offers various discounts, such as for the Le Grand Tour tourist bus.

58 38). An all-inclusive ticket costs €5/2.50 per adult/student.

Be blown away by the celestial bay and city views, and knockout 19th-century architecture at the hilltop **Basilique Notre Dame de la Garde** (☎ 04 91 13 40 80; montée de la Bonne Mère; admission free; ♥ basilica & crypt 7am-7pm, longer hours in summer), the opulent Romano-Byzantine basilica that dominates Marseille's skyline.

Immortalised in Alexandre Dumas' classic 1840s novel *Le Comte de Monte Cristo* (The Count of Monte Cristo), the 16th-century fortress-turned-prison **Château d'If** (☎ 04 91 59 02 30; adult/student €5/3.50; ♥ 9.30am-6.30pm May-Aug, 9.30am-5.30pm Tue-Sun Sep-Mar, 9.30am-5.30pm daily Apr) sits on a 3-hectare island 3.5km west of the Vieux Port. Boats run by **Frioul If Express** (☎ 04 91 46 54 65; www.frioul-if-express.com; 1 quai des Belges, 1er) leave for the Château d'If from the Vieux Port at the corner of quai de la Fraternité and quai de Rive Neuve. Boats to the Château d'If also serve the **Îles du Frioul** (€10 return; €15 for a combined ticket; 35 minutes).

TOURS

Le Grand Tour (☎ 04 91 91 05 82; adult/student/child €16/13/8; ♥ 10am-4pm) is handy for getting around as well as for seeing the city. This hop-on, hop-off, open-topped double-decker bus travels between the main sights and museums. Buy tickets from the tourist office or on the bus.

Croisières Marseille Calanques (☎ 08 25 13 68 00; www.croisieres-marseille-calanques .com, in French; 74 quai du Port, 2e) runs boat

Marseille

BRUCE BI

THE CALANQUES, SOON A NATIONAL PARK?

Just a few miles east of Marseille lies the **Calanques**, a small piece of perfectly unspoilt Mediterranean landscape: turquoise, translucent water lapping the sheer cliffs of the indented coast, interrupted every now and then by a small idyllic beach.

The area is cherished by Marseillais who love to come here to soak up some rays or go for a long Sunday walk. The site has always been protected but a project is now underway to turn the Calanques into a national park by 2010.

Whether or not the project goes ahead, you will still be able to go hiking along the many maquis-lined trails from October to June, and when the fire risks are too high over the summer months, you can take a boat trip. From Marseille, heading to the nearby village of Cassis makes for a great day trip – after a glorious morning travelling along the Calanques' coves, lunch and a bottle of crisp Cassis white at one of the port-side restaurants is just the ticket. If you're interested in wines of the area, **Cassis' tourist office** (☎ 04 42 01 71 17; quai des Moulins; ☉ 9am-12.30pm & 2-6pm Tue-Sat) supplies a free list and map of all the cellars you can visit for tastings.

trips (with French commentary only) from the Vieux Port to Cassis and back (€25).

SLEEPING

our pick **Vertigo** (☎ 04 91 91 07 11; www.hotel vertigo.fr; 42 rue des Petites Maries, 1er; Ⓜ Gare St-Charles SNCF; dm €23.90, d €55-65; 🖳) This new boutique hostel has kissed goodbye to dodgy bunk beds, itchy blankets and hospital-like decor. Here it's 'hello' to vintage posters, a designer chrome kitchen, groovy communal spaces and trendy multilingual staff.

Hôtel Le Richelieu (☎ 04 91 31 01 92; www .lerichelieu-marseille.com; 52 corniche Président John F Kennedy, 7e; d €46-110) This beach-house-like hotel has gone a little over the top on the old bright-coloured walls during its recent refurbishment, but the balconies, sea views, idyllic breakfast terrace and adjacent beach (June to September only) are still there.

Hôtel Le Corbusier (☎ 04 91 16 78 00; www.hotellecorbusier.com; 280 bd Michelet, 8e; cabin with shared toilet €59, d €94-120; 🎿 ✗)

It's not for everyone, but staying at the 20-room hotel within this iconic concrete monolith is an architectural experience, and a chance to absorb Le Corbusier's legacy. Double rooms look very sharp indeed with sublime sea views and Le Corbusier chairs.

Villa Monticelli (☎ 04 91 22 15 20; www .villamonticelli.com; 96 rue du Commandant Rolland, 8e; d €85-110) Colette and Jean are passionate about their city and will share with you all their secrets and best addresses. The five exquisite *chambre d'hôte* (B&B) rooms in their stunning villa are absolutely worth the slightly outer-city location. It is probably the best value for money that you will find for this type of accommodation.

Le Petit Nice-Passédat (☎ 04 91 59 25 92; www.passedat.fr; Anse de Maldormé, 7e; d low/high season from €230/370; 🎿 🖳 🎿) Nestled into the rocks above a petite cove, this is an idyllic hideaway of just 16 individually and exquisitely appointed rooms overlooking the mosaic-tiled saltwater pool and cacti

Aix-en-Provence

GLENN BEANLAND

garden. It's also home to Gerald Passédat's virtuoso restaurant.

EATING

Marseille's signature dish *bouillabaisse* is a fish soup made from five different fish, along with tomatoes, white wine, fennel and saffron, and served with *rouille* (garlic mayonnaise) and croutons. Any less than €35 and it won't be the genuine article.

The Vieux Port overflows with restaurants. For fare as diverse as Marseille itself, cours Julien and its surrounding streets are jammed with French, Indian, Antillean, Pakistani, Thai, Armenian, Lebanese, Tunisian and Italian restaurants.

La Part des Anges (☎ 04 91 33 55 70; 33 rue Sainte; mains €15, ☼ lunch & dinner Mon-Sat, dinner Sun) The name *la part des anges* (angels'

share) refers to the amount of alcohol that evaporates through a barrel during wine (or whisky) fermentation. But at this gem of a wine bistro in Marseille's centre, you'd be best not to lose an ounce or a drop of whatever you eat or drink: the French fare is cooked to perfection and the wine list is an oenologist's dream.

Chez Jeannot (☎ 04 91 52 11 28; 129 rue du Vallon des Auffes; mains €15-22; ☼ lunch & dinner Tue-Sat, lunch Sun, closed Mon) An institution among Marseillais, the rooftop terrace overlooking the stunning Vallon des Auffes is booked out days in advance. The atmosphere is jovial and uncomplicated, just like the thin-crust pizzas, *grillades* (grilled meats) and seafood that land on your plate.

Au Bord de l'Eau (☎ 04 91 72 68 04; 15 rue des Arapèdes, port de la Madrague Montredon, 8e; menus €25-30; ☼ lunch & dinner Mon & Thu-Sun, lunch Tue Sep–mid-Jun, lunch & dinner Thu-Sun, dinner Mon-Wed mid-Jun–Aug) At the water's edge' is the kind of place Marseillais cherish: easy on the frills, heavy on outdoor space, steady on the price and artistic on the plate. Catch bus 83 along the coast to av du Prado (by the statue of David), then take bus 19 further south along the coast.

Chez Fonfon (☎ 04 91 52 14 38; 140 rue du Vallon des Auffes, 7e; mains around €40; ☼ lunch & dinner Tue-Sat, dinner Mon) Overlooking the enchanting little harbour Vallon des Auffes, Chez Fonfon is famed for its *bouillabaisse*. The place is quite formal, although the wonderful views brighten things up.

ENTERTAINMENT

La Caravelle (☎ 04 96 17 05 40; 34 quai du Port, 2e; Ⓜ Vieux Port; ☼ 7am-2am) Live jazz and chilled vibes are what's waiting for you at Hôtel Belle-Vue's 1st-floor bar. On balmy nights, a mojito on the small balcony overlooking the port is just the ticket.

SHOPPING

The small but enthralling **fish market** (quai des Belges; Ⓜ Vieux Port; ☯ 8am-1pm) is a daily fixture at the Vieux Port docks.

Marseille's biggest market, the daily **Prado Market** (Ⓜ Castellane or Périer; ☯ 8am-1pm) stretches from the Castellane metro station along av du Prado to the Périer metro station, with a staggering array of clothes, fruit, vegetables and speciality items – and a flower market on Friday morning.

GETTING THERE & AWAY

Aéroport Marseille-Provence (☎ 04 42 14 14 14; www.marseille.aeroport.fr) is 25km northwest of town in Marignane.

Marseille's **passenger ferry terminal** (☎ 04 91 39 40 00; www.marseille-port.fr; Ⓡ Joliette) is 250m south of place de la Joliette (1er).

Marseille's train station, **Gare St-Charles** is served by both metro lines. From Marseille there are trains to pretty much anywhere in France and beyond.

GETTING AROUND

Navette (Marseille ☎ 04 91 50 59 34; airport ☎ 04 42 14 31 27) shuttle buses link Aéroport Marseille-Provence (€8, 25 minutes) with Marseille's train station.

Pick up a bike from more than 100 bike stations across the city, and drop it off at one of those same stations. The system is called **le vélo** (www.levelo-mpm.fr).

AIX-EN-PROVENCE

pop 141,200

Aix-en-Provence is to Provence what the Left Bank is to Paris: a pocket of Bohemian chic with an edgy student crowd. In 123 BC the military camp was named Aquae Sextiae (Waters of Sextius) for the thermal springs, which still flow today. The city be-

came a centre of culture under King René (1409–80); two of Aix' most famous sons are painter Paul Cézanne and novelist Émile Zola.

INFORMATION

Tourist Office (☎ 04 42 16 11 61; www.aixenprovencetourism.com; 2 place du Général de Gaulle; ☯ 8.30am-7pm Mon-Sat, 10am-1pm & 2-6pm Sun)

SIGHTS & ACTIVITIES

The tourist office has some great DIY walking tour maps. Otherwise, just follow your nose: Aix is a stroller's heaven.

The graceful **cours Mirabeau** is the literal and spiritual heart of Aix. The mossy **fontaine d'Eau Thermale**, at the intersection of cours Mirabeau and rue du 4 Septembre, spouts 34°C water, a pleasant hint of what's awaiting you at the **Thermes Sextius** (Thermal Spa; ☎ 04 42 23 81 82; www.thermes-sextius.com; 55 av des Thermes; day pass incl 4 treatments from €84).

The pride and joy of **Musée Granet** (☎ 04 42 52 88 32; place St-Jean de Malte; ☯ 11am-7pm Wed-Mon Jun-Sep, noon-6pm Wed-Mon Oct-May) is its nine Cézanne paintings (although none of his masterworks).

The awesome **Fondation Victor Vasarely** (☎ 04 42 200 109; 1 av Marcel Pagnol; adult/student €7/4; ☯ 10am-1pm & 2-6pm Tue-Sat), 4km west of the city, was designed

---

AIX-CELLENT

Brilliant savings come in the form of the **Aix City Pass**, which costs €15, lasts five days and includes admission to **Atelier Paul Cézanne** (Cézanne's studio; p255), **Bastide du Jas de Bouffan** (Cézanne's former family home; p255) and **Musée Granet** (p253).

AIX-EN-PROVENCE

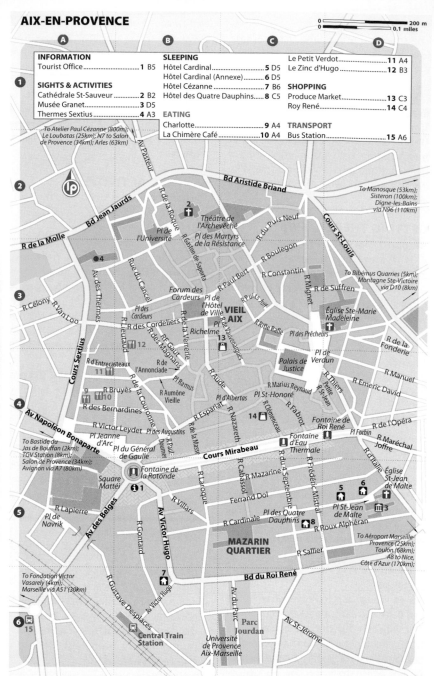

INFORMATION		**SLEEPING**		Le Petit Verdot.............................**11** A4
Tourist Office.................................**1** B5		Hôtel Cardinal..............................**5** D5		Le Zinc d'Hugo...........................**12** B3
		Hôtel Cardinal (Annexe)...........**6** D5		
SIGHTS & ACTIVITIES		Hôtel Cézanne.............................**7** B6		**SHOPPING**
Cathédrale St-Sauveur..............**2** B2		Hôtel des Quatre Dauphins......**8** C5		Produce Market..........................**13** C3
Musée Granet...............................**3** D5				Roy René.......................................**14** C4
Thermes Sextius.........................**4** A3		**EATING**		
		Charlotte.......................................**9** A4		**TRANSPORT**
		La Chimère Café........................**10** A4		Bus Station...................................**15** A6

0 _____ 200 m
0 _____ 0.1 miles

by the Optical Art leader himself. Take bus 4 to the Vasarely stop.

Cézanne's last studio, **Atelier Paul Cézanne** (☎ 04 42 21 06 53; www.atelier-cezanne.com; 9 av Paul Cézanne; adult/student €5.50/2; ☷ 10am-noon & 2-5pm Oct-Mar, to 6pm Apr-Jun & Sep, 10am-6pm Jul & Aug) is a must for any Cézanne fan. The atelier is 1.5km north of the tourist office on a hilltop; take bus 20 to the Atelier Cézanne stop. Otherwise, it's a 20 minute-walk from the centre.

The other two main Cézanne sights in Aix are the **Bastide du Jas de Bouffan** (on the western fringes of the city), the former family home where Cézanne started painting as a young man, and the **Bibémus quarries**, where he did most of his Montagne Ste-Victoire paintings. Head to the tourist office for bookings (required) and information on how to get to these sites.

SLEEPING

Hôtel des Quatre Dauphins (☎ 04 42 38 16 39; www.lesquatredauphins.fr; 54 rue Roux Alphéran; s €55-65, d €65-100; ☷) Close to cours Mirabeau, this sweet 13-room hotel is a symphony of Wedgwood blue, pale-pink and beige.

Hôtel Cardinal (☎ 04 42 38 32 30; www.hotel-cardinal-aix.com; 24 rue Cardinale; d €70, self-catering ste €110) Beneath stratospheric ceilings, Hôtel Cardinal's 29 romantic rooms are beautifully furnished with antiques, tasselled curtains, and newly tiled bathrooms.

Hôtel Cézanne (☎ 04 42 91 11 11; www.hotelaix.com; 40 av Victor Hugo; d €170-195; ☷ ☐) Apart from the beautifully crafted designer rooms and artistic surroundings, perhaps the best thing about Aix' hippest pad is the breakfast: smoked salmon and Champagne (bring on the Buck's Fizz!).

EATING

Charlotte (☎ 04 42 26 77 56; 32 rue des Bernardines; 2-/3-course menu €14/17.50; ☷ lunch & dinner Tue-Sat) Townspeople congregate like a big extended family at this bustling place. It turns out delicious, simple home cooking, including terrines, homemade soups, grilled meat and savoury tarts, from its open kitchen. In summer, feasting takes place outdoors in the garden.

Le Zinc d'Hugo (☎ 04 42 27 69 69; 22 rue Lieutaud; mains €14-18; ☷ lunch & dinner Tue-Sat; ☒) This rustic bistro of stone walls, wooden tables and a blackboard menu chalked with daily specials gets a little overwhelmed on market days when shoppers come up for the €14 lunchtime *menu*.

Le Petit Verdot (☎ 04 42 27 30 12; 7 rue Entrecasteaux; menu €17; ☷ dinner Mon-Sat; ☒) At this cosy establishment decorated with wine cases, you'll choose food to accompany your wine (not the other way around). The wine list includes 100-odd choices, through which the staff will expertly guide you.

Café la Nuit, Arles

BETHUNE CARMICHAEL

La Chimère Café (☎ 04 42 38 30 00; 15 rue Brueys; 3-course menu €29.50; ☼ dinner Mon-Sat) Aix' yuppies lap up the cabaret atmosphere of this former nightclub: starry-night vaulted ceiling in the underground room, grand chandeliers with crimson, velvety furnishings above.

Trestle tables set up each morning for a **produce market** (place Richelme), displaying olives, goat's cheese, garlic, lavender, honey, peaches, melons and other sun-kissed products.

GETTING THERE & AWAY

Aéroport Marseille-Provence (☎ 04 42 14 14 14; www.marseille.aeroport.fr), aka Aéroport Marseille-Marignane, is 25km from Aix-en-Provence and has regular shuttle buses.

Aix' tiny **city centre train station** (☼ 7am-7pm) is at the southern end of av Victor Hugo and has services to Marseille (€6.50, 50 minutes).

Aix' **TGV station**, 8km from the city centre and accessible by shuttle bus, has many more services (only 12 minutes to Marseille, €8).

ARLES

pop 52,400

Long before Van Gogh captured this Grand Rhône River spot on canvas, the Romans had already been turned on to its charms. Within a century and a half, it boasted a 12,000-seat theatre and a 20,000-seat amphitheatre to entertain its citizens with gruesome gladiatorial spectacles and chariot races.

Still impressively intact, the two structures now stage huge events including Arles' famous *ferias*, with their controversial bullfights and three-day street parties.

INFORMATION

Tourist Office (☎ 04 90 18 41 20; www.tourisme.ville-arles.fr; esplanade Charles de Gaulle; ☼ 9am-6.45pm Apr-Sep, 9am-4.45pm Mon-Sat, 10am-12.45pm Sun Oct-Mar)

SIGHTS & ACTIVITIES

Arles' remarkable Roman amphitheatre, **Les Arènes** (☎ 04 90 49 59 05; adult/student €5.50/4; ☼ 9am-6.30pm May-Sep, 9am-6pm Mar,

Apr & Oct, 10am-5pm Nov-Feb), was built around the late 1st or early 2nd century.

Still regularly used for projections and plays, the **Théâtre Antique** (Roman Theatre; ☎ 04 90 49 59 05; entrance is on rue de la Calade; adult/student €3/2.20; ◷ 9am-6.30pm May-Sep, 9am-noon & 2-6pm Mar, Apr & Oct, 10am-noon & 2-5pm Nov-Feb) dates from the end of the 1st century BC.

Within a striking, state-of-the-art cobalt-blue building, the **Musée de l'Arles et de la Provence Antiques** (☎ 04 90 18 88 88; av de la 1ère Division Française; adult/student/under 18yr €5.50/4/free; ◷ 9am-7pm May-Oct, 10am-5pm Nov-Apr) is perched on the edge of what used to be the Roman chariot racing track (circus), 1.5km southwest of the tourist office. It has amassed a rich collection of pagan and Christian art, including stunning mosaics.

Housed in a former 15th-century priory, the splendid **Musée Réattu** (☎ 04 90 96 37 68; 10 rue du Grand Prieuré; adult/student €4/3, temporary exhibitions €6/4.50; ◷ 10am-12.30pm & 2-6.30pm Mar-Jun & mid-Sep–Oct, 10am-7pm Jul–mid-Sep, 1-5pm Nov-Feb) has two Picasso paintings, and 57 of his sketches from the early 1970s. It also has works by 18th- and 19th-century Provençal artists, but it's best known for its cutting-edge photographic displays.

Fitting tributes to Van Gogh's art include **Fondation Vincent Van Gogh** (☎ 04 90 49 94 04; 24bis Rond Point des Arènes; adult/student €7/5; ◷ 10am-6pm Apr-Jun, 10am-7pm Jul-Sep, 11am-5pm Tue-Sun Oct-Mar), where important modern-day artists pay homage to the artist's distinctive style.

The best way to get a sense of Van Gogh's time in Arles is to take the excellent **Van Gogh Trail**, a walking circuit of the city marked by footpath-embedded plaques.

SLEEPING

Hôtel du Musée (☎ 04 90 93 88 88; www.hotel dumusee.com; 11 rue du Grand Prieuré; d €48-68, tr & q €65-85; ◷ closed mid-Jan–mid-Feb; 🖳)

The 28 rooms in this gorgeous 12th- to 13th-century building are all individually decorated and have been fitted with brand-new bathrooms.

our pick **Hôtel Le Cloître** (☎ 04 90 96 29 50; www.hotelcloitre.com; 16 rue du Cloître; d €50-70, tr/q €70/80; ◷ mid-Mar–Oct) It has taken 18 years of painstaking renovation to get this old convent to be in its current stunning state. The rooms all feel like a little piece of history, from the grand dining room to rooms 18 and 20 with their prized views of the stone and marble St-Trophime cloister.

Hôtel Arlatan (☎ 04 90 93 56 66; www.hotel -arlatan.fr; 26 rue du Sauvage; d €85-155; ◷ closed mid-Jan–mid-Feb; 🖳 🖳) The heated swimming pool, pretty garden and plush rooms decorated with antique furniture are just some of the things going for this hotel. Add to that a setting steeped in history, with Roman foundations visible through a glass floor in the lobby and 15th-century paintings on one of the lounges' ceilings; this is a very classy choice.

EATING

The Roman place du Forum, shaded by outstretched plane trees, turns into a giant dining table at lunch and dinner during summer. It's also where you'll find **Café la Nuit**, thought to be the café captured on canvas by Van Gogh in his Café Terrace at Night (1888), now mostly a tourist trap.

Au Jardin du Calendal (☎ 04 90 96 11 89; 22 place Pomme; mains €11-19; ◷ lunch Tue-Sun May-Oct) Hôtel Calendal's restaurant is summer bliss for its wholesome fresh food as much as for its lush garden setting. It also serves afternoon tea, with scrumptious cakes.

La Mule Blanche (☎ 04 90 93 98 54; 8 rue du Président Wilson; mains €12.20-20; ◷ lunch Tue-Sun, dinner Wed-Sun summer, lunch Tue-Sat, dinner Wed-Sat winter) Jazz is often performed at the piano in the White Mule's domed interior, but the hottest tables are on the pavement terrace, the prettiest in town, perfect to savour a king-size salad or simple Mediterranean fare.

Le Cilantro (☎ 04 90 18 25 05; 31 rue Porte de Laure; mains €32; ☻ lunch Tue-Fri & Sun, dinner Tue-Sat) Arles' most buzzing tables are a result of the homecoming of Arlésian chef Jérôme Laurent, cooking accomplished dishes that change seasonally – ginger or cocoa pigeon, lard-roasted potatoes (yum!) and excellent veggie courses, too.

GETTING THERE & AWAY

Nîmes airport is 20km northwest of the city.

Some major rail destinations from Arles' **train station** include Nîmes (€7.20, 30 minutes), Marseille (€12.70, 55 minutes) and Avignon (€6.30, 20 minutes).

THE CAMARGUE

Just half an hour from Arles, Provence's rolling and brightly coloured landscapes morph into the flat, bleached, desolate wilderness of the Camargue.

The area is particularly famous for its teeming birdlife. King of all is the pink flamingo, which likes to winter in the Camargue's expansive wetlands. Other nature-lovers will revel in horse-riding trips across the patchwork of pink and purple salt-pans, meadows with grazing bulls and rice fields.

Enclosed by the Petit Rhône and Grand Rhône Rivers, most of the Camargue wetlands are within the 850-sq-km Parc Naturel Régional de Camargue.

The Camargue's two largest towns are the seaside pilgrim's outpost, Les Stes-Maries-de-la-Mer, and to the northwest, the walled town of Aigues Mortes.

INFORMATION

Réserve Nationale de Camargue Office (☎ 04 90 97 00 97; La Capelière; ☻ 9am-

1pm & 2-6pm Apr-Sep, 9am-1pm & 2-5pm Wed-Mon Oct-Mar) Along the D36B, on the eastern side of Étang de Vaccarès, with exhibits on the Camargue's ecosystems, flora and fauna. Many trails and paths fan out from here.

SIGHTS & ACTIVITIES

Inside an 1812-built sheep shed, the **Camargue Museum** (☎ 04 90 97 10 82; Mas du Pont de Rousty; adult/student €5/2.50; ☻ 9am-6pm Apr-Sep, 10am-5pm Wed-Mon Oct-Mar) covers the area's history and ecosystems, as well as traditional lifestyle in the new *gardian* (the Camargue version of cowboy!) room. From here, a 3.5km nature trail leads to an observation tower with bird's-eye views. The museum is 10km southwest of Arles on the D570 to Les Stes-Maries-de-la-Mer.

Get up close with some 2000 pink flamingos at the wonderful **Parc Ornithologique du Pont de Gau** (☎ 04 90 97 82 62; adult/child €7/4; ☻ 9am-sunset Apr-Sep, 10am-sunset Oct-Mar), a semi-wild natural reserve 4km north of Les Stes-Maries on the D570.

Saddle up for a *promenade à cheval* (horse ride) along the beach on the region's white horses. Farms along the D570 (Rte d'Arles) leading into Les Stes-Maries have signs advertising riding and lessons.

Bicycles are perfect for traversing the Camargue's flat (if windy) terrain.

SLEEPING & EATING

Low-rise 'ranch-style' hotels line the D570 heading into Les Stes-Maries.

L'Auberge Cavalière (☎ 04 90 97 88 88; www.aubergecavaliere.com; D570; s €130-160, d €140-170, half-board available; ☒ ☐ ☒) Approximately 1.5km north of Les Stes-Maries, this stunning, yet salt-of-the-earth, hotel spreads out over a typical Camargue landscape of wetlands and meadows. Rooms 340 to 345 look over a pond teeming with birdlife while the thatched *cabanes de gardian* (cabins) offer cosy independent quarters. The restaurant serves great local fare, from bull-meat stews to Camargue rice.

Le Delta (☎ 04 90 97 81 12; 1 place Mireille; mains €11-15; ☼ lunch & dinner Tue-Sat, lunch Sun) A local favourite, Le Delta is a great place to try Camargue specialities like *gardianne de taureau* (bull stew) and the area's thumbnail-sized clams called *tellines*.

NÎMES

pop 145,000

Plough your way through the bleak, traffic-clogged outskirts of Nîmes to reach its true heart, still beating where the Romans established their town more than two millennia ago. Here you'll find some of France's best-preserved classical buildings, together with some stunning modern constructions.

INFORMATION

Tourist Office (☎ 04 66 58 38 00; www.ot-nimes.fr; 6 rue Auguste; ☼ 8.30am-8pm Mon-Fri, 9am-7pm Sat, 10am-6pm Sun Jul & Aug, core hours 8.30am-6.30pm Mon-Fri, 9am-6.30pm Sat, 10am-5pm Sun Sep-Jun)

SIGHTS

Nîmes' magnificent **Roman Amphitheatre** (adult/7-17yr/under 7yr incl audioguide €7.70/5.90/ free; ☼ 9am-7pm Jun-Aug, 9am-6pm or 6.30pm Mar-May, Sep & Oct, 9.30am-5pm Nov-Feb) is the best preserved in the whole of the Roman Empire and was built around AD 100 to seat 24,000 spectators.

The **Maison Carrée** (Square House; place de la Maison Carrée; adult/7-17yr/under 7yr €4.50/3.70/ free; ☼ 10am-7pm or 7.30pm Apr-Sep, 10am-6.30pm Mar & Oct, 10am-1pm & 2-5pm Nov-Feb) is a remarkably preserved rectangular Roman temple, constructed around AD 5 to honour Emperor Augustus' two adopted sons.

The striking glass-and-steel building across the square is the **Carré d'Art** (Art Square), which houses the municipal library and **Musée d'Art Contemporain** (Contemporary Art Museum; place de la Maison Carrée; adult/7-17yr/under 7yr €5.10/3.70/free).

Roman Amphitheatre, Nîmes

RUSSELL MOUNTFORD

RUSSELL MOUNTFORD

Fortified walls, Carcassonne

⬊ CARCASSONNE

From afar, Carcassonne looks like some fairy-tale medieval city. Bathed in late-afternoon sunshine and highlighted by dark clouds, La Cité, as the old walled city is known, is truly breathtaking. But once you're inside, La Cité loses its magic and mystery. Luring an estimated four million visitors annually, it can be a tourist hell in high summer. That said, you'll have to be fairly stone-hearted not to be moved.

But Carcassonne is more than La Cité. The Ville Basse (Lower Town), altogether more tranquil, and established in the 13th century, is a more modest stepsister to camp Cinderella up the hill, and also merits more than a browse. Borrow an audioguide to the Ville Basse (€3 for two hours) from the **main tourist office**.

Even if it's a boiling summer's day, don't leave town without trying the cassoulet, a piping-hot dish with white beans, juicy pork cubes, even bigger cylinders of meaty sausage and, in the most popular local variant, a hunk of duck.

Step down to semi-basement level in the **L'Écu d'Or** to dine in style within the thick stone walls of this friendly spot. It serves, among many other delightful dishes, five varieties of cassoulet and a delicious range of creative desserts.

Things you need to know: Main Tourist Office (☎ 04 68 10 24 30; www.carcassonne -tourisme.com; 28 rue de Verdun; 🕑 9am-7pm Jul & Aug, 9am-6pm Mon-Sat, 9am-1pm Sun Sep-Jun); L'Écu d'Or (☎   04 68 25 49 03; www.restaurant-ecudor.fr, in French; 7-9 rue Porte d'Aude; lunch menu €18, menus €25-33, mains €18-20)

The work of British architect Sir Norman Foster, it is a wonderful, light and airy building.

GETTING THERE & AWAY

Nîmes' **airport** (☎ 04 66 70 49 49), 10km southeast of the city on the A54, is served only by Ryanair, which flies to/

from London (Luton), Liverpool and Nottingham East Midlands in the UK.

The **bus station** (☎ 04 66 38 59 43; rue Ste-Félicité) connects with the train station. Regional destinations include Pont du Gard (€6.50, 30 minutes, five daily).

PONT DU GARD

The **Pont du Gard**, a Unesco World Heritage site, is an exceptionally well-preserved, three-tiered Roman aqueduct, once part of a 50km-long system of canals built around 19 BC to bring water from nearby Uzès to Nîmes.

At the **visitors centre** (☎ 08 20 90 33 30; www.pontdugard.fr; 🕑 9.30am-7pm Tue-Sun, 1-7pm Mon May-Sep, to 5pm or 6pm Oct-Apr) on the left, northern bank, there's an impressive, high-tech **museum** (admission €7), a 25-minute large-screen **film** (admission €4) showing the bridge from land and air, and **Ludo** (per hr €5), a children's activity play area. A **combination ticket** (adult/6-17yr/under 6yr €12/9/free) gives access to all three activities.

You can walk, for free, **Mémoires de Garrigue**, a 1.4km trail with interpretive signs that winds through this typical Mediterranean bush and scrubland – though you'll need the explanatory booklet in English (€4) to get the most out of it.

In July and August, for an extra €2 on top of your museum entry or combination ticket, it's possible to walk the bridge's topmost tier.

The Pont du Gard is 21km northeast of Nîmes and 26km west of Avignon.

RIVER GARD

The wild, unpredictable River Gard descends from the Cévennes mountains.

The river has sliced itself a meandering 22km gorge (Les Gorges du Gardon) through the hills from **Russan** to the village of **Collias**, about 6km upstream from

the Pont du Gard. The GR6 hiking trail runs beside it most of the way.

You can paddle 8km down to the Pont du Gard (€19.50 per person, two hours), or arrange to be dropped upstream at Russan, from where a great descent leads back to Collias through Gorges du Gardon (€33, full day), usually possible only between March and mid-June, when the river is high enough.

AVIGNON

pop 90,800

Hooped by 4.3km of superbly preserved stone ramparts, this graceful city is the belle of Provence's ball. Its turn as the papal seat of power has bestowed Avignon with a treasury of magnificent art and architecture, none grander than the massive medieval fortress and papal palace, the Palais des Papes.

Famed for its annual performing arts festival, these days Avignon is an ideal spot from which to step out into the surrounding region.

INFORMATION

Tourist Office (☎ 04 32 74 32 74; www .avignon-tourisme.com; 41 cours Jean Jaurès; 🕑 9am-5pm Mon-Sat, 9.45am-5pm Sun Apr-Oct, 9am-7pm Mon-Sat, 9.45am-5pm Sun Jul, 9am-6pm Mon-Fri, 9am-5pm Sat & 10am-noon Sun Nov-Mar) Around 300m north of the train station.

SIGHTS & ACTIVITIES

The fabled **Pont St-Bénezet** (St Bénezet's Bridge; ☎ 04 90 27 51 16; adult/student 8-18yr/under 8yr €4.50/3.50/free; 🕑 9am-9pm Aug, 9am-8pm Jul & early–mid-Sep, 9am-7pm Apr-Jun & mid-Sep–Oct, 9.30am-5.45pm Nov-Mar), immortalised in the nursery rhyme *Sur le Pont d'Avignon,* was completed in 1185. The 900m-long wooden structure was repaired and rebuilt several times before all but four of its 22 spans were washed away in the mid-1600s.

THE SOUTH OF FRANCE

AVIGNON

AVIGNON

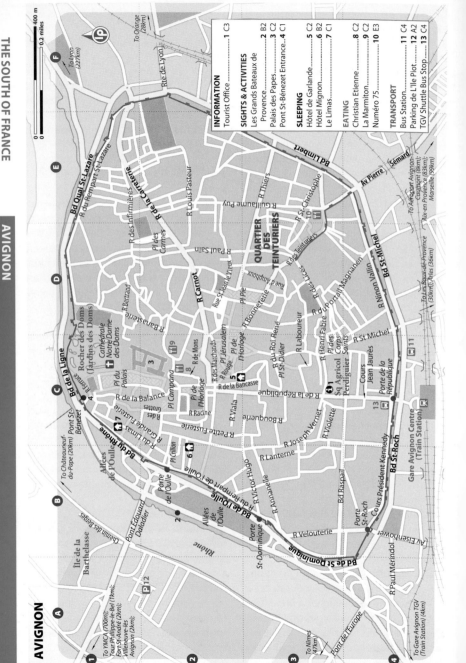

To Orange (28km)

To Lyon (227km)

Rte de Lyon

Bd Limbert

Av Pierre Sémard

Bd Quai St-Lazare

R du Rempart St-Lazare

R des Infirmières

R de la Carreterie

R Louis Pasteur

R Thiers

R St-Christophe

R Guillaume Puy

R des Teinturiers

Pl des Carmes

R Paul Sain

QUARTIER DES TEINTURIERS

R Bertrand

R Banasterie

Rue St-Baile Vieux

R Pipe

Rue d'Amphoux

R Bonneterie

R des Lices

R du Portail Magnanen

Bd St-Michel

R Ninon Vallin

Rocher des Doms (Jardins des Doms)

Cathédrale Notre-Dame des Doms

R Carnot

Pl Pie

R du Roi René

R St-Didier

R Laboureur

R St Michel

Bd de la Ligne

Pont St-Bénezet

Pl du Palais

R Ferruce

R Rouge

Pl de l'Horloge

R des Marchands

R P Jérusalem

R de Mons

R de la Bancasse

Pl de l'Horloge

R de la République

Sq Agricol Perdiguier

Cours Jean Jaurès

Porte de la République

Bd du Rhône

R de la Balance

R des Grottes

R Grande Fusterie

R Radne

R Viala

R Bouquerie

R Violette

R Joseph Vernet

R Lanterne

Cours Président Kennedy

Bd St-Roch

Gare Avignon Centre (Train Station)

Pl Crillon

Pl de l'Horloge

Pl Compana

Pl St-Didier

To Châteauneuf-du-Pape (20km); Pont St-Bénezet

Allées de l'Oulle

Porte de l'Oulle

Pont Édouard Daladier

R du Rempart de l'Oulle

R Victor Hugo

R Annanelle

R Velouterie

Porte St-Dominique

Bd de St Dominique

Porte St-Roch

Île de la Barthelasse

Chemin des Berges

Rhône

To YMCA (700m); Tour Phillippe-le-Bel (1km); Fort St-André (2km); Villeneuve-lès Avignon (2km)

To Nîmes (47km)

Pont de l'Europe

To Gare Avignon TGV (Train Station) (4km)

R Paul Mérindol

Av Eisenhower

To Les Baux-de-Provence (30km); Arles (36km)

To Aéroport Avignon-Caumont (8km); Aix-en-Provence (83km); Marseille (99km)

P12

P

400 m
0.2 miles

A   B   C   D   E   F
1   2   3   4

Flanked by the sprawling courtyard cours d'Honneur, the cavernous stone halls and extensive grounds of the **Palais des Papes** (Palace of the Popes; ☎ 04 90 27 50 00; place du Palais; adult/Avignon Passion pass, student & 12-18yr/under 12yr €6/3/free; ☷ 9am-9pm Aug, 9am-8pm Jul & early–mid-Sep, 9am-7pm Apr-Jun & mid-Sep–Oct, 9.30am-5.45pm Nov-Mar) testify to the fortune amassed by the papacy during the 'Babylonian Captivity'. Built during the 14th century and intended as a fortified palace for the pontifical court, it's the largest Gothic palace in Europe.

Les Grands Bateaux de Provence (☎ 04 90 85 62 25; www.mireio.net, in French; allées de l'Oulle) runs year-round excursions down the Rhône to Arles or the vineyard area of Châteauneuf-du-Pape on two restaurant boats (adult/Avignon Passion pass €46.50/41.85, including a meal).

FESTIVALS & EVENTS
Festival d'Avignon (www.festival-avignon .com) Hundreds of artists take to the stage and streets during this world-famous festival, founded in 1946 and held every year from early July to early August.
Festival Off (☎ 04 90 85 13 08; www.avignon leoff.com, in French) Paralleling the official Avignon festival, fringe event.

SLEEPING
Hôtel Mignon (☎ 04 90 82 17 30; www.hotel -mignon.com; 12 rue Joseph Vernet; s €42-62, d €59-72; ☒ ☐) Cute and comfy, this 16-room place within the walled city is a favourite for its small rooms in pretty shades, friendly, helpful staff, wi-fi, and a decent breakfast of croissants and rolls (€5).

Hôtel de Garlande (☎ 04 90 80 08 85; www. hotelgarlande.com; 20 rue Galante; d €75-115; ☒ ☒) Centrally located, Hôtel de Garlande is a sweet, familial little 12-room place housed in a historic *hôtel particulier* (private mansion) overlooking a narrow street.

ourpick Le Limas (☎ 04 90 14 67 19; www. le-limas-avignon.com; 51 rue du Limas; d incl breakfast €100-160, tr incl breakfast €150-180; ☒ ☐) Behind its discreet lavender door, this chic B&B, in an 18th-century town house, is like something out of *Vogue Living*.

EATING
Place de l'Horloge is a riot of cafés. They're popular with tourists, but the food is nothing to write home about.

Numéro 75 (☎ 04 90 27 16 00; 75 rue Guillaume Puy; mains from €10; ☷ lunch & dinner Mon-Sat) Whether in the lush garden or inside the stunning dining room of absinthe inventor Jules Pernod's former *hôtel particulier*, the food at Numéro 75 is everything you'd want Mediterranean

Palais des Papes, Avignon

JOHN ELK III

DONALD C. & PRISCILLA ALEXANDER EASTMAN

Théâtre Antique, Orange

⇘ THÉÂTRE ANTIQUE

Orange's **Roman theatre** is by far the most impressive Roman sight in France. Its sheer size and age are awe-inspiring: designed to seat 10,000 spectators, it's thought to have been built during Augustus Caesar's rule (27 BC–AD 14). The 103m-wide, 37m-high stage wall is one of only three in the world still standing in its entirety – the other two are in Syria and Turkey – minus a few mosaics and the roof (its replacement is a modern addition). Admission includes a seven-language audioguide.

The theatre still regularly stages theatrical and musical performances (see p272). Do catch a performance, if you can; balmy summer nights in this millennia-old venue are truly magical.

Follow montée Philbert de Chalons or montée Lambert to the top of **Colline St-Eutrope** (St Eutrope Hill; elevation 97m) for a bird's-eye view of the theatre, and for phenomenal views of the Mont Ventoux and the Dentelles de Montmirail.

Things you need to know: ☎ 04 90 51 17 60; adult/student €7.70/5.90; ☷ 9am-7pm Jun-Aug, 9am-6pm Apr, May & Sep, 9.30am-5.30pm Mar & Oct, 9.30am-4.30pm Nov-Feb

cuisine to be: super-fresh, packed with flavours, and ever so cheap.

Christian Etienne (☎ 04 90 86 16 50; 10 rue de Mons; mains €28-45; ☷ lunch & dinner Tue-Sat Aug-Jun, lunch & dinner Jul) This is Avignon's top table. The restaurant's elevated dining room and leafy outdoor terrace are found in a 12th-century palace near the Palais des Papes. The refined

Provençal cuisine (including an amazing and highly unusual starter-to-dessert tomato menu) is prepared by its eponymous master chef.

Le Marmiton (☎ 04 90 14 20 20; www.la -mirande.fr; 4 place de l'Amirande; lunch/dinner menus €38/49, table d'hôte €92; ☷ restaurant lunch & dinner Thu-Mon, table d'hôte dinner Tue-Sat) Dine in one of France's famous gastronomic restaurants. Even better, try your hand in the exquisite 19th-century kitchen – Le Marmiton puts on a roll-call of visiting chefs who run phenomenal cooking courses year-round.

GETTING THERE & AWAY

Gare Avignon TGV is 4km southwest. From central **Gare Avignon Centre** (42 bd St-Roch), local trains to/from Orange (€5.20, 20 minutes), Arles (€6.30, 20 minutes) and Nîmes (€8.10, 30 minutes) arrive and depart.

Some TGVs to/from Paris stop at Gare Avignon Centre, but TGVs to/from Marseille (€23.10, 35 minutes) and Nice (€51.80, three hours) only use Gare Avignon TGV.

AROUND AVIGNON
LES BAUX-DE-PROVENCE
pop 457

At the heart of the Alpilles and spectacularly perched above picture-perfect rolling hills of vineyards, olive groves and orchards is the intricate Provençal village of Les Baux-de-Provence, 30km south of Avignon.

Clawing precariously onto a 245m-high grey limestone *baou* (Provençal for rocky spur) is the rambling **Château des Baux** (☎ 04 90 54 55 56; adult/child €7.60/5.70; ⏲ 9am-8.30pm summer, 9.30am-6pm autumn, 9.30am-5pm winter, 9am-6.30pm spring).

Les Baux-de-Provence is one of the most visited villages in France – aim for early evening after the caterpillar of tourist coaches has crawled back downhill. The **tourist office** (☎ 04 90 54 34 39; www.les bauxdeprovence.com; ⏲ 9.30am-1pm & 2-5.30pm Mon-Fri, 10am-noon & 2-5pm Sat & Sun) can give visitors information on Les Baux' handful of accommodation options.

MONT VENTOUX

Visible from miles around, Mont Ventoux (1909m), nicknamed *le géant de Provence* (Provence's giant), stands like a sentinel over northern Provence. From its summit, accessible by road between May and October, vistas extend to the Alps and – on a clear day – as far as the Camargue. The relentless mistral wind blows 130 days a year, sometimes at a speed of 250km/h. The snow has generally all but melted by April, so the white glimmering stuff you can see in summer is not snow but *lauzes* – broken white stones covering the top.

FONTAINE DE VAUCLUSE
pop 650

Aptly named, Fontaine (meaning 'fountain') is Provence's main tap: all the rain that falls within 1200 sq km gushes out here as the River Sorgue. It is the world's fifth most powerful spring – and France's most powerful. It is most dazzling after heavy rain, but in drought times, the normally surging hole looks like something out of a Harry Potter book, with calm emerald water.

Most visitors come to see the spring, but this tiny village also has an eclectic collection of museums.

Tourist Office (☎ 04 90 20 32 22; www. oti-delasorgue.fr; chemin de la Fontaine; ⏲ 9.30am-12.30pm & 1.30-5.30pm)

Just off the main village square, **La Figuière** (☎ 04 90 20 37 41; www.la-figuiere. com; chemin de la Grangette; menus €20 & €28) has set up shop in a beautiful stone house. In summer, you can savour the Provençal dishes (rabbit, aïoli, sea bass etc) in the lovely front garden, or if you're staying in one of the three lovely *chambres d'hôtes*, wake up to the trickle of the fountain and a riot of cicadas.

Fontaine de Vaucluse is 21km southeast of Carpentras, 30km west of Apt, and 7km east of L'Isle-sur-Sorgue.

THE LUBERON

The Luberon's lush hills shot to fame following Peter Mayle's 1989 bestseller *A*

Year in Provence, a light-hearted account of how he renovated a crumbling old farmhouse in deep rural Provence (just outside the village of Ménerbes).

Provence fans come here for the area's rugged beauty, its relentless hills and cliffs, riot of purple, ochre, red and green, inhospitable forests and gastronomic treats.

The region's capital, Apt, is a good base from which to explore the area. The Luberon stretches from Cavaillon in the west to Manosque in the east, and from St-Saturnin-lès-Apt southwards to the River Durance. You'll undoubtedly come across many charming *chambres d'hôtes* and restaurants as you go: stumbling across them is what Provence is all about.

Le Luberon en Vélo (www.veloloisir luberon.com) network has signposted a 236km cycling itinerary with suggested stops in towns and villages across the park.

GORGES DU VERDON

Europe's largest canyon, the plunging Gorges du Verdon (also known as the Grand Canyon du Verdon) slices a 25km swath through Provence's limestone plateau.

The gorges begin at Rougon near the confluence of the Verdon and the Jabron Rivers, and wind westwards until the Verdon's green waters flow into Lac de Ste-Croix. A dizzying 250m to 700m deep, the gorges' floor is just 8m to 90m wide, with its overhanging rims 200m to 1500m apart.

WORTH A TRIP

You'll see beehive-shaped *bories* while you're buzzing around Provence, but the **Village des Bories** (☎ 04 90 72 03 48; adult/child €5.50/3; ☺ 9am-sunset) has some of the finest models.

Reminiscent of Ireland's *clochàn*, these one- or two-storey dry-walled huts constructed from slivers of limestone were first built in the area in the Bronze Age. Their original purpose isn't known (shelter would seem most likely), but over time they've also been used as workshops, wine cellars and storage sheds. This 'village' contains about 20, dating back to the 18th century. You'll find the village 4km southwest of **Gordes** (population 2100), just off the D2. Gordes' **tourist office** (☎ 04 90 72 02 75; www.gordes-village.com; place du Château; ☺ 9am-noon & 2-6pm Mon-Sat, 10am-noon & 2-6pm Sun) has information.

About 5km north of Gordes is the stunning **Abbaye de Sénanque** (☎ 04 90 72 02 05; www.senanque.fr, in French; adult/student/under 18yr €7/5/3). Fronted by a huge lavender field at the bottom of an isolated valley, it features on every postcard rack in Provence – but seeing it with your own eyes is a different thing altogether.

For another Provençal colour to add to your palette, head to ochre-rich **Roussillon** (population 1200), between the Vaucluse plateau and the Luberon Range. Two millennia ago the Romans used this distinctive earth to produce pottery glazes. These days the whole village, even the cemetery's gravestones, is built of the reddish stone.

From Roussillon, take a 45-minute walk along the fiery-coloured **Sentier des Ocres** (Ochre Trail; admission €2.50; ☺ 9am-5pm Mar-11 Nov). The trail leads you through nature's powdery sunset-coloured palette of ochre formations that were created over centuries by erosion and winds. Don't wear white!

The two main jumping-off points for exploring the gorges are the villages of Castellane (population 1592) and the magical Moustiers Ste-Marie (population 705), which has a centuries-old gold star on a 227m-long chain strung between its cliffs.

INFORMATION

Castellane Tourist Office (☎ 04 92 83 61 14; www.castellane.org; rue Nationale; ☉ 9am-1pm & 2-7pm Jul & Aug, 9.15am-noon & 2-6pm Mon-Fri Sep-Jun)

Moustiers Ste-Marie Tourist Office (☎ 04 92 74 67 84; www.moustiers.fr; ☉ daily, hours vary monthly) This tip-top tourist office has resourceful staff and excellent documentation for exploring the area.

SIGHTS & ACTIVITIES

The gorges' depths are only accessible by foot or raft. Motorists and cyclists can take in staggering panoramas from two vertigo-inducing cliff-side roads.

The D952 corkscrews along the northern rim, past **Point Sublime**, which offers a fisheye-lens view of serrated rock formations falling away to the river below. The best view from the northern side is from **Belvédère de l'Escalès**, along rte de Crêtes (D23). Drive to the third bend and steel your nerves for the stunning drop-off into the gorge.

Also heart-palpitating, **La Corniche Sublime** (the D19 to the D71) twists along the southern rim, taking in landmarks such as the **Balcons de la Mescla** (Mescla Terraces) and **Pont de l'Artuby** (Artuby Bridge), the highest bridge in Europe.

OUTDOOR SPORTS

Castellane's and Moustiers' tourist offices have lists of companies offering rafting, canyoning, horse-riding, mountaineering, biking and more. Activities are unsuitable for children under the age of eight.

BILL BACHMANN
Verdon River, Castellane

Aboard Rafting (☎ /fax 04 92 83 76 11; www.aboard-rafting.com; place de l'Eglise, Castellane; ☉ Apr-Sep) runs white-water rafting (€33 to €75) as well as canyoning trips (€33 to €65).

The newest thrill-seeking pursuit is 'floating' (€50/90 per half-/full day) – it's like white-water rafting minus the raft, with a buoyancy bag strapped to your back. Contact **Guides Aventure** (www.guidesaventure.com) for details.

SLEEPING & EATING

La Ferme Rose (☎ 04 92 74 69 47; www.lafermerose.com; chemin de Quinson; d €78-148, 🍽) This fabulous converted farmhouse contains wonderfully quirky collections including antique toys, a Wurlitzer jukebox with 45rpm records, a display case of coffee grinders, and old telephones, telex machines, theatre lighting, projectors and a puppet theatre. Its dozen boutique rooms with their Provençal-colonial styles all have spectacular bathrooms. It's off the D952, 1km from Moustiers.

La Bastide de Moustiers (☎ 04 92 70 47 47; www.bastide-moustiers.com; d €160/335; ❌ ᵭ) This Provençal nest belonging to legendary chef Alain Ducasse is known up and down the country for its very fine cuisine (menus €42-57) – hence the helicopter pad in the garden. Rooms are equally sophisticated and breakfast is served on a terrace shaded by an old plane tree.

THE FRENCH RIVIERA

The Côte d'Azur (Azure Coast), with its glistening seas, idyllic beaches and lush hills, is a gift from the heavens. Greeks and Ligurians were quick to spot this. Queens, tsars and assorted crowns followed a few centuries later, coming for mild winters and hedonistic lifestyles on what became known as the French Riviera. The monarchs gone, celebrated artists and writers (Matisse, Chagall, Picasso, F Scott Fitzgerald, Cocteau) took over. These days the Riviera is the destination de rigueur for the celebrity set.

NICE

pop 346,900

The light here is magical. The city also offers an exceptional quality of life: shimmering Mediterranean shores, the very best of Mediterranean food, a rich historical heritage and Alpine wilderness within an hour's drive.

Thanks to its busy international airport, Nice has a very cosmopolitan and diverse crowd. Bars reverberate with a Babylonian hubbub of merry punters, the seafront is lined with strollers, in-line skaters, beach-goers, and businesspeople working on their laptop by the Promenade. Fortunately, Nice has way too much attitude to become such a polished product, and that's just fine by us: we like a good bit of French attitude.

RUSSELL MOUNTFORD

Quai des États-Unis, Nice

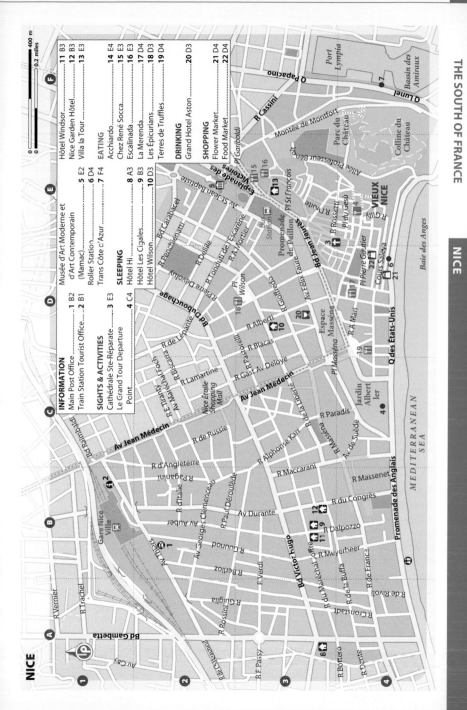

INFORMATION

Nice Tourism (www.nicetourisme.com) The tourist office's website.

Main Tourist Office (☎ 08 92 70 74 07; 5 promenade des Anglais; ☺ 8am-8pm Mon-Sat, 9am-7pm Sun Jun-Sep, 9am-6pm Mon-Sat Oct-May)

Train Station Tourist Office (☎ 08 92 35 35 35; av Thiers; ☺ 8am-8pm Mon-Sat, 9am-7pm Sun Jun-Sep, 8am-7pm Mon-Sat, 10am-5pm Sun Oct-May)

SIGHTS

There is something really unique about **Vieux Nice's** tangle of alleyways and backstreets packed with shops and holes in the wall, all claiming to sell *spécialités Niçoises* more genuine than their neighbours'. Jutting above the rooflines are the spires of baroque **Cathédrale Ste-Réparate** (place Rossetti). Perpendicular to rue Rossetti is the notorious **Rue Benoît Bunico**, Nice's old Jewish ghetto, where a 1430 law ordered Jews to be locked in by gates at each end of the street from sunset to dawn.

From **Parc du Château** the glittering views of Vieux Nice spires and the Baie des Anges are mesmerising. To reach the park you can walk up montée Lesage or climb the steps at the eastern end of rue Rossetti, or take the **ascenseur** (lift; per person €1; ☺ 9am-8pm Jun-Aug, 9am-7pm Apr, May & Sep, 10am-6pm Oct-Mar) under Tour Bellanda.

Mamac (Museum of Modern & Contemporary Art; ☎ 04 97 13 42 01; www.mamac-nice.org; Promenade des Arts; admission free; ☺ 10am-6pm Tue-Sun) is worth a visit for its stunning architecture alone, but it also houses some fantastic avant-garde art from the 1960s to the present.

Heading northeast from the Chagall museum (about 2.5km from the city centre) brings you to the **Musée Matisse** (☎ 04 93 81 08 08; www.musee-matisse-nice .org; 164 av des Arènes de Cimiez; admission free;

☺ 10am-6pm Wed-Mon), housed in a 17th-century Genoese mansion.

ACTIVITIES

Established by English expats in 1822, wide, palm-lined **promenade des Anglais** (English promenade) is a timelessly elegant place for a beachfront stroll. Smooth and flat, the promenade des Anglais provides 7km of perfect skating ground between the port and the airport. **Roller Station** (☎ 04 93 62 99 05; 49 quai des États-Unis) rents out skates and kneepads for €8 a day and bikes for €15 a day.

You'll need at least a beach mat to cushion your tush from Nice's **beaches**, which are made up of round pebbles. Free sections of beach alternate with 15 sunlounge-lined **plages concédées** (private beaches; ☺ late Apr or early May-15 Sep).

TOURS

With headphone commentary in several languages, the open-topped **Le Grand Tour** (☎ 04 92 29 17 00; adult/student/child €20/18/10) buses give you a good overview of Nice.

Trans Côte d'Azur (☎ 04 92 00 42 30; www .trans-cote-azur.com; quai Lunel; ☺ Apr-Oct) runs scenic one-hour coastal cruises as well as day trips to the Îles de Lérins, St-Tropez (adult/child €52/39) and Monaco (adult/child €29/21).

To tour the coast in style, take a DIY day trip in a classic convertible. **Le Road-Show** (☎ 04 92 04 01 05; www.azur-roadshow .com, in French) offers packages for two people including car rental, lunch at a gourmet restaurant en route, and a detailed driving itinerary plus fuel and insurance for €390.

FESTIVALS & EVENTS

Carnaval de Nice (www.nicecarnaval.com) This two-week carnival, held in Febru-

Cannes (p276)

RICHARD I'ANSON

ary, is particularly famous for its battles of the flowers, where thousands of blooms are tossed into the crowds from passing floats.

Nice Jazz Festival (www.nicejazzfestival. fr) In July Nice swings to the week-long jazz festival held at the Arènes de Cimiez, amid the Roman ruins.

SLEEPING

our pick **Hôtel Wilson** (☎ 04 93 85 47 79; www .hotel-wilson-nice.com; 39 rue de l'Hôtel des Postes; s €29-50, d €34-65) Many years of travelling, an experimental nature and exquisite taste have turned Jean-Marie's rambling flat into a compelling place to stay. The 16 rooms have individual, carefully crafted decor, and share the eclectic dining room where photo albums, African statues and paintings offered by previous guests decorate the walls.

Villa la Tour (☎ 04 93 80 08 15; www.villa-la -tour.com; 4 rue de la Tour; s €45-129, d €48-139; ⬚) Small but perfectly formed, the Villa la Tour is delightful, with warm, romantic Provençal rooms, a location at the heart of the Vieux Nice, and a diminutive, flower-decked

roof-terrace with views of the Colline du Château and surrounding roofs.

Nice Garden Hôtel (☎ 04 93 87 35 63; www.nicegardenhotel.com; 11 rue du Congrès; d €60-98; ⬚ ⬚) Behind heavy iron gates hides this little gem of a hotel has nine beautifully appointed rooms overlooking an equally exquisite garden with a glorious orange tree.

Hôtel Les Cigales (☎ 04 97 03 10 70; www .hotel-lescigales.com; 16 rue Dalpozzo; s €75-160, d €79-160, ⬚) The Cicadas' brightly coloured rooms may be spacious and well located, but the hotel's real asset is its roof terrace: think chilled rosé wine on long summer evenings or lazy breakfasts in the morning sun.

Hôtel Windsor (☎ 04 93 88 59 35; www .hotelwindsornice.com; 11 rue Dalpozzo; d €90-175; ⬚ ⬚ ⬚) This original boutique hotel has let rip artists' imaginations – be it with the graffiti mural by the pool; the weird and wonderful artists' rooms customised from bathroom to bedspread; or the luxurious garden with its unconventional exotic plants.

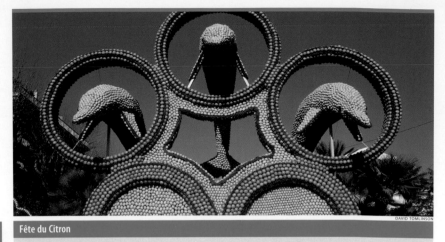

DAVID TOMLINSON

Fête du Citron

↘ IF YOU LIKE...

If you've a penchant for the fun-packed frolics of **Carnival de Nice** (p270) and **Festival d'Avignon** (p263), you'll have a ball at these festivals:

- **Fête du Citron** (www.feteducitron.com; Menton) Since the 1930s lemon cultivation in the exceptionally warm seaside town of Menton near the Italian border has been celebrated each February with this lemon extravaganza. Kitsch lemon-adorned floats weave processions along the seafront, and gargantuan wire-framed sculptures bearing zillions of lemons speckle the town.
- **Courses Camarguaises** (www.arenes-arles.com; Arles) Camargue bullfights (*courses Camarguaises*) do not end with a dead bull. Rather, amateur *razeteurs* remove rosettes and ribbons tied to the bull's horns using a hooked comb clasped between their fingers. Arles' bullfighting season begins at Easter with the **Féria Pascale** and charges through to September's rice harvest festival.
- **Les Chorégies d'Orange** (www.choregies.asso.fr; Orange) Balmy summer nights in July and August usher in a series of magical operas, classical concerts and choral performances to Orange's exceptional Roman amphitheatre. Reserve festival tickets months ahead.
- **Féria de Pentecôte** (www.arenesdenimes.com; Nîmes) Roman Nîmes becomes more Spanish than French during this five-day Whitsuntide *féria* (bullfighting festival) in June; the three-day **Féria des Vendanges** celebrates the grape harvest the third weekend in September. Each is marked by daily (bloody) *corridas* (bullfights).

Hôtel Hi (☎ 04 97 07 26 26; www.hi-hotel .net; 3 av des Fleurs; s from €195, d €210-395; ⊠ ▯ ⊠) Think of what the most techno-funk, whacky, futuristic designer place would look like in your wildest dreams. Now quadruple that, and you have Hôtel Hi. Oh, and you can also ask for a goldfish in your room, if you are feeling a liitle lonely.

EATING

Niçois nibbles include *socca, salade Niçoise,* ratatouille and *farcis* (stuffed vegetables, each with a unique filling).

Chez René Socca (☎ 04 93 92 05 73; 2 rue Miralhéti; dishes from €2; ❧ 9am-9pm Tue-Sun, to 10.30pm Jul & Aug, closed Nov) Forget about presentation and manners. Grab a portion of *socca* or a plate of *petits farçis* and head across the street to the bar for a *grand pointu* (glass) of red, white or rosé.

La Merenda (4 rue Raoul Bosio; starters from €9, mains €12-15; ❧ lunch & dinner Mon-Fri) You'd think that being closed at weekends, and not having a phone number or a credit card machine would be a recipe for disaster, but La Merenda is doing just fine. In fact, you'll have to be pretty determined to bag one of the house's 26 seats (queuing is what it comes down to) and feast on the unusual fare scribbled on a blackboard.

Escalinada (☎ 04 93 62 11 71; 22 rue Pairolière; mains €12-20; ❧ lunch & dinner) Lunch under a stripy awning or dine on the candle-lit terrace with a decent bottle of wine and good, unpretentious local fare such as *daube,* delicious homemade gnocchi, or, if you're game, the house speciality – *testicules de mouton panés* (sheep's testicles in batter).

Acchiardo (☎ 04 93 85 51 16; 38 rue Droite; mains €14-20; ❧ lunch & dinner Mon-Fri) Going strong since 1927, locals flock to Acchiardo for the *plat du jour* (daily special), a glass of wine and a load of gossip served straight up on the counter.

Les Épicuriens (☎ 04 93 80 85 00; 6 place Wilson; mains €18-45.50; ❧ lunch & dinner Mon-Fri, dinner Sat) Famous for its *cocottes* (casseroles cooked in cast-iron dishes), it also excels in pretty much everything else – from the *pâté de foie gras* (duck or goose liver pâté) served with grape compote to *brandade de cabillaud* (cod

that is cooked in the oven with crème fraîche, olive oil, garlic, lemon juice and herbs), and whatever daily special takes the chef's fancy.

Terres de Truffes (☎ 04 93 62 07 68; 11 rue St-François de Paule; mains €30; ❧ lunch & dinner Tue-Sat) At this small, exquisite place, the head chef Arnaud Leclercq uses Provençal truffles to create seasonal sensations ranging from pastry-wrapped pigeon stuffed with *foie gras* and truffles to brie layered with truffles, to caramel of truffles.

DRINKING

Vieux Nice's streets runneth over with local bars and cafés: from a morning espresso to a lunchtime pastis (aniseed-flavoured aperitif, the tipple of choice in the south of France), a chilled evening beer or a midnight cocktail, the choice is yours.

If you're above those sorts of shenanigans, head for the rarefied rooftop bar at the **Grand Hotel Aston** (☎ 04 92 17 53 00; 12 av Félix Faure; ❧ 8am-11pm, closed Sun & Mon in winter), which has Champagne views over Nice and the Med.

SHOPPING

Cours Saleya is split between its famous **flower market** (❧ 6am-5.30pm Tue-Sat, to 1.30pm Sun) selling bucketfuls of blooms in the western half, and a magnificent **food market** (❧ 6am-1.30pm Tue-Sun) at the eastern end, with long trestle tables displaying exotic spices, shiny fruit and veg, pastries, *fruits glacés* (glazed or candied fruits such as figs, ginger, tangerine and pears) and more.

GETTING THERE & AWAY

Nice's international airport, **Aéroport International Nice-Côte d'Azur** (☎ 08 20 42 33 33; www.nice.aeroport.fr), is about 6km west of the city centre.

Antibes

IZZET KERIBAR

ANTIBES
pop 75,000

Antibes is a concentrate of Mediterranean history. The town's sea walls bear witness to a defensive past (neighbouring Nice had switched allegiance to rival Savoy). Picasso painted in the Château Grimaldi and F Scott Fitzgerald wrote his seminal novel *Tender is the Night* based on life in Antibes.

Its marina is the second biggest in Europe.

INFORMATION
Antibes Tourist Office (☎ 04 92 90 53 00; www.antibesjuanlespins.com; 11 place de Gaulle, Antibes; ☼ 9am-7pm Jul & Aug, 9am-12.30pm & 1.30-6pm Mon-Fri, 9am-noon & 2-6pm Sat Sep-Jun)

SIGHTS & ACTIVITIES
Picasso used the 12th-century Château Grimaldi as a studio in 1946. It's now home to the **Musée Picasso** (☎ 04 92 90 54 28; Château Grimaldi, Antibes; adult/concession/under 18yr €6/3/free; ☼ 10am-noon & 2-6pm Tue-Sun mid-Sep–mid-Jun, 10am-6pm Tue-Sun mid-Jun–mid-Sep).

Antibes' small, sandy beach, **Plage de la Gravette**, gets packed; you'll find the best beaches in **Juan-les-Pins**.

Cap d'Antibes' 4.8km of wooded shores are the perfect setting for a walk-swim-walk-swim afternoon.

SLEEPING & EATING
Hôtel La Jabotte (☎ 04 93 61 45 89; www.jabotte.com; 13 av Max Maurey, Cap d'Antibes; d incl breakfast from €81) A hotel with a *chambre d'hôte* (B&B) feel, La Jabotte is Antibes' hidden gem. A mere 50m from the beautiful Plage de la Salis, its 10 Provençal rooms all look out onto an exquisite patio where breakfast is served.

Auberge Provençale (☎ 04 93 34 13 24; www.aubergeprovencale.com; 61 place Nationale, Antibes; d €120-200) Famed for its fabulous Provençal cuisine – seafood in particular –

Gare Nice Ville (av Thiers) is 1.2km north of the beach. There are fast and frequent services to coastal towns including Antibes (€3.80, 30 minutes), Cannes (€5.70, 30 to 40 minutes), Menton (€4.30, 35 minutes), Monaco (€3.20, 20 minutes). Direct TGV trains link Nice with Paris' Gare de Lyon (€110, 5½ hours).

GETTING AROUND
Ligne d'Azur runs two airport bus services (€4). Route 99 shuttles approximately every half-hour direct between Gare Nice Ville and both airport terminals. Route 98 takes the slow route and departs from the bus station every 20 minutes.

A taxi from the airport to the centre of Nice will cost €25 to €30.

this *auberge* (inn) also features six grand, antique-filled romantic rooms.

Hôtel Belles Rives (☎ 04 93 61 02 79; www .bellesrives.com; 33 bd Edouard Baudoin, Juan-les-Pins; d €255-740; ⚡) In the mid-1920s, F Scott and Zelda Fitzgerald rented this villa. Since the early 1930s it's housed this classic Riviera establishment with its private beach and pier, top-notch restaurants and jazz bar.

Marché Provençal (cours Masséna, Antibes; ⚡ mornings daily Jun-Aug, Tue-Sun Sep-May) Antibes' heady Provençal marketplace is perfect for picking up picnic supplies.

ENTERTAINMENT

La Siesta-Le Pearl (☎ 04 93 33 31 31; rte du Bord de Mer, Antibes; cover €15-20; ⚡ 11pm-5am) This establishment is famous up and down the coast for its beachside nightclub (Le Pearl) and all-night dancing under the stars. Open from early June to mid-September only, you can still party at the indoor bar-lounge (Le Flamingo) during the rest of the year.

GETTING THERE & AWAY

Antibes is an easy day trip by train from Nice (€3.80, 30 minutes) or Cannes (€2.40, 15 minutes).

ST-PAUL DE VENCE & AROUND

pop 3300

St-Paul de Vence's cobblestone streets and 16th-century fortifications draw 2.5 million visitors a year. But what's distinguished the medieval hilltop village of St-Paul de Vence from every other medieval hilltop village around is its phenomenal art legacy.

Browsing the gallery-lined village streets is a fine entrée for art lovers, but the main course is the **Fondation Maeght** (☎ 04 93 32 81 63; adult/student €11/9; ⚡ 10am-7pm Jul-Sep, 10am-6pm Oct-Jun), outside the old village. Its extraordinary permanent collection of 40,000 works is exhibited on a rotating basis.

Matisse's stunning Chapelle du Rosaire and his former home Villa Le Rêve (see below) are 4.8km north of St-Paul de Vence on rte de St-Jeannet (the D2210).

SLEEPING & EATING

Chez Andréas (☎ 04 93 32 54 50; Rempart Ouest; tapas €5, mains €10; ⚡ noon-midnight) Perched on the ramparts, this popular bar teems with locals who come to feast on chilled beer, tasty tapas and panoramic views.

MAGICAL MATISSE TOUR

During WWII, Matisse rented **Villa Le Rêve** in Vence, where he was visited by Picasso and Aragon, among others. To unleash your own creative streak, you can take a **painting course** (☎ 04 93 58 82 68, www.mclean.dk; ⚡ Mar-Nov) at the villa, with seven nights' accommodation, from around €650. While living here, Matisse's friendship with his former model-turned Dominican Sister Jacques-Marie inspired him to design his masterwork, the nearby **Chapelle du Rosaire** (Rosary Chapel; ☎ 04 93 58 03 26; www.vence.fr/the-rosaire-chapel.html; 466 av Henri Matisse, Vence; admission €3; ⚡ 2-5.30pm Mon, Wed & Sat, 10-11.30am & 2-5.30pm Tue & Thu, closed mid-Nov–mid-Dec), completed in 1951. Mid-morning is the prime time to see sunlight streaming through the vast stained-glass windows.

Matisse is buried at the **Monastère Notre Dame de Cimiez** (Cimiez Notre Dame Monastery; ☎ 04 93 81 00 04; ⚡ 8.30am-12.30pm & 2.30-6.30pm), near Nice's Musée Matisse; signs lead to his grave.

La Colombe d'Or (The Golden Dove; ☎ 04 93 32 80 02; www.la-colombe-dor.com, in French; lunch mains €20-60, dinner mains €60-70; ⏰ lunch & dinner) La Colombe d'Or was the party headquarters of many artists (Chagall, Braque, Matisse, Picasso etc) who often paid for their meals in kind, resulting in an incredible private art collection. Don't expect to get a table (or room; €280 to €350) unless you book weeks in advance.

GETTING THERE & AWAY

From Nice, the frequent bus 400 stops in St-Paul de Vence (€1, 55 minutes) and Vence (€1, one hour).

CANNES

pop 70,400

Most people have heard of Cannes and its eponymous film festival. The latter only lasts for two weeks in May, but the buzz and glitz are there year round, mostly thanks to regular visits from celebrities enjoying the creature comforts of bd de la Croisette's palaces.

INFORMATION

Tourist Office (☎ 04 92 99 84 22; www .cannes.travel; bd de la Croisette; ⏰ 9am-8pm Jul & Aug, 9am-7pm Mon-Sat Sep-Jun) On the ground floor of the Palais des Festivals.

SIGHTS & ACTIVITIES

Perched at the top of the Suquet old town, you could spend as long studying the beautifully presented ethnographic collections of the **Musée de la Castre** (☎ 04 93 38 55 26; place de la Castre, Le Suquet; adult/concession/student & under 18yr €3.20/2/free; ⏰ 10am-7pm Jul & Aug, 10am-1pm & 2-6pm Tue-Sun Apr-Jun & Sep, 10am-1pm & 2-5pm Tue-Sun Oct-Mar) as you would admiring the view of the Baie de Cannes from the museum's grounds.

The central, sandy **beaches** along bd de la Croisette are sectioned off for hotel patrons. A microscopic strip of sand near the Palais des Festivals is free, but you'll find better free sand on **Plages du Midi** and **Plages de la Bocca**, west from the Vieux Port along bd Jean Hibert and bd du Midi.

ÎLES DE LÉRINS

Although just 20 minutes away by boat, the tranquil Îles de Lérins feel far from the madding crowd.

The closest of these two tiny islands is the 3.25km-by-1km **Île Ste-Marguerite**, where the mysterious Man in the Iron Mask was incarcerated during the late 17th century. Its shores are an endless succession of perfect castaway beaches and fishing spots, eucalyptus and pine forest.

Smaller still, **Île St-Honorat** has been a monastery since the 5th century. Its Cistercian monks welcome visitors all year round.

Boats for the islands leave Cannes from quai des Îles (along from quai Max Laubeuf) located on the western side of the harbour.

TOURS

In summer, **Trans Côte d'Azur** (☎ 04 92 98 71 30; www.trans-cote-azur.com; quai Max Laubeuf) runs day trips to St-Tropez, Monaco and the stunning red cliffs of the Massif de l'Estérel.

SLEEPING

Le Chanteclair (☎ /fax 04 93 39 68 88; 12 rue Forville; d from €48; ⏰ closed mid-Nov–mid-Jan) Right in the heart of Le Suquet, this sweet, simple 15-room place has an enchanting courtyard garden, and is handy for the harbourside restaurants.

Hôtel Splendid (☎ 04 97 06 22 22; www .splendid-hotel-cannes.com; 4-6 rue Félix Faure; s/d from €115/128; ⏰) This elaborate 1871 building has beautifully decorated rooms,

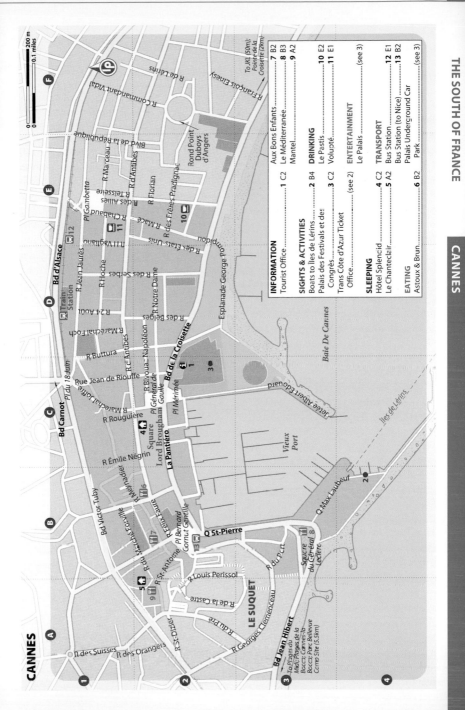

CANNES

INFORMATION

Tourist Office **1** C2

SIGHTS & ACTIVITIES

Boats to Îles de Lérins **2** B4
Palais des Festivals et des
  Congrès **3** C2
Trans Côte d'Azur Ticket
  Office .... (see 2)

SLEEPING

Hôtel Splendid **4** C2
Le Chanteclair **5** A2

EATING

Astoux & Brun **6** B2

Aux Bons Enfants **7** B2
Le Méditerranée **8** B3
Mantel **9** A2

DRINKING

Le Pastis **10** E2
Volupté **11** E1

ENTERTAINMENT

Le Palais .... (see 3)

TRANSPORT

Bus Station **12** E1
Bus Station (to Nice) **13** B2
Palais Underground Car
  Park .... (see 3)

great location, stunning views: 15 of the 62 rooms are equipped with kitchenettes.

In a stratosphere of their own, there are the amazing beachfront palaces garlanding bd de la Croisette

EATING

Aux Bons Enfants (80 rue Meynadier; menu €23; ☾ lunch & dinner Tue-Sat) This familial little place doesn't have a phone, and there are no plans to get one any time soon: it's always full. The lucky ones who get a table (get there early or late) can feast on regional dishes made from ingredients picked up at the adjacent market.

Le Pastis (☎ 04 92 98 95 40; 28 rue Commandant André; mains €25-30; ☾ 7.30am-11.30pm) With a name like this, it would be a crime if you didn't have an *apéritif* or two at this establishment. But you'd miss out if you stopped there – Le Pastis serves fabulous brasserie food (creamy risottos, tender steaks, delicious fish) in a setting of stone walls and vintage posters.

ourpick Mantel (☎ 04 93 39 13 10; 22 rue St-Antoine; lunch menus €25, dinner menus €36-58; ☾ lunch & dinner, closed Wed & lunch Tue & Thu) The Italian maître d' will make you feel like a million dollars and you'll melt at Noël Mantel's divine cuisine and great value prices.

Astoux & Brun (☎ 04 93 39 21 87; 27 rue Félix Faure; menus from €28; ☾ noon-1am) Seafood connoisseurs seldom need an introduction to this world-renowned place. And for those less familiar with bivalve mollusc consumption (read: shells), this is *the* place to try a fabulous seafood platter (oysters in particular).

Le Méditerranée (☎ 04 92 99 73 02; 2 bd Jean Hibert; lunch menu €42, dinner menus €52-72; ☾ lunch & dinner) On top of the port-side Sofitel hotel, adjoining the rooftop pool, it's hard to say which makes more of an impression – this contemporary French restaurant's cuisine or its 360-degree views across the Med to the red Massif de l'Estérel mountains.

DRINKING

The party bloc in town is located between rue Macé and the Grand Hôtel, just north of La Croisette.

Volupté (☎ 04 93 39 60 32; 32 rue Hoche; snacks €4.50, mains €13-15; ☾ 9am-8pm Mon-Sat) This is *the* place to be seen in town. With its 140 types of teas, all neatly stocked in red-and-white tins spanning an entire wall, this elegant tearoom draws an all-happening crowd of young and beautiful things.

To mingle with the rich and famous, Cannes' hotel palaces all have drop-dead-posh bars.

ENTERTAINMENT

Dress up or you won't get in, and warm up your credit card.

Le Palais (www.palais-club.com; Palais des Festivals, bd de la Croisette; ☾ midnight-dawn) Where else but in Cannes would you dance on 2000 sq metres of suspended gardens overlooking the sea? This ephemeral nightclub (it's open only for 50 nights each year, in July and August) has become the hottest ticket in DJ land, a combination of the most happening names in music and its spectacular setting at the heart of the Palais des Festivals.

GETTING THERE & AWAY

Destinations within easy train reach include Nice (€5.70, 30 to 40 minutes), Grasse (€3.60, 25 minutes) and Marseille (€24.80, two hours).

GRASSE

pop 49,100

Surrounded by fields of lavender, jasmine, centifolia roses, mimosa, orange blossom and violets, Grasse is one of France's leading perfume producers.

The **Tourist Office** (☎ 04 93 36 03 56; www
.grasse.fr; 22 cours Honoré Cresp; ☻ 9am-7pm Mon-
Sat, 9am-1pm & 2-6pm Sun Jul-Sep, 9am-12.30pm
& 2-6pm Mon-Sat Oct-Jun) is inside the Palais
de Congrès.

Fragonard (☎ 04 93 36 44 65; 20 bd
Fragonard; ☻ 9am-6pm Feb-Oct, 9am-12.30pm &
2-6pm Nov-Jan) is the easiest perfumery to
reach by foot; the tourist office provides
information about other perfumeries that
can be visited further afield.

For the ultimate field trip, the **Domaine
de Manon** (☎ 04 93 60 12 76; www.domaine
-manon.com; admission €6) runs tours of its rose
fields from mid-May to mid-June, and its
jasmine fields from July to late October.

MASSIF DE L'ESTÉREL

Punctuated by pine, oak and eucalyptus
trees, the rugged red mountain range
Massif de l'Estérel contrasts dramatically
with the brilliant blue sea.

Extending east from **St-Raphaël** to
Mandelieu-La Napoule (near Cannes), a
curling coastal road, the famous **corniche
de l'Estérel** (also known as the corniche
d'Or and the N98), passes through summer villages and inlets that are ideal for
swimming. More than 100 hiking trails
criss-cross the Massif de l'Estérel.

ST-TROPEZ

pop 5635

For centuries St-Tropez remained a peace-
ful little fishing village, attracting painters
like pointillist Paul Signac, but few tourists.
That changed dramatically in 1956 when
Et Dieu Créa la Femme (And God Created
Woman) was shot here starring Brigitte
Bardot, catapulting the village into the
international limelight.

INFORMATION
Tourist Office (☎ 04 94 97 45 21; www.
ot-saint-tropez.com; quai Jean Jaurès; ☻ 9.30am-

Massif de l'Estérel
IZZET KERIBAR

8pm Jul & Aug, 9.30am-12.30pm & 2-7pm Apr-Jun
& Sep–mid-Oct, 9.30am-12.30pm & 2-6pm mid-
Oct–Mar)

SIGHTS
Dramatically displayed in a chapel that
is disused, the **Musée de l'Annonciade**
(☎ 04 94 17 84 10; place Grammont, Vieux Port;
adult/student €5/3, exhibitions €6/4; ☻ 10am-
noon & 3-7pm Wed-Mon Jun Sep, 10am-noon &
2-6pm Wed-Mon Oct & Dec-May) displays an
impressive collection of art works by
Matisse, Bonnard, Dufy and especially
Signac, who set up his home and studio
in St-Tropez.

The panoramas of St-Tropez' bay that
you get from the elevated 17th-century
Citadelle de St-Tropez (☎ 04 94 97 59 43;
admission €2.50; ☻ 10am-6.30pm Apr-Sep, 10am-

JOHN ELK III

Vaison-la-Romaine

⤸ IF YOU LIKE...

If you love the hubbub of St-Tropez's aromatic place des Lices *marché* (p281), you'll be mad with an equal passion over these smaller market towns:

- **Carpentras** (tourist office ☎ 04 90 63 00 78; www.carpentras-ventoux.com) Each Friday morning rue d'Inguimbert, av Jean Jaurès and streets spilling off the latter overflow with 350-odd stalls laden with breads, honeys, cheeses, olives, nuts, fruit, nougat and a rainbow of *berlingots* (local striped, pillow-shaped hard-boiled sweets). Winter ushers in the pungent smell and hushed-tones transactions of Carpentras' Friday-morning truffle market on place Ariside Briand.

- **Narbonne** (tourist office ☎ 04 68 65 15 60; www.narbonne-tourisme.com) Once a coastal port but now 13km inland because of silting up, this Languedoc town was capital of Gallia Narbonensis and a principal Roman city in Gaul. Its imposing art-nouveau covered market, Les Halles, is an architectural jewel gem and a colourful place to stock up on fresh local produce.

- **Vaison-la-Romaine** (tourist office ☎ 04 90 36 02 11; www.vaison-la-romaine.com) Nestled in a valley at the crossroads of seven hills, this quintessential Provençal village split by the River l'Ouvèze has long been a traditional exchange place. The tradition endures at its magnificent Tuesday-morning market, which has become an attraction in its own right. Post-shop, pay homage to Vaison's trove of Roman vestiges; the tourist office has a map.

12.30pm & 1.30-5.30pm Oct-Mar) are definitely worth the climb.

ACTIVITIES

The glistening sandy beach **Plage de Tahiti**, 4km southeast of town, morphs into the 5km-long **Plage de Pampelonne**, which in summer incorporates a sequence of exclusive restaurant/clubs.

Marked by yellow blazes, a 35km **sentier du littoral** (coastal trail) starts from St-Tropez' sandy fishing cove to the east of the 15th-century Tour du Portalet, in the old fishing quarter La Ponche, and arcs around to Cavalaire-sur-Mer along a spectacular series of rocky outcrops and hidden bays. If you're short on time or energy, you can walk as far as Ramatuelle and return by bus.

SLEEPING

La Mistralée (☎ 04 98 12 91 12; www.hotel -mistralee.com; 1 av du Général Leclerc; d low season €190-390, high season €460-790; ❄ ☜) The flamboyant former home of hairdresser to the stars, Alexandre (famously *sans* surname), this totally over-the-top 1960s-decorated hotel includes, for example, fabric presented to Alexandre by the king of Morocco.

Pastis (☎ 04 98 12 56 50; www.pastis-st -tropez.com; 61 av du Général Leclerc; d low season €200-350, high season €350-600; ❄ ✕ ☜) This stunning hotel is the brainchild of an English couple besotted with Provence and passionate about modern art: you'll die for the pop-art-inspired interior and long for a swim in the emerald green pool and a snooze under the centenary palm trees.

EATING

Quai Jean Jaurès, on the old port, is littered with restaurants and cafés.

La Table du Marché (☎ 04 94 97 85 20; 38 rue Georges Clémenceau; mains €24-36; ❂ lunch & dinner) Chef Christophe Leroy's St-Tropez pad is a must, be it for scrumptious tea time *pâtisseries* (pastries and cakes) or heavenly cuisine come dinner time. Take a leaf of out Leroy's recipe book at one of his cooking lessons (5-person minimum, €100 per person).

La Nouvelle Bohème (☎ 04 94 95 12 63; 3 rue Charrons; menus €25; ❂ dinner Tue-Sun) With its corset-shaped fluffy cushions, candlelit atmosphere, low-beamed ceiling and

whitewashed walls, this irreverent, superfriendly restaurant serves the best seafood tagliatelle in town.

Auberge de l'Oumède (☎ 04 94 44 11 11; Chemin de l'Oumède, Ramatuelle; menu €75; ❂ dinner Apr-Oct, closed Mon Apr–mid-Jun, Sep & Oct) Epicureans come from far and wide to savour Jean-Pierre Frezia's divine Provençal cuisine in the idyllic setting of his hilltop *mas* (traditional Provençal stone building). Red mullet and spinach cannelloni, grilled catch of the day and sensational desserts, all accompanied by some *very* fine wines – dining at l'Oumède is a once in a lifetime treat.

CAFÉS

Sénéquier (☎ 04 94 97 00 90; cnr quai Jean Jaurès & place aux Herbes; dishes €5-12.50; ❂ 8am-2am Apr-Oct, 8am-7pm Nov-Mar) This quintessential St-Tropez quay-side café opened in 1887, and Sartre worked on *Les Chemins de la Liberté* (Roads to Freedom) here. Its fire-engine-red terrace is a prized drinking spot.

Le Café (☎ 04 94 97 44 69; place des Lices; mains €20, menu €30; ❂ lunch & dinner) If you've been itching to have a go at *pétanque,* Le Café will lend you a set of bowls to play out front while you sip a glass of rosé or an evening kir.

SELF-CATERING

The **place des Lices market** (❂ mornings Tue & Sat) is a big highlight of local life here; the **fish market** (❂ Tue-Sun, daily in summer) situated on place aux Herbes is joined by a fruit-and-veg market in summer.

A must-try is *tarte Tropézienne,* an orange-blossom-flavoured double-sponge cake filled with a thick cream. **La Tarte Tropézienne** (☎ 04 94 97 71 42; 36 rue Georges Clémenceau; ❂ 7am-7.30pm) turns them out

DAVID TOMLINSON

Île de Porquerolles

⤷ ÎLES D'HYÈRES

For some inexplicable reason, these islands (aka Îles d'Or – Golden Islands – for their shimmering mica rock) have remained mostly unknown to foreign crowds.

The easternmost and largest of this trio is the discreet **Île du Levant**, split into an odd combination of army land and nudist colony. **Île de Port-Cros**, the middle and smallest island, is the jewel in the islands' crown. France's only marine *parc national* (national park), it boasts exceptional marine fauna and flora, which makes it a **snorkelling** paradise. The island is also covered with 30km of marked trails through thick forest, ragged clifftops and deserted beaches.

The largest and westernmost island is **Île de Porquerolles**. There are plenty of walking trails, but the best way to get around is by cycling. There are several bicycle-rental places, as well as a few restaurants and hotels.

For more information check www.provence-azur.com.

Boats to the Îles d'Hyères leave from various towns along the coast. **Vedettes Îles d'Or** in Le Lavandou operates boats to all three islands (Porquerolles return adult/child €30.60/23.90, 40 minutes each way; Port-Cros and Île du Levant return adult/child €23.50/19.60, 35 and 60 minutes respectively). In summer, there are boats between Port-Cros and Porquerolles.

TLV-TVM has services from Hyères' two ports: La Tour Fondue, at the bottom of the Giens Peninsula, 10 minutes from Porquerolles (return adult/child €16/14), while Hyères' port at the top of the peninsula has services to Port-Cros (60 minutes, summer only) and Le Levant (adult/child return €23.50/20.50; 50 to 90 minutes).

Things you need to know: Île de Port-Cros (☎ 04 94 12 82 30; www.portcrosparcnational .fr, in French; 50 rue St Claire, Hyères); Île de Porquerolles (www.porquerolles.com); Vedettes Îles d'Or (☎ 04 94 71 01 02; www.vedettesilesdor.fr); TLV-TVM (☎ for Porquerolles 04 94 58 21 81, for Port-Cros & Levant 04 94 57 44 07; www.tlv-tvm.com)

along with freshly filled sandwiches on home-baked bread.

GETTING THERE & AWAY

Les Bateaux Verts (☎ 04 94 49 29 39; www .bateauxverts.com) operates a shuttle-boat service from St-Tropez to Ste-Maxime and Port Grimaud. Trans Côte d'Azur runs day trips from Nice and Cannes between Easter and September.

St-Tropez' **bus station** (av Général de Gaulle) is on the southwestern edge of town. Bus 111 serves Toulon-Hyères' airport (€20.90, one hour), April to October only.

THE CORNICHES

Some of the Côte d'Azur's most spectacular scenery stretches between Nice and Menton. A trio of corniches (coastal roads) hugs the cliffs, each higher up the hill than the last. The middle corniche ends in Monaco; the upper and lower continue to Menton.

CORNICHE INFÉRIEURE

Skimming the villa-lined waterfront, the Corniche Inférieure (also known as the Basse Corniche, the Lower Corniche or the N98) sticks pretty close to the train line, passing (west to east) through Villefranche-sur-Mer, St-Jean-Cap Ferrat, Beaulieu-sur-Mer, Èze-sur-Mer and Cap d'Ail.

VILLEFRANCHE-SUR-MER

pop 6650

This picturesque little pastel-coloured, terracotta-roof fishing port overlooking the Cap Ferrat peninsula was a favourite with Jean Cocteau, who painted the frescoes in the 17th-century Chapelle St-Pierre. Steps split the steep cobblestone streets that weave through the old town, including the oldest, rue Obscure, an eerie vaulted passageway built in

1295. Looking down on the township is the 16th-century citadel. Beyond the port is a sandy **beach** offering picture-perfect views of the town.

ST-JEAN-CAP FERRAT

pop 2100

On the Cap Ferrat peninsula, the fishing-village-turned-playground-for-the-wealthy St-Jean-Cap Ferrat conceals an enclave of millionaires' villas. On the narrow isthmus of the town, the extravagant Musée de Béatrice Ephrussi de Rothschild (☎ 04 93 01 33 09; www.villa -ephrussi.com; adult/student €10/7.30; ☉ 10am-7pm Jul & Aug, to 6pm mid-Feb–Jun, Sep & Oct, 2-6pm Mon-Fri & 10am-6pm Sat & Sun Nov–mid-Feb) gives you an appreciation of the area's wealth. Housed in a 1912 Tuscan-style villa built for the Baroness de Rothschild, it's full of 18th-century furniture, paintings, tapestries and porcelain. The peninsula also has three **walking trails** with glimmering seascapes, and secluded coves for swimming.

MOYENNE CORNICHE

The middle coastal road (the N7) clings to the hillside. It was here that Alfred Hitchcock filmed *To Catch a Thief*, which starred Grace Kelly. The actress met Prince Rainier of Monaco at that time, and it was here that she later lost her life in a car crash.

ÈZE

pop 2930

At the pinnacle of a 427m peak is the medieval stone village of Èze. The high point is the Jardin Èze (admission €5; ☉ 9am-sunset), a slanting cliff-side garden of exotic cacti with views of the Med all the way to Corsica (on a good day).

To explore the village's nooks and crannies after the tour buses have left, donkeys can cart your luggage uphill from the car park to **Château Eza** (☎ 04 93 41 12 24; www.chateaueza.com; rue de la Pise; d from €180; ⊠ ⊠), which also has a lofty gastronomic restaurant and terrace (lunch *menus* €45 to €55, dinner mains €45), with views of the Med on a plate.

GRANDE CORNICHE
The Grande Corniche, whose panoramas are the most dramatic of all, leaves Nice as the D2564. It passes **La Turbie** (population 3150), which sits on a promontory directly above Monaco and offers vertigo-inducing views of the principality. The best views are from the town's **Trophée des Alpes** (☎ 04 93 41 20 84; cours Albert 1; adult/child €5/3.50; ☺ 10am-1.30pm & 2.30-5pm

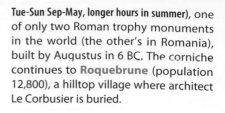

Tue-Sun Sep-May, longer hours in summer), one of only two Roman trophy monuments in the world (the other's in Romania), built by Augustus in 6 BC. The corniche continues to **Roquebrune** (population 12,800), a hilltop village where architect Le Corbusier is buried.

MONACO
pop 32,000

Monaco has a surprising amount to offer, much more, in fact, than the customary spin at its casino's roulette table. In its 1.95 sq km, the world's second-smallest state has managed to squeeze in a thriving performing art and sport scene (Formula One, but also a world-famous circus festival and a tennis open), a world-class aquarium, a beautiful old town, stunning gardens, interesting architecture throughout and a royal family on a par with British royals for best gossip fodder.

Monaco is a sovereign state but there is no border control. It has its own flag (red and white), national holiday (19 November), postal system (good for the card home to grandma) and telephone country code (☎ 377), but the official language is French and the country uses the euro. It is not part of the European Union.

INFORMATION
Tourist Office (☎ 92 16 61 16; www.visit monaco.com; 2a bd des Moulins; ☺ 9am-7pm Mon-Sat, 10am-1pm Sun)

SIGHTS
At 11.55am every day, guards are changed at Monaco's **Palais du Prince** (Prince's Palace; ☎ 93 25 18 31). For a half-hour inside glimpse into royal life, tour the **state apartments** (adult/child €7/3.50; ☺ 9.30am-6.30pm May-Sep, 10.30am-6pm Apr, 10am-5.30pm Oct) with an 11-language audioguide.

NEIL SETCHFIELD

Casino de Monte Carlo (p286)

MONACO

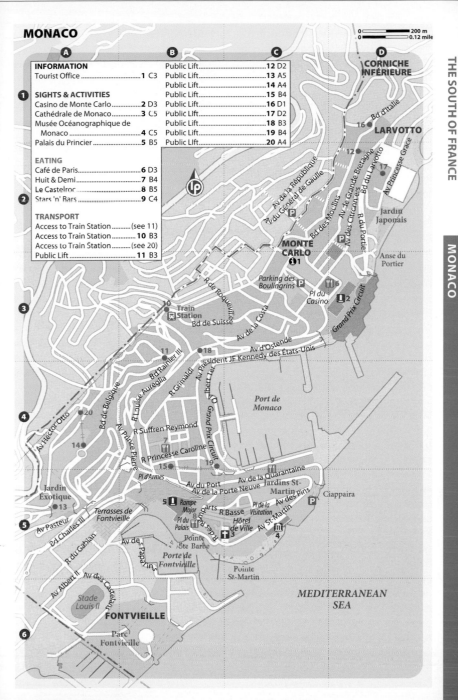

0 — 200 m
0 — 0.12 mile

INFORMATION
Tourist Office **1** C3

SIGHTS & ACTIVITIES
Casino de Monte Carlo.................**2** D3
Cathédrale de Monaco..................**3** C5
Musée Océanographique de
  Monaco **4** C5
Palais du Princier **5** B5

EATING
Café de Paris.....................................**6** D3
Huit & Demi......................................**7** B4
Le Castelroc.......................................**8** B5
Stars 'n' Bars **9** C4

TRANSPORT
Access to Train Station ....(see 11)
Access to Train Station **10** B3
Access to Train Station ....(see 20)
Public Lift **11** B3

Public Lift..**12** D2
Public Lift..**13** A5
Public Lift..**14** A4
Public Lift..**15** B4
Public Lift..**16** D1
Public Lift..**17** D2
Public Lift..**18** B3
Public Lift..**19** B4
Public Lift..**20** A4

CORNICHE INFÉRIEURE

LARVOTTO

Jardin
Japonais

Anse du
Portier

MONTE CARLO

Parking des
Boulingrins

Pl du
Casino

Grand Prix Circuit

Train Station

Bd de Suisse

Av de la Costa

Av d'Ostende

Av Président JF Kennedy des États-Unis

Port de
Monaco

R Suffren Reymond

R Princesse Caroline

Pl d'Armes

Jardin
Exotique

Terrasses de
Fontvieille

Av Pasteur

Bd Charles III

R du Gabian

Av de
Papalin

Av Albert II

Av des Castelans

Stade
Louis II

FONTVIEILLE

Parc
Fontvieille

Porte de
Fontvieille

Pointe
Ste Barbe

Pointe
St-Martin

Av du Port

Av de la Porte Neuve

Rampe
Major

Pl du
Palais

R Basse

Pl de la
Visitation

Hôtel
de Ville

Jardins St-
Martin

Av des Pins

Av St-Martin

Ciappaira

Av de la Quarantaine

**MEDITERRANEAN
SEA**

Av de la République
du Général de Gaulle

Bd des Moulins

Av de la Grande Bretagne

Av des Citronn ers

Bd du Portier

Av Princesse Grace

Bd du Larvotto

Bd d'Italie

R de Roqueville

Bd Rainier III

R Grimaldi

Grand Prix Circuit

Q Albert 1er

R Louis Auréglia

Bd de Belgique

Av Hector Otto

Av Prince Pierre

Propped on a sheer cliff-face, the graceful **Musée Océanographique de Monaco** (☎ 93 15 36 00; av St-Martin; adult/student €12.50/6; ☯ 9.30am-7pm Jul & Aug, to 6.30pm Apr-Jun & Sep, to 6pm Oct-Mar), built in 1910, houses a fantastic aquarium.

An adoring crowd continually shuffles past Prince Rainier's and Princess Grace's graves, located on the western side of the cathedral choir of the 1875 Romanesque-Byzantine **Cathédrale de Monaco** (4 rue Colonel).

FESTIVALS & EVENTS

Brazilian triple-world champion Nelson Piquet famously likened driving Monaco's **Formula One Grand Prix** with 'riding a bicycle around your living room'. If you're dead keen, you can walk the 3.2km circuit; the tourist office has maps.

EATING

Huit & Demi (☎ 93 50 97 02; cnr rue Langlé & rue Princesse Caroline; mains €13-27; ☯ noon-3pm & 7-11pm Mon-Fri, 7-11pm Sat) Very chic and very popular. You can savour your Italian fare indoors amid crimson-coloured walls lined with celebrity B&W portraits, or on the street-side terrace when the sun is shining.

Le Castelroc (☎ 93 30 36 68; place du Palais; mains €22-27; ☯ 9am-3pm daily, dinner Tue-Sat May-Sep) Right across from the palace, and behind the souvenir stalls, hides the authentic Le Castelroc. Its alfresco terrace is the perfect place to try genuine Monégasque specialities like *barbajuan* (a beignet filled with spinach and cheese) and *cundyun* (Monaco's version of *salade Niçoise*).

DRINKING

Café de Paris (☎ 98 06 76 23; place du Casino; mains €17-53; ☯ 7am-2am) Adjacent to the opulent Monte Carlo Casino, this is a fabulous spot for a classy lunch or a decadent coffee with liqueur and pastry whilst limo-spotting from the sprawling 300-seat terrace.

Stars 'n' Bars (☎ 97 97 95 95; 6 quai Antoine 1er; mains €14.50-22; ☯ noon-2.30am Tue-Sun) Any star worth his or her reputation has partied at this American western saloon.

ENTERTAINMENT

Pack your evening wear for concerts, opera and ballet at various venues.

Living out your James Bond fantasies just doesn't get any better than at Monte Carlo's monumental, richly decorated showpiece, the 1910-built **Casino de Monte Carlo** (☎ 98 06 21 21; www.casinomonte carlo.com; place du Casino; ☯ European Rooms from noon Sat & Sun, from 2pm Mon-Fri). You have to pay even before you play: admission is €10 for the European Rooms, with poker/slot machines, French roulette and *trente et quarante* (a card game), and €20 for the Private Rooms, which offer baccarat, blackjack, craps and American roulette. The jacket-and-tie dress code kicks in after 10pm. Minimum entry age for both types of rooms is 18; bring photo ID.

GETTING THERE & AWAY

Trains to and from Monaco's **train station** (av Prince Pierre) are run by the French SNCF. There are frequent trains to Nice (€3.20, 20 minutes), and east to Menton (€1.80, 10 minutes), and to the first town across the border in Italy, Ventimiglia (€3.20, 20 minutes).

BORDEAUX & THE SOUTHWEST

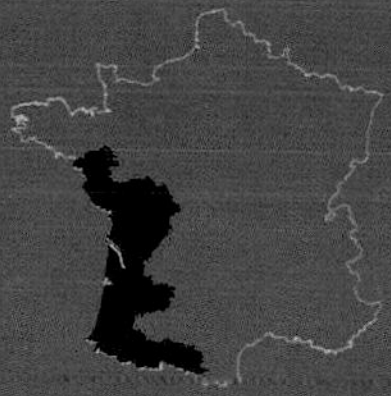

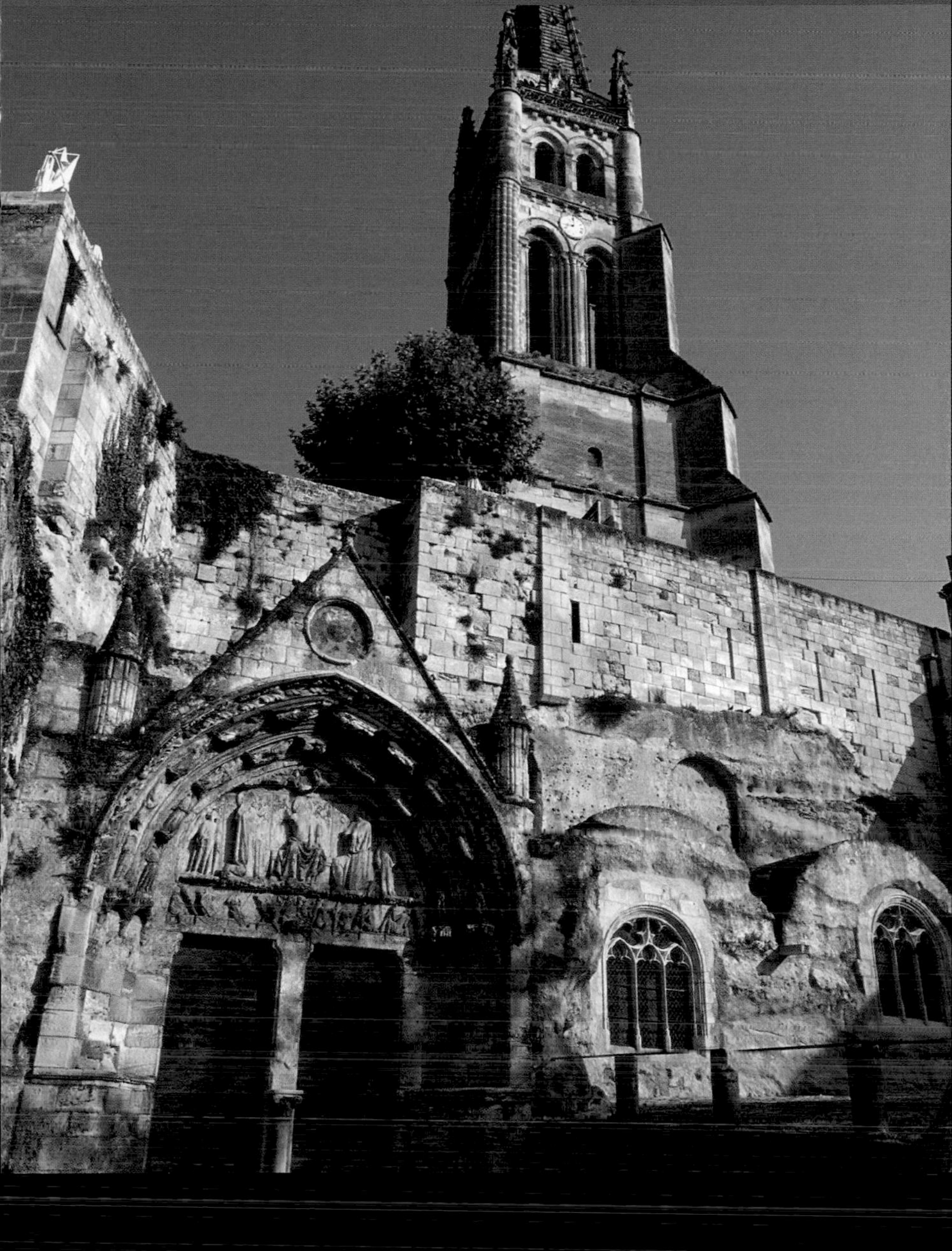

BORDEAUX & THE SOUTHWEST

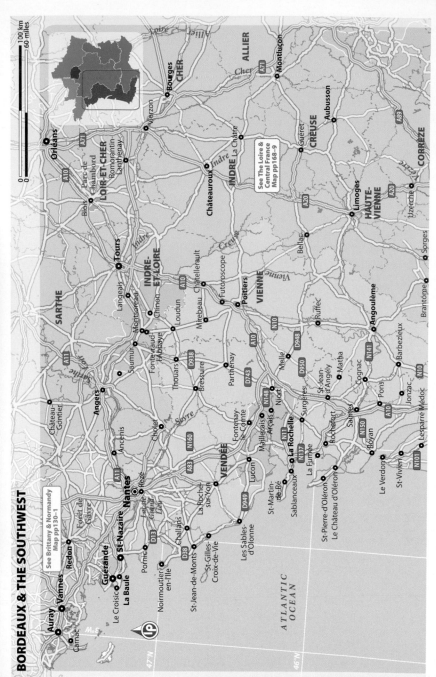

See Brittany & Normandy
Map pp130–1

See The Loire &
Central France
Map pp168–9

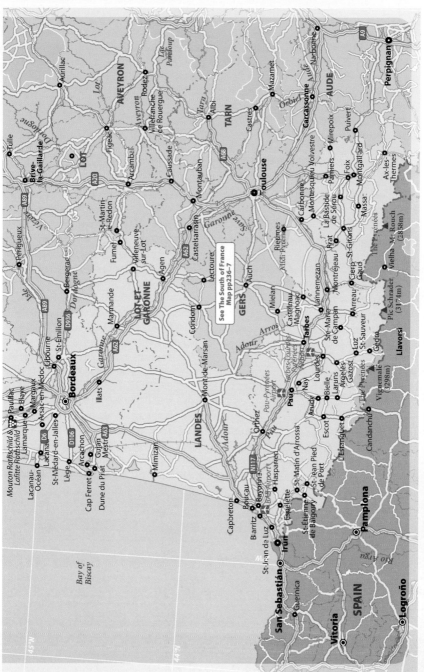

HIGHLIGHTS

1 BORDELAISE CUISINE

BY JEAN-PIERRE XIRADAKIS, CULINARY WRITER & CELEBRITY RESTAURANT OWNER SINCE 1968

For me the best moment is when I catch the *bonheur* (happiness) in people's eyes, usually as they are eating a particular dish. I was born in Blaye, 50km from Bordeaux and my cuisine is *paysanne* (a country cuisine), rustic; using only the best products and traditional recipes from the southwest.

⤣ JEAN-PIERRE XIRADAKIS' DON'T MISS LIST

❶ MARCHÉ DES CAPUCINS

Cuisine bordelaise (Bordeaux cuisine) originates from the south, from Basque-country women who came to work in the great Bordelaise houses. And the diversity of produce is enormous. We have river and sea fish, shellfish, oysters, fowl (duck and geese), lamb, beef, mushrooms, vegetables, poultry, truffles… We really have everything, although we miss cheese. I buy my produce from local producers and markets: **Marché des Capucins** in Bordeaux and the twice-weekly market in **Blaye** (Wednesday and Saturday mornings).

❷ CASSOULET, MACARONADE & EELS

I love **cassoulet**, typical to the rural southwest and traditionally eaten to celebrate; it's a heart-warming haricot bean stew with a few giblets, a bit of sausage and pork thrown in. Then there's **macaronade aux cèpes et au foi gras**, fresh macaroni with local *cèpes* (boletus mushrooms), foie gras and cream. It is very rich, very delicious and demands a healthy appe-

Clockwise from top: Vineyards, St-Émilion (p302); Fish for sale; Fermentation barrels at Mouton Rothschild, Pauillac (p302), Médoc; Fresh oysters; Market vegetable stall

tite! **Lamproie à la Bordelaise** (eel-like lamprey), a migratory river fish cooked with wine and leeks, is very typical of our local cuisine.

❸ LA SOUPE

In winter at **La Tupina** (p301) we always have a cauldron of soup cooking in the fireplace; the fire burns all day just as it did at my grandparents'. We throw in cabbage, carrots, beans, a bit of duck or pork to give it taste and so on, just as peasants did centuries ago. For them it provided all the daily nutrition they needed – water, vegetables and a little meat.

❹ WINE & OYSTERS

Bordelaise essentials! **L'Essentiel** (☎ 05 57 24 39 76; 6 rue Guadel) in St-Émilion is

the place to taste wine and **La Boîte à Huitres** (☎ 05 56 81 64 97; 35 cours du Chapeau Rouge), a seafood and shellfish restaurant in Bordeaux, is the *dégustation* (tasting) address for oysters. Favourite wine producers to taste and buy include **Château Mayne Lalande** (7 route du Mayne) and **Château Lestage** (☎ 05 56 58 02 43; www

↘ THINGS YOU NEED TO KNOW

Markets Villages have a food market at least once a week **Saucy!** Anything *à la Bordelaise* comes in a wine-based sauce spiced with parsley, shallots and bone marrow **Cooking lessons** With Bordelaise chef Nicolas Frion at École de Cuisine au Chapon Fin (☎ 05 56 90 91 92; www.chapon-fin.com; 5 rue Montesquie, Bordeaux).

HIGHLIGHTS

2

↘ DUNE DU PILAT

No natural feature is more magnificent or soul-stirring than this colossal **sand dune** (p308) within cycling distance from Arcachon. Europe's largest, the sand mountain approximately 2.8km long and 500m wide is apparently spreading eastwards at 4.5m a year – it has swallowed trees, a road junction and even a hotel. Scale it for a panorama once seen.

3

↘ COGNAC

Complement your Bordeaux tippling with at least a day in this riverside town where the double-distilled spirit known the world over is carefully blended and matured in age-old cellars. Learn step-by-step how grapes end up in the brandy bottle at the **Musée des Arts du Cognac** (p306), followed by a tour of and tasting session at a big-name **Cognac house** (p306).

4

⬊ URBAN BORDEAUX

Since 2007 half of southwest France's largest city was Unesco listed, making **Bordeaux** (p298) the largest urban World Heritage site. Touring its dramatically flood-lit buildings and monuments is well worth the foot power, as are the city's richly varied tours, river cruises, fine wines and dining temptations.

5

⬊ FRENCH BASQUE TRADITION

Bullfighting, 'running of the cows', *jambon de Bayonne, pelota* (p312), Espelette chillies and Izarra liquor: the traditions of France's Basque country make this region unique. Food markets in **Bayonne** (p309) and **St-Jean-Pied-de-Port** (p313) are a fabulous affair. Then, there's **Biarritz** (p311), as flamboyant in a flash, cool surfer type of way.

6

⬊ LOURDES

Immersing yourself in an icy **bath** (p316) at the spiritual sanctuary of Lourdes in the Pyrenees. Often used by invalids seeking miraculous cures but open to all comers of any or no religious affiliation, these baths are among the world's key pilgrimage sites. Later, summit Pic du Jer aboard the funicular for views of the busy town and central snow-capped Pyrenees.

2 ANDREW BAIN; 3 OLIVER STREWE; 4 OLIVER STREWE; 5 GREG JOHNSTON; 6 BRIAN HAMILTON/ALAMY.

2 Dune du Pilat (p308); 3 Barrels of Hennessey Cognac (p306), Cognac; 4 Bordeaux (p298); 5 St-Jean-Pied-de-Port (p313), French Basque Country; 6 Statue of Mary, Lourdes (p316), Pyrenees

THE BEST...

⌁ BIRD'S EYE VIEWS

- **Bordeaux city panorama** (p298) Atop the cathedral belfry.
- **St-Émilion rooftops** (p303) Trip up the bell tower for tip-top views of this hilltop hamlet.
- **Basque coastline** (p312) Scale Biarritz lighthouse for a superb view.
- **Spanish Basque Country** (p312) Best seen from Rocher de la Vierge.

⌁ SOUVENIRS

- **L'Intendant, Bordeaux** (p301) 15,000 bottles of regional wine.
- **La Winery, Arsac-en-Médoc** (p303) Groundbreaking winery with 1000 different Bordeaux wines.
- **St-Émilion** (p302) With one wine shop for every eight old-city inhabitants, wine shopping's a breeze.
- **Pierre Ibaïalde & Bayonne covered market** (p310) Taste/buy cured Bayonne ham.
- **Para Gabia** (p313) Basque espadrilles handcrafted here since 1935.

⌁ LOCAL FAVOURITES

- **L'Entrecôte, Bordeaux** (p300) Going strong since 1966 with one *menu* and a queue every day at noon.
- **L'Envers du Décor, St-Émilion** (p305) Seasonal market cuisine alfresco or before the hearth.
- **Ttipia, Bayonne** (p310) One *menu*, endless cider and shared tables.
- **Brasserie Le Berry, Pau** (p316) A local fave since the 1950s.

⌁ EASY WALKS

- **St-Émilion** (p304) Eight hikes, 4km to 14km long, loop this beautiful Unesco-protected hamlet in the Bordeaux region.
- **Plage d'Arcachon to Dune de Pilat** (p307) Beach to sand dune along a tree-shaded pedestrian promenade makes for the perfect afternoon stroll.
- **Pic de Jer, Lourdes** (p318) Skip the funicular and walk.

LEFT: GREG ELMS; RIGHT: ANDREW BAIN

Left: St-Émilion (p302), Bordeaux; Right: Biarritz (p311), French Basque Country

THINGS YOU NEED TO KNOW

⬆ VITAL STATISTICS

- **Population** 4,529,642 (The Atlantic Coast), 600,000 (French Basque Country), 3,050,000 (The Pyrenees)
- **Best time to visit** April, June and September
- **Points of entry** Bordeaux, Bayonne and Pau

⬆ ADVANCE PLANNING

- **As early as possible** Book accommodation, particularly for Bayonne and Biarritz in July and August.
- **Two weeks before** Take your pick of Bordeaux tourist office's 101 thematic guided tours (p300) and reserve; book the city's *Découverte* hotel package at least 10 days before to cash in on the good-value accommodation deal.
- **One week before** Reserve your guided visit of a Cognac house (p306); organise your Bordeaux wine-tasting (p303); and book a table for that quintessential French lunch (p311).

⬆ RESOURCES

- **Maison du Tourisme de la Gironde** (☎ 05 56 52 61 40; www .tourisme-gironde.cg33.fr; 21 cours de l'Intendance) Regional tourist information on the Bordeaux region.

⬆ GETTING AROUND

- **Budget flights** from the UK to/from Bordeaux (p301), Angoulême-Cognac (p306), Bayonne (p310) and Pau (p315).
- **TGV train** to/from Paris to main transport hub Bordeaux and other main towns.
- **Car** means more freedom (and spitting) for any wine-tasting trail.
- **Bicycle** is *the* way to access the Dune du Pilat from Arcachon (p307).

⬆ BE FOREWARNED

- **St-Émilion** Wear flat comfy shoes: the village's steep, uneven streets are hard-going.
- **Baie d'Arachon** Take care swimming in this area: powerful currents swirl out to sea from the deceptively tranquil *baïnes* (little bays).
- **Bordeaux wine-making châteaux** generally close their doors to visitors during October's grape harvest.
- **Finding a hotel bed** in Bayonne is tough mid-July to mid-August and near impossible during the Fêtes de Bayonne.
- **Lourdes** is so quiet in winter that most hotels shut down.

ITINERARIES

More sunshine than anywhere in France, apart from the Mediterranean, coupled with exceptional wining and dining and a smorgasbord of mountain vistas make this region an enticing place to visit.

CITY TO SEA Three Days

Start your long weekend with **(1) Bordeaux** (p298), a city so *belle* with its Unesco-loved architecture and feast of fine dines: devote the morning to urban meandering, not missing **(2) Cathédrale St-André** (p298) and **(3) Tour Pey-Berland** (p298) or – for foodies – uncover the city with a **(4) Gourmet Trail Tour** (p300). Lunch local at **(5) L'Entrecôte** (p300) or on cheese at **(6) Baud et Millet** (p301), and spend the afternoon **(7) shopping** (p301) or afloat a **(8) river cruise** (p300). There is no more magical spot to dine after dark than at **(9) L'Estaquade** (p301), against a backdrop of twinkling city lights.

On day two catch a train to seaside **(10) Arcachon** (p307). Walk its piers, ride the art-deco lift up to **(11) Ville d'Hiver** (p307) and crack open local oysters at **(12) La Calypso** (p309). Post-lunch, rent a bike and pedal to the mind-blowing **(13) Dune du Pilat** (p308).

Final day find out for yourself just how fine Bordeaux wine is with wine-tasting in **(14) The Médoc** (p302) and **(15) St-Émilion** (p302); see the next itinerary for detailed suggestions.

WINE TASTING Five Days

Begin your oenological holiday with a two-hour tasting course at Bordeaux's **(1) École du Vin** (p303), followed by a browse around specialist wine shop **(2) L'Intendant** (p301). Then drive northwest to **(3) Arsac-en-Medoc** (p303) where **(4) La Winery** (p303) captivates wine lovers with innovative tastings and an exceptional wine list in its gastronomic restaurant **(5) Le Wy** (p302).

Spend your second day exploring the **(6) Médoc** (p302) wine region, stopping at **(7) Pauillac** (p302) to pick up a map and list of local chateaux from its **(8) Maison du Tourisme et du Vin** (p302). Come dusk backtrack to **(9) Bordeaux** (p298), in preparation for an early start to beat the crowds at **(10) St-Émilion** (p302): overnight in the beautiful medieval village and devote day four to touring the area's wine-making châteaux – on foot with a day hike, by car or with a tourist-office-organised tour.

Final day, en route back to Bordeaux, spoil yourself rotten with a day of red-wine baths and merlot wraps at the luxurious château spa, hotel and restaurant **(11) Spa de Vinothérapie Caudalie** (p303).

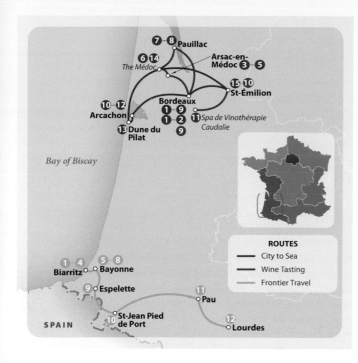

FRONTIER TRAVEL One Week

The majestic snow-capped peaks of France and Spain's Pyrenees as a backdrop are a constant during this majestic week-long tour. Pick it up on the coast in hip (1) Biarritz (p311) with an invigorating walk to (2) Rocher de la Vierge (p312) – the wonderful views of Spanish Basque Country instantly tantalise. Just to remind yourself where you are, buy some (3) espadrilles (p313) and feast on chorizo-spiced dishes at (4) Le Corsaire (p313).

Day two get lost in the maze of medieval streets and alleys of (5) Bayonne (p309) and pinch yourself –you're really in France! Lunch on typical Basque dishes at (6) La Criée (p316), watch a game of (7) pelota (p312) and jig after dark to (8) traditional Basque music (p310).

Over the next few days head southeast along the French–Spanish frontier (D918) via chilli-pepper hot (9) Espelette to (10) St-Jean-Pied-de-Port (p313), just 8km from Spain. Then head inland to (11) Pau (p315) where every Pyreneen peak can be seen from atop a funicular. Further east, (12) Lourdes (p316) lures pilgrims by the coach-load with its invigorating waters and equally invigorating Pyrenees panorama.

DISCOVER BORDEAUX & THE SOUTHWEST

Wine aficionados fall passionately in love with this southern region, through which country roads wiggle past vine-striped hills to countless gastronomic treats, among them, the town of Cognac, tantamount with its double-distilled spirit; the country's largest wine-growing area, encompassing magnificent Médoc châteaux and golden-hued St-Émilion; and the tranquil Bay of Arcachon, home to a sand dune and weather-beaten oyster shacks. The gateway to all this tasteful splendour is the city of Bordeaux, a name synonymous with some of France's finest wine.

Snug against the lower reaches of the Atlantic Coast sizzles French Basque country, a feisty region like no other. Best known for its surfing mecca, Biarritz, bronzed surfers zoom around hilly coastline on mopeds while oiled sun-seekers pack beaches. Yet there is another side to this traditional part of France, personified by humble pilgrims who follow in the footsteps of their ancestors on foot to St-Jean-Pied-de-Port and through the Pyrenees into neighbouring Spain.

BORDEAUX

pop 229,500

The new millennium was a major turning point for the city long known as La Belle Au Bois Dormant (Sleeping Beauty), when the mayor, ex-Prime Minister Alain Juppé, roused Bordeaux, pedestrianising its boulevards, restoring its neoclassical architecture, and implementing a high-tech public transport system.

Bolstered by its high-spirited university-student population (not to mention 2.5 million tourists annually), La Belle Bordeaux now scarcely seems to sleep at all.

INFORMATION

Main Tourist Office (☎ 05 56 00 66 00; www.bordeaux-tourisme.com; 12 cours du 30 Juillet; ☺ 9am-7.30pm Mon-Sat, 9.30am-6.30pm Sun Jul & Aug, 9am-6.30pm Mon-Sat, 9.30am-6.30pm Sun May, Jun, Sep & Oct, 9am-6.30pm Mon-Sat, 9.45am-4.30pm Sun Nov-Apr)
Train Station Tourist Office (☺ 9am-noon & 1-6pm Mon-Sat, 10am-noon & 1-3pm Sun May-Oct, 9.30am-12.30pm & 2-6pm Mon-Fri Nov-Apr)

SIGHTS

Lording over the city is **Cathédrale St-André**. A Unesco World Heritage site, the cathedral's oldest section dates from 1096; most of what you see today was built in the 13th and 14th centuries. Even more imposing than the cathedral itself is the gargoyled, 50m-high Gothic belfry, **Tour Pey-Berland** (adult/student/child €5/3.50/free; ☺ 10am-1.15pm & 2-6pm Jun-Sep, 10am-12.30pm & 2-5.30pm Tue-Sun Oct-May). Scaling the tower's 232 narrow steps rewards you with a spectacular panorama of the city.

Gallo-Roman statues and relics dating back 25,000 years are among the highlights at the impressive **Musée d'Aquitaine** (Museum of Aquitaine; ☎ 05 56 01 51 00; 20 cours Pasteur; ☺ 11am-6pm Tue-Sun). Built in 1824 as a warehouse for French colonial produce like coffee, cocoa, peanuts

BORDEAUX & THE SOUTHWEST

BORDEAUX

BORDEAUX

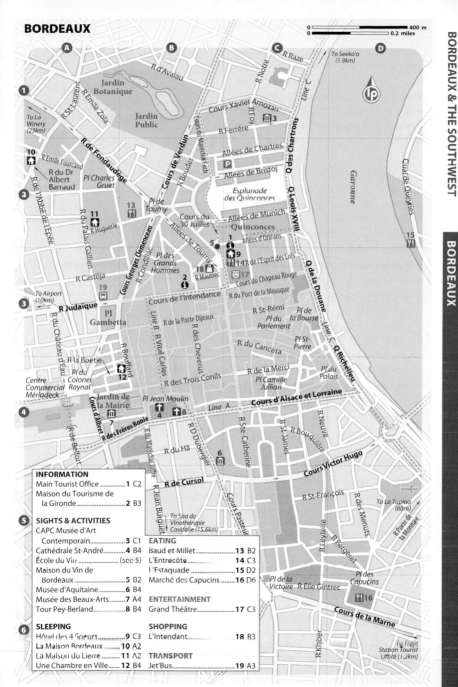

0 ____ 400 m
0 ____ 0.2 miles

INFORMATION
Main Tourist Office	**1** C2
Maison du Tourisme de la Gironde	**2** B3

SIGHTS & ACTIVITIES
CAPC Musée d'Art Contemporain	**3** C1
Cathédrale St-André	**4** B4
École du Vin	(see 5)
Maison du Vin de Bordeaux	**5** B2
Musée d'Aquitaine	**6** B4
Musée des Beaux-Arts	**7** A4
Tour Pey-Berland	**8** B4

SLEEPING
Hôtel des 4 Sœurs	**9** C3
La Maison Bordeaux	**10** A2
La Maison du Lierre	**11** A2
Une Chambre en Ville	**12** B4

EATING
Baud et Millet	**13** B2
L'Entrecôte	**14** C3
l 'Estaquade	**15** D2
Marché des Capucins	**16** D6

ENTERTAINMENT
Grand Théâtre	**17** C3

SHOPPING
L'Intendant	**18** B3

TRANSPORT
Jet'Bus	**19** A3

and vanilla, the cavernous Entrepôts Lainé creates a dramatic backdrop for post-1960s works by European and American artists at the **CAPC Musée d'Art Contemporain** (Museum of Contemporary Art; ☎ 05 56 00 81 50; Entrepôt 7, rue Ferrére; 🕒 11am-6pm Tue, Thu-Sun, to 8pm Wed, closed Mon). The rooftop **café** (brunch €25, menus €20-32, mains €13-21; 🕒 11am-6pm Tue-Sun) does a fantastic Sunday brunch.

The evolution of Occidental art from the Renaissance to the mid-20th century is on view at Bordeaux's **Musée des Beaux-Arts** (Museum of Fine Arts; ☎ 05 56 10 20 56; 20 cours d'Albret; 🕒 11am-6pm Wed-Mon).

Pretty **place Gambetta** also has its share of history – during the Reign of Terror that followed the Revolution, a guillotine placed here severed the heads of 300 alleged counter-revolutionaries.

TOURS

The tourist office runs a packed program of bilingual tours, including a **gourmet trail tour** (tickets €22; 🕒 9.45am 1st & 3rd Sat of each month), where you can learn about the region's cuisine the best way there is – by sampling it (four tastings are included in the price). Contact the tourist office for details of dozens of other tour options, including **river cruises** in the warmer months.

SLEEPING

The *Découverte* (Discover Bordeaux) package is a neat little offering from the tourist office that bundles up two nights at your choice of participating hotels along with free public transportation, a guided city tour, a vineyard tour including wine tasting (both tours in English and French), and a bottle of wine.

Hôtel des 4 Soeurs (☎ 05 57 81 19 20; 4soeurs.free.fr; 6 cours du 30 Juillet; s/d from €65/75; 🔀 🖳 🔀) A romantic relic from the reign of Louis-Philippe, Hôtel des 4 Soeurs' sophisticated rooms recall the private home

it once was. Try room 22, where Richard Wagner stayed in 1850.

La Maison du Lierre (☎ 05 56 51 92 71; www.maisondulierre.com; 57 rue Huguerie; d €78-99; 🔀) The delightfully restored 'House of Ivy' has a welcoming *chambre d'hôte* (B&B) feel. A beautiful Bordelaise stone staircase leads to sunlit rooms with polished floorboards, rose-printed fabrics and sparkling bathrooms. The vine-draped garden is a perfect spot to breakfast.

Une Chambre en Ville (☎ 05 56 81 34 53; www.bandb-bx.com; 35 rue Bouffard; d €89, junior ste €99, 6-person apt per week €1300) Within the walls of a former gallery and an adjoining Bordelaise town house, each of these five *chambres en ville* (rooms in the city) is an individual work of art.

La Maison Bordeaux (☎ 05 56 44 00 45; www.lamaisonbordeaux.com; 113 rue du Docteur Albert Barraud; s €145-195, d €180-230) You'd expect to find a sumptuous 18th-century château with a conifer-flanked courtyard and stable house in the countryside, but this stunning *maison d'hôte* is right in the middle of the city. A *table d'hôte* is available by arrangement (*menus* €30 to €150 including wine). Breakfast is included in the price.

ourpick Seeko'o (☎ 05 56 39 07 07; www .seekoo-hotel.com; 54 quai de Bacalan; d €180-220, ste €360; 🔀) The monochrome lobby of Bordeaux's iceberg-shaped, first-ever design hotel leads to 45 retro-futuristic vinyl-and-leather- decorated rooms (some with circular beds), fitted out by Bordeaux designers.

EATING

L'Entrecôte (☎ 05 56 81 76 10; 4 cours du 30 Juillet; menu €16.50; 🕒 lunch & dinner) Opened in 1966, this unpretentious place doesn't take reservations, and it only has one menu option. But Bordeaux locals continue to queue for its succulent thin-sliced meat

Médoc vineyards (p302)

OLIVER STREWE

BORDEAUX & THE SOUTHWEST

BORDEAUX

(heated underneath by tea-light candles and topped with a 'secret recipe' sauce made from shallots and bone marrow), salad and unlimited home-made *frites* (fries).

Baud et Millet (☎ 05 56 79 05 77; 19 rue Huguerie; menus €19-24; ⏰ 10am-11pm Mon-Sat) Over 250 different cheeses are offered at this cosy, mostly vegetarian place, with almost as many international wines lining the walls. Serious *fromage* fans should go for the all-you-can-eat cheese buffet.

La Tupina (☎ 05 56 91 56 37; 6 rue Porte de la Monnaie; mains €19-44, menus €32-48; ⏰ lunch & dinner) Filled with the aroma of soup simmering inside an old *tupina* ('kettle' in Basque) over an open fire, this white-tableclothed place is feted far and wide for its seasonal southwestern French specialities.

L'Estaquade (☎ 05 57 54 02 50; quai de Queyries; mains €22-26; ⏰ lunch & dinner) Set on stilts, jutting out off the river's eastern bank, the seafood and meat dishes here can't help but be eclipsed by the magical views of Bordeaux's neoclassical architecture.

SHOPPING

Europe's longest pedestrian shopping street, **rue Ste-Catherine**, is paved with raised, polished Bordelaise stone, becoming increasingly upmarket as it stretches 1.2km north from place de la Victoire to place de la Comédie.

Speciality wine shops include **L'Intendant** (☎ 05 56 48 01 29; 2 allées de Tourny). The latter has a spiral staircase climbing four floors, surrounded by cylindrical shelves holding 15,000 bottles of regional wine.

GETTING THERE & AWAY

Bordeaux airport (☎ 05 56 34 50 50; www .bordeaux.aeroport.fr) is in Mérignac, 10km west of the city centre.

Bordeaux station, Gare St-Jean, is about 3km from the city centre. Destinations include Paris' Gare Montparnasse (€66.20, three hours).

GETTING AROUND

The train station, place Gambetta and the main tourist office are connected to the

Wine grapes

SALLY DILLON

airport (one-way €7) by **Jet'Bus** (☎ 05 56 34 50 50). The trip takes approximately 45 minutes. A taxi from the airport into town costs about €20.

THE MÉDOC

Northwest of Bordeaux, along the western shore of the Gironde Estuary lie some of Bordeaux's most celebrated vineyards. To their west, fine-sand beaches, bordered by dunes and *étangs* (lagoons), stretch from Pointe de Grave south along the Côte d'Argent (Silver Coast) to the Bassin d'Arcachon and beyond, with great surf.

ORIENTATION & INFORMATION

On the banks of the muddy Gironde, the port town of **Pauillac** (population 1300) is at the heart of the wine coun-try, surrounded by the distinguished Haut-Médoc, Margaux and St-Julien ap-pellations. The Pauillac wine appellation encompasses 18 *crus classés* (see p303) including the world-renowned Mouton Rothschild, Latour and Lafite Rothschild.

Pauillac's tourist office houses the **Maison du Tourisme et du Vin** (☎ 05 56 59 03 08; www.pauillac-medoc.com, in French; La Verrerie; ☾ seasonal hours vary annually), which has information on châteaux and how to visit them.

SLEEPING & EATING

From Bordeaux, the Médoc makes an easy and enjoyable day trip.

Le Pavillon de Margaux (☎ 05 57 88 77 54; www.pavillonmargaux.com; 3 rue Georges Mandel, Margaux; d €70-120) In an old school-house, this welcoming, family-run place has 14 rooms styled according to famous local châteaux. You can taste the family's wines at the on-site restaurant under a canopy of fairy lights.

Le Wy (☎ 05 56 39 04 91; La Winery; 3-course menus €23, discovery menu €63, mains €19-26; ☾ lunch Tue-Sun, dinner Tue-Sat) Gastronomic fare like truffle-infused risotto and foie gras with green apples blends with a relaxed at-mosphere (not a white tablecloth in sight) and over 400 different wines by the glass.

GETTING THERE & AWAY

The region is best explored by car; from Bordeaux, take *sortie* (exit) 7 to get off the Bordeaux Rocade (ring road).

Trains run from Bordeaux's Gare St-Jean station to Margaux (€6.80, 50 minutes) and Pauillac (€9.60, one hour 10 minutes) several times a day.

ST-ÉMILION

pop 2345

The medieval village of St-Émilion perches above vineyards renowned for producing full-bodied, deeply coloured red wines. Named after Émilion, a miracle-working Benedictine monk who lived in a cave here between 750 and 767, it soon became a stop on pilgrimage routes, and the village and its vineyards are now Unesco-listed. Today, it's well worth venturing 40km east from Bordeaux to experience St-Émilion's magic, particularly when the sun sets over the valley and the limestone buildings glow with halolike golden hues.

ORIENTATION & INFORMATION

Tourist Office (☎ 05 57 55 28 28; www .saint-emilion-tourisme.com; place des Créneaux; ⏲ 9.30am-8pm Jul-Aug, to 7pm mid–late Jun &

ON THE WINE TRAIL

Bordeaux has over 5000 châteaux (also known as *domaines*, *crus* or *clos*), referring not to palatial residences but rather to the properties where grapes are raised, picked, fermented and then matured as wine. You have to make advance reservations. Many close during the *vendange* (grape harvest) in October.

Whet your palate with the tourist office's informal introduction to wine and cheese courses (adult/concession €23/20), every Thursday at 4.30pm yearround, where you sip two to three different wines, and sup on cheese straight out of the cellar.

Serious students of the grape can enrol at the **École du Vin** (Wine School; ☎ 05 56 00 22 66; ecole.vins-bordeaux.fr), within the **Maison du Vin de Bordeaux** (Bordeaux House of Wine; 3 cours du 30 Juillet; ☎ 8.30am-4.30pm Mon-Fri), located across the street from the tourist office. Introductory two-hour courses are held June and September (€25). To really develop your nose (and your dinner-party skills), sign up for more complex two- to three-day courses (from €335/218 per adult/student).

Châteaux visits are also included in many tours run by Bordeaux's tourist office. Day trips generally start at €72 per adult for those closest to town, and around €83 for areas such as the **Médoc** (p302) or **St-Émilion** (p302), including wine tastings and lunch.

For DIY wine trailing, the Maison du Vin de Bordeaux supplies free, colourcoded maps. A good starting point is Philippe Raoux's **La Winery** (☎ 05 56 39 04 90; www.lawinery.fr, in French; Rond-point des Vendangeurs, D1, Arsac-en-Médoc; ⏲ 11am-7pm Tue-Sun Sep-Jun, to 8pm Tue-Sun Jul & Aug), 23km from Bordeaux. A first for France, this vast glass-and-steel wine centre mounts concerts and contemporary-art exhibits alongside various fee-based tastings, including innovative tastings that determine your *signe œnologique* ('wine sign'; booking required).

If you'd rather imbibe than drive, **Bordeaux Excursions** (www.bordeaux-excur sions.com) customises private wine-country tours, starting from €190 for one to four people (excluding châteaux fees) for a half-day trip.

And to immerse yourself, literally, in the local liquid, at the **Spa de Vinothérapie Caudalie** (☎ 05 57 83 83 83; www.sources-caudalie.com; chemin de Smith Haut Lafitte, Martillac; treatments from €58) you can try a red-wine bath, a merlot wrap or a cabernet body scrub. The spa is 20 minutes south of Bordeaux. It's best reached by your own wheels; exit the A62 at junction 1.

early-late Sep, 9.30am-12.30pm & 1.45-6.30pm Apr–mid-Jun & late Sep-Oct, 9.30am-12.30pm & 1.45-6pm Nov-Mar) Details on visiting over 100 nearby châteaux.

SIGHTS

The only (but highly worthwhile) way to visit the town's most interesting historical sites – many of them concealed beneath the village streets in a labyrinth of cata-combs – is with one of the tourist office's 45-minute **guided tours** (adult/student/child incl site entry €6.50/4.10/3.20). Highlights are the hermit saint's famous cave, **Grotte de l'Ermitage**, and the 11th-century church **Église Monolithe**, carved out of limestone between the 9th and 12th centuries.

For captivating views of the hilltop hamlet, collect the key from the tourist office to climb the **clocher** (bell tower; ☎ 05 57 55 28 28; admission €1) above the church. The entrance is on place des Créneaux.

A domed Romanesque 12th-century nave dominates the former **Collégiale** (Collegiate Church). **Cloître de l'Église Collégiale**, the church's tranquil 12th-to 14th- century cloister, is the venue for special events.

Within the ruined monastery, **Cloître des Cordeliers** (rue Porte Brunet; admission free; ☼ year-round), the winery **Les Cordeliers** (☎ 05 57 24 58 32; guided cellar tours €4; ☼ tour hours vary daily) has made sparkling wine for over a century.

The 13th-century donjon known as the **Castel daou Rey** (Tour du Roi, King's Tower; admission €1; ☼ 11am-7.15pm Jul & Aug, variable hours out of season) has exceptional views of the town and the Dordogne Valley.

ACTIVITIES

Blind tastings and games (available in English) are a fun and informative intro-duction to wine tasting at **L'École du Vin de St-Émilion** (☎ 05 57 24 61 01; www.vignobles

chateaux.fr; 4 rue du Clocher; tasting courses €29; ☼ 3pm daily Apr-Oct, by reservation Nov-Mar). The adjacent **Maison du Vin** (☎ 05 57 55 50 55; place Pierre Meyrat; classes €17; ☼ mid-Jul–mid-Sep) also offers bilingual, 1½-hour classes starting at 11am.

Eight **hiking circuits** loop, from 4km to 14km, through the greater World Heritage jurisdiction; the tourist office has maps.

TOURS

The tourist office organises two-hour af-ternoon **château visits** (adult/child €9.60/6; ☼ Mon-Sat May-Sep) in French and English. It also runs various events throughout the year, such as **Les Vendredis Vignerons** (Winemakers' Friday; tickets €68; ☼ 11am-5pm Fri Jun-Sep) that combines a day in the vine-yards and lunch with a local winemaker.

SLEEPING & EATING

Hôtel-Restaurant du Palais Cardinal (☎ 05 57 24 72 39; www.palais-cardinal.com; place du 11 Novembre 1918; s €67-208, d €70-266; ☒) Run by the same family for five gen-erations. The hotel's heated pool is set in rambling flower-filled gardens and framed by sections of the original medi-eval town-wall fortifications. Gastronomic fare at its restaurant includes the likes of Cognac-glazed shrimp and spiced St-Émilion wine plums accompanied by blackcurrant sorbet.

ourpick **Hostellerie de Plaisance** (☎ 05 57 55 07 55; www.hostellerie-plaisance.com; place du Clocher; d €310-520, ste €620; ☼ closed Jan; ☒ ☐) With a spice-coloured bar open-ing to a wraparound terrace, this intimate gem in the shadow of the bell tower re-cently expanded to house 17 whimsical rooms. Its two-Michelin-star restaurant (menus €55 to €120; closed Wednesday lunch and all day Sunday and Monday) is now housed in a dining room of egg-shell blue and white gold.

Antique shop, St-Martin-de-Ré, Île de Ré

RACHEL LEWIS

L'Envers du Décor (☎ 05 57 74 48 31; 11 rue du Clocher; lunch menus €18-28, dinner menu €28; ☺ lunch & dinner) Warmed by a wood fire in the cooler months, this local favourite serves market-fresh *menus* and opens to a quiet rear courtyard garden.

SHOPPING

St-Émilion's sloping streets and squares are lined with about 50 wine shops. The best value is **Maison du Vin** (☎ 05 57 55 50 55; place Pierre Meyrat; ☺ 9.30am-12.30pm & 2-6pm Sep-Jul, 9.30am-7pm Aug).

Ursuline nuns brought the recipe for *macarons* (macaroons – almond biscuits) to St-Émilion in the 17th century. Specialist shops around town charge €6 per two dozen.

GETTING THERE & AWAY

Trains run three times daily from Bordeaux (€7.70, 40 minutes); the train station is 1km south of the base of the village.

Year-round the tourist office rents out bicycles for €10/14.70 per half-/full day.

Call for a **taxi** (☎ 05 57 25 17 59; www.taxi-st-emilion.com).

ÎLE DE RÉ

pop 16,000

Spanning 30km from its most easterly and westerly points, and just 5km at its widest section, Île de Ré is scattered with 10 villages of traditional green-shuttered, whitewashed buildings with red Spanish-tile roofs. Even with the advent of the bridge linking it to La Rochelle, Île de Ré retains an isolated feel.

On the northern coast, the quaint fishing port of **St-Martin-de-Ré** (population 2500) is the island's main town. St-Martin's **Tourist Office** (☎ 05 46 09 20 06; www.iledere .com; av Victor Bouthillier; ☺ 10am-6pm Mon-Sat, to noon Sun May-Sep, 10am-noon & 2-6pm Mon-Sat Oct-Apr) is about 100m on your right, across the port, from the Rébus stop. The island's best **beaches** are along the southern edge and the pancake-flat island is ideal for **cycling**. Bikes can be delivered to the bridge by **Cycland** (☎ 05 46 09 65 27).

COGNAC

pop 19,400

On the banks of the River Charente amid vine-covered countryside, Cognac is known worldwide for the double-distilled spirit that bears its name.

Cognac's central, café-ringed roundabout place François 1er, is 200m northeast of the **Tourist Office** (☎ 05 45 82 10 71; www.tourism-cognac.com; 16 rue du 14 Juillet; ☺ 9am-7pm Mon-Sat, 10am-4pm Sun Jul & Aug, 9.30am-5.30pm Mon-Sat May, Jun & Sep, 10am-5pm Mon-Sat Oct-Apr).

Half-timbered 15th- to 17th-century houses line the narrow streets of the **Vieille Ville** (old city). At the southern corner of the leafy **Jardin Public** (Public Park) is the **Musée de Cognac** (☎ 05 45 32 07 25; 48 bd Denfert Rochereau; adult/child €4.50/ free; ☺ 10am-6pm Apr-Oct, 2-5.30pm Wed-Mon Nov-Mar), showcasing the town's history. Admission here also covers **Le Musée des Arts du Cognac** (☎ 05 45 32 07 25; 48 bd Denfert Rochereau; ☺ 10am-6pm Apr-Oct, 2-5.30pm Tue-Sun Nov-Mar), taking you step by step through the production of cognac.

Hôtel Héritage (☎ 05 45 82 01 26; www .hheritage.com; 25 rue d'Angoulême; d €68-74) This wi-fi'd 17th-century mansion in the heart of town proves period elegance and contemporary style don't have to be mutually exclusive. The hotel's restaurant, La Belle Époque, specialises in reintroducing long-lost regional classics (menus €18 to €29).

Angoulême-Cognac airport (www .aeroport-angouleme-cognac.com) is about

---

THE HOME OF COGNAC

According to local lore, divine intervention plays a role in the production of Cognac. Made of grape *eaux-de-vie* (brandies) of various vintages, Cognac is aged in oak barrels and blended by an experienced *maître de chai* (cellar master). Each year some 2% of the casks' volume – *la part des anges* (the angels' share) – evaporates through the pores in the wood, nourishing the tiny black mushrooms that thrive on the walls of cognac warehouses.

The best-known **Cognac houses** are open to the public, and also run tours of their cellars and production facilities, ending with a tasting session. Opening times vary annually; it's a good idea to reserve in advance.

Camus (☎ 05 45 32 28 28; www.camus.fr; 29 rue Marguerite de Navarre; adult from €7, under 18yr free)

Hennessy (☎ 05 45 35 72 68; www.hennessy-cognac.com; 8 rue Richonne; adult from €9, 12-18yr €7, under 12yr free; ☺ closed Jan & Feb) Tours include a film (in English) and a boat trip across the Charente to visit the cellars.

Martell (☎ 05 45 36 33 33; www.martell.com; place Édouard Martell; adult/12-18yr/under 12yr €7/3/free) Found 250m northwest of the tourist office.

Otard (☎ 05 45 36 88 86; www.otard.com; 127 bd Denfert Rochereau; adult/12-18yr/under 12yr €7/3.50/free) Housed in the 1494 birthplace of King François I, the Château de Cognac, 650m north of place François 1er.

Rémy Martin (☎ 05 45 35 76 66; www.remymartin.com) Two locations: the **estate** (adult/12-18yr/under 12yr €14/7/free; ☺ closed Oct-Apr), 4km southwest of town towards Pons; and, in town, the **house** (adult/12-18yr/under 12yr €25/14/7; ☺ year-round by appointment), for intimate tastings in groups of eight.

30km northwest of town and is connected to London (Stansted). A shuttle to/from Cognac costs €5 one-way (bring euros with you).

ARCACHON
pop 11,800

A long-time oyster-harvesting area on the southern side of the tranquil, triangular Bassin d'Arcachon (Arcachon Bay), this seaside town lured bourgeois Bordelaise at the end of the 19th century. Its four little quarters are romantically named for each of the seasons, with villas that evoke the town's golden past amid a scattering of 1950s architecture.

Arcachon seethes with sun-seekers in summer, but you'll find practically deserted beaches a short bike ride away.

INFORMATION
Tourist Office (☎ 05 57 52 97 97; www .arcachon.com; Esplanade Georges Pompidou; ☾ 9am-7pm Jul & Aug, 9am-6.30pm Mon-Fri, to 5pm Sat, 10am-noon & 1-5pm Sun Apr-Jun & Sep, 9am-6pm Mon-Fri, 9am-5pm Sat Oct-Mar)

SIGHTS
In the **Ville d'Été** (Summer Quarter) Arcachon's beautiful sandy beach, **Plage d'Arcachon**, is flanked by two piers.

On the tree-covered hillside south of the Ville d'Été, the century-old **Ville d'Hiver** (Winter Quarter) has over 300 villas, many decorated with delicate wood tracery, ranging in style from neo-Gothic through to colonial. It's an easy stroll or a short ride up the **art-deco public lift** (admission free; ☾ 9am-12.45pm & 2.30-7pm) in Parc Mauresque.

A tree-lined **pedestrian promenade** runs west from the Plage d'Arcachon to **Plage Pércire**, **Plage des Abatilles** and the **Dune du Pilat** (p308). **Cycle paths** link Arcachon with the Dune du Pilat

Sandboarding, Dune du Pilat (p308)

and Biscarosse (30km to the south), and around the Bassin d'Arcachon to Cap Ferret. From here, a cyclable path parallels the beaches north to Pointe de Grave.

The tourist office has details of stacks of other activities including **tandem parachuting**, **seaplane flights**, **wakeboarding** and more.

TOURS
Les Bateliers Arcachonnais (UBA; ☎ 05 57 72 28 28; www.bateliers-arcachon.asso.fr, in French) runs daily, year-round cruises around the **Île aux Oiseaux** (adult/child €13.50/9.50), the uninhabited 'bird island' in the middle of the bay. It's a haven for tern, curlew and redshank, so bring your binoculars. In summer there are regular all day excursions (11am to 5.30pm) to the

Dune du Pilat

ANDREW BAIN

◥ DUNE DU PILAT

This colossal sand dune (sometimes referred to as the Dune de Pyla because of its location in the resort town of Pyla-sur-Mer), 8km south of Arcachon, stretches from the mouth of the Bassin d'Arcachon southwards for almost 3km.

The view from the top, approximately 114m above sea level, is magnificent. To the west you can see the sandy shoals at the mouth of the Bassin d'Arcachon, including the **Banc d'Arguin bird reserve** and **Cap Ferret**. Dense dark-green pine forests stretch from the base of the dune eastwards almost as far as the eye can see.

Hôtel Yatt, built in 1950 and renovated with a designer's eye, is a hip hotel in the café-clad Moulleau fishing village, 400m north of Pyla-sur-Mer, footsteps from the jetty and the beach.

Côte du Sud is a chic little beachside boutique hotel that has eight exotic rooms inspired by a spectrum of continents.

Cycling is the most popular way to reach the dune from Arcachon (see p307).

Things you need to know: Hôtel Yatt (☎ 05 57 72 03 72; www.yatt-hotel.com, in French; 253 bd Côte D'Argent, Moulleau village; d €45-105, tr €60-105, q €70-115, mini ste €80-135; 🕑 closed mid-Nov–week before Easter; 🌠 🗙); Côte du Sud (☎ 05 56 83 25 00; www.cote-du-sud.fr; 4 av du Figuier; d €59-130; 🕑 closed Dec-early Feb; 🌠)

Banc d'Arguin, the sand bank off the Dune du Pilat (€16/11 per adult/child).

SLEEPING

Arcachon has scads of accommodation options. Many are chintzy mid-20th-century time warps, though not without charm.

Hôtel le Dauphin (☎ 05 56 83 02 89; www.dauphin-arcachon.com; 7 av Gounod; d €57-88, tr €64-95, q €71-107; 🌠 🚊) Don' miss this late-19th-century gingerbread place with patterned red-and-cream brickwork. An icon of its era, it's graced by twin semi-circular staircases, magnolias and palms.

Plain but spacious rooms are well set up for families.

Hôtel Point France (☎ 05 56 83 46 74; www
.hotel-point-france.com; 1 rue Grenier; s €82-140, d
€85-181; ❄) All 34 rooms at this retro-chic
place near the beach have balconies. Rooms
facing the sea have knock-out views.

EATING

The bay's oysters (served raw and accompanied by the local small, flat sausages, *cre-
pinettes*) appear on *menus* everywhere.

Aux Mille Saveurs (☎ 05 56 83 40 28; 25 bd
du Général Leclerc; menus €18-35, tasting menu €45;
❄ closed dinner Tue & Wed low season) In a light-
filled space of flowing white tablecloths,
this genteel restaurant is renowned for
traditional French fare artistically presented on fine china.

La Calypso (☎ 05 56 83 65 08; 84 bd de la
Plage; menu €25; ❄ closed Wed & Thu Sep-Jun)
Beneath beamed ceilings, with a cosy
open fire flickering in the chillier months,
this is an amiable place to tuck in to specialities like sole stuffed with crab, honey-
glazed duck, and a delicious *bouillabaisse
arcachonnaise* (fish soup) made from local
sea critters.

GETTING THERE & AROUND

Locabeach (☎ 05 56 83 39 64; www.locabeach
.com, in French; 326 bd de la Plage; ❄ 9am-12.30pm
& 2.30-7pm) rents out mopeds from €25/39
per half-/full day, and bicycles per half-
/full day from €7/10.

Frequent trains between Bordeaux and
Arcachon (€9.90, 50 minutes) coordinate
with TGVs from Paris' Gare Montparnasse.

FRENCH BASQUE COUNTRY

Gently sloping from the western foothills
of the Pyrenees into the deep sapphire-
blue Bay of Biscay, the Basque Country

(Euskal Herria in the Basque language; Le
Pays Basque in French) straddles modern-
day France and Spain. Yet this feisty, independent land remains profoundly different from either of the nation states that
have adopted it.

The French side is famed for its glitzy
beach resort, Biarritz. Its cultural and
economic capital is Bayonne, whose au-
thentically preserved old town is bisected
by bridges arcing over its confluence of
rivers.

Up in the lush hills, little one-street
villages and green valleys traversed by
hiking trails are easily explored from
the walled town of St-Jean-Pied-de-
Port, an age-old pit stop for pilgrims
heading over the border to Santiago de
Compostela.

BAYONNE

pop 44,200

Bayonne (Baiona in Basque) is defined by
the so-named 'river junction' of the River
Adour and the smaller River Nive. Until
1907, it was forbidden to build outside
the town's fortifications, resulting in the
narrow, curved streets of Petit Bayonne,
with riverside buildings clad in red-and-
green shutters and shoals of waterside
restaurants.

In addition to its chocolates, Bayonne is
famous for its prime cured ham.

INFORMATION

Tourist Office (☎ 08 20 42 64 64; www.bay
onne-tourisme.com; place des Basques; ❄ 9am-
7pm Mon-Sat, 10am-1pm Sun Jul & Aug, 9am-
6.30pm Mon-Fri, 10am-6pm Sat Sep-Jun)

SIGHTS

The twin towers of Bayonne's Gothic
cathedral (❄ 8am-noon & 3-7pm Mon-Sat)
soar above the city. Construction began
in the 13th century. Above the north aisle

are three lovely stained-glass windows. The entrance to the stately 13th-century cloister (☼ 9am-12.30pm & 2-6pm Jun-Sep, to 5pm Oct-May) is on place Louis Pasteur.

The seafaring history and cultural identity of the unique Basque people are all explored at the **Musée Basque et de l'Histoire de Bayonne** (☎ 05 59 59 08 98; www .musee-basque.com, in French; 37 quai des Corsaires; adult/student/under 18yr €5.50/3/free; ☼ 10am-6.30pm daily Jul & Aug, closed Mon Sep-Jun).

FESTIVALS & EVENTS
Ham Fair During Easter week, the town hosts a Ham Fair, honouring *jambon de Bayonne,* the acclaimed local ham.

Fêtes de Bayonne The town's premier fiesta is the five-day Fêtes de Bayonne, the first Wednesday in August. They do a 'running of the bulls', as in Pamplona, Spain, only here they use cows not bulls and most of the time participants are chasing the frisky heifers rather than vice versa.

SLEEPING & EATING
Hôtel des Arceaux (☎ 05 59 59 15 53; www .hotel-arceaux.com, in French; 26 rue Port Neuf; r from €79) These 17 spick-and-span rooms are decorated in a fresh palette of colours reflecting the Basque sky, green hills, warm earth and golden sands, and some can accommodate families.

ourpick La Criée (☎ 05 59 59 56 60; 14 quai Chaho; mains €8-13.50; ☼ lunch Mon-Sat, dinner Tue-Sat) Decked out in marine colours, this unassuming little find does delicious Basque seafood specialities (such as *les chipirons à l'espagnole* – squid with sweet peppers served with finely ground rice). For dessert, don't miss the *ardi gasna* (local cheese with cherry jam).

Le Chistera (☎ 05 59 59 25 93; 42 rue Port Neuf; mains €10-16; ☼ lunch Tue-Sun, dinner Thu-Sun) A local gathering spot, this aromatic,

traditional Basque place is named for the *chistera* (basket) that *pelota* players strap to their wrists, and is decorated with motifs from the sport, thanks to two generations of owners who are ex-professional players.

Ttipia (☎ 05 59 46 13 31; 27 rue des Cordeliers; menu €28; ☼ lunch Tue-Sun, dinner Mon-Sat) Help yourself to unlimited cider direct from the huge barrels and take a seat at long communal tables to tuck into Ttipia's only offering, a set menu comprising an omelette with *morue* (salt cod) and *merlu* (hake) wrapped in paper, and salted pork with salad, followed by local cheese and nuts.

ENTERTAINMENT
Every Thursday in July and August, there's traditional **Basque music** (admission free; ☼ from 9.30pm) in place Charles de Gaulle.

Between October and June **Trinquet St-André** (☎ 05 59 59 18 69; rue du Jeu de Paume; tickets around €9) stages *main nue pelota* matches (see boxed text, p312) every Thursday at 4.30pm.

In summer, bullfights are held at **Les Arènes** (☎ 05 59 25 65 30; 19 av du Maréchal Foch). The tourist office has details.

SHOPPING
To buy Bayonne's famous ham visit specialist shop **Pierre Ibaïalde** (☎ 05 59 25 65 30; 41 rue des Cordeliers), where you can taste before you buy.

GETTING THERE & AWAY
Biarritz-Anglet-Bayonne airport (☎ 05 59 43 83 83; www.biarritz.aeroport.fr) is 5km southwest. Bus 6 links both Bayonne and Biarritz with the airport. A taxi from the town centre costs around €15 to €20.

TGVs run between Bayonne and Paris' Gare Montparnasse (€75.60, five hours).

BORDEAUX & THE SOUTHWEST

OLIVER STREWE

St-Jean-de-Luz

FRENCH BASQUE COUNTRY

⤵ IF YOU LIKE...

If you were bowled over by the **Dune du Pilat** (p308), you'll love these equally dramatic coastal spots:

- **Cap Ferret** (www.lege-capferret.com) Hidden beneath pine trees at the tip of the Cap Ferret peninsula (population 6392), this tiny village spans a mere 2km between tranquil bay and crashing Atlantic surf. Scale its red-and-white lighthouse for coastal stunning views. Catch a **ferry** (www.bateliers-arcachon.asso .fr) from Arcachon or enjoy the scenic drive around Bassin d'Arcachon.

- **Gujan Mestras** (www.ville-gujanmestras.fr) Flat-bottomed oyster boats moored to weathered wooden shacks dot the pretty ports around this town (population 15,367), 15km east of Arcachon. Learn about oyster farming at its **Maison de l'Huître** (☎ 05 56 66 23 71; adult/child €4.50/2.50; ☯ 10am-12.30pm & 2.30-6pm Mon-Sat year-round plus 10am-12.30pm & 2.30-6pm Sun Jun-Aug) and savour local oysters at nearby waterside restaurant terraces.

- **St-Jean-de-Luz** (www.saint-jean-de-luz.com) With its narrow streets, beach sprouting bathing huts, sheltered bay, surf and lively fishing port pulling in shoals of sardines, tuna and anchovies, St-Jean-de-Luz (population 13,600), 24km southwest of Bayonne, is your quintessential French Basque seaside town. Join locals gorging on fresh sardines and tuna slabs at **Grillerie du Port** (☎ 05 59 51 18 29; quai du Maréchal Leclerc; ☯ mid-Jun–mid-Sep) and learn about Izarra (Basque for 'star'), a liquor made from 20 different local plants, at the **Écomusée Basque** (☎ 05 59 51 06 06; adult/student/child €5.50/5/2.30), 2km north on the N10.

There are five trains daily to St-Jean-Pied-de-Port (€8.20, 1¼ hours) and fairly frequent services to St Jean de-Luz (€4.30, 25 minutes) via Biarritz (€2.30, nine minutes).

BIARRITZ

pop 30,700

As ritzy as its name suggests, this stylish coastal town, 8km west of Bayonne, took off as a resort in the mid-19th century when

PELOTA

Even in the tiniest of Basque villages, you'll find a church, a cemetery, a town hall and at least one *pelota* court.

The term *pelota* (*pelote basque* in French) is actually the generic name for a group of 16 different native Basque games. The courts differ, but all are played using a hard ball with a rubber core (the *pelote*), which is struck with bare hands (*mains nues*), a wooden paddle (*pala* or *paleta*), or a scooplike racquet made of wicker, leather or wood and strapped to the wrist (*chistera*). The latter is used in *cesta punta*, also known as *jaï alaï*, which, with its three-walled court, is the world's fastest ball game (up to 250km/h) and electrifying to watch.

Napoléon III and his Spanish-born wife, Eugénie, visited regularly. Along its rocky coastline are architectural hallmarks of this golden age, and the belle-époque and art-deco eras that followed. Although it retains a high glamour quotient (and high prices to match), it's also a magnet for vanloads of surfers, with some of Europe's best waves.

INFORMATION
Tourist Office (☎ 05 59 22 37 00; www.biarritz .fr; square d'Ixelles; ☼ 9am-7pm daily Jul & Aug, 9am-6pm Mon-Sat, 10am-5pm Sun Sep-Jun)

SIGHTS & ACTIVITIES
Biarritz' fashionable beaches, particularly the **Grande Plage** and **Plage Miramar**, are end-to-end bodies on hot summer days. North of Pointe St-Martin, the adrenaline-pumping surfing beaches of **Anglet** (the final 't' is pronounced) continue northwards for more than 4km.

Biarritz' **Musée de la Mer** (Sea Museum; ☎ 05 59 22 33 34; www.museedelamer.com; Esplanade du Rocher de la Vierge; adult/child €7.80/5; ☼ 9.30am-12.30pm & 2-6pm, closed Mon Nov-Mar) has tanks seething with underwater life from the Bay of Biscay (Golfe de Gascogne), as well as exhibits recalling Biarritz' whaling past.

If the swell's big, you might get a drenching as you cross the footbridge at the end

of Pointe Atalaye to **Rocher de la Vierge** (Rock of the Virgin). Views from this impressive outcrop, named after its white statue of the Virgin and child, extend to the mountains of the Spanish Basque Country.

Climbing the 258 twisting steps inside the 73m-high **Phare de Biarritz** (admission €2; ☼ 10am-noon & 3-7pm daily Jul & Aug, 2-6pm Sat & Sun Sep-Jun plus 2-5pm weekdays during school holidays), the town's 1834 lighthouse, rewards you with sweeping views of the Basque coast.

SLEEPING
Hôtel Maïtagaria (☎ 05 59 24 26 65; www .hotel-maitagaria.com; 34 av Carnot; s €49-54, d €57-69, tr €76-90) Spotless modern rooms with art-deco furniture and immaculate bathrooms make this friendly place good value. Not least of its charms is its summer terrace opening off the comfy guest lounge.

Hôtel Mirano (☎ 05 59 23 11 63; www .hotelmirano.fr, in French; 11 av Pasteur; r €70-110) Squiggly purple, orange and black wallpaper and oversize orange perspex light fittings are some of the rad '70s touches at this boutique retro hotel, a 10-minute stroll from the town centre.

Villa Le Goëland (☎ 05 59 24 25 76; www .villagoeland.com; 12 plateau de l'Atalaye; r €130-280; ▯ ✕) This family home, with its châteaulike spires, perches high on a plateau above

Pointe Atalaye. Rooms have panoramic views of town, the sea and across to Spain. Advance booking is essential.

EATING

See-and-be-seen cafés and restaurants line Biarritz' beachfront.

Le Corsaire (☎ 05 59 24 63 72; Port des Pêcheurs; mains €11-23.50; ☽ lunch & dinner Tue-Sat) Down by the water's edge, sit out on the terrace to savour dishes like grilled cod with chorizo. On either side, the neighbouring seafood restaurants in this little harbourside setting offer similar quality and prices, and are equally appealing.

Bistrot des Halles (☎ 05 59 24 21 22; 1 rue du Centre; mains €14.50-17; ☽ lunch & dinner) One of a cluster of decent restaurants along rue du Centre that get their produce directly from the nearby covered market, this bustling place serves excellent fish and other fresh fare from the blackboard menu in an interior adorned with old metallic advertising posters.

SHOPPING

At **Pare Gabia** (☎ 05 59 24 22 51; 18 rue Mazagran), Vincent Corbun continues his grandfather's business, established in 1935, making and selling espadrilles in a rainbow of colours and styles (customised with ribbons and laces while you wait). A pair starts from €10.

GETTING THERE & AWAY

Biarritz-La Négresse train station is about 3km south of the town centre; buses 2 and 9 connect the two. Times, fares and destinations are much the same as Bayonne's, a nine-minute train journey away.

ST-JEAN-PIED-DE-PORT

pop 1700

At the foot of the Pyrenees, the walled town of St-Jean-Pied-de-Port, 53km southeast of Bayonne, was for centuries the last stop in France for pilgrims heading south over the Spanish border, a mere 8km away, and on to Santiago de Compostela in western Spain.

St-Jean-Pied-de-Port makes an ideal day trip from Bayonne, particularly on Monday when the market is in full swing. Half the reason for coming here is the scenic journey south of Cambo-les-Bains, as both railway and road (the D918) pass through rocky hills, forests and lush meadows dotted with white farmhouses selling *ardi* ('cheese' in Basque).

INFORMATION

Tourist Office (☎ 05 59 37 03 57; www .pyrenees-basque.com; place Charles de Gaulle;

Biarritz
GREG JOHNSTON

BORDEAUX & THE SOUTHWEST

FRENCH BASQUE COUNTRY

⊙ 9am-7pm Mon-Sat, 10am-4pm Sun Jul & Aug, 9am-noon & 2-6pm Mon-Sat Sep-Jun)

SIGHTS
OLD TOWN

The **Église Notre Dame du Bout du Pont**, with foundations as old as the town itself, was rebuilt in the 17th century. Beyond **Porte de Notre Dame** is the photogenic **Vieux Pont** (Old Bridge), from where there's a fine view of whitewashed houses with balconies leaning out above the water.

Rue de la Citadelle is edged by substantial, pink-granite, 16th- to 18th-century houses. A common motif is the scallop shell, symbol of St Jacques (St James or Santiago) and of the Santiago de Compostela pilgrims. Pilgrims would enter the town through the **Porte de St-Jacques** on the northern side of town, then, head for Spain through the **Porte d'Espagne**, south of the river.

LA CITADELLE

From the top of rue de la Citadelle, a rough cobblestone path ascends to the massive citadel itself, from where there's a spectacular panorama of the town and the surrounding hills. Constructed in 1628, the fort was rebuilt around 1680 by military engineers of the Vauban school. If you've a head for heights, descend by the steps signed *escalier poterne* (rear stairway). Steep and slippery after rain, they plunge beside the moss-covered ramparts to **Porte de l'Échauguette** (Watchtower Gate).

SLEEPING & EATING

ourpick **Maison E Bernat** (☎ 05 59 37 23 10; www.ebernat.com; 20 rue de la Citadelle; d incl breakfast €66-86, extra person €24; 🖳) There are only four bedrooms in this welcoming 17th-century place with thick stone walls, but they're airy, well furnished and meticulously kept. There's a great little restaurant on-site, spilling onto a tiny terrace (*menus* from €11).

Chez Arrambide (menus €40-85, mains €20-49) This twin Michelin-starred restaurant, the real reason to stop by Hôtel les Pyrénées, is where chef Firmin Arrambide does wonders with market produce, such

Frozen lake, Pyrenees

DAVID ELSE

as pan-fried duck breast with ginger and cinnamon- or foie-gras-stuffed hare.

Farmers from the surrounding hills bring fresh produce – chilli peppers and local cheeses and much more – to the town's **Monday market** (place Charles de Gaulle).

GETTING THERE & AWAY

Train is the best option to/from Bayonne (€8.20, 1¼ hours).

THE PYRENEES

Snow-capped for much of the year, the jagged peaks of the Pyrenees (les Pyrénées) form a natural, 430km-long boundary between France and Spain. Their rugged ridges and precarious cols fall within the narrow strip of the Parc National des Pyrénées that shadows the frontier for about 100km. Disappear into these protected mountains for days and spot only other walkers, marmots, izards (cousin to the chamois) and, perhaps, one of the Pyrenees' few brown bears.

Rising steadily from the Atlantic through mist and cloud, the Pyrénées-Atlantiques cradle the mountains' largest and most stylish town, Pau. To the southeast sits Lourdes, one of Christianity's most revered pilgrimage sites.

PAU

pop 80,600

Palm trees might seem out of place in this mountainous region, but its chief city, Pau (rhymes with 'so'), has long been famed for its mild climate. In the 19th century it was a favourite wintering spot for wealthy English and Americans, who left behind grand villas, English-style flower-filled public parks and promenades that had with dizzying vistas of the snow-dusted peaks.

INFORMATION

Tourist Office (☎ 05 59 27 27 08; www.tourismepau.com; place Royale; ☺ 9am-6pm Mon-Sat, 9.30am-noon & 2-6pm Sun, closed Sun afternoon Sep-Jun)

SIGHTS

Pau's **château** (☎ 05 59 82 38 02; www.musee-chateau-pau.fr, in French; adult/18-25yr/under 18yr €5/3.50/free; ☺ 9.30am-12.15pm & 1.30-5.45pm mid-Jun–mid-Sep, 9.30-11.45am & 2-5pm mid-Sep–mid-Jun) holds one of Europe's richest collections of 16th- to 18th-century Gobelins tapestries.

A mesmerising panorama of the Pyrenean summits unfolds from the majestic bd des Pyrénées. An **orientation table** details the names of the peaks. For information on the funicular, see p316.

Pau's old centre is rich in restored medieval and Renaissance buildings. The **Musée Bernadotte** (☎ 05 59 27 48 42; 8 rue Tran; adult/student/child €3/1.50/free; ☺ 10am-noon & 2-6pm Tue-Sun) has exhibits illustrating the improbable yet true story of how a French general, Jean-Baptiste Bernadotte, born in this very building, became king of Sweden and Norway in 1810, when the Swedish Riksdag (parliament) reckoned that the only way out of the country's dynastic and political crisis was to stick a foreigner on the throne.

SLEEPING

Hôtel Montpensier (☎ 05 59 27 42 72; www.hotel-montpensier-pau.com; 36 rue Montpensier; s €75-95, d €85-95; 🅿 ✕) Sunlit, coir-carpeted rooms spill over with shimmering taffeta and silk cushions, and metallic and timber furniture at this boutique gem. In fine weather you can take breakfast (€9) on the garden terrace.

Hôtel Parc de Beaumont (☎ 05 59 11 84 00; www.hotel-parc-beaumont.com; 1 av Edouard VII; r from €195; 🅿 🖳 ✕ 🛎) Built from striking

ECO EATING & DRINKING

Artisan produce abounds along the **Route Gourmande de Basque** (Basque Gourmand Route; ☎ 05 59 54 56 70; www.routegourmandebasque.com). The route links 10 producers over 126km, but if you're short on time you can cherry-pick among them. Along the way, you can learn about and taste Basque specialities including ham, trout, wine, cheese, chilli peppers, Basque cake, cider, Izarra liquor, chocolate and honey, all utilising traditional methods for minimal environmental impact and deliciously rich, natural flavours.

materials including steel, wood and glass, public areas at this ultracontemporary hotel are hung with original works of art.

EATING

ourpick **Pau Golf Club** (☎ 05 59 13 18 56; www .paugolfclub.com; rue du Golf; menus €10-20, mains €7-15; ☺ lunch daily) A veritable museum, this 1856-built, still-operating golf course was the first ever on the European continent. Dining at its brass-and-timber restaurant allows you to survey its antique golf clubs, artworks painted at various stages of its history, and cabinets full of old trophies. The food is hearty and regional, and diners often break spontaneously into song (it's a Pyrenean thing…).

Brasserie Le Berry (☎ 05 59 27 42 95; 4 rue Gachet; mains €13-18; ☺ lunch & dinner) Adored by locals for its top value, original 1950s ambience and classical brasserie fare including scrumptious homemade desserts, Le Berry's tables are hotly contested (they don't take reservations). Be sure to arrive early, especially at lunchtime, when there's a €7.80 *plat du jour*.

La Table d'Hôte (☎ 05 59 27 56 06; 1 rue Hédas; menus €18-31; ☺ lunch & dinner Wed-Sun) On a little country lane, this 17th-century tannery is all beams, mellow exposed brickwork and rough plaster. Service is cheerful, and dishes – such as *cochon noir Gascon*, locally reared pork stuffed with frilly mushrooms and soaked in its juices – are creative and delightfully presented.

Look out for the local **Jurançon wines** (www.cavedejurancon.com), whose vineyards ribbon the surrounding countryside.

GETTING THERE & AWAY

The **Aéroport Pau-Pyrénées** (☎ 05 59 33 33 00; www.pau.aeroport.fr) is about 10km northwest of town. A taxi costs around €25.

Around 10 direct trains run to Bayonne (€15, 1¼ hours). There are five daily TGVs to Paris' Gare Montparnasse (from €79.70, 5½ hours).

The train station is linked to bd des Pyrénées by a free **funicular railway** (☺ 6am-10pm, approximately every 3min), a wonderful creaky little contraption dating from 1908. (The short walk, even uphill, takes much the same time.)

LOURDES

pop 15,700 / elevation 400m

Lourdes, 43km southeast of Pau, has become one of the world's most important pilgrimage sites since 1858, when 14-year-old Bernadette Soubirous (1844–79) saw the Virgin Mary in a series of 18 visions that came to her in a grotto. The Vatican confirmed them as bona-fide apparitions and the little country girl turned nun was beatified in 1933.

Catering to some six million visitors annually, the town is now awash with neon-signed hotels and over 220 souvenir shops selling cut-price statues, rosaries and crucifixes and Virgin Mary–shaped plastic bottles (just add holy water at the shrine).

INFORMATION
Forum Information office (☎ 05 62 42 78 78; www.lourdes-france.com; Esplanade des Processions; ☒ 8.30am-6.30pm Apr-Oct, 9am-noon & 2-6pm Nov-Mar) For information on the Sanctuaires Notre Dame de Lourdes.
Tourist Office (☎ 05 62 42 77 40; www.lourdes -infotourisme.com; place Peyramale; ☒ 9am-7pm Mon-Sat, 10am-6pm Sun Jul & Aug, 9am-6.30pm Mon-Sat, 10am-12.30pm Sun Apr-Jun & Sep, 9am-noon & 2-6pm Mon-Sat Jan-Mar & Oct-Dec)

SIGHTS
The development of the Sanctuaries of Our Lady of Lourdes began within a decade of Ste Bernadette's apparitions in 1858. The most revered site is known variously as the **Grotte de Massabielle** (Massabielle Cave or Grotto), the Grotte Miraculeuse (Miraculous Cave) and the Grotte des Apparitions (Cave of the Apparitions). Open 24 hours, its walls are worn smooth by the touch of millions of hands over the years. Hundreds of candles, donated by pilgrims, flicker. Adjacent are 19 individual **baths** (☒ generally 9-11am & 2.30-4pm Mon-Sat, 2-4pm Sun & holy days), separated into men's and women's areas. Volunteers in the change rooms shield you with blue cloaks as you strip off your clothes (yep, all of them), swaddle you in a wet, white, cotton

MARTIN MOOS

Notre Dame de Lourdes

sheet, then, after you step into the bath, walk to the end and kiss the Virgin Mary statue, they take you by the arms and lower you backwards, dipping you into the bath's seriously icy stream water for a few seconds.

HATS OFF?
The archetypal beret-wearing, baguette-carrying Frenchman may be a caricature, but berets are still sported by plenty of folk in these parts (often carrying baguettes, too).

This quintessential headgear is honoured at the **Musée du Béret** (Beret Museum; ☎ 05 59 61 91 70; place St-Roch; adult/child under 10yr €4/free; ☒ 10am-noon & 2-6pm Tue-Sun Apr-Oct, 2-6pm Tue-Sat Nov-Mar), in the bustling little market town of Nay (a well-signed 24km west of Lourdes along the D937 towards Pau), and have been made here since 1812. Cap off a visit by browsing its boutique's rainbow of colours.

Café patrons, St-Jean-de-Luz (p311)

WAYNE WALTON

Also called Chemin du Calvaire (Way of Calvary), the 1.5km Chemin de Croix (Way of the Cross), leading up the forested hillside from near the Basilique Supérieure, is punctuated by the 14 **Stations of the Cross**. Especially devout pilgrims mount to the first station on their knees.

The **Musée de Lourdes** (☎ 05 62 94 28 00; adult/child €5.50/2.70; ⏰ 9am-noon & 1.30-6.30pm Apr-Oct), in the Parking de l'Égalité, portrays the life of Ste Bernadette as well as the general history of Lourdes. To learn yet more about Ste Bernadette (or to simply rest your feet), **Cinéma Bernadette** (☎ 05 62 42 79 19; 6 av Monseigneur Schoepfer; adult/disabled/child €6.50/5/4.50) shows the two-hour feature film *Bernadette* (with optional English dialogue) at 2pm, 4.30pm and 8.30pm daily from Easter to mid-October.

Panoramic views of Lourdes and the central chain of the Pyrenees unfurl from the summit of **Pic du Jer** (948m). It's a six-minute ride from valley level by the **funicular railway** (☎ 05 62 94 00 41; bd d'Espagne; adult/child one-way €6.50/5, return €9/6.50; ⏰ 10am-6pm Mar-Nov). The signed trail to the summit from the lower station is a more strenuous route (allow 2½ to three hours for the return journey) or simply ride up and walk down.

SLEEPING

Mercure Impérial (☎ 05 62 94 06 30; www .mercure.com; 3 av du Paradis; r €69-145; ⏰ Feb–mid-Dec; ✗ ▣ ✗) This 1930s hotel preserves its original ambience, and its roof terrace is a sublime place to sip an aperitif, overlooking the river and Pont Vieux. The lounge opens out onto a rear garden, and the restaurant is splendid.

ourpick Grand Hôtel de la Grotte (☎ 05 62 94 58 87; www.hotel-grotte.com; 66 rue de la Grotte; s/d/tr from €71/80/94; ⏰ mid-Feb–mid-Oct; ✗ ▣) Established in 1871, Lourdes' first-ever hotel has belonged to the same family for four generations. With richly coloured rooms and suites, a gorgeous garden, a bar and a couple of restaurants, it embodies old-world courtesy.

Hôtel Gallia et Londres (☎ 05 62 94 35 44; www.hotelgallialondres.com; 26 av Bernadette Soubirous; d €120-240; ⏰ Apr-Oct; ✗ ▣) The spacious bedrooms (some with sanctuary views) are individually and attractively decorated à la Louis XVI. You'll gasp at the chandeliers and the wooden panelling of the dining room with its side alcoves for intimate eating. Equally seductive is the lovely little garden.

EATING

Le Cardinal (☎ 05 62 42 05 87; 11 place Peyramale; dishes from €5, daily menu €8.50; ☼ Mon-Sat) Popular with locals, this unpretentious bar-brasserie is great for a drink or for tucking in to huge, healthy salads and filling daily *menus*.

Restaurant le Magret (☎ 05 62 94 20 55; 10 rue des Quatre Frères Soulas; weekday lunch menu €13, dinner menus €26-33, mains €17-23; ☼ Tue-Sun Feb-Dec) Rustic decor embellished with early photos of Lourdes makes an evoca-tive backdrop for dining on innovative regional cuisine including a crayfish 'cappuccino' with wild nettles, served in a glass, raw Pyrenean black-pork ham, and Vallée d'Ossau cheese.

GETTING THERE & AWAY

Tarbes-Lourdes-Pyrénées airport (www .tarbes-lourdes.aeroport.fr) is 10km north of Lourdes on the N21. It mainly handles charter flights, but has up to three scheduled daily Air France flights to/from Paris (Orly). The airport is not served by public transport.

Lourdes is well connected by train lines to French cities including Bayonne (€17.70, 1¾ hours, up to four daily), Pau (€6.80, 30 minutes, 10-plus daily) and Paris' Gare Montparnasse (from €88.80, six hours).

FRANCE IN FOCUS

ARCHITECTURE

GLENN VAN DER KNIJFF

Cathédrale St-Étienne (p127), Metz

From the awe-inspiring prehistoric megaliths around Carnac in Brittany to Vauban's star-shaped citadels built all over France to defend its 17th-century frontiers, French architecture has always been of giant proportions. No surprise then that French political leaders have long sought to immortalise themselves through the erection of huge public edifices, otherwise called *grands projects*.

Georges Pompidou commissioned Paris' Centre Pompidou in 1977; Valéry Giscard d'Estaing transformed a derelict Seine-side train station into the Musée d'Orsay; and François Mitterrand commissioned the capital's best-known contemporary architectural landmarks, including IM Pei's glass pyramid at the Louvre, the Opéra Bastille, the Grande Arche in the skyscraper district of La Défense, and the national library. Best up perhaps is the groundbreaking Musée du Quai Branly on the Seine, a wonderful mirage of glass and green foliage outside.

ROMAN TO GOTHIC

The south is the place to track France's Gallo-Roman architectural legacy: the Pont du Gard, amphitheatres in Nîmes and Arles, the theatre at Orange and Nîmes' Maison Carrée. Several centuries later, architects adopted elements from Gallo-Roman buildings to create *roman* (Romanesque) masterpieces.

Northern France's extraordinary wealth in the 12th century lured the finest architects, engineers and artisans, who created impressive Gothic structures with ribbed vaults carved with great precision, pointed arches, slender verticals, chapels along the nave and chancel, refined decoration and stained-glass windows. Avignon's pontifical palace is Gothic architecture on a gargantuan scale. With the introduction of flying buttresses around 1230, Gothic masterpieces such as the seminal cathedral at Chartres and its successors at Reims, Amiens and Strasbourg appeared.

RENAISSANCE TO ART NOUVEAU

By the 15th century architects had shelved size for ornamentation, conceiving the beautifully lacy Flamboyant Gothic. For an example of such decorative overkill,

BILL WASSMAN

Maison Carrée (p259), Nîmes

FRANCE IN FOCUS

ARCHITECTURE

⤵THE BEST

OWEN FRANKEN/CORBIS

Ice Kube Bar, Kube Hôtel (p82), Paris

THE BEST URBAN DESIGN HOTELS

- **Hôtel du Petit Moulin**, Paris (p80)
- **Kube Hôtel**, Paris (p82)
- **Collège Hôtel**, Lyon (p219)
- **Hôtel Le Corbusier**, Marseille (p251)
- **Seeko'o**, Bordeaux (p300)

check out the spire of Strasbourg cathedral. To trace the shift from late Gothic to Renaissance, travel along the Loire Valley: Château de Chambord illustrates the mix of classical components and decorative motifs typical of early Renaissance architecture. In the mid-16th century, François I had Italian architects design Fontainebleau.

In 1635 early baroque architect François Mansart (1598–1666) designed the classical wing of Château de Blois, while his younger rival, Louis Le Vau (1612–70), started work on Louis XIV's palace at Versailles. A quest for order, reason and serenity through the adoption of the forms and conventions of Greco-Roman antiquity defined neoclassical architecture from 1740 until well into the 19th century. Nancy's place Stanislas is France's loveliest neoclassical square. Under Napoléon meanwhile many of Paris' best-known sights – the Arc de Triomphe, La Madeleine, the Arc du Carrousel at the Louvre and the Assemblée Nationale building – rose out the ground.

Art nouveau (1850–1910) combined iron, brick, glass and ceramics in ways never before seen. See for yourself in Paris with Hector Guimard's noodle-like metro entrances or the fine art-nouveau interiors in the Musée d'Orsay.

CONTEMPORARY

In the 1950s France's most celebrated architect, Le Corbusier (1887–1965) rewrote the architectural style book with the sweeping lines and functionalised forms, adapted to fit the human form, which characterised his structures. Marseille's Hôtel Le Corbusier, inside his iconic concrete monolith, the 337-apartment Unité d'Habitation.

In the provinces, notable buildings include Strasbourg's European Parliament, Dutch architect Rem Koolhaas's Euralille and Jean Nouvel's glass-and-steel Vesunna Musée Gallo-Romain in Périgueux, a 1920s art-deco swimming-pool-turned-art-museum in Lille and the fantastic Louvre in unknown Lens, 37km south of Lille. Also noteworthy is an 11th-century abbey-turned-monumental sculpture gallery in Angers. Then, of course, there's one of the world's tallest bridges, the Pont de Millau in Languedoc, designed by Sir Norman Foster. In Metz meanwhile in northeast France, locals hope the new Centre Pompidou covered by an undulating, translucent membrane of teflon-coated fibreglass, designed to trap rainwater for irrigation, will do for Metz what the Guggenheim did for Bilbao. Architecture aficionados might just say yes.

ART & LITERATURE

SALLY DILLON
Gobelins tapestry, Château de Cheverny (p183), Loire Valley

In a country where natural style and panache counts, it comes as no surprise to learn that art and literature matter deeply to French people and are an important focus of individual and national identity. France's art and literature legacy is great and contemporary artists very much ride on the back of this extraordinary heritage.

No country moreover has inspired so many outsiders to write, paint, compose and fantasise: be it a packed sun-flooded café terrace in Arles (Van Gogh's *Café Terrace At Night*), bohemian Paris between the wars (Ernest Hemingway's *A Movable Feast*) or murder on the mythical *Train Bleu* from the capital to the French Riviera (Agatha Christie's *The Mystery*), France is both timeless and tireless for artists all over the world.

PAINTING FRANCE
CLASSICAL TO ROMANTIC

According to Voltaire, French painting proper began with Nicolas Poussin (1594–1665), known for his classical mythological and biblical scenes bathed in golden light. Wind forward a couple of centuries and modern still life pops onto the scene with Jean-Baptiste Chardin (1699–1779), the first to see still life as an essay in composition rather than a show of skill in reproduction. A century later, neoclassical artist Jacques Louis David (1748–1825) wooed the public with his vast portraits; some are in the Louvre.

While Romantics such as Eugène Delacroix (buried in Paris' Cimetière du Père Lachaise) revamped the subject picture, the Barbizon School effected a parallel transformation

THE BEST

JOHN HAY

Musée du Louvre (p63), Paris

THE BEST ART MUSEUMS

- **Musée d'Orsay**, Paris (p74)
- **Musée du Louvre**, Paris (p63)
- **Musée des Beaux-Arts**, Lyon (p216)
- **CAPC Musée d'Art Contemporain**, Bordeaux (p300)
- **Musée de l'Annonciade**, St-Tropez (p279)
- **MAMAC**, Nice (p270)

of landscape painting. Barbizons included landscape artist Jean-Baptiste Camille Corot (1796–1875) and Jean-François Millet (1814–75). The son of a peasant farmer from Normandy, Millet took many of his subjects from peasant life, and reproductions of his *L'Angélus* (The Angelus; 1857) – the best-known French painting after the *Mona Lisa* – are strung above mantelpieces all over rural France. The original hangs in Paris' Musée d'Orsay.

THE IMPRESSIONISTS

It was in a flower-filled garden in a Normandy village that Claude Monet (1840–1926) expounded Impressionism, a term of derision taken from the title of his experimental painting *Impression: Soleil Levant* (Impression: Sunrise; 1874).

An arthritis-crippled Renoir painted out his last Impressionist days in a villa on the Côte d'Azur. With a warmth and astonishing intensity of light hard to equal, the French Riviera inspired dozens of artists post-Renoir: Paul Cézanne (1839–1906) is particularly celebrated for his post-Impressionist still lifes and landscapes done in Aix-en-Provence where he was born and worked.

In St-Tropez pointillism took off: Georges Seurat (1859–91) was the first to apply paint in small dots or uniform brush strokes of unmixed colour, producing fine mosaics of warm and cool tones, but it was his pupil Paul Signac (1863–1935) who is best known for his pointillist works. See them both in St-Tropez's Musée de l'Annonciade.

MATISSE & PICASSO

Twentieth-century French painting is characterised by a bewildering diversity of styles, including fauvism, named after the slur of a critic who compared the exhibitors at the 1906 autumn Salon in Paris with *fauves* (wild animals) because of their radical use of intensely bright colours, and cubism.

Henri Matisse (1869–1954) was the man behind the former, and Spanish prodigy Pablo Picasso (1881–1973), the latter. Both chose southern France to set up studio, Matisse living in Nice and Picasso opting for a 12th-century château (now the Musée Picasso) in Antibes. Cubism, developed by Picasso and Georges Braque (1882–1963), deconstructed the subject into a system of intersecting planes and simultaneously presented various aspects of it.

SURREALIST PARIS & NEW REALIST NICE

No piece of French art better captures Dada's rebellious spirit than Marcel Duchamp's *Mona Lisa,* complete with moustache and goatee. In 1922 German Dadaist Max Ernst

JOHN HAY

Monet's garden, Giverny (p159)

moved to Paris and worked on surrealism, a Dada offshoot that drew on the theories of Freud to reunite the conscious and unconscious realms and permeate daily life with fantasies and dreams.

With the close of WWII, Paris' role as the artistic capital of the world ended, leaving critics ever since wondering where all the artists have gone. The focus shifted back to southern France in the 1960s with new re-alists such as Arman (1928–2005) and Yves Klein (1928–62), both from Nice. In 1960 Klein famously produced *Anthropométrie de l'Époque Bleue,* a series of imprints made by naked women (covered from head to toe in blue paint) rolling around on a white canvas – in front of an orches-tra of violins and an audience in evening dress. A decade on the Supports/Surfaces movement deconstructed the concept of a painting, transforming one of its struc-tural components (such as the frame or canvas) into a work of art instead.

URBAN MINUTIAE

Artists in the 1990s turned to the minu-tiae of everyday urban life to express so-cial and political angst, using every media other than paint to let rip. Conceptual artist Daniel Buren (b 1938) reduced his painting

DAN HERRICK

Musée Matisse (p270), Nice

THE BEST ART TRAILS

- **Cézanne** in and around Aix-en-Provence (p255)
- **Van Gogh** in Arles' (p257)
- **Matisse** in and around Nice (p270)
- **Picasso** in Paris (p67) and Anti-bes (p274)

to a signature series of vertical 8.7cm-wide stripes that he applies to every surface imaginable – white marble columns in the courtyard of Paris' Palais Royal included. The painter (who in 1967, as part of the radical *groupe BMPT*, signed a manifesto declaring he was not a painter) was the *enfant terrible* of French art in the 1980s. Partner-in-crime Michel Parmentier (1938–2000) insisted on monochrome painting for a while – blue in 1966, grey in 1967 and red in 1968.

> ### TIP OFF
>
> Come 2010, when the Louvre-Lens (www.louvrelens.fr) is set to open in **Lens** (☎ **tourist office 03 21 67 66 66; www.tourisme-lenslievin.fr**) in northern France you'll no longer have to go to Paris to visit the world's most-visited museum. The new museum, which will occupy the site of long-closed coal mine, shaft No 9, is being designed by the Japanese architectural firm Sanaa.

LITERARY LOVE & TRAGEDY

COURTLY TO CLASSICAL

Lyric poems of courtly love composed by troubadours dominated medieval French literature, while the *roman* (literally 'romance', now meaning 'novel') drew on old Celtic tales such as King Arthur, the search for the Holy Grail and so on. With the *Roman de la Rose*, a 22,000-line poem by Guillaume de Lorris and Jean de Meung, the allegorical figures of Pleasure and Riches, Shame and Fear popped on the scene.

La Pléiade, Rabelais and de Montaigne made French Renaissance literature great: La Pléiade was a group of lyrical poets active in the 1550s and 1560s, of whom the best known is Pierre de Ronsard (1524–85), author of four books of odes. The highly exuberant narrative of Loire Valley–born François Rabelais (1494–1553) blends coarse humour with encyclopaedic erudition in a vast panorama of subjects that includes every kind of person, occupation and jargon existing in mid-16th-century France. Michel de Montaigne (1533–92) wrote essays on everything from cannibals, war horses and drunkenness to the uncanny resemblance of children to their fathers.

Le grand siècle ushered in the great French classical writers with their lofty odes to tragedy. François de Malherbe (1555–1628) brought a new rigour to the treatment of

> ### CURRENT ART TRENDS
>
> Paris-born conceptual artist Sophie Calle (b 1953), born to shock, brazenly exposes her private life with her eye-catching installations, which most recently involved 107 women (including Carla Bruni before she became First Lady) reading and interpreting an email she received from her French lover, dumping her.
>
> Track current trends at Paris' **Palais de Tokyo** (www.palaisdetokoyo.com), an art space that's open noon to midnight six days a week and encourages art visitors to feel, touch, talk and interact. **La Maison Rouge** (www.lamaisonrouge.org) is the other key address that bends over backwards to turn every expectation of painting and art on its head.

Mona Lisa, Musée du Louvre (p63), Paris

FRANCE IN FOCUS

ART & LITERATURE

rhythm in poetry; and Marie de La Fayette (1634–93) penned the first major French novel, *La Princesse de Clèves* (1678).

FRENCH ROMANTICISM

The philosophical work of Voltaire (1694–1778) dominated the 18th century. A century on gave birth to Victor Hugo, the key figure of French romanticism. The breadth of interest and technical innovations exhibited in his poems and novels – *Les Misérables* and *Notre Dame de Paris* (The Hunchback of Notre Dame) among them – was phenomenal: after his death, his coffin was laid beneath the Arc de Triomphe for an all-night vigil.

In 1857 literary landmarks *Madame Bovary* by Gustave Flaubert (1821–80), and Charles Baudelaire's (1821–67) collection of poems, *Les Fleurs du Mal* (The Flowers of Evil), were published. Émile Zola (1840–1902) strove to convert novel-writing from an art to a science in his powerful series, *Les Rougon-Macquart*.

The expression of mental states was the ideal of symbolist Paul Verlaine (1844–96) whose poems (alongside those of Arthur Rimbaud with whom Verlaine shared a tempestuous homosexual relationship) were French literature's first modern poems.

CHEEKY COLETTE ET AL

The world's longest novel, a seven-volume 9,609,000-character giant by Marcel Proust (1871–1922), dominated the early 20th century. *À la Recherche du Temps Perdu* (Remembrance of Things Past) explores in evocative detail the true meaning of past experience recovered from the unconscious by 'involuntary memory'.

Surrealism proved a vital force until WWII, André Breton (1896–1966) capturing its spirit, a fascination with dreams, divination and all manifestations of 'the marvellous', in his autobiographical narratives. In Paris the bohemian Colette (1873–1954) captivated

THE NEW GENERATION

No French writer better delves into the mind 'n' mood of France's ethnic population than Faïza Guène. A born-and-bred Paris suburbs ghetto gal', the literary sensation stunned with her debut novel, *Kiffe Kiffe Demain* (Just Like Tomorrow). In 1952 her father, then 17, moved from western Algeria to northern France to work in the mines. Only in the 1980s could he return to Algeria where he met his wife, whom he brought back to France – to a housing estate in Seine-St-Denis where 6000-odd immigrants live like sardines in high-rise blocks. Such is the setting for Guène's first book and her second semiautobiographical novel, *Dreams from the Endz* (2008).

and shocked with her titillating novels detailing the amorous exploits of heroines such as schoolgirl Claudine.

After WWII, existentialism developed around the lively debates of Jean-Paul Sartre (1905–80), Simone de Beauvoir (1908–86) and Albert Camus (1913–60) in Left Bank cafés of Paris' St-Germain-des-Prés.

ANYTHING GOES

The 1950s' *nouveau roman* saw experimental young writers seek new ways of organising narratives, with Nathalie Sarraute slashing identifiable characters and plot in *Les Fruits d'Or* (The Golden Fruits). *Histoire d'O* (Story of O), an erotic sadomasochistic novel written by Dominique Aury under a pseudonym in 1954, sold more copies outside France than any other contemporary French novel. In the 1960s it was Philippe Sollers' experimental novels that raised eyebrows.

Contemporary authors include Françoise Sagan, Pascal Quignard, Anna Gavalda, Emmanuel Carrère, Stéphane Bourguignon and Martin Page, whose novel *Comment Je Suis Devenu Stupide* (How I Became Stupid) explores a 25-year-old Sorbonne student's methodical attempt to become stupid. Also popular are Frédéric Dard (alias San Antonio), Léo Malet and Daniel Pennac, widely read for his witty crime fiction such as *Au Bonheur des Ogres* (The Scapegoat) and *La Fée Carabine* (The Fairy Gunmother).

CAUGHT ON FILM

Sign for Cannes Film Festival (p46)

RICHARD CUMMINS

Watching French classics in the factory in Lyon where the cinematographic pioneers, the Lumière brothers, shot the world's first motion picture in March 1895, is a must for cinema buffs – as is a trip to Cannes, that iconic Riviera town where the biggest and best names in the industry gather each year in May.

France, with its dramatic gaggle of medieval villages teetering precariously atop rocky crags and Unesco-endorsed treasure chest of stunning monuments and natural features, has in fact made the perfect cinema set on many an occasion. Delve into French cinematic history and tour this fascinating country from a filmmaker's perspective.

The French film industry honours its directors and actors with the Césars, named after the Marseille-born artist who created the prestigious statue awarded to winners.

ITS GLORIOUS BIRTH

Cinema's glorious beginnings are showcased in Lyon at the **Musée Lumière** (www.institut -lumiere.org), the art-nouveau home of Antoine Lumière who moved to Lyon with his sons Auguste and Louis in 1870 and shot the first reels of the world's first motion picture, *La Sortie des Usines Lumières* (Exit of the Lumières Factories) in one of their factories here on 19 March 1895. Today classic films are screened in the Hangar du Premier Film (the film set for *La Sortie des Usines Lumières*), which somehow escaped demolition when the rest of the Lumière factories were bulldozed in the 1970s.

French film flourished in the 1920s. Abel Gance (1889–1981) was king of the decade with his antiwar blockbuster *J'Accuse!* (I Accuse!; 1919) – all the more impressive for its location filming on actual WWI battlefields. The switch to sound ushered in René Clair (1898–1981) and his world of fantasy and satirical surrealism.

Montmartre (p77), Paris

JEAN-PIERRE LESCOURRET

WOES OF WAR

WWI inspired the 1930s classic *La Grande Illusion* (The Great Illusion; 1937), a devastating portrayal of the folly of war based on the trench warfare experience of director Jean Renoir (1894–1979). Indeed, portraits of ordinary people and their lives dominated film until the 1950s, when realism was eschewed by surrealist Jean Cocteau (1889–1963) in two masterpieces: *La Belle et la Bête* (Beauty and the Beast; 1945) and *Orphée* (Orpheus; 1950) are unravelled in Menton's Musée Jean Cocteau on the Côte d'Azur.

THE BEST CINEMATIC SETS & SITES

- **La Croisette & Palais des Festivals**, Cannes (p278)
- **American Film Festival**, Deauville (p162)
- **Musée Lumière**, Lyon (p331)
- **Montmartre**, Paris (p77)

Sapped of talent and money after WWII, France's film industry found new energy by the 1950s, and so the *nouvelle vague* (new wave) burst forth. With small budgets and no extravagant sets or big-name stars, film-makers produced uniquely personal films using real-life subject matter: Claude Chabrol (b 1930) explored poverty and alcoholism in rural France in *Le Beau Serge* (Bitter Reunion; 1958); Alain Resnais (b 1922) portrayed the problems of time and memory in *Hiroshima, Mon Amour* (1959); and François Truffaut (1932–84) dealt with love.

A TIMELESS ROMANCE

By the 1970s the new wave had lost its experimental edge, handing over the limelight to lesser-known directors such as Éric Rohmer (b 1920), who made beautiful but uneventful films in which the characters endlessly analyse their feelings.

Two 1960s movies ensured France's invincibility as the land of romance: Claude Lelouch's *Un Homme et une Femme* (A Man and a Woman; 1966), a love story set in Deauville; and Jacques Demy's *Les Parapluies de Cherbourg* (The Umbrellas of Cherbourg; 1964), a wise and bittersweet love story, likewise filmed in Normandy.

PURE NOSTALGIA

Big-name stars, slick production values and a strong sense of nostalgia were the dominant motifs in the 1980s, as generous state subsidies saw film-makers switch to costume dramas and comedies in the face of growing competition from the USA.

Claude Berri's portrait of prewar Provence in *Jean de Florette* (1986), Jean-Paul Rappeneau's *Cyrano de Bergerac* (1990) and *Bon Voyage* (2003), set in 1940s Paris, and *Astérix et Obélix: Mission Cléopâtre* (2002), all starring France's best-known (and biggest-nosed) actor, Gérard Depardieu, found huge audiences in France and abroad.

RENAISSANCE

French film has enjoyed a massive renaissance in the new millennium thanks to films such as *Le Fabuleux Destin d'Amélie Poulain* (Amélie), directed by Jean-Pierre Jeunet of *Delicatessen* (1991) fame; Jacques Perrin's animal film *Le Peuple Migrateur* (Winged Migration; 2001), about bird migration; the big-name (Omar Sharif and Isabelle Adjani) *Monsieur Ibrahim et les Fleurs du Coran* (Mr Ibrahim and the Flowers of Coran; 2003), about an Arab grocer living on rue Bleue; and the giggle-guaranteed Marseille comedy *Taxi 3* (2003) and *Les Choristes* (The Chorus; 2004), a sentimental tale of a new teacher arriving at a school for troublesome boys in 1949.

Astérix et les Vikings (2005), by Danish director Stefan Fjeldmark, wooed French cinema-goers as Europe's most expensive feature-length cartoon – its budget was €22 million – proving once and for all that France's cartoon industry, which currently produces about 15 films a year, means business. Three years later it was another Astérix film, *Astérix aux Jeux Olympiques* (2008), which became the most expensive film (its budget: €78 million) to be made in the history of French cinema.

LEADING LIGHTS

Charismatic comic actor Jean Dujardin (b 1972) has been the hottest thing since sliced bread since starring in *Brice de Nice* (2005), a piss-take of cult surfing movie *Point Break* in which surfing dude and poseur Brice waits for *sa vague* (his wave) to come in waveless Nice on the French Riviera. The film features great shots of the town. Dujardin went on to play the sexist, racist, macho, uncultured and cringingly outdated 1950s Bond…James Bond, or rather Bonisseur de la Bath…Hubert Bonisseur de la Bath, in *OSS 117: Le Caire, Nid d'Espions* (OSS 117: Cairo Nest of Spies; 2006). The Bond parody was an instant hit. His latest comedy, *Lucky Luke* (2008), is a guaranteed classic.

France's leading lady of the moment, meanwhile, the sexy, pouting, dark-haired Marion Cotillard (b 1975), was catapulted to stardom in 2007 by her role as Édith Piaf in *La Môme* (La Vie en Rose), a hugely successful film portraying the life of the French singer, from Paris waif to New York

Amélie film poster, Paris

superstar. The film landed her an Oscar for best actress in 2008.

RUNAWAY HITS

The runaway hit of the decade was indisputably American film director Ron Howard's *The Da Vinci Code* (2006). Not only did the film bring international acclaim to Audrey Tautou, the waifish French actress of *Amélie* fame, who costarred with Tom Hanks in the film, it also brought American tourists in their droves back to Paris. The odds are now on as to whether Dany Boon's hilarious French comedy *Bienvenue chez les Ch'tis* – the film rights of which Warner Brothers bought to make an American equivalent – will do the same for northern France.

The 2008 Cannes film festival (www .festival-cannes.fr) saw a French film win the Palme d'Or, arguably the world's most coveted film prize, for the first time since 1987. Set in a rough Parisian neighbourhood, Laurent Cantet's *Entre Les Murs* (The Class) used real pupils and teachers and portrayed a year in their school life. The documentary-drama was based on the autobiographical novel of teacher François Bégaudeau (he plays the teacher in the film) and stays firmly in the classroom (hence its French title 'Between the Walls'). The kids are a real mix of cultures and attitudes (an illegal Chinese immigrant, a boy from Mali and another from the Caribbean and so on) rendering the film a brilliant reflection of multiethnic society in contemporary France.

FRENCH CINEMA IN 10 FILMS

- **La Règle du Jeu** (The Rules of the Game; 1939)
- **Les Enfants du Paradis** (Children of Paradise; 1945)
- **Et Dieu Créa la Femme** (And God Created Woman; 1956)
- **Les Quatre Cents Coups** (The 400 Blows; 1959)
- **Les Vacances de M Hulôt** (Mr Hulôt's Holiday; 1953)
- **Diva** (1981)
- **Shoah** (1985)
- **37°2 le Matin** (Betty Blue; 1986)
- **Indochine** (Indochina; 1993)
- **Code Inconnu** (Code Unknown; 2001)

FAMILY TRAVEL

BETHUNE CARMICHAEL

Parc de la Villette (p75), Paris

Be it dining, celebrating or travelling, the French are great believers in doing it *en famille* (as a family) – making France a great place to kid around. Big cities, especially Paris, present their own challenges but the upside is a stack of unique activities to indulge *les enfants* in. Rural France is a family-travel dream.

WAY TO GO

Paris' narrow streets and metro stairways are, in short, a trial if you have a pram or pushchair in tow. Car-rental firms have children's safety seats for hire at a nominal cost; book in advance.

The choice of baby food, infant formula, soy and cow's milk, nappies (diapers) and the like in French supermarkets is similar to that in any developed country, but remember that opening hours may be more limited: run out of nappies on Saturday evening and you could be facing a long and messy weekend. (Should disaster strike, pharmacies, of which there is always one open for at least a few hours on a Sunday, also sell baby paraphernalia, and in Paris a number of pharmacies are open 24/7.)

À TABLE

Few restaurants in France have high chairs but a fair few serve a *menu enfant* (children's set menu) – more often than not comprising a beef burger or chicken nuggets and fries, and a ball of ice cream for around €6 – to kids aged under 12. In addition a whole

DENNIS JONES

Jardin du Luxembourg (p73), Paris

rash of American-style fast-food restaurants, *cafétérias* and French chain restaurants, like Hippopotamus and Bistro Romain, cater to parents with kids in tow.

Take drinks and snacks with you on sightseeing days if you want to avoid costly stops in cafés. Picnics are a great way to feed the troops cheaply and enjoy local produce.

KIDDING AROUND

There is no shortage of things to do *en famille:* in kid-friendly capital extraordinaire Paris, scale the Eiffel Tower (p76), sail the Seine (p73), romp round the Jardin du Luxembourg (great playground; p73), meet *Mona Lisa* (kids must see her once; p66), discover wildlife in the Musée National d'Histoire Naturelle (p73), and watch horses dance in Versailles (p95) or Chantilly (p96). Prioritise Parc de la Villette and its interactive, action-packed Cité des Sciences et de l'Industrie (p75) if you want your children to love Paris forever.

Elsewhere, the Loire Valley's fairy-tale châteaux are the stuff of little kids' dreams, as is a visit to Saumur's Cadre Noir riding school (p190) and a perfume-creation workshop in Grasse (p278). For the vehicle-mad, there's Monaco (for a razz around the F1 Grand Prix track in a Ferrari, contact the tourist office; p284).

◥ THE NITTY GRITTY

- **Cots** Available upon request in many midrange and top-end hotels
- **Highchairs** Rare; bring your own screw-on seat
- **Kids' menu** A standard in most restaurants
- **Nappies (diapers)** Easy to buy in supermarkets and pharmacies
- **Changing facilities** Rare; bring a towel and improvise (no one minds)
- **Strollers (pushchairs)** A strict no-no inside Château de Versailles; bring a baby sling

The French Alps also have lots of outdoor activities year-round, like horse riding, snow-shoeing, light hiking and biking (most bike rental places carry children's bicycles).

The coastlines drum up bags of old-fashioned fun: meet sharks in Monaco's Musée Océanographique (p286), party at the Carnival de Nice (p270) and see how oysters grow at an oyster farm in Brittany (p153). Beaches are natural kid-pleasers: the sandy Mediterranean coast is especially popular with families, as are beaches on the Atlantic Coast, although some have strong undertows.

Include the kids in the trip planning: Lonely Planet's *Travel with Children* is a useful source of information.

BEDTIME

Staying in a *chambre d'hôte* (B&B; p372) that also does a *table d'hôte* is fab for families; little kids can sweetly slumber upstairs while weary parents wine and dine in peace downstairs (don't forget your baby monitor!) Fancier hotels have a pool and facilities for kids.

In Paris, weekly magazine *L'Officiel des Spectacles* advertises babysitting services *(gardes d'enfants* means baby-sitting). Elsewhere, tourist offices often have lists of babysitters, or try www.bebe-annonce.com (in French).

↘THE BEST

JEAN-BERNARD CARILLET

Horse-riding, Camargue (p258)

THE BEST CHILDREN'S ACTIVITIES

- Canoe beneath the **Pont du Gard** (p261)
- Horse ride in the **Camargue** (p258)
- Pedal, be pedalled and/or snorkel on **Île de Porquerolles** (p282),
- Watch **medieval builders at work** (p198)
- Ride a little red train to an **ice cave** in the French Alps (p222)

THE FRENCH

Place de la Sorbonne, Paris

WILL SALTER

Arrogant, bureaucratic, chauvinistic and stylish… France is a country whose people have attracted more stubborn myths and stereotypes than any other in Europe, and over the centuries, dozens of tags have been pinned on the garlic-eating, beret-wearing, *sacrebleu*-swearing French. (The French, by the way, don't wear berets or use old chestnuts such as '*sacrebleu*' anymore.)

Suckers for tradition, the French are slow to embrace new ideas and technologies: it took the country an age to embrace the internet, clinging on for dear life to their own at-the-time innovative Minitel system for eons. Yet the French are also incredibly innovative – a dichotomy reflected in every facet of French life: they drink and smoke more than anyone else, yet live longer. They eat like kings, but are not fat…

SUPERIORITY COMPLEX

Most people are extremely proud to be French and are staunchly nationalistic to boot, a result of the country's republican stance that places nationality – rather than religion, for example – at the top of the self-identity list. This has created an overwhelmingly self-confident nation, both culturally and intellectually, that invariably comes across as a French superiority complex.

Contrary to popular belief, many French speak a foreign language fairly well, travel and are happy to use their language skills should the need arise. Of course, if monolingual English-speakers don't try to speak French, there's no way proud French linguists will let on they speak fluent English with a great sexy accent! French men, incidentally, deem an English gal's heavily accented French as irresistibly sexy as women deem a Frenchman speaking English. Hard to believe, but true.

SEX

On the subject of sex, not all French men ooze romance or light Gitanes all day. Nor are they as civilised about adultery as French cinema would have you believe. Adultery, illegal in France until 1975, was actually grounds for automatic divorce until as late as mid-2004.

Kissing is an integral part of French life. (The expression 'French kissing', as in tongues, doesn't exist in French, incidentally.) That said, put a Parisian in Provence and there's no saying they will know when to stop. Countrywide, people who know each other reasonably well, really well, a tad or barely at all greet each other with a glancing peck on each cheek. Southern France aside (where everyone kisses everyone), two men rarely kiss but always shake hands. Boys and girls start kissing as soon as they're out of nappies, or so it seems.

LIFESTYLE

Be a fly on the wall in the 5th-floor bourgeois apartment of Monsieur et Madame Tout le Monde and you'll see them dunking croissants in bowls of *café au lait* for breakfast, buying a baguette every day from the bakery (Monsieur nibbles the top off on his way home) and recycling nothing bar a few glass bottles.

They go to the flicks once a month, work precisely 35 hours a week and view the web-radio production company their 24-year-old son set up and heads in Paris with a mix of pride, amusement and pure scepticism. Their 20-year-old daughter, who is

---

FRENCH BALLS

France's traditional ball games include *pétanque* and the more formal boules, which has a 70-page rule book. Both are played by village men in work clothes on a gravel or sand pitch, scratched out wherever a bit of flat and shady ground can be found. World championships are held for both sports. In the Basque Country, the racquet game of *pelota* (p312) is the thing to do with your balls.

FRENCH KISSING

Kissing French-style is not completely straightforward, 'how many' and 'which side first' potentially being problematic. In Paris it is definitely two: anything more is deemed affected. That said, in certain trendy 20-something circles, friends swap three or four cheek-skimming kisses, as do many young teenagers at school *parce qu'ils ont que ça à faire*…

Travel south and the *bisous* (kisses) multiply, three being the norm in Provence and the bits of France neighbouring Switzerland around Lake Geneva, and four in the Loire Valley.

Hot tip: to avoid locked lips, start with the right cheek like everyone else in France.

FAUX PAS

- **Forget the school-textbook French** *'S'il vous plaît'* – never *'garçon'* (meaning 'boy') – is the *only* way to summon a waiter.
- **Don't split the restaurant bill** It's so uncivilised! The person who invites pays, although close friends often go Dutch.
- **Don't fondle** fruit, veg, flowers or clothing in shops. Ask if you want to touch.
- **Get the name right** *'Monsieur'* for men; *'madame'* for 'Mrs'; *'mademoiselle'* for unmarried women.

so BCBG (*bon chic, bon genre* – a Sloane Ranger in non-Parisian speak) darling, is a student: France's overcrowded state-run universities are free and open to anyone who passes the *baccalauréat,* although Sarkozy had a stab at changing this by giving universities the autonomy to select students and seek outside funding.

Madame buys a load of hot-gossip weekly mags, Monsieur meets his mates to play boules (p339), and August is the *only* month to summer holiday (with the rest of France). Dodging dog poo on pavements is a sport practised from birth and everything goes on the *carte bleue* (credit or debit card) when shopping: this *is* the society, after all, that microchipped credit cards long before anyone else even dreamt of scrapping the swipe-and-sign system. The couple have a landlord: with a tradition of renting rather than buying, home ownership is low (57% of households own their own home; the rest rent).

BLOGGER CLOUT

If there's one country in Europe that deems blogging a national pastime (so *that's* what they do outside their 35-hour work week), it's France. The underbelly of what French people think right now, the French blogosphere is gargantuan, with everyone

WILL SALTER

Rue Vieille du Temple, Marais (p67), Paris

TONY WHEELER

Horseman and woman at festival, Arles (p256)

and everything from streets and metro stops to bars, bands and the president having their own blog. For an informative overview (did someone say three million bloggers in France and counting?) see **LeMondeduBlog.com** (**www.lemondedublog.com**) covering just that, the blog world (in English and French), with loads of links.

French bloggers have serious clout. In the days preceding France's historic vote on the EU constitution, it was the powerful 'No' blog of a humble French law professor that lured an online crowd of 25,000 a day and contributed enormously to France's eventual rejection of the constitution, say political analysts (there was no equivalent 'Yes' blog). The so-called 'workers' revolt' in Paris and elsewhere against the government's proposed new employment law in 2006 was likewise charted in English by French bloggers.

FRENCH CUISINE

A stack of baguettes

FRANK CARTER

'The French think mainly about two things – their two main meals', a well-fed bon-vivant Parisian was once heard to say. 'Everything else is in parentheses.' And it's true. While not every French man, woman and child is a walking bible of things culinary, eating and drinking well is of prime importance to most French who spend an inordinate amount of time thinking, discussing and feasting on good food and wine (p366).

But don't suppose for a moment that this food obsession means dining out in France has to be a ceremonious occasion or one full of pitfalls for the uninitiated. Approach food and wine here with half the zest *les français* do, and you will be welcomed, encouraged and exceedingly well fed indeed.

THINK CHEESE

Think France. Think cheese. The country counts upwards of 500 varieties of *fromage* (cheese) made from raw, pasteurised or *petit-lait* milk (the whey left over after the milk fats and solids have been curdled with rennet). The choice at a *fromagerie* (cheese shop) can be overwhelming – ask to sample before buying.

Goat's cheese *(chèvre)* is creamy and both sweet and a little salty when fresh, but harder and saltier as it matures and dries out. Among the best are Ste-Maure de Touraine from the Loire region; Crottin de Chavignol from Burgundy; Rocamadour, often served warm with salad or marinated in oil and rosemary; and St-Marcellin, a soft white creamy cheese runny enough to eat with a spoon from Lyon.

Roquefort, a ewe's-milk veined blue cheese from Languedoc, is to many the king of French cheese, while Camembert, made from unpasteurised cow's milk, is the classic moulded cheese from Normandy that is synonymous with French cheese for most. Munster from Alsace and the strong (read stinky) Époisses de Bourgogne are rind-washed, fine-textured cheeses.

Among the most popular hard cheeses – always cooked and pressed – are Beaufort (a grainy cow's-milk cheese with a slightly fruity taste) and Comté, both from around the Alps; Emmental, a cow's-milk cheese made all over France; and Mimolette, an Edam-like bright-orange cheese from Lille that can be aged for as long as 36 months.

To serve, cut a small circular cheese such as a Camembert into wedges like a pie. If a larger cheese like Brie comes already sliced into a wedge shape, cut from the tip to the rind – cutting off the tip is just not on. Slice cheeses whose middle is the best part (eg blue or veined cheeses) in such a way as to take your fair share of the rind. A flat piece of semihard cheese like comté from the French Alps is usually just cut horizontally in hunks.

In general, strong, pungent cheeses require a young, full-bodied red or a sweet wine, while soft cheeses with a refined flavour call for more quality and age in the wine.

AND A CRUST OF BREAD

Nothing is more French than *pain* (bread), eaten with gusto – and *sans beurre* (without butter) – at practically every meal. All bakeries have crusty baguettes (and the fatter *flûtes*) which are long and thin, and wider loaves *(pains)*, softer on the inside and less crispy than a baguette. Both are best eaten within four hours of baking. You can store them for longer in a plastic bag, but the crust becomes soft and chewy; if you leave them out, they'll be rock-hard within hours. A *ficelle* is a skinnier version of a baguette.

Most bakeries also carry heavier, more expensive breads made with all sorts of grains and cereals, and studded with nuts, raisins or herbs. These keep much longer than baguettes and standard white-flour breads.

PIGGY PARTS

Diverse as it is, French cuisine is typified by certain regions, most notably Normandy, Burgundy, the Dordogne, Lyon and, to a

THE BEST

OLIVER STREWE

Blood sausage

THE BEST CHARCUTERIE DECODER

- **Andouillette** Pig's small intestines in a sausage; best eaten in Lyon (p200) and Troyes (p121)
- **Boudin noir** Pig's blood sausage, with onions and spices
- **Jambon** The safe bet: bog-standard ham, simply cooked, smoked or salt-cured
- **Saucisse** A fresh small sausage, boiled, grilled or fried before eating

BILL WASSMAN

Cured meats for sale

lesser extent, the Loire region, Alsace and Provence. Still others – Brittany, Languedoc and the Basque country – have made incalculable contributions to what can generically be called French food.

While every region in France produces standard *charcuterie* favourites (meat products, traditionally pork-based), Alsace, Lyon and the Auvergne in central France produce the best sausages, and the Dordogne and north of France some of the most acclaimed pâtés, terrines and *rillettes* (coarsely shredded potted meat spread cold over bread or toast). Indeed there is no better initiation into the art of French piggy-part cuisine than in Lyon, France's third-largest city and *temple de gastronomie extraordinaire,* where one bite of a big fat *saucisson de Lyon* or tripe-stuffed *andouillette* (p343) ensures you love it (or hate it) forever.

ATLANTIC OYSTER TASTE TEST

Oysters from the Bassin d'Arcachon's four oyster-breeding zones in the Atlantic hint at subtly different flavours. Shuck, slurp and see if you can detect these:

- **Banc d'Arguin** – milk and sugar
- **Île aux Oiseaux** – minerals
- **Cap Ferret** – citrus
- **Grand Banc** – roasted hazelnuts

SOMETHING FISHY

Another Lyonnais speciality is the *quenelle,* an unusual poached dumpling made of freshwater fish (usually pike) and served with *sauce Nantua,* made with cream and paste from freshwater crayfish.

Brittany, with its abundance of oyster farms, is France's paradise for lovers of seafood. Combine the royalty of Breton cuisine – the sweet crêpe (p142) and its savoury sister, the galette (made from buckwheat and

RESTAURANT TALK

Restaurants open six days a week, orders being taken from around noon to 3pm and 7pm to 11pm. Any 'resto' worth its salt has a *carte* (menu) displayed outside, allowing potential diners to do a quick dish and price check before committing. Most serve a cheaper *menu* (not to confused with an English 'menu') comprising two or three courses at a fixed-price; a *menu du jour* (daily menu) features the *plat du jour* (daily special). Many restaurants only serve *menus* at lunchtime; come dusk it is strictly à la carte.

An *entrée* (starter) starts a meal, followed by a *plat* (main course), cheese and dessert. Dessert is never eaten *before* the cheese.

stuffed/topped with various fillings such as ham, egg and cheese) – and the Brittany-bound are in gastronomic heaven.

Seafood, cream and apples are essentials in neighbouring Normandy where specialities include *moules à la crème normande* (mussels in cream with a dash of cider) and *canard à la rouennaise* ('Rouen-style duck'; duck stuffed with its liver and served with a red-wine sauce), preferably interrupted by a *trou normand* (literally 'Norman hole'; a glass of Calvados) to allow room for more courses.

Hop to the hot south where fish likewise thrives in the kitchen. The Roman legacy of olives, wheat and wine remain the holy trinity of Provencal cuisine, along with a generous pinch of olive oil, garlic and tomatoes. But Provence's most famous contribution to French cuisine has to be *bouillabaisse,* a chowder made with at least five kinds of fresh saltwater fish, cooked for about 10 minutes in a broth containing onions, tomatoes, saffron and various herbs, and eaten as a main course with toasted bread and *rouille,* a spicy mayonnaise of olive oil, garlic and chilli peppers. There is no better spot on the coast to taste this meal-in-itself fish soup than Marseille (p252).

BEANS & TRUFFLES

Moving southwest along the Mediterranean, good old-fashioned 'peasant' cooking starts with Languedoc's most evocative dish, *cassoulet* (a cockle-warming

THE BEST

JEAN-BERNARD CARILLET

Plate of fresh oysters

THE BEST REGIONAL TASTES

- **Lyon & French Alps** Lyonnais *bouchon* fare and Alpine cheese fondue
- **Brittany** Oysters fresh from their beds
- **Dordogne** Snails stuffed with foie gras
- **Alsace** *Wädele* (ham knuckles) and *choucroute* (sauerkraut) in a cosy Alsatian *winstub*

RUSSELL MOUNTFORD

Cakes at pâtisserie

casserole of beans and meat). There are at least three major *cassoulet* varieties but the favourite is arguably that from Toulouse, which throws *saucisse de Toulouse* (a fat, mild-tasting pork sausage) into the cooking pot.

Among the essential ingredients of Basque cooking are the deep-red chillies, which add an extra bite to many of the region's dishes, including the dusting on the signature *jambon de Bayonne,* the locally prepared Bayonne ham. Basques also love cakes and pastries; the most popular is *gâteau basque,* a relatively simple layer cake filled with cream or cherry jam.

Moving towards central France, the Dordogne is famous for its luxurious *diamants noirs* (black diamonds) aka truffles (p200) and poultry, especially ducks and geese whose fattened livers are turned into *pâté de foie gras* (duck- or goose-liver pâté), sometimes flavoured with cognac and truffles. *Confit de canard* and *confit d'oie* are duck or goose

SNAILS

One of France's trademark culinary habits, the consumption of gastropod molluscs – preferably with butter, garlic, parsley and fresh bread – is inextricably linked in the public mind with Burgundy because *Helix pomatia,* though endemic in much of Europe, is best known as *escargot de Bourgogne* (the Burgundy snail). Once a regular – and unwelcome – visitor to the fine-wine vines of Burgundy and a staple on Catholic plates during Lent, the humble hermaphroditic crawler has been decimated by overharvesting and the use of agricultural chemicals, and is now a protected species. As a result, the vast majority of *escargots* (snails) impaled on French snail forks (the ones with two tongs) are now imported from Turkey, Greece and Eastern Europe.

DINING LEXICON

- **Auberge** (inn) Often attached to a rural B&B or small hotel; serves traditional country fare
- **Ferme-auberge** A working farm serving diners dishes made farm produce
- **Bistro** A small cosy restaurant serving traditional food
- **Bar à vins** Wine bar
- **Brasserie** Lots of brass fittings and dishes like *choucroute* (sauerkraut) and sausages
- **Café** Just that, often with munch options like a *croque-monsieur* (ham and toasted cheese sandwich)
- **Crêperie** Sweet crêpes and savoury galettes

joints cooked very slowly in their own fat. The preserved fowl is then left to stand for some months before being eaten.

MUSTARD & TARTE TATIN

Specialities of central France include *lentilles vertes du Puy aux saucisses fumées* (smoked pork sausages with green Puy lentils) and *clafoutis,* a custard and cherry tart baked upside down and often served for breakfast. The trinity of Burgundy's kitchen is beef, red wine and mustard. *Bœuf bourguignon* (beef marinated and cooked in young red wine with mushrooms, onions, carrots and bacon) combines the first two; Dijon, the capital of Burgundy, has been synonymous with mustard for centuries.

JULIET COOMBE

The cuisine of the Loire Valley, refined in the kitchens of the region's châteaux from the 16th century onwards, ultimately became the cuisine of France; *rillettes* (potted meat), *coq au vin* (chicken cooked in wine), *beurre blanc* sauce and *tarte Tatin* (a caramelised upside-down apple pie) are specialities from this area, but are now considered generic French cuisine. The Loire region is also known for its *pruneaux de Tours,* prunes dried from luscious damson plums and used in poultry, pork or veal dishes.

FESTIVE TREATS

Food itself makes French people celebrate. There are, of course, also birthdays

Escargots (snails)

and engagements and weddings and christenings and, like everywhere, special holidays, usually based in religion.

One tradition that is very much alive is *Jour des Rois* (Day of the Kings), which falls on 6 January and marks the feast of the Épiphanie (Epiphany), when the Three Wise Men paid homage to the infant Jesus. Placed in the centre of the table is a *galette des rois* (literally 'kings' cake'; a puff-pastry tart with frangipane cream), which has a tiny porcelain figurine hidden inside and is topped with a gold paper crown. The person who gets the figurine is named king or queen, dons the crown and chooses his or her consort. This tradition is popular among families, and at offices and dinner parties.

At Chandeleur (Candlemas, marking the Feast of the Purification of the Virgin Mary) on 2 February, family and friends gather together in their kitchens to make *crêpes de la Chandeleur* (sweet Candlemas pancakes).

HARD FACTS

- Smoking is banned inside cafés, bars and restaurants; light up on the terrace
- Tap water in France is safe to drink
- Save cents in restaurants by ordering *une carafe d'eau* (a jug of water)
- *Un café* (slug of espresso) is the only way to end a meal
- Mid-morning order *un café au lait* (spot of coffee with loads of hot milk)
- Tea comes black; sometimes with a slice of lemon, never with milk
- Summer refresher: *un citron pressé* (iced water with freshly squeezed lemon juice and sugar)

Pâques (Easter) is marked as elsewhere with *œufs au chocolat* (chocolate eggs) – here filled with candy fish and tiny chickens – and there is always an egg hunt for the kids. The traditional meal at Easter is lamb or *jambon de Pâques* (Easter ham).

After the *dinde aux marrons* (turkey stuffed with chestnuts) eaten at lunch on Noël (Christmas), a *bûche de Noël,* a 'yule log' of chocolate and cream or ice cream, is served.

FRESH-AIR FROLICS

CHRISTIAN ASLUND

Snowboarder, Le Brévent (p222), French Alps

From the peaks, rivers and canyons of the French Alps to the mountains and volcanic peaks of the Massif Central – not to mention 3200km of coastline stretching from Italy to Spain and from the Basque country to the Straits of Dover – France offers a cornucopia of exhilarating outdoor adventure.

Be it canyoning, diving, ice-driving or kite-surfing on snow or water, France sets the pulse racing. In larger cities and picturesque regions like the French Riviera and the French Alps, local activity companies offer all kinds of high-adrenaline pursuits. Yet for those who prefer less heart-pounding activities there is no end of fresh-air frolics just made for exploring and discovering rural France from a very different perspective.

GRAB A BIKE

The French take cycling very seriously with whole parts of the country grinding to a halt during the famous annual Tour de France. Indeed a *vélo tout-terrain* (VTT, or mountain bike) is a fantastic tool for roaming the countryside.

Some of the best areas for mountain biking (with varying gradients and grades of difficulty) are around Annecy in the Alps and throughout the Pyrenees. In southwest France, the Dordogne offers a vast network of scenic, tranquil roads for pedal-powered tourists. The Loire Valley, Alsace, Burgundy, the Lubéron in Provence and coastal regions like Brittany, Normandy and the Atlantic coast offer easier, flatter options.

Lonely Planet's *Cycling France* includes essential maps, advice, directions and technical tips. For information on transporting your bicycle by train and bike rental, see p388.

FRANCE IN FOCUS

FRESH-AIR FROLICS

↘THE BEST

Vélib' bike rental station (p94), Paris

THE BEST BIKING TIPS & TRAILS

- **Vélib'** (p94) Freewheel Paris
- **Île de Porquerolles** (p282) Pedal around a Mediterranean island
- **Champagne Domi Moreau** (p118) Vineyard bike tours
- **Association Française de Développement des Véloroutes et Voies Vertes** (www.af3v.org) Database of 250 signposted *véloroutes* (bike paths) and *voies vertes* (greenways)

Details on places that rent out bikes – but rarely helmets – appear in each city or town listing under Getting Around.

SKATE THE CITY

Over 10,000 in-line skaters – accompanied by skating police – race through the streets of Paris from 10pm to 1am every Friday night. The free, 30km ride, whose purpose – in addition to fun – is to promote in-line skating as a mode of urban transport, is the largest such event in the world. For details see the website of **Pari Roller** (www.pari-roller.com).

The **Fédération Française de Roller Skating** (http://parcours.ffrs.asso.fr, in French) can provide details on routes suitable for in-line skating.

SKI HARD

The ski season in France's 400-odd resorts generally lasts from mid-December to late March or April. January and February tend to have the best overall conditions but the slopes get very crowded during the February–March school holidays.

The high Alps have some of the world's priciest and most fashionable resorts, although smaller, low-altitude stations in the Alps and Pyrenees are cheaper. Cross-country skiing is best done in the valleys. Some lower-altitude stations are examining their options should global warming make the ski season too short and/or unpredictable.

One of the cheapest ways to ski or snowboard is with a package deal, though thanks to budget airlines flying to/from Lyon, Grenoble, Chambéry and Geneva (Switzerland),

TOP THREE NATURAL CURIOSITIES

Explore the best of France's astonishing natural patrimony on foot, by bike or boat:

- Europe's highest **sand dune** (which moves and swallows trees), the Dune du Pilat (p308)
- Europe's highest **tides**, with – incredibly – a difference of up to 15m between low and high tides, around Mont St-Michel (p164) in Normandy
- The navigable **underground river** – over 100m beneath the surface – that flows through the Gouffre de Padirac (p199)

arranging Alpine breaks independently is equally viable.

LEG IT

The French countryside is criss-crossed by 120,000km of *sentiers balisés* (marked walking paths) through every imaginable terrain in every region of the country. No permit is needed to hike. The best-known trails are the *sentiers de grande randonnée* (GR), long-distance paths marked by red-and-white-striped track indicators.

The *grandes randonnées de pays* (GRP) trails, whose markings are yellow, are designed for intense exploration of one particular area. Other types of trails include *sentiers de promenade randonnée* (PR), walking paths marked in yellow; *drailles,* paths used by cattle to get to high-altitude summer pastures; and *chemins de halage,* canal towpaths. Shorter day-hike trails are *sentiers de petites randonnées* or *sentiers de pays.*

The **Fédération Française de la Randonnée Pédestre** (FFRP; French Ramblers' Association; www.ffrp.asso.fr, in French) has an **information centre** (Map pp52-3; ☎ 01 44 89 93 93; 64 rue du Dessous des Berges, 13e, Paris; Ⓜ Bibliothèque François Mitterrand) in Paris.

▶THE BEST

Vallée Blanche (p225), French Alps
CHRIS MELLOR

THE BEST SKIING SUPERLATIVES

France can claim a fair few superlatives in the world of skiing:

- One of France's longest off-piste trails (20km) is the legendary Vallée Blanche (p225) at Chamonix.
- The world's largest ski area is Les Portes du Soleil (p227).
- Europe's largest skiable glacier, with 120 hectares of marked slopes, is at Les Deux Alpes in the spectacular Parc National des Écrins (p224).

SURF

France has fine beaches along all its coasts – the English Channel, the Atlantic and the Mediterranean. The beautifully sandy beaches stretching along the family-oriented Atlantic Coast are less crowded than their rather pebbly counterparts on the Côte d'Azur. Brittany, Normandy and the Channel coast are also popular, albeit cooler, beach destinations. The general public is free to use any beach not marked as private.

The best surfing is on the Atlantic Coast around Biarritz (p312), where waves reach heights of 4m. Windsurfing is popular wherever there's water and a breeze, and equipment is often rented out near beaches and lakes.

White-water rafting, canoeing and kayaking are practised on many French rivers, especially in the Alps, but also in Burgundy along the Gorges de l'Allier, Gorges de l'Ardèche, Gorges du Tarn and Gorges du Verdon.

⤵ HISTORY

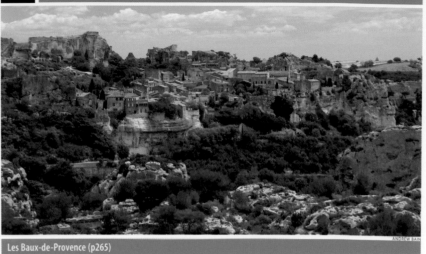

Les Baux-de-Provence (p265)

Neanderthals were the first people to live in France; in the late 19th century Neanderthal skeletons were found in caves in the Vézère Valley in Dordogne. Cro-Magnons, a taller *Homo sapiens* variety who notched up 1.7m on the height chart, followed 35,000 years ago.

These people had larger brains than their ancestors and short, wide faces. Their hands were nimble, and with the aid of improved tools they hunted reindeer, bison, horses and mammoths to eat. They played music, danced and had fairly complex social patterns. They were also artists: Tour Grotte de Lascaux II (p201) and view their drawings and animal engravings. Dubbed 'Périgord's Sistine Chapel', it is one of 25 known decorated caves in the area.

MENHIRS & DOLMENS

The Neolithic Period produced France's incredible collection of menhirs and dolmens: the Morbihan Coast in Brittany is an ode to megalithic monuments. During this era, warmer weather caused great changes in flora and fauna, and ushered in farming

c 30,000 BC	1500–500 BC	c AD 100–300
Cro-Magnons decorate their homes in the Vézère Valley, Dordogne, with the world's best cave paintings.	The Celtic Parisii tribe build wattle-and-daub huts on what is now Île de la Cité, Paris.	The Romans revel in their heyday with a riot of splendid public buildings.

and stock rearing. Cereals, peas, beans and lentils were grown, and villages were settled. Decorated pottery, woven fabrics and polished stone tools became commonplace household items.

GAULS & ROMANS

The Celtic Gauls moved into the region between 1500 and 500 BC and traded with the Greeks whose colonies included Massilia (Marseille) on the Mediterranean coast.

It was from Wissant in far northern France that Julius Caesar launched his invasion of Britain in 55 BC. Centuries of conflict between the Gauls and the Romans ended in 52 BC when Caesar's legions crushed a revolt by many Gallic tribes led by Celtic Arverni tribe chief Vercingétorix. For the next couple of years the Gauls hounded the Romans with guerrilla warfare and stood up to them in several match-drawn pitched battles. But gradually Gallic resistance collapsed and Roman rule in Gaul reigned supreme.

▼**THE BEST**

GLENN BEANLAND

Roman Amphitheatre (p259), Nîmes

THE BEST ROMAN SITES

- Pont du Gard, near Nîmes (p261)
- Les Arènes (p256) & Théâtre Antique, Arles (p257)
- Roman Theatre, Orange (p264)
- Arènes de Cimiez, Nice (p271)
- Trophée des Alpes, Le Turbie (p284)
- Musée Gallo-Romain Vesunna & Amphitheatre, Périgueux (p196)

Roman France is magnificent, climaxing with the almighty Pont du Gard aqueduct, built to bring water to the city of Nîmes in southern France. Post-Romans, the Franks adopted important elements of Gallo-Roman civilisation (including Christianity).

DYNASTY

The Frankish Merovingian and Carolingian dynasties ruled from the 5th to the 10th centuries. Charles Martel's grandson, Charlemagne (742–814), extended the boundaries of the kingdom and was crowned Holy Roman Emperor (Emperor of the West) in 800. But during the 9th century Scandinavian Vikings (also called Norsemen, thus Normans) raided France's western coast, settling in the lower Seine Valley and forming the duchy of Normandy a century later.

The tale of how William the Conqueror and his Norman forces occupied England in 1066 is told on the Bayeux Tapestry. In 1152 Eleanor of Aquitaine wed Henry of Anjou (see ornate polychrome effigies of the royal couple in Abbaye Royale de Fontevraud,

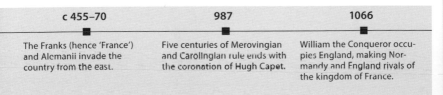

c 455–70	987	1066
The Franks (hence 'France') and Alemanii invade the country from the east.	Five centuries of Merovingian and Carolingian rule ends with the coronation of Hugh Capet.	William the Conqueror occupies England, making Normandy and England rivals of the kingdom of France.

FRANCE IN FOCUS

HISTORY

Cathédrale Notre Dame (p155), Rouen

CHRISTOPHER WOOD

p191), bringing a further third of France under the control of the English crown. The subsequent rivalry between France and England for control of Aquitaine and the vast English territories in France lasted three centuries.

GOOD OLD JOAN

During the Hundred Years' War (1337–1453) the French suffered nasty defeats. Abbey-studded Mont St-Michel (p164) was the only place in northern and western France not to fall into English hands.

Five years later the dukes of Burgundy (allied with the English) occupied Paris and in 1422 John Plantagenet was made regent of France for England's King Henry VI, then an infant. Less than a decade later he was crowned king of France at Paris' Notre Dame (p71).

Luckily for the French, a 17-year-old virginal warrior called Jeanne d'Arc (Joan of Arc) came along. At a chateau in the Loire Valley she persuaded French legitimist Charles VII in 1429 that she had a divine mission from God to expel the English from France and bring about Charles' coronation in Reims. Convicted of witchcraft and heresy by a tribunal of French ecclesiastics following her capture by the Burgundians and subsequent sale to the English in 1430, Joan was burned at the stake. Charles VII returned to Paris in 1437, but it wasn't until 1453 that the English were driven from French territory.

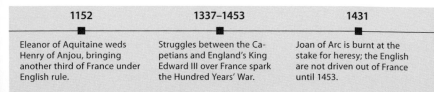

1152	1337–1453	1431
Eleanor of Aquitaine weds Henry of Anjou, bringing another third of France under English rule.	Struggles between the Capetians and England's King Edward III over France spark the Hundred Years' War.	Joan of Arc is burnt at the stake for heresy; the English are not driven out of France until 1453.

FRANCE IN FOCUS

HISTORY

RENAISSANCE TO REVOLUTION

With the arrival of Italian Renaissance culture during the reign of François I (r 1515–47), the focus shifted to the Loire Valley where Italian artists decorated royal castles like there was no tomorrow. The Reformation swept through Europe in the 1530s and in 1598 Henri IV (r 1589–1610) issued the controversial Edict of Nantes guaranteeing Huguenots (French Protestants who received help from the English) freedom of conscience.

At the tender age of five, the Roi Soleil (Sun King) ascended the throne as Louis XIV (r 1643–1715). He quashed the ambitious, feuding aristocracy; created the first centralised French state; and in Versailles built an extravagant palace. In 1685 he revoked the Edict of Nantes.

REVOLUTION TO REPUBLIC

Social and economic crises marked the 18th century, a Parisian mob taking to the streets in 1789, raiding the Invalides for weapons and storming the prison at Bastille (now a very busy roundabout; p70). France was declared a constitutional monarchy and reforms enacted. But before long the moderate republican Girondins lost power to the radical Jacobins and in September 1792 France's First Republic was declared. Louis XVI was publicly guillotined in January 1793 on Paris' place de la Concorde and the head of his queen, the vilified Marie-Antoinette, rolled several months later.

The Reign of Terror between September 1793 and July 1794 saw churches closed, cathedrals turned into 'Temples of Reason' and thousands incarcerated in dungeons in Paris' Conciergerie (p72) before being beheaded.

DASHING NΛPOLÉON

Beheadings done and dusted, a five-man delegation of moderate republicans set itself up as a Directory to rule the republic until Napoléon Bonaparte (1769–1821)

> **THE BEST**

Château de Blois (p180), Loire Valley
SALLY DILLON

THE BEST HISTORIC SITES

- Bayeux Tapestry & Musée Mémorial 1944 Bataille de Normandie, Bayeux (p158)
- Musée National du Moyen Âge, Paris (p73)
- Renaissance châteaux, Loire Valley (p189)
- Château de Versailles, Versailles (p95)
- Verdun Battlefields (p128) & Battle of the Somme Memorials (p124)

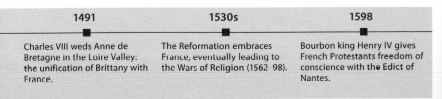

1491	1530s	1598
Charles VIII weds Anne de Bretagne in the Loire Valley: the unification of Brittany with France.	The Reformation embraces France, eventually leading to the Wars of Religion (1562–98).	Bourbon king Henry IV gives French Protestants freedom of conscience with the Edict of Nantes.

came along. His skills and military tactics quickly turned him into an independent political force and in 1799 he overthrew the Directory. In 1804 he was crowned emperor of the French by Pope Pius VII at Paris' Notre Dame and two years on he commissioned the world's largest triumphal arch (p77). But in 1814 allied armies entered Paris, exiled Napoléon to Elba and restored the House of Bourbon to the French throne at the Congress of Vienna (1814–15).

In 1815 Napoléon escaped, triumphantly entering Paris on 20 May. His glorious 'Hundred Days' back in power ended with the Battle of Waterloo and his return to exile.

OFF WITH HIS HEAD

To make public executions more humane (read: instead of roping the victim's limbs to four oxen, which then ran in four different directions), a French physician invented the guillotine.

Highwayman Nicolas Jacques Pelletie was the first in France to have his head sliced off by the 2m falling blade on 25 April 1792. During the Reign of Terror, at least 17,000 met their death this way. By the time the last was given the chop in 1977 (behind closed doors – the last public execution was in 1939), the contraption could slice off a head in two hundreths of a second.

SECOND REPUBLIC TO SECOND EMPIRE

Following the 1848 Revolution the Second Republic was established and elections brought in Napoléon's almost useless nephew, Louis Napoléon Bonaparte, as president. But in 1851 Louis Napoléon led a coup d'état and proclaimed himself Emperor Napoléon III of the Second Empire (1852–70).

France enjoyed significant economic growth at this time. Paris was transformed under urban planner Baron Haussmann (1809–91); Napoléon III threw glittering parties at his royal palace in northern France and breathed in fashionable sea air at Biarritz and Deauville. Like his uncle, he embroiled France in various catastrophic conflicts, including the Crimean War (1853–56) and the humiliating Franco-Prussian War (1870–71).

A BEAUTIFUL AGE

Born as a provisional government of national defence in September 1870, the Third Republic was quickly besieged by the Prussians who besieged Paris and demanded National Assembly elections be held. Unfortunately, the first move made by the resultant monarchist-controlled assembly was to ratify the Treaty of Frankfurt (1871), the harsh terms of which – a 5-billion-franc war indemnity and surrender of the provinces of Alsace and Lorraine – prompted revolt. During the Semaine Sanglante (Bloody Week), several

1643–1715	1789–94	1851
Louis XIV assumes the French throne and shifts his royal court from Paris to Versailles.	Revolutionaries storm the Bastille. Louis XVI and Marie-Antoinette are beheaded.	Louis Napoléon proclaims himself Emperor Napoléon III of the Second Empire (1852–70).

FRANCE IN FOCUS

HISTORY

RUSSELL MOUNTFORD

Conciergerie (p72), Paris

thousand rebel Communards (supporters of the hard-core insurgent Paris Commune) were killed and a further 20,000 or so executed.

Despite the bloody start, the Third Republic ushered in the glittering belle époque (beautiful age), with art-nouveau architecture, a whole field of artistic 'isms' from Impressionism onwards, and advances in science and engineering, including the construction of the first metro line in Paris. World Exhibitions were held in the capital in 1889, showcased by the Eiffel Tower.

THE GREAT WAR

A trip to the Somme (p124) or Verdun (p128) battlefields goes some way to revealing the unimaginable human cost of WWI.

Paris sparkled as the centre of the avant-garde in the 1920s and 1930s, with artists pushing into the new fields of cubism and surrealism, Le Corbusier rewriting the architectural textbook, foreign writers such as Ernest Hemingway and F Scott Fitzgerald drawn to the liberal atmosphere of Paris, and nightlife establishing a cutting-edge reputation for everything from jazz to striptease. In 1922 the luxurious *Train Bleu* (Blue Train) made its first run from Calais, via Paris, to the French Riviera.

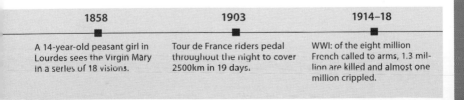

1858	1903	1914–18
A 14-year-old peasant girl in Lourdes sees the Virgin Mary in a series of 18 visions.	Tour de France riders pedal throughout the night to cover 2500km in 19 days.	WWI: of the eight million French called to arms, 1.3 million are killed and almost one million crippled.

Normandy American Cemetery & Memorial (p161), Omaha Beach

DENNIS JOHNSON

WWII

Two days after Germany invaded Poland in 1939 France joined Britain in declaring war on Germany. By June 1940 France had capitulated. The British expeditionary force sent to help the French barely managed to avoid capture by retreating to Dunkirk and crossing the English Channel in small boats.

The demarcation line between the Nazi-occupied and Vichy zones ran through Château de Chenonceau (p186) in the Loire Valley. The Vichy regime was viciously anti-Semitic, and local police proved very helpful to the Nazis in rounding up French Jews and others for deportation to Auschwitz and other death camps.

During the D-Day landings on 6 June 1944, 100,000-plus Allied troops stormed the coastline to liberate most of Normandy and Brittany. Paris was liberated on 25 August.

POVERTY TO PROSPERITY

The magnitude of France's postwar economic devastation required a strong central government with broad powers to rebuild the country's industrial and commercial base. But progress was slow. By 1947 rationing remained and France was forced to turn to the USA for loans as part of the Marshall Plan to rebuild Europe.

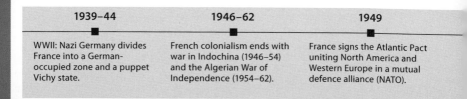

1939–44	1946–62	1949
WWII: Nazi Germany divides France into a German-occupied zone and a puppet Vichy state.	French colonialism ends with war in Indochina (1946–54) and the Algerian War of Independence (1954–62).	France signs the Atlantic Pact uniting North America and Western Europe in a mutual defence alliance (NATO).

THE BIRTH OF THE BIKINI

Almost called *atome* (French for atom) because of its miniscule size, the bikini was the 1946 creation of Cannes fashion designer Jacques Heim and automotive engineer Louis Réard.

Top-and-bottom swimsuits had existed for centuries, but it was the French duo who made them briefer than brief and plumped for the name 'bikini' – after Bikini, an atoll in the Marshall Islands chosen by the USA in 1946 as the testing ground for atomic bombs.

Once wrapped around the curvaceous buttocks of 1950s sex-bomb Brigitte Bardot in St-Tropez there was no looking back. The bikini was born.

The economy gathered steam in the 1950s. The French government invested in hydroelectric and nuclear-power plants, oil and gas exploration, petrochemical refineries, steel production, naval construction, auto factories and building construction to accommodate a baby boom and consumer goods.

YESTERDAY'S MAN

The Fourth Republic was hampered by a weak presidential branch and the debilitating Algerian War of Independence (1954–62). French President Charles de Gaulle remedied the first problem by drafting the Fifth Republic, which gave considerable powers to the president at the expense of the National Assembly.

The struggle for Algerian independence was a tougher nut to crack. De Gaulle's attempts at according the Algerians political equality and recognising their right in principle to self-determination only infuriated right-wingers. The Organisation de l'Armée Secrète (OAS; a group of French settlers and sympathisers opposed to Algerian independence) tried to assassinate de Gaulle several times and in 1961 violence broke out on the streets of Paris.

By the late 1960s loss of the colonies and a surge in immigration and unemployment had seriously weakened de Gaulle's government. Student protests in 1968 turned violent and a general strike by 10 million workers countrywide paralysed France: The government decentralised the higher-education system and followed through in the 1970s with other reforms (lowering the voting age to 18, instituting legalised abortion and so on). De Gaulle resigned from office in 1969 and died the following year.

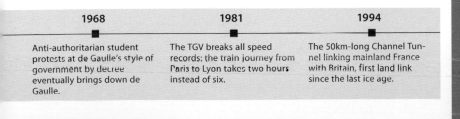

1968	1981	1994
Anti-authoritarian student protests at de Gaulle's style of government by decree eventually brings down de Gaulle.	The TGV breaks all speed records; the train journey from Paris to Lyon takes two hours instead of six.	The 50km-long Channel Tunnel linking mainland France with Britain, first land link since the last ice age.

FRANCE IN FOCUS

HISTORY

THE FRENCH RESISTANCE

Despite the myth of 'la France ré-sistante' (the French Resistance), the underground movement never actually included more than 5% of the population. The other 95% either collaborated or did nothing. Resistance members engaged in railway sabotage, collected intelligence for the Allies, helped Allied airmen who had been shot down and published anti-German leaflets, among other activities. The impact of their pursuits might have been modest but the Resistance served as an enormous boost to French morale – not to mention fresh fodder for numerous literary and cinematic endeavours.

POMPIDOU TO CHIRAC

Georges Pompidou (1911–74) stepped onto the presidential podium in 1969 and Valéry Giscard d'Estaing (b 1926) in 1974. In 1981 d'Estaing was ousted by long-time Socialist Party head François Mitterrand (1916–96).

Mitterrand gave France sparkle. The Minitel – a potent symbol of France's advanced technological savvy – was launched in 1980; the death penalty was abolished; homosexuality was legalised; a 39-hour work week was instituted, annual holiday time was upped from four to five weeks and the right to retire at 60 was guaranteed.

Presidential elections ushered Chirac into the Élysée Palace in 1995 and again in 2002.

THE HEAT IS ON

France's outright opposition to the US-led war in Iraq in 2003 stirred up anti-French sentiment among Americans: many restaurants in the US changed 'French fries' to 'freedom fries' on their menus, while US defence secretary Donald Rumsfeld publicly dismissed France (along with Germany) as 'old Europe'.

In November 2002 strikes brought France to a standstill as public-sector workers hit out at the government's ambitious privatisation plans aimed at raising cash to reduce an increasingly too-high budget deficit. Spring 2003 ushered in more strikes, this time over the government's proposed pension reform. An extreme heatwave that summer, sending temperatures in the capital soaring above 40° and claiming 11,000 predominantly elderly lives, did little to cool rising temperatures.

The last quarter of 2005 was the final helter-skelter downhill. Riots broke out after two teenagers of North African descent were electrocuted while hiding in an electricity substation in a northeast Paris suburb after allegedly running from the police. Within days violence was countrywide. Two weeks later the government introduced emergency measures restricting people's movements and imposing curfews in 30 French towns and cities. Nine thousand burnt cars and buildings later, Chirac assured France

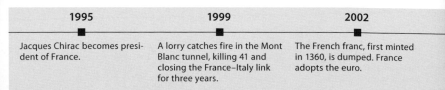

1995	1999	2002
Jacques Chirac becomes president of France.	A lorry catches fire in the Mont Blanc tunnel, killing 41 and closing the France–Italy link for three years.	The French franc, first minted in 1360, is dumped. France adopts the euro.

there would be no more urban violence, and swore steps would be taken to create equal opportunities for immigrants and better opportunities for their youth.

A NEW BREED OF PRESIDENT

Presidential elections, held every five years, threw a woman into the arena in 2007. Socialist Ségolène Royal grabbed the country's attention with her glam, squeaky-clean image and tough talk about leading France in a ground-breaking new direction where no man had dared set foot before. Discredited French president *Le Grand Jacques,* now in his 70s and with a twinset of terms under his presidential belt, did not stand again.

Then there was 'Sarko', as the French press quickly dubbed the highly ambitious Nicolas Sarkozy (b 1955) of Chirac's UMP party. Interior minister and ruling party chairman, centre-right candidate Sarkozy spoke about job creation, lowering taxes, crime crackdown and helping the country's substantial immigrant population, which, given he himself was the son of a Hungarian immigrant, had instant appeal. In the second round of voting 84% of France's 44.7 million eligible voters cast their ballots, which saw the charismatic, silky tongued, 52-year-old Nicolas Sarkozy bagging the Élysée Palace. A new breed of personality-driven, American-style French president was born.

BLING-BLING

Far from knuckling down to implementing the rigorous economic reform platform he was elected on, Sarkozy devoted his first months in office to personal affairs, falling out of love, divorcing, falling in love, and remarrying Italian singer and former model Carla Bruni all in a few months – hence the media quickly dubbing him President Bling-Bling. Sarkozy's popularity and national morale plummeted.

◥THE BEST

HULTON-DEUTSCH COLLECTION/CORBIS

Allied troops, July 1944

THE BEST HISTORIC READS

- **The Discovery of France** (Graham Robb) Epic portrait of contemporary France; the author cycled 20,000km around France to research it.
- **Birdsong** (Sebastian Faulks) The horror of WWII trench warfare.
- **La Reine Margot** (Queen Margot; Alexander Dumas) Murder and intrigue in the Renaissance royal French court.

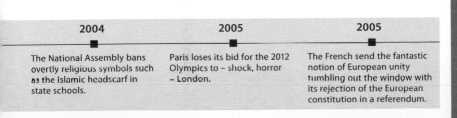

2004	2005	2005
The National Assembly bans overtly religious symbols such as the Islamic headscarf in state schools.	Paris loses its bid for the 2012 Olympics to – shock, horror – London.	The French send the fantastic notion of European unity tumbling out the window with its rejection of the European constitution in a referendum.

FRANCE IN FOCUS

SARKOSIS

It's hardly the stuff French people expect of their president. Hardly respectable at all, in fact, say most who've reacted to the Sarkozy soap opera with shock, shame and dismay.

First there was Cécilia, his second wife of 11 years and mother of one of his three children. Within three months of the couple divorcing, Sarkozy had met, wooed and married Italian Carla Bruni, a former supermodel, folk singer, songwriter and multimillionaire.

Dozens of biographies have been published on the couple, including one in which Bruni spills the beans on the intimacies of their relationship. Bling-bling, yes, but no one can get enough of the unpopular, but charismatic, French president and his First Lady.

In 2008 a psychiatrist in Paris identified people's unhealthy obsession condition with Sarkozy as 'Sarkosis'.

HISTORY

Local elections in spring 2008 confirmed opinion polls as the ruling UMP party lost key seats to the Socialists. Several high-profile members of Sarkozy's cabinet in Paris moreover failed to snag a mayorship. Justice Minister Rachida Dati provided France's disgruntled and substantial ethnic population with a glimmer of hope by becoming the first mayor of North African origin to head up the 7e.

As national morale moped about at an all-time low, French box-office smash-hit film *Bienvenue chez les Ch'tis* provided a spot of light relief and boosted national pride. A couple of months on, a nation mourned the death of Parisian fashion designer Yves Saint Laurent (1936–2008), the last stalwart of France's Chanel and Dior heyday. Most of the women at his funeral at Paris St-Roch's Church wore a trouser suit in homage to the 20th century's most iconic fashion designer.

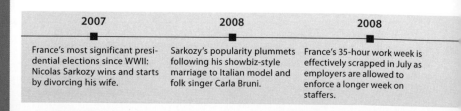

2007

France's most significant presidential elections since WWII: Nicolas Sarkozy wins and starts by divorcing his wife.

2008

Sarkozy's popularity plummets following his showbiz-style marriage to Italian model and folk singer Carla Bruni.

2008

France's 35-hour work week is effectively scrapped in July as employers are allowed to enforce a longer week on staffers.

◨ SHOPPING

Galeries Lafayette (p91), Paris

France is a wonderful place to shop, whether you're in the market for a diamond-encrusted original Cartier bracelet or you're an impoverished *lèche-vitrine* (literally, 'window-licker') who just enjoys what you see from the outside looking in. From the ultrachic couture houses of Paris' av Montaigne and the cubby-hole boutiques of the Marais to the vast underground shopping centre at Les Halles and the flea-market bargains at St-Ouen, the capital is a city that knows how to make it, how to display it and how to charge for it.

Indeed, renowned for its luxury goods it might be – think haute couture, high-quality clothing accessories such as Hermès scarves, lingerie, perfume and cosmetics – but goods are not necessarily cheaper in France than at home.
For the best of French shopping see p40.

OPENING HOURS

Opening hours for Paris shops are generally 10am to 7pm Monday to Saturday. Smaller shops in the city and in most smaller towns often shut all day Monday; other days, their proprietors may simply close from noon to around 2pm for a long lunch. Many larger stores hold *nocturnes* (late nights) on Thursdays, remaining open until around 10pm. Sunday shopping is something of a no go in France, except for in Paris where Champs-Élysées, Montmartre, the Marais and Bastille areas remain fairly lively.

ON THE CHEAP

Soldes (sales) – held, by law, countrywide for three weeks in January and July – offer significant discounts and can be a gold mine for fashionistas. The budget-conscious should also look out for the words *degriffés* (name-brand products with the labels cut out) or *dépôt-vente* (ex-showroom garments sold at steep mark-downs). Factory-outlet shops can be found in Troyes (p123) and Calais in far northern France.

In some shops and department stores, non-EU residents can arrange a rebate of some of the 19.6% value-added tax (VAT) if they spend enough. There are forms to fill out in-store, and these must be shown, with the purchases, as you leave the country (eg at an airport).

SHOPPING LIST

- **Boulangerie** Fresh bread, fruit tarts and mouth-watering pastries
- **Pâtisserie** Often bakes bread too; creamy and ornate cakes to die for
- **Fromagerie** The place to buy cheese that is *fait* (ripe) to the precise degree you request
- **Traiteur** Delicatessen selling *charcuterie* (sliced meats), pâtés and other great picnic food
- **Épicerie** Every neighbourhood has a greengrocer, selling a bit of everything
- **Boucherie** A general butcher; buy fish and seafood from the neighbouring **poissonnerie**

SOUVENIRS

For local arts and crafts, go directly to the source. In Brittany, look for colourful Quimper *faïence* (earthenware), and in Normandy you can pick up Rouen *faïence* or intricate lace from Alençon. Other possibilities include deluxe crystal and glassware from Baccarat in southern Lorraine, or enamel and porcelain from Limoges in Limousin.

Wines from Bordeaux, Burgundy, Alsace and Champagne are available all around France but you'll find a better selection at local wine shops. Buying direct from wineries – after a *dégustation* (tasting session), of course – is an even more enjoyable option! Local brandies make good souvenirs since they may not be available in your home country; look out for Cognacs (from Cognac!), Calvados (apple brandy), *pommeau* (a mixture of unfermented apple juice and Calvados) or Fécamp Bénédictine (from Normandy).

Goodies that travel well include macaroons from St-Émilion and Alsace, *calissons* (a chewy, marzipan-like sweet) from Aix-en-Provence, and candied fruit from Nice. For information on local shopping options, see the individual towns and cities.

MARKET TALK

Shopping for food is one of France's unique joys. Most French people buy a good part of their food from small neighbourhood shops, each with its own speciality – an important ritual and part of French people's daily lives. Each *commerçant* (shopkeeper) specialises in one type of food, meaning they can almost always provide all sorts of useful tips: which round of Camembert is ripe, which wine will complement a certain food, which type of pot to cook rabbit in and so on, which fish to oven-bake and so on.

These shops are geared to people buying small quantities of fresh food each day, so it's perfectly acceptable to buy just meal-size amounts: a few *tranches* (slices) of meat to

ELLIOT DANIEL
Rue Mouffetard (p85), Paris

FRANCE IN FOCUS

SHOPPING

make a sandwich, perhaps, or a *petit bout* (small hunk) of sausage. You can also request just enough for *une/deux personne(s)* (one/two persons). If you want a bit more, ask for *encore un petit peu,* and if you are being given too much, say *'C'est trop'.*

But it is food markets *(marchés alimentaires)* – both open-air street ones *(marchés découverts)* and covered markets *(marchés couverts)* – that are the life and soul of daily life in France. Practically every village, town and city hosts a weekly market that spills across main squares or streets in a riot of colour, noise, hustle and bustle one or two mornings a week, from around 7am to noon. Little bargaining goes on but it is worth a try. Take your own bag or basket.

WINE

Sharing wine

HÖLGER LEUE

The stereotypical Frenchman might no longer start the day with a shot of red wine to *tuer le ver* (kill the worm), followed by an espresso, but France still ranks in the top 10 of the world boozing stakes. Wine, predictably, is the favourite tipple and there are dozens of wine-producing regions throughout France, the seven principal regions being Alsace, Bordeaux, Burgundy, Champagne, Languedoc, the Loire region and the Rhône. With the exception of Alsatian wines, wines in France are generally named after the location of the vineyard rather than the grape varietal.

Appellation d'Origine Contrôlée (AOC; literally, 'label of inspected origin') is bestowed on wines that have met stringent regulations governing where, how and under what conditions they are grown, fermented and bottled. They can cover a wide region, such as Bordeaux, a subregion such as Haut-Médoc, or a commune or village as in Pomerol. Some wine regions only have a single AOC, such as Alsace, while Burgundy is chopped into scores of individual AOCs. AOC wines are almost always good and usually superb. About a third of all French wine produced carries an AOC guarantee.

A FINE ART

Grapes and the art of wine-making were introduced to Gaul by the Romans. In the Middle Ages, important vineyards developed around monasteries as the monks needed wine to celebrate Mass. Large-scale wine production later moved closer to ports (eg Bordeaux), from where it could be exported.

In the mid-19th century, phylloxera aphids were accidentally brought to Europe from the USA. These pests ate through the roots of France's grapevines, destroying some 7000 sq km – 60% of the total – of vineyards. Wine production appeared to be doomed until root stocks resistant to phylloxera were brought from California and original cuttings grafted onto them.

Wine-making is a complicated chemical process, but ultimately the taste and quality of the wine depend on four key factors: the type(s) of grape, the climate, the soil and the art of the vigneron (winemaker). Some viticulturists have honed their skills and techniques to such a degree that their wine is known as a *grand cru* (literally 'great growth'). If this wine has been produced in a year of optimum climatic conditions it becomes a *millésime* (vintage) wine. *Grands crus* are aged first in small oak barrels and then in bottles, sometimes for 20 years or more, before they develop their full taste and aroma. These are the memorable (and pricey) bottles that wine experts talk about with such passion.

↘**THE BEST**

Hennessy Cognac (p306)

OLIVER STREWE

THE BEST ALCOHOLIC-TIPPLE DRIVING TRAILS

- **Champagne houses** (p115) & **Route du Champagne** (p116), Reims & Épernay
- **Route du Cidre** (p164), near Caen
- **Route des Grands Crus** (p194), around Dijon
- **Cassis** (p251), near Marseille
- **Cognac houses** (p306), Cognac
- **Bordeaux wine trail** (p303), Bordeaux

FRANCE IN FOCUS

WINE

BURGUNDY

Burgundy developed its reputation for viticulture during the reign of Charlemagne, when monks first began to make wine here. The vignerons of Burgundy generally only

APÉRITIFS & DIGESTIFS

Meals are often preceded by an *apéritif* such as kir (white wine sweetened with cassis or blackcurrant syrup), *kir royale* (Champagne with cassis) or *pineau* (Cognac and grape juice). Pastis, a 90-proof, anise-flavoured alcoholic drink from the south of France, is hot in summer.

After-dinner drinks are ordered with coffee. France's most famous brandies are Cognac and Armagnac. *Eaux de vie*, literally 'waters of life', can be made with grape skins and the pulp left over after being pressed for wine (Marc de Champagne, Marc de Bourgogne), apples (Calvados) and pears (Poire William).

ELLIOT DANIEL
Mumm Champagne (p115)

have small vineyards (rarely more than 10 hectares) and produce small quantities of wine. Burgundy reds are produced with pinot noir grapes; the best vintages need 10 to 20 years to age. White wine is made from the chardonnay grape. The five main wine-growing areas are Chablis, Côte d'Or, Côte Chalonnaise, Mâcon and Beaujolais, which alone produces 13 different types of light gamay-based red wine.

BORDEAUX

Britons have had a taste for the full-bodied wines of Bordeaux, known as clarets in the UK, since the mid-12th century when King Henry II, who controlled the region through marriage, tried to gain the favour of the locals by granting them tax-free trade status with England. Thus began a roaring business in wine exporting that continues to this day.

Bordeaux has the perfect climate for producing wine and as a result its 1100 sq km of vineyards produce more fine wine than any other region in the world. Bordeaux red wines are often described as well balanced, a quality achieved by blending several grape varieties. The grapes that are predominantly used are merlot, cabernet sauvignon and cabernet franc. Bordeaux's foremost wine-growing areas are Médoc, Pomerol, Saint Émilion and Graves. The nectar-like sweet whites of the Sauternes area are the world's finest dessert wines.

CÔTES DU RHÔNE

The Rhône region is divided into northern and southern areas. The different soil, climate, topography and grapes used means there are dramatic differences in the wines produced by each.

Set on steep hills by the river, the northern vineyards produce red wines exclusively from the ruby-red syrah (shiraz) grape; the aromatic viognier grape is the most popular for producing white wines. The southern region is better known for quantity rather than quality. The vineyards are also more spread out and interspersed with fields of lavender and orchards of olives, pears and almonds. The grenache grape, which ages well when blended, is used in the red wines, while the white wines use the ugni blanc grape.

CHAMPAGNE

Champagne, northeast of Paris, has been the centre for what is arguably France's best-known wine since the 17th century when the innovative monk Dom Pierre Pérignon perfected a technique for making sparkling wine.

Champagne is made from the red pinot noir, the black pinot meunier or the white chardonnay grape. Each vine is vigorously pruned and trained to produce a small quantity of high-quality grapes. Indeed, to maintain exclusivity (and price), the designated areas where grapes used for Champagne can be grown and the amount of wine produced each year is limited. In 2008 the borders that confine the Champagne AOC label were extended to include another 40 villages, increasing the value of their vineyards and its produce by tens of millions of euros (and making party-goers around the world forever grateful).

Champagne is labelled *brut* (extra dry with just 1.5% sugar content), *extra-sec* (dry, but not as dry as *brut*), *sec* (dry), *demi-sec* (slightly sweet) or *doux* (sweet) Famous Champagne houses include Dom Pérignon, Moët & Chandon, Veuve Clicquot, Mercier, Mumm, Krug, Laurent-Perrier, Piper-Heidsieck, Taittinger, De Castellane and Pommery.

THE LOIRE VALLEY

The Loire's 700 sq km of vineyards rank it as the third-largest area in France for the production of quality wines. Although sunny, the climate here is humid and not all grape varieties thrive. Still, the Loire produces the greatest variety of wines of any region in the country (a particular speciality of the region is rosé). The most common grapes are the Muscadet, cabernet franc and chenin blanc varieties. Wines tend to be light and delicate. The most celebrated areas are Pouilly-Fumé, Vouvray, Sancerre, Bourgueil, Chinon and Saumur.

LANGUEDOC

This is the country's most productive wine-growing region, with up to 40% of France's wine – mainly cheap red table wine – produced here. About 2500 sq km of the region is 'under vine', which represents just over a third of France's total.

About 10% of the wine produced now is AOC standard. In addition to the well-known Fitou label, the area's other quality wines are Coteaux du Languedoc, Faugères, Corbières and Minervois. The region also produces about 70% of France's *vin de pays,* most of which is labelled Vin de Pays d'Oc.

FRANCE IN FOCUS

WINE

JOHNNY HAGLUND

Cheese for sale

THE BEST

▶THE BEST

THE BEST WINE & CHEESE PAIRINGS

- Alsatian **gewürztraminer** (p370) and Munster
- **Côtes du Rhone** (p368) with Roquefort
- A Burgundy **Côte d'Or** (p194) with Brie or Camembert
- A mature **Bordeaux** (p368) with Emmental or Cantal
- **Champagne** (p369) and mushroom-like Chaource.

FRANCE IN FOCUS

BEER & CIDER

Alsace, with its close cultural ties to Germany, produces some excellent local beers (eg Bière de Scharrach, Schutzenberger Jubilator and Fischer d'Alsace, a hoppy brew from Schiltigheim). Northern France, close to Belgium and the Netherlands, has its own great beers as well, including St-Sylvestre Trois Monts, Terken Brune and the barley-based Grain d'Orge.

Normandy and Brittany are the home of *cidre* (apple cider) and pear-based *poiré* (perry).

WINE

ALSACE

Alsace produces almost exclusively white wines – mostly varieties produced nowhere else in France – that are known for their clean, fresh taste and compatibility with the often heavy local cuisine. Unusually, some of the fruity Alsatian whites also go well with red meat. The vineyards closest to Strasbourg produce light red wines from pinot noir that are similar to rosé and are best served chilled.

Alsace's four most important varietal wines are riesling, known for its subtlety; the more pungent and highly regarded gewürztraminer; the robust pinot gris, which is high in alcohol; and muscat d'Alsace, which is not as sweet as that made with muscat grapes grown further south.

↘ DIRECTORY & TRANSPORT

DIRECTORY

ACCOMMODATION

Be it a fairy-tale château, an urban boutique hideaway or a mountain refuge, France has accommodation to suit every taste and pocket.

In this guide, accommodation options listed as 'budget' have doubles with private bathroom costing up to €60 (€70 in Paris); 'midrange' hotels charge €60 to €140 (to €160 in Paris); and top-end rooms cost anything upwards of €140 (€160 in Paris).

During periods of heavy tourism, popular destinations are packed out and prices soar. Ski resorts charge their highest rates over Christmas and New Year and the February–March school holidays, while beach resorts are priciest in summer, especially July and August, and particularly from 14 July to 15 August. On the other hand, hotels in inland cities charge low-season rates while everyone is on the coast. In cities whose hotels get mainly business clients, rooms are most expensive from Monday to Thursday and cheaper over the weekend. Rates listed in this guide are generally high-season rates.

Some tourist offices make room reservations, often for a fee of €5, but many

SMOKE-FREE HOTEL ROOMS

Almost all French hotels, except a few budget ones, now have at least some nonsmoking rooms. The nonsmoking icon (✕) appears only when an establishment is 100% nonsmoking.

only do so if you stop by in person. In the Alps, tourist offices for ski resorts run a central reservation service for booking accommodation.

B&BS

Some of France's most charming accommodation comes in the form of *chambres d'hôtes* (B&Bs) – up to five bed-and-breakfast rooms attached to a private home. Many hosts cook up a homemade evening meal *(table d'hôte)* for an extra charge (usually €20 to €25). Tourist offices have lists of local *chambres d'hôtes,* which are urban rarities but plentiful in rural areas.

Gîtes de France acts as an umbrella organisation for B&B properties. Ask at local tourist offices about Gîtes de France brochures and offices, or contact the **Fédération Nationale des Gîtes de France** (Map pp64-5; ☎ 01 49 70 75 75; www .gites-de-france.fr; 59 rue St-Lazare, 9e, Paris; Ⓜ Trinité). Check out their annual catalogue *Gîtes de Charme* (€20; online at www.gites-de-france-charme.com).

Bienvenue à la Ferme (Map pp64-5; ☎ 01 53 57 11 44; www.bienvenue-a-la-ferme.com; 9 av George V, 8e, Paris; Ⓜ Alma-Marceau, George V) has *chambres d'hôte* on farms. Search online or order a catalogue.

Other useful websites are **Fleurs de Soleil** (http://fleursdesoleil.fr, in French), **Samedi Midi Éditions** (www.samedimidi. com) and **...en France** (www.bbfrance.com).

☝ BOOK YOUR STAY ONLINE

For more accommodation reviews and recommendations by Lonely Planet authors, check out the online booking service at www.lonely planet.com. You'll find the true, insider lowdown on the best places to stay. Reviews are thorough and independent. Best of all, you can book online.

HOTELS

French hotels almost never include breakfast in their advertised nightly rates. Unless specified otherwise, prices quoted in this guide don't include breakfast, which costs around €6.50/8/18 in a budget/midrange/top-end hotel. When you book, hotels usually ask for a credit-card number.

A double room generally has one double bed (often two pushed-together singles!); a room with twin beds *(deux lits)* is usually more expensive, as is a room with a bathtub instead of a shower. Triples and quads usually have two or three beds.

The small, often family-run hotels rated by **Logis de France** (☎ 01 45 84 83 84; www.logis-de-france.fr) are known for their charm and warm welcome.

Independent hotels, each with its own unique local character, are grouped by **Arcantis** (www.arcantis-hotels.com), which brings together two- and three-star places; **Best Western** (www.bestwestern.com), whose hotels are generally on the upper end of midrange; **Citôtel** (www.citotel.com); **Contact Hôtel** (www.contact-hotel.com); and **Inter-Hotel** (www.inter-hotel.fr). Superluxury establishments can be found through **Relaix & Châteaux** (www.relaischateaux.com) and **Grandes Étapes Françaises** (www.grandesetapes.fr).

RENTAL ACCOMMODATION

Renting a furnished studio, apartment or villa can be an economical alternative for stays of a few days or more, plus it gives you the chance to live a little bit like a local, with trips to the farmers market and the *boulangerie*. Cleaning, linen rental and electricity fees usually cost extra.

In rural areas, Gîtes de France (p372) handles some of the most charming *gîtes ruraux* (self-contained holiday cottages).

CLIMATE CHARTS

France has a temperate climate with generally mild winters, except in mountainous areas and the far northeast.

DIRECTORY

CLIMATE CHARTS

PRACTICALITIES

- France uses the metric system for weights and measures.
- Plugs have two round pins, so visitors from the English-speaking lands will need an adaptor; the electric current is 220V at 50Hz AC (you may need a transformer for 110V electrical appliances).
- Videos in France work on the PAL system; TV is Secam.
- Locals read their news in centre-left, highly intellectual *Le Monde* (www.lemonde.fr), right-leaning *Le Figaro* (www.lefigaro.fr) or left-leaning *Libération* (www.liberation.fr).
- For radio news, tune in to the French-language Radio France Info (105.5MHz or thereabouts in most areas), the multilanguage RFI (738kHz or 89MHz in Paris) or, in northwestern France, the BBC World Service (648kHz) and BBC Radio 4 (198kHz).
- In many areas, Autoroute Info (107.7MHz) has round-the-clock information on autoroute travel conditions.
- Popular national FM music stations include NRJ (pronounced 'energy'; www.nrj.fr, in French), Skyrock (www.skyrock.fm, in French) and Nostalgie (www.nostalgie.fr, in French).

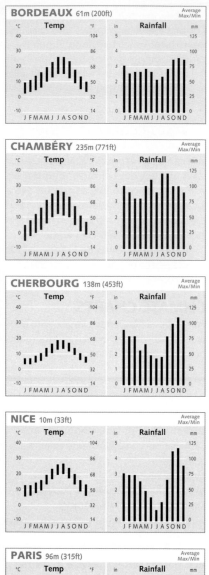

COURSES
COOKING

Cooking courses are available for different levels and lengths of time and the cost of tuition varies widely. In Paris one of the most popular – and affordable – for beginners is the **Cours de Cuisine Olivier Berté** (Map pp64-5; ☎ 01 40 26 14 00; www.coursdecuisineparis.com; 2nd fl, 7 rue Paul Lelong, 2e; Ⓜ Bourse; 3hr course adult/12-14 yr €100/30), which offers three-hour courses at 10.30am from Wednesday to Saturday with an additional class from 6pm to 9pm on Friday. *Carnets* of five/20 courses cost €440/1500.

Much more expensive are the **Cooking Classes with Patricia Wells** (www.patriciawells.com; US$5000) led by the incomparable American food critic and author (p238) at her Parisian cooking studio in rue Jacob, 6e, and her farmhouse in Provence.

Other cooking schools in Paris:
École Le Cordon Bleu (Map pp52-3; ☎ 01 53 68 22 50; www.cordonbleu.edu; 8 rue Léon Delhomme, 15e; Ⓜ Vaugirard or Convention) Dating back to 1895, the Cordon Bleu school has one-day themed workshops.
École Ritz Escoffier (Map pp64-5; ☎ 01 43 16 30 50; www.ritzescoffier.com; 38 rue Cambon, 1er; Ⓜ Concorde) This prestigious cooking school is based in what is arguably Paris' finest hotel, the Hôtel Ritz Paris.

CUSTOMS

Goods brought in and out of countries within the EU incur no additional taxes provided duty has been paid somewhere within the EU and the goods are for personal consumption. Duty-free shopping is available only if you're leaving the EU.

Coming from non-EU countries (including the Channel Islands), duty-free allowances (for adults) are: 200 cigarettes, 50 cigars, 1L of spirits, 2L of wine, 50ml of perfume, 250ml *eau de toilette* and other goods up to the value of €175 (€90 for under 15s). Anything over these limits must be declared.

DANGERS & ANNOYANCES

France is generally a safe place in which to travel but crime has risen dramatically in the last few years. Although property crime is a major problem, it's extremely unlikely that you will be physically assaulted while walking down the street. Safety advice for women travellers is on p383.

HUNTERS

The hunting season runs from September to February. If you see signs reading *'chasseurs'* or *'chasse gardée'* strung up or tacked to trees, think twice about wandering into the area.

Hunting is traditional and commonplace in all rural areas in France.

NATURAL DANGERS

There are powerful tides and strong undertows at many places along the Atlantic Coast, from the Spanish border north to Brittany and Normandy.

Only swim in *zones de baignade surveillée* (beaches monitored by life guards). Be aware of tide times and, if sleeping on a beach, always make sure you are above the high-tide mark.

Thunderstorms in the mountains and the hot southern plains can be extremely sudden and violent. Check the weather report before setting out on a long walk and be prepared for sudden storms and temperature drops if you're heading into the high country of the Alps or Pyrenees.

Avalanches pose an enormous danger in the French Alps.

SMOKING

As of 2007, smoking is illegal in all public spaces, including restaurants and pubs –

RAIN, HAIL, SNOW OR SHINE

Check out the French weather forecasts at www.meteofrance.com (in French) or call one of the following, which will cost you €0.34 per minute:

National, city, marine and mountain forecasts ☎ 3250

Local & département forecasts ☎ 08 92 68 02 plus two-digit *département* number

---

and, to the surprise of some, the law is actually obeyed!

THEFT

The security problem that you're most likely to encounter is theft, including pickpocketing and bag snatching (eg in dense crowds and public places). A common ploy is for one person to distract you while another steals your wallet, camera or bag. Tired tourists on the train from the airport are a frequent target for thieves. Big cities, notably Paris, Marseille and Nice, have the highest crime levels. Particularly in Paris, museums are beset by organised gangs of seemingly innocuous children who are actually trained pickpockets.

TRAVELLING BY CAR

Break-ins to parked cars are a widespread problem. Gangs cruise seemingly tranquil tourist areas for unattended vehicles – out-of-town or foreign plates and rental stickers are a dead giveaway. *Never, ever* leave anything valuable – or anything not valuable – inside your car. Hiding your bags in the trunk is risky; in hatchbacks it's practically an open invitation to theft.

Aggressive theft from cars stopped at red lights (eg by motorcycle-borne thieves) is occasionally a problem, especially in the south (specifically in and around Marseille and sometimes Nice).

EMBASSIES & CONSULATES

FRENCH EMBASSIES & CONSULATES

France's diplomatic and consular representatives abroad are listed on the website www.diplomatie.gouv.fr/en.

Australia Canberra (☎ 02-6216 0100; www.ambafrance-au.org; 6 Perth Ave, Yarralumla, ACT 2600); Sydney Consulate (☎ 02-9268 2400; Level 26, St Martin's Tower, 31 Market St, Sydney, NSW 2000) Plus seven consular agencies.

Canada Ottawa (☎ 613-789-1795; www.ambafrance-ca.org; 42 Sussex Drive, Ottawa, Ontario K1M 2C9); Toronto Consulate (☎ 416-847-1900; www.consulfrance-toronto.org; 2 Bloor St East, Ste 2200, Toronto M4W 1A8)

New Zealand Wellington (☎ 04-384 2555; www.ambafrance-nz.org; 13th fl, Rural Bank Bldg, 34-42 Manners St, PO Box 11-343, Wellington)

South Africa Pretoria (☎ 012-425 1600; www.ambafrance-rsa.org; 250 Melk St, New Muckleneuk, 0181 Pretoria)

UK London Embassy (☎ 020-7073 1000; www.ambafrance-uk.org; 58 Knightsbridge, London SW1X 7JT); London Consulate (☎ 020-7073 1200; www.consulfrance-londres.org; 21 Cromwell Rd, London SW7 2EN); London Visa Section (☎ 020-7073 1250; 6A Cromwell Pl, London SW7 2EW)

USA Washington (☎ 202-944-6000; www.ambafrance-us.org; 4101 Reservoir Rd NW, Washington, DC 20007); New York Consulate (☎ 212-606-3600; www.consulfrance-newyork.org; 934 Fifth Ave, New York, NY 10021)

EMBASSIES & CONSULATES IN FRANCE

Australia Paris (Map pp52-3; ☎ 01 40 59 33 00; www.france.embassy.gov.au; 4 rue Jean Rey, 15e; Ⓜ Bir Hakeim)

Canada Paris (Map pp64-5; ☎ 01 44 43 29 00; www.amb-canada.fr; 35 av Montaigne, 8e; Ⓜ Franklin D Roosevelt); Nice (☎ 04 93 92 93 22; 10 rue Lamartine)

Japan Paris (Map pp64-5; ☎ 01 48 88 62 00; www.amb-japon.fr; 7 av Hoche, 8e; Ⓜ Courcelles)

New Zealand Paris (Map pp52-3; ☎ 01 45 01 43 43; www.nzembassy.com; 7ter rue Léonard de Vinci, 16e; Ⓜ Victor Hugo)

South Africa Paris (Map pp52-3; ☎ 01 53 59 23 23; www.afriquesud.net; 59 quai d'Orsay, 7e; Ⓜ Invalides)

UK Paris Embassy (Map pp64-5; ☎ 01 44 51 31 00; www.amb-grandebretagne.fr; 35 rue du Faubourg St- Honoré, 8e; Ⓜ Concorde); Paris Consulate (Map pp64-5; ☎ 01 44 51 31 00; 18bis rue d'Anjou, 8e; Ⓜ Madeleine); Marseille Consulate (☎ 04 91 54 92 00; place Varian Fry, 6e)

USA Paris Embassy (Map pp64-5; ☎ 01 43 12 22 22; http://france.usembassy.gov; 2 av Gabriel, 8e; Ⓜ Concorde); US citizen services (☎ 01 43 12 26 71; 4 av Gabriel, 8e; Ⓜ Concorde; Ⓨ 9am-noon Mon-Fri except US & French holidays); Nice Consular Agency (☎ 04 93 88 89 55; 3rd fl, 7 av Gustave V); Marseille Consulate (☎ 04 91 54 92 00; place Varian Fry, 6e)

FESTIVALS & EVENTS

Most French cities and towns have at least one major music, dance, theatre, cinema or art festival each year and many have several. Villages hold *foires* (fairs) and *fêtes* (festivals) to honour anything from a local saint to the year's garlic crop. We list many of these important annual events in city and town sections; more details are available from tourist-office websites. During big events towns get extremely busy and accommodation can get booked out in advance.

GAY & LESBIAN TRAVELLERS

France is one of Europe's most liberal countries when it comes to homosexuality. Paris has been a thriving gay and lesbian centre since the late 1970s. Attitudes towards homosexuality tend to be more conservative in the countryside and villages.

Gay Pride marches are held in major cities between mid-May and early July.

ORGANISATIONS

Most major gay and lesbian organisations are based in Paris:

Act Up-Paris (☎ 01 48 06 13 89; www.act upparis.org, in French; 45 rue Sedaine, 11e; Ⓜ **Voltaire**) An activist group focusing on the battle against HIV/AIDS and the rights of people who are *séropositif* (have tested positive for HIV).

Association des Médecins Gais (☎ 01 48 05 81 71; www.medecins-gays.org, in French; 63 rue Beaubourg, 3e; Ⓜ **Rambuteau**) Association of Gay Doctors, based in the Centre Lesbien Gai Bi & Trans; deals with gay-related health issues.

Centre Lesbien Gai Bi & Trans (LGBT; ☎ 01 43 57 21 47; www.cglparis.org, in French; 63 rue Beaubourg, 3e; Ⓜ **Rambuteau**) A welcome and support centre.

HEALTH

France is a healthy place so your main risks are likely to be sunburn, foot blisters, insect bites and mild stomach problems from eating and drinking with too much gusto.

BEFORE YOU GO

Prevention is the key to staying healthy while abroad. A little planning before departure, particularly for pre-existing illnesses, will save trouble later. See your dentist before a long trip, carry a spare pair of contact lenses and glasses, and take your optical prescription with you. Bring medications in their original, clearly labelled, containers. A signed and dated letter from your physician describing your medical conditions and medications, in-

cluding generic names (French medicine names are often completely different from those in other countries), is also a good idea. If carrying syringes or needles, be sure to have a physician's letter documenting their medical necessity.

INSURANCE

Citizens of the EU, Switzerland, Iceland, Norway or Liechtenstein receive free or reduced-cost state-provided health-care cover with the European Health Insurance Card (EHIC) for medical treatment that becomes necessary while in France. (The EHIC replaced the E111 in 2006.) Each family member will need a separate card. In the UK, get application forms from post offices, or download them from the Department of Health website (www.dh.gov.uk), which has comprehensive information about the card's coverage.

Citizens from other countries will need to check if there is a reciprocal arrangement for free medical care between their country and France. If you need health insurance, consider a policy covering the worst possible scenario, such as an accident requiring an emergency flight home. Find out in advance if your insurance plan will make payments directly to providers or reimburse you later for health expenditures.

RECOMMENDED VACCINATIONS

No vaccinations are required to travel to France. However, the World Health Organization (WHO) recommends that all travellers be covered for diphtheria, tetanus, measles, mumps, rubella and polio, regardless of their destination.

IN FRANCE

AVAILABILITY & COST OF HEALTH CARE

Visitors to France can get excellent health care from the emergency room/casualty ward *(salle des urgences)* of a hospital *(hôpital)* and at a doctors' office *(cabinet médical)*, and for minor illnesses, trained staff in pharmacies – flagged in every village and town with a green-cross sign that's outside and flashes when open – give valuable advice and sell medications.

They can also tell you when more specialised help is needed and point you in the right direction. Dental care is usually good; however, it is sensible to have a dental check-up before a long trip.

SEXUAL HEALTH

Emergency contraception is available with a doctor's prescription in France. Condoms *(les préservatifs)* are readily available. Be sure to keep them in a cool dry place or they may crack.

It is estimated that 0.4% of France's adult population (aged 15 to 49) is living with HIV/AIDS (in French: *VIH/SIDA*).

HOLIDAYS

The following *jours fériés* (public holidays) are observed in France:

New Year's Day (Jour de l'An) 1 January; parties in larger cities; fireworks are subdued by international standards.

Easter Sunday & Monday (Pâques & lundi de Pâques) Late March/April.

May Day (Fête du Travail) 1 May; traditional parades.

Victoire 1945 8 May; commemorates the Allied victory in Europe that ended WWII.

Ascension Thursday (Ascension) May; celebrated on the 40th day after Easter.

Pentecost/Whit Sunday & Whit Monday (Pentecôte & lundi de Pentecôte) Mid-May to mid-June; celebrated on the seventh Sunday after Easter.

Bastille Day/National Day (Fête Nationale) 14 July; *the* national holiday.

Assumption Day (Assomption) 15 August.

All Saints' Day (Toussaint) 1 November.

Remembrance Day (L'onze novembre) 11 November; marks the WWI armistice.

Christmas (Noël) 25 December.

The following days are *not* public holidays in France: Shrove Tuesday (Mardi Gras; the first day of Lent); Maundy (or Holy) Thursday and Good Friday, just before Easter; and Boxing Day (26 December).

INSURANCE

See p347 for health insurance and p390 for car insurance.

TRAVEL INSURANCE

Getting travel insurance to cover theft, loss and medical problems is highly recommended. Some policies specifically exclude dangerous activities such as scuba diving, motorcycling, skiing and even trekking so read the fine print. Check that the policy covers ambulances or an emergency flight home.

You may prefer a policy that pays doctors or hospitals directly rather than reimbursing you for expenditures after the fact. If you have to claim later, make sure you keep all documentation.

INTERNET ACCESS

Wireless access points can now be found at major airports, in many (if not most) hotels and at lots of cafés. Many tourist offices tout wi-fi hot spots that let laptop owners hook up for free.

Internet cafés can be found in towns and cities countrywide. Prices range from €2 to €6 per hour.

If you'll be accessing dial-up ISPs with your laptop, you'll need a telephone-plug adaptor, available at large supermarkets.

WHAT THE COMPUTER ICON MEANS

Throughout this guide, only accommodation providers that have an actual computer that guests can use to access the internet are flagged with a computer icon (🖳); those that offer wi-fi access, but have no computer, are not. Paris is the exception: places offering wi-fi only as well as places offering the use of a computer receive the 🖳 icon in the Paris chapter.

LEGAL MATTERS

DRUGS & ALCOHOL

Contrary to popular belief, French law does not distinguish between 'hard' and 'soft' drugs. The penalty for any personal use of *stupéfiants* (including cannabis, amphetamines, ecstasy and heroin) can be a one-year jail sentence and a €3750 fine, but depending on the circumstances it might be anything from a stern word to a compulsory rehab program.

Importing, possessing, selling or buying drugs can get you up to 10 years' prison and a fine of up to €500,000. Police have been known to search chartered coaches, cars and train passengers for drugs just because they're coming from Amsterdam.

Ivresse (drunkeness) in public is punishable by a €150 fine.

POLICE

French police have wide powers of search and seizure and can ask you to prove your identity at any time – whether or not there is 'probable cause'. Foreigners must be able to prove their legal status in France (eg passport, visa) without delay.

If the police stop you for any reason, be polite and remain calm. Verbally (and of course physically) abusing a police officer can lead to a hefty fine, and even imprisonment. You may refuse to sign a police statement, and have the right to ask for a copy. People who are arrested are considered innocent until proven guilty, but can be held in custody until trial.

Because of the threat of terrorism, French police are very strict about security. Do not leave baggage unattended, especially at airports or train stations: suspicious objects may be summarily blown up.

LOCAL GOVERNMENT

Metropolitan France (the mainland and Corsica) is made up of 22 *régions* (regions), which group the country's 96 *départements* (departments), each ruled by a Paris-appointed *préfet* (prefect) who rules from the departmental capital, the *préfecture*. *Départements* are subdivided into 324 arrondissements, which are in turn subdivided into *cantons*, which are split into 36,400 *communes*.

Almost always named after a geographic feature, *départements* have two-digit codes that do extra duty as the first two digits of all postcodes.

MAPS

France's two major map publishers are **Michelin** (http://boutiquecartesetguides .michelin.fr, in French, www.viamichelin.com for online maps) and the **Institut Géographique National** (IGN; www.ign.fr). Countrywide, road and city maps are available at Maisons de la Presse (large newsagencies), bookshops, tourist offices and newspaper kiosks. In Paris, the full range of IGN maps is on offer at **Espace IGN** (Map pp64-5; ☎ 01 43 98 80 00; 107 rue la Boétie, Paris 8e; Ⓜ Franklin D Roosevelt).

Michelin's green-jacketed *Environs de Paris* and *Banlieue de Paris* maps (€4.30), both available from airport newsagents,

DIRECTORY

MONEY

LEGAL AGE

- Driving: 18
- Buying alcohol: 16
- Age of majority: 18
- Age of sexual consent for everyone: 15
- Age considered minor under anti-child-pornography and child-prostitution laws: 18
- Voting: 18

will help you with the very confusing drive into and out of Paris. Michelin's yellow-orange 1:200,000 scale (1cm = 2km) regional maps (€6.50) are perfect for cross-country driving; if you'll be covering more than a few regions the national *Atlas Routier France* (€15.90) is better value.

The IGN also has regional fold-out maps as well as an all-France volume, *France – Routes, Autoroutes*.

MONEY
ATMS

ATMs – known as *distributeurs automatiques de billets* (DAB) or *points d'argent* in French – are the cheapest and most convenient way to get money. ATMs connected to international networks are situated in all cities and towns and usually offer an excellent exchange rate.

CASH

You always get a better exchange rate in-country but it's a good idea to arrive in France with enough euros to take a taxi to a hotel if you have to.

CREDIT & DEBIT CARDS

Credit and debit cards are convenient, relatively secure and usually offer a better exchange rate than travellers cheques or cash exchanges. Credit cards issued in France have embedded chips – you have to type in a PIN code to make a purchase.

Credit cards are accepted almost everywhere in France. Visa, MasterCard and Amex can be used in shops and supermarkets and for train travel, car rentals and motorway tolls, though some places (eg 24-hour petrol stations, some autoroute toll machines) only take French-style credit cards with chips and PINs (for security reasons, these are now being issued by more and more banks worldwide). Don't assume that you can pay for a meal or a budget hotel with a credit card – inquire first.

For lost cards, these numbers operate 24 hours:

Amex (☎ 01 47 77 72 00)
Diners Club (☎ 08 10 31 41 59)
MasterCard (☎ 08 00 90 13 87)
Visa (Carte Bleue; ☎ 08 00 90 11 79)

CURRENCY
The euro has been the official currency of France since 2002. One euro is divided into 100 cents or centimes, with one-, two-, five-, 10-, 20- and 50-centime coins. Notes come in denominations of five, 10, 20, 50, 100, 200 and 500 euros. Euro notes and coins issued in France are valid throughout the other 14 countries in the euro zone: Austria, Belgium, Cyprus, Finland, Germany, Greece, Ireland, Italy, Luxembourg, Malta, the Netherlands, Portugal, Slovenia and Spain.

MONEYCHANGERS
Commercial banks usually charge a stiff €3 to €5 fee per foreign-currency transaction – if they even bother to offer exchange services any more. In Paris and major cities, *bureaux de change* (exchange bureaux) are faster and easier, open longer hours and often give better rates than banks.

DIRECTORY

TELEPHONE

TIPPING

By law, restaurant and bar prices are *service compris* (include a 15% service charge) so there's no expectation of a *pourboire* (tip), though if you're satisfied you might leave a few coins (for a cup of coffee) or round up to the nearest euro or two. Except in very upscale establishments, that is, where 5% is the norm. Taxi drivers are usually tipped 10%. If you stay in a hotel for several days, it's good form to leave €1 or €2 for the people who clean your room (more in top-end places, where the porter, the bellboy and other staff should be tipped if you've asked them to carry out extra services).

TRAVELLERS CHEQUES

Travellers cheques, a relic of the 19th and 20th centuries, cannot be used to pay most French merchants directly and so have to be changed into euro banknotes at banks, exchange bureaux or post offices.

TELEPHONE
DOMESTIC DIALLING

French telephone numbers have 10 digits, except for a few commercial access numbers that have four digits and some emergency numbers that have just two or three. Emergency numbers (see inside the front cover) can be dialled from public phones without a phonecard.

Dialling a mobile phone (ie a number that begins with ☎ 06) from a fixed-line phone or another mobile can be very expensive.

For France Telecom's *service des renseignements* (directory inquiries) dial ☎ 11 87 12 (€1.18 per call from a fixed-line phone). Not all operators speak English. For help in English with all France Telecom's services, see www.francetelecom.com or call ☎ 08 00 36 47 75.

PUBLIC PHONES & TELEPHONE CARDS

To get explanations in English and other languages on how to use a public telephone, push the button engraved with a two-flags icon.

For both international and domestic calling, most public phones operate using either a credit card or two kinds of *télécartes* (phonecards): *cartes à puce* (cards with a magnetic chip) issued by France Télécom and sold at post offices for €8 or €15; and *cartes à code* (cards that you can use from public or private phones by dialling a free access number and then the card's scratch-off code), marketed by an array of companies and sold at *tabacs*, newsagents and post offices.

Phonecards with codes offer *much* better international rates than do France Télécom chip cards or Country Direct services (for which you're billed at home by your long-distance carrier). The shop you buy a phonecard from should be able to tell you which type is best for the country you'd like to call. Using phonecards from a home phone is much cheaper that using them from public phones or mobile phones.

INTERNATIONAL DIALLING

To call France from another country, dial your country's international access code, then ☎ 33 (France's country code), then the 10-digit local number *without* the initial ☎ 0.

To call internationally from France, dial ☎ 00 (the international access code), the *indicatif* (country code), the area code (without the initial zero if there is one) and the local number. Some country codes are posted in public telephones.

For directory inquiries for numbers outside France, dial ☎ 11 87 00 (€2 or €3).

To make a reverse-charges (collect) call *(en PCV)* or a person-to-person call *(avec préavis)* from France, dial ☎ 31 23. For the USA and Canada you can dial ☎ 08 00 99 00 11, and for Australia (Telstra) ☎ 08 00 99 00 61.

MOBILE PHONES

French mobile phones have numbers that begin with ☎ 06.

France uses GSM 900/1800, which is compatible with the rest of Europe and Australia but not with the North American GSM 1900 or the totally different system in Japan (though some North Americans have tri-band phones that work here). Check with your service provider about roaming charges – using a mobile phone outside your home country can be hideously expensive!

TIME

France uses the 24-hour clock and is on Central European Time, which is one hour ahead of GMT/UTC. During daylight-saving time, which runs from the last Sunday in March to the last Sunday in October, France is two hours ahead of GMT/UTC.

TOURIST INFORMATION

LOCAL TOURIST OFFICES

Almost every city, town, village and hamlet has an *office de tourisme* (a tourist office run by some unit of local government) or *syndicat d'initiative* (a tourist office run by an organisation of local merchants). Both are excellent resources and can supply you with local maps as well as details on accommodation, restaurants and activities. Many tourist offices make local hotel and B&B reservations, sometimes for a small fee. Details on tourist offices appear under Information at the beginning of each city, town or area listing.

Comités régionaux de tourisme (CRTs; regional tourist boards), their *départemental* analogues (CDTs), and their websites are a superb source of information and hyperlinks. CRT websites can be found at www.fncrt.com (in French).

TOURIST OFFICES ABROAD

French government tourist offices (usually called Maisons de la France) provide every imaginable sort of tourist information on France. See www.franceguide.com for links to country-specific websites.

Australia (☎ 02-9231 5244; Level 13, 25 Bligh St, Sydney, NSW 2000)

Canada (☎ 514-288 2026; Suite 1010, 1800 McGill College Ave, Montreal, Quebec H3A 3J6)

UK (☎ 09068-244 123; Lincoln House, 300 High Holborn, London WC1V 7JH)

USA New York (☎ 514-288-1904; 29th fl, 825 Third Ave, entrance on 50th St, New York, NY 10022); Los Angeles (☎ 310-271-6665; 9454 Wilshire Bd, Ste 210, Beverly Hills, CA 90212-2967)

TRAVELLERS WITH DISABILITIES

France is not well equipped for *handicapés* (people with disabilities): cobblestone streets are a nightmare to navigate in a wheelchair; kerb ramps are often lacking; older public facilities and budget hotels frequently lack lifts; and the Paris metro, most of it built decades ago, is hopeless. But travellers with disabilities who would like to visit France can overcome these difficulties.

Tourisme et Handicaps (☎ 01 44 11 10 41; www.tourisme-handicaps.org, in French; 43 rue Marx Dormoy, 18e, Paris) issues the 'Tourisme et Handicap' label to tourist sites, restaurants and hotels that comply with strict accessibility and usability standards.

Details on rail access for people with disabilities appear in the SNCF's French-language booklet *Guide des Voyageurs Handicapés et à Mobilité Réduite,* available at train stations. You can also contact the **Centre du Service Accès Plus** (☎ 08 90

64 06 50; www.accessibilite.sncf.fr, in French), to check station accessibility or to arrange for a *fauteuil roulant* (wheelchair) or to receive help getting on or off a train. For the Paris region, contact **Accès Plus Transilien** (☎ 08 10 76 74 33; www.infomobi.com).

Mobile en Ville (www.mobile-en-ville.asso.fr) works to make Paris wheelchair accessible and publishes *Paris Comme sur les Roulettes*, which showcases 20 tours of the city.

Michelin's *Guide Rouge* uses icons to indicate hotels with lifts and with facilities that make them at least partly accessible to people with disabilities, while Gîtes de France (see p372) can provide details on *gîtes ruraux* and *chambres d'hôtes* with 'disabled access' (this is one of their website's search criteria).

VISAS

For up-to-date details on visa requirements, see the **French Foreign Affairs Ministry site** (www.diplomatie.gouv.fr) and click 'Going to France'.

EU nationals and citizens of Iceland, Norway and Switzerland need only a passport or a national identity card in order to enter France and stay in the country. However, nationals of the 12 countries that joined the EU in 2004 and 2007 are subject to various limitations on living and working in France.

Citizens of Australia, Canada, Israel, Hong Kong, Japan, Malaysia, New Zealand, Singapore, the USA and many Latin American countries do not need visas to visit France as tourists for up to 90 days.

Other people wishing to come to France as tourists have to apply for a **Schengen Visa**, named after the agreements that abolished passport controls between 15 European countries: Austria, Belgium, Denmark, Finland, France, Germany, Greece, Iceland, Italy, Luxembourg, the Netherlands, Norway, Portugal, Spain and Sweden. It allows unlimited travel throughout the entire zone for a 90-day period. Application should be made to the consulate of the country you are entering first, or that will be your main destination.

Tourist visas *cannot* be extended except in emergencies (such as medical problems). When your visa expires you'll need to leave and reapply from outside France.

WOMEN TRAVELLERS

Women tend to attract more unwanted attention than men but need not walk around in fear; people are rarely assaulted on the street. Be aware of your surroundings and of situations that could be dangerous: empty streets, lonely beaches, dark corners of large train stations. Using metros late at night is generally OK, as stations are rarely deserted, but there are a few in Paris that it's best to avoid (see p61).

In some places women may have to deal with what might be called low-intensity sexual harassment: 'playful' comments and invitations that can become overbearing or aggressive, and which some women find threatening or offensive. Remain polite and keep your distance. Hearing a foreign accent may provoke further unwanted attention.

Be alert to vibes in cheap hotels, sometimes staffed by unattached men who may pay far more attention to your comings and goings than you would like. Change hotels if you feel uncomfortable, or allude to the imminent arrival of your husband (whether you have one or not).

On overnight trains, you may prefer to ask (when reserving) if there's a women's compartment available. If your compartment companions are overly attentive, don't hesitate to ask the conductor for a change of compartment. Sleeping cars, which have their own bathrooms, offer greater security than a couchette.

In an emergency, contact the **police** (☎ 17), who'll take you to the hospital if you've been injured. You can reach France's national **rape crisis hotline** (☎ 08 00 05 95 95; ☺ **10am-7pm Mon-Fri**) toll-free from any telephone without using a phonecard.

TRANSPORT
GETTING THERE & AWAY
ENTERING THE COUNTRY

Entering France from other parts of the EU is usually a breeze – no border checkpoints and no customs – thanks to the Schengen Agreements, signed and fully implemented by all of France's neighbours except the UK and the Channel Islands. For these two entities, old-fashioned document and customs checks are still the norm, at least when exiting France.

If you're arriving from a non-EU country, you will have to show your passport (and your visa if you need one – see p383) or EU identity card, and clear customs.

AIR
AIRPORTS

France's two major international airports, both just outside Paris, are **Roissy Charles de Gaulle** (☎ 01 48 62 22 80; www.aeroportsdeparis.fr; airport code CDG) and **Orly** (☎ 01 49 75 15 15; www.aeroportsdeparis.fr; airport code ORY). For details, see p92.

Relevant regional airports are listed in destination chapters.

TICKETS
AUSTRALIA & NEW ZEALAND

Both **Flight Centre** (Australia ☎ 133 133; www.flightcentre.com.au; New Zealand ☎ 0800 24 35 44; www.flightcentre.co.nz) and **STA Travel** (Australia ☎ 1300 733 035; www.statravel.com.au; New Zealand ☎ 0508 782 872;

www.statravel.co.nz) have branches throughout Australia and New Zealand. For online bookings, try www.travel.com.au.

CANADA

Travel Cuts (☎ 800-667-2887; www.travelcuts.com) is Canada's national student travel agency. For online bookings try www.expedia.ca and www.travelocity.ca.

UK & IRELAND

Advertisements for travel agencies appear in the travel pages of the weekend broadsheet newspapers, *Time Out* and the *Evening Standard,* as well as in the free online magazine *TNT* (www.tntmagazine.com), but some of the best deals are available direct from budget airlines.

Recommended travel agencies and online ticket sales:

ebookers.com (www.ebookers.com)
Flight Centre (www.flightcentre.co.uk)
Trailfinders (www.trailfinders.com)
USIT (www.usit.ie)

USA

San Francisco is the ticket consolidator capital of America, although some good

---

THINGS CHANGE…

The transport information in this chapter is particularly vulnerable to change, especially as the price of oil skyrockets. Check directly with the transport provider or a travel agent to make sure you understand how a fare (and the ticket you may buy) works, and be aware of the security requirements for international travel. The details given in this chapter should be regarded as pointers and are not a substitute for your own careful, up-to-date research.

TRANSPORT

⇲ CLIMATE CHANGE & TRAVEL

Travel – especially air travel – is a significant contributor to global climate change. At Lonely Planet, we believe that all who travel have a responsibility to limit their personal impact. As a result, we have teamed with Rough Guides and other concerned industry partners to support Climate Care, which allows people to offset the greenhouse gases they are responsible for with contributions to energy-saving projects and other climate-friendly initiatives in the developing world. Lonely Planet offsets all staff and author travel.

For more information, turn to the responsible travel pages on www.lonely planet.com. For details on offsetting your carbon emissions and a carbon calculator, go to www.climatecare.org.

deals can be found in Los Angeles, New York and other big cities.

The following agencies are recommended for online bookings:

CheapTickets (www.cheaptickets.com)
Expedia (www.expedia.com)
lowestfare.com (www.lowestfare.com)
Orbitz (www.orbitz.com)
STA Travel (www.statravel.com)
Travelocity (www.travelocity.com)

Other rock-bottom options for discounted trans-Atlantic air travel include stand-by and courier flights. For details:

Airhitch (www.airhitch.org)
Courier Travel (www.couriertravel.org)
International Association of Air Travel Couriers (www.courier.org)

LAND

CAR & MOTORCYCLE

Arriving in France by car is easy. At some border points you may be asked for a passport or EU national identity card (your driver's licence will not be sufficient ID). See p389 for details about driving in France.

EUROTUNNEL

The Channel Tunnel, inaugurated in 1994, is the first dry-land link between England and France since the last ice age.

High-speed **Eurotunnel shuttle trains** (☎ in UK 08705-35 35 35, in France 08 10 63 03 04; www.eurotunnel.com) whisk bicycles, motorcycles, cars and coaches from Folkestone through the Channel Tunnel to Coquelles, 5km southwest of Calais, in airconditioned and soundproofed comfort in just 35 minutes.

Depending on the date and, especially, the time of day, one-way car fares range from UK£49 to UK£145 (€69 to €217), including all passengers, unlimited luggage and taxes.

TRAIN

Thanks to the long-awaited high-speed track recently put into operation in England, the highly civilised **Eurostar** (☎ in UK 08705-186 186, in France 08 92 35 35 39; www.eurostar.com) now whisks you between London and Paris in just 2¼ hours. Trains link London (St Pancras International) with Paris (Gare du Nord), Lille (Gare Lille Europe; 1½ hours, 10 daily) and Disneyland Resort Paris (2½ hours, one or two daily), with less frequent services departing from Ebbsfleet and Ashford, both in Kent. Ski trains connect London and Ashford with the French Alps on weekends from late December to mid-April.

LEFT-LUGGAGE FACILITIES

Because of security concerns, French train stations no longer have left-luggage lockers, but in some larger stations you can leave your bags in a *consigne manuelle* (staffed left-luggage facility), where items are handed over in person and x-rayed before being stowed. To find out which stations let you leave your bags and when their *consignes* are open, go to www .gares-en-mouvement.com (in French), choose a city, click 'Infos Pratiques' and then 'Services'.

Eurostar offers a bewildering array of fares. A standard 2nd-class one-way/return ticket from London to Paris costs a whopping UK£154.50/309 (€232.50/435), but super- discount returns go for as little as UK£59.

SEA

Tickets for car- and passenger-ferry travel to/from France are available from most travel agencies, though it's generally cheapest to book online.

Except where noted, the prices given here are for standard one-way tickets. Prices vary tremendously according to the season (July and August are priciest) and demand. People under 25 and over 60 may qualify for discounts. Many companies charge a supplement if you book by phone.

THE UK

To get the best fare by comparing prices on various trans-Channel options, try the booking service offered by **Ferry Savers** (☎ in UK 0844-576 8835; www.ferrysavers.com). Booking by phone incurs a UK£25 fee.

If you pay the foot-passenger fare, transporting a bicycle is often (but not always) free.

TO BRITTANY

Condor Ferries runs car ferries from Poole to St-Malo (from 4½ hours) and from Weymouth to St-Malo (5¼ hours).

Brittany Ferries links Plymouth with Roscoff (6½ hours by day, nine hours overnight) and Portsmouth with St-Malo (8¾ hours by day, 10¾ hours overnight).

TO FAR NORTHERN FRANCE

The extremely popular Dover-Calais crossing is handled by SeaFrance (80 to 90 minutes, 15 daily) and P&O Ferries (75 to 90 minutes, 35 daily). Foot passengers, who are not allowed on night sailings (ie sailings departing after sometime between 7pm and 9.30pm and before 7am or 8am), pay about UK£14 one-way on SeaFrance and UK£20 one-way on P&O (less if you reserve ahead). Car fares vary greatly – for a vehicle and up to nine passengers they can be as low as UK£25 or as high as UK£70.

Car ferries run by Norfolk Line link Loon Plage, about 25km west of Dunkirk (Dunkerque), with Dover (1¾ hours) for UK£19 to UK£93 one-way for a vehicle and up to four passengers. Foot passengers are not allowed.

Ultramodern, ultrafast, low-cost car catamarans run by Speed Ferries link Dover with Boulogne-sur-Mer (50 minutes, three to five daily). The one-way fare for a car with up to five passengers ranges from UK£18 to UK£67. Foot passengers and camping trailers cannot be accommodated but cyclists can.

TO NORMANDY

Transmanche Ferries operates year-round car ferries from Newhaven to Dieppe (four hours). A one-way foot-passenger

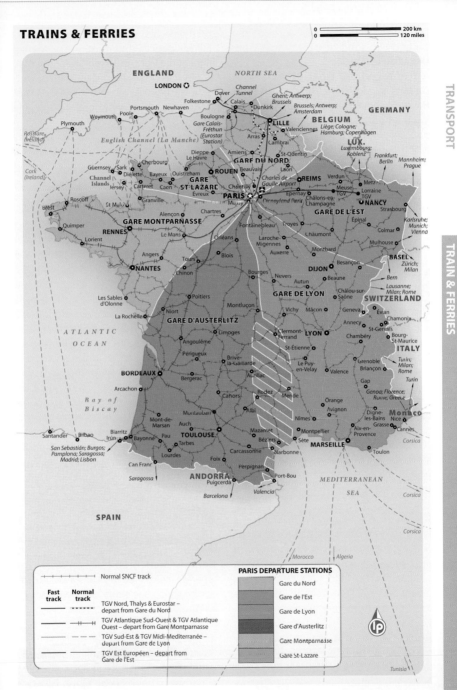

TRAINS & FERRIES

fare starts at €19; the one-way fare for a car and two adults usually ranges from UK£37.50 to UK£90.

Year-round, LD Lines offers a 5pm car ferry service from Portsmouth to Le Havre (5½ hours) and an overnight crossing (eight hours) in the opposite direction. One-way passage for a car and two adults generally costs from UK£32.50 to UK£89.50.

Brittany Ferries links Cherbourg with both Poole (high-speed ferry 2¼ hours, regular ferry 4½ to 6½ hours, two or three daily) and Portsmouth (three hours, one or two sailings daily).

Condor Ferries links Portsmouth with Cherbourg (5½ hours).

GETTING AROUND

This section provides details on travelling both by car – the simplest way to get around except in traffic-plagued, parking-starved city centres – and on the excellent public transport network, which covers every corner of the land except some rural areas. In addition to its environmental benefits, travelling by train, metro, tram and bus lets you experience France the way many ordinary French people do, taking in the sights, encountering the unexpected and meeting locals at a pace set by the leisurely rhythm of day-to-day life.

BICYCLE

France is generally a great place to cycle. Not only is much of the countryside drop-dead gorgeous but it has a growing number of urban and rural *pistes cyclables* (bike paths and lanes), some linking one town to the next, and an extensive network of secondary and tertiary roads with relatively light traffic.

French law dictates that bicycles must have two functioning brakes, a bell, a red reflector on the back, and yellow reflectors on the pedals. After sunset and when visibility is poor, cyclists must turn on a white light at the front and a red one at the rear.

Never leave your bicycle locked up outside overnight if you want to see it or most of its parts again. Some hotels can provide enclosed bicycle parking.

The **Fédération Française des Usagers de la Bicyclette** (French Bicycle Users Federation; www.fubicy.org, in French) promotes cycling for transport.

BIKE RENTAL

Most French cities and towns have at least one bike shop that rents out *vélos tout terrains* (mountain bikes; generally €10 to €20 a day), popularly known as VTTs; more road-oriented *vélos tout chemin* (VTCs); or cheaper city bikes. You usually have to leave ID and/or a deposit (often a credit-card slip) that you forfeit if the bike is damaged or stolen. For details on rental options, see Getting Around in the city and town sections throughout this book.

A growing number of cities – most famously, Paris and Lyon – have automatic bike rental systems, intended to encourage cycling as a form of urban transport, with computerised pick-up and drop-off sites all over town. In general, you have to sign up either short-term or long-term, providing credit-card details, and can then use the bikes for no charge for the first half hour.

BOAT

For information on ferry services that operate along France's coasts and to offshore islands, see individual town and city sections.

CANAL BOATING

Transportation and tranquillity are usually mutually exclusive – but not if you rent a houseboat and cruise along France's canals and navigable rivers, stopping at whim to pick up supplies, dine at a village restaurant or check out a local château by bicycle. Changes in altitude are taken care of by a system of *écluses* (locks).

Boats generally accommodate from two to 12 passengers and are fully outfitted with bedding and cooking facilities. Anyone over 18 can pilot a riverboat but first-time skippers are given a short instruction session so they qualify for a *carte de plaisance* (a temporary cruising permit).

Prices start at around €450 a week for a small boat and can top €3000 for a large, luxurious craft. Except in July and August, you can often rent over a weekend (Friday to Monday; from €280) or from Monday to Friday.

Advance reservations are essential for holiday periods, over long weekends and in July and August, especially for larger boats.

Online rental agencies include **Canal Boat Holidays** (www.canalboatholidays.com), **H2olidays** (Barging in France; www.bargingin france.com) and **Worldwide River Cruise** (www.worldwide-river-cruise.com). For more rental companies, see the Burgundy (p192) and the Dordogne (p196) sections in this book.

BUS
Buses are widely used for short-distance travel within *départements*, especially in rural areas with relatively few train lines (eg Brittany and Normandy). Unfortunately, services in some regions are infrequent and slow.

CAR & MOTORCYCLE
Having your own wheels gives you exceptional freedom and makes it easy to visit more remote parts of France. Unfortunately driving can be expensive, and in the cities traffic and finding a place to park are frequently a major headache. Motorcyclists will find France great for touring, with winding roads of good quality and lots of stunning scenery. Just make sure your wet-weather gear is up to scratch.

France has the densest highway network in Europe. There are four types of intercity roads, which have alphanumeric designations:

Autoroutes (highway names beginning with A) Multilane divided highways, that usually have tolls *(péages)* and are generously outfitted with rest stops.
Routes Nationales (N, RN) National highways that often have sections with a divider strip.
Routes Départementales (D) Local roads.
Routes Communales (C, V) Minor rural roads.

Information on tolls, rest areas, traffic and weather is available from www.autoroutes. fr. The websites www.viamichelin.com and www.mappy.fr plot itineraries between your departure and arrival points.

Theft from cars is a major problem in France, especially in the south – see p375.

Make sure your car is fitted with winter or all-season tyres if there's a chance you'll be driving through snow. During holiday periods and over long weekends, roads throughout France get backed up with *bouchons* (traffic jams).

BRINGING YOUR OWN VEHICLE
A right-hand-drive vehicle brought to France from the UK or Ireland must have deflectors affixed to the headlights to avoid dazzling oncoming traffic.

A foreign motor vehicle entering France must display a sticker or licence plate identifying its country of registration.

CAR HIRE

To hire a car in France, you'll generally need to be over 21 years old, have had a driver's licence for at least a year, and have an international credit card.

Car-rental companies provide mandatory third-party liability insurance but things such as collision-damage waivers (CDW, or *assurance tous risques*) vary greatly from company to company. When comparing rates and conditions (ie the fine print), the most important thing to check is the *franchise* (excess), which for a small car is usually around €600 for damage and €800 for theft. With many companies, you can reduce the excess to zero (or at least to half) by paying a daily insurance supplement of between €10 and €16. Your credit card may cover CDW if you use it to pay for the car rental but the rental company won't know anything about this – verify conditions and details with your credit-card issuer to be sure.

Arranging your car rental or fly/drive package before you leave home is usually considerably cheaper than a walk-in rental but beware of website offers that don't include a CDW or you may be liable for up to 100% of the car's value.

Major rental companies:

ADA (☎ 08 25 16 91 69; www.ada.fr, in French)

Avis (☎ 08 20 05 05 05; www.avis.com)

Budget (☎ 08 25 00 35 64; www.budget.com or www.budget.fr, in French)

Easycar (☎ in UK 0906-333 333 3; www.easycar.com)

Europcar (☎ 08 25 35 83 58; www.europcar.com)

Hertz (☎ 01 39 38 38 38; www.hertz.com)

National-Citer (www.nationalcar.com, www.citer.fr)

Renault Rent (☎ 08 10 40 50 60; www.renault-rent.com, in French) Renault's new car-rental arm.

Sixt (☎ 08 20 00 74 98; www.sixt.fr, in French)

Deals can be found on the internet, with travel agencies and through companies like **Auto Europe** (☎ in USA 1-888-223-5555; www.autoeurope.com) in the US, **DriveAway Holidays** (☎ in Australia 1300 723 972; www.driveaway.com.au) in Australia and **Holiday Autos** (☎ in UK 0871-472 5229; www.holidayautos.co.uk) in the UK.

Note that rental cars with automatic transmission are very much the exception in France. You will usually need to order one well in advance, with a much smaller (and invariably costlier) range of models to choose from.

DRIVING LICENCE & DOCUMENTS

All drivers must carry at all times: an EU national ID card or passport; a valid driver's licence (*permis de conduire;* most foreign licences can be used in France for up to a year); car-ownership papers, known as a *carte grise* (grey card); and proof of third-party liability *assurance* (insurance).

FUEL & SPARE PARTS

Essence (petrol), also known as *carburant* (fuel), costs around €1.40/L for 95 unleaded (Sans Plomb 95 or SP95, usually available from a green pump) and €1.30 for diesel (*diesel, gazole* or *gasoil,* usually available from a yellow pump). Filling up *(faire le plein)* is most expensive at the rest stops along the autoroutes and often cheapest at hypermarkets.

INSURANCE

Third-party liability insurance *(assurance au tiers)* is compulsory for all vehicles in France, including cars brought in from abroad.

If you get into a minor accident with no injuries, the easiest way for drivers to sort things out with their insurance companies is to fill out a Constat Aimable d'Accident Automobile (European Accident Statement), a standardised way of recording important details about what happened. In rental cars it's usually in the packet of documents in the glove compartment. Don't sign anything you don't fully understand. If problems crop up, call the **police** (☎ 17).

MOTORBIKE HIRE
Motorcycle and moped rental is popular in southern France, especially in the beach resorts, but accidents are all too common. Where relevant, details on rental options appear at the end of city and town sections.

To rent a moped, scooter or motorcycle, you usually have to leave a large *caution* (deposit), which you then forfeit – up to the value of the damage – if you cause an accident or if the bike is damaged or stolen.

PARKING
In city centres, most on-the-street parking places are *payant* (metered) from about 9am to 7pm (sometimes with a break from noon to 2pm) from Monday to Saturday, except bank holidays.

ROAD RULES
French law requires that all passengers, including those in the back seat, wear seat belts. Babies weighing less than 13kg must travel in the rear in backward-facing child seats; children up to 18kg must ride in child seats. Children under 10 must sit in the back unless it's already occupied by other children under 10. North American drivers should remember that turning right on a red light is illegal in France.

Speed limits outside built-up areas:
- 90km/h (80km/h if it's raining) on undivided N and D highways
- 110km/h (100km/h if it's raining) on nonautoroute divided highways
- 130km/h (110km/h in the rain, 60km/h in icy conditions) on autoroutes

Unless otherwise posted, a limit of 50km/h applies in *all* areas designated as built up, no matter how rural they may appear. You must slow to 50km/h the moment you come to a white sign with a red border and a place name written on it; you can resume your previous speed when you pass an identical sign with a horizontal bar through it. You can be fined for going 10km over the speed limit.

Under the *priorité à droite* rule, any car entering an intersection from a road on your right has the right of way, unless the intersection is marked *vous n'avez pas la priorité* (you do not have right of way) or *cédez le passage* (give way). *Priorité à droite* is also suspended on priority roads, which are marked by an yellow square with a black square in the middle.

It is illegal to drive with a blood-alcohol concentration over 0.05% (0.5g per litre of blood) – the equivalent of two glasses of wine for a 75kg adult. Police often conduct breathalyser tests at random and penalties can be severe, including imprisonment. Mobile phones may only be used when accompanied by a hands-free kit or speakerphone.

Since July 2008, all French vehicles must now carry a reflective safety jacket and a reflective triangle; the fine for not carrying one/both is €90/135.

Riders of any type of two-wheeled vehicle with a motor (except motor-assisted bicycles) must wear a helmet. No special licence is required to ride a motorbike whose engine is smaller than 50cc, which is why you often find places renting scooters rated at 49.9cc.

LOCAL TRANSPORT

France's cities and larger towns have excellent public-transport systems.

TAXI

All medium and large train stations, and many small ones, have a taxi stand out front. In small cities and towns, where taxi drivers are unlikely to find another fare anywhere near where they let you off, one-way and return trips often cost the same. Tariffs are about 30% higher at night and on Sundays and holidays. There may be a surcharge to get picked up at a train station or airport and a small additional fee for a fourth passenger and/or for suitcases.

TRAIN

Travelling by train is a comfortable, classy, urbane and environmentally sustainable way to see France. Since many train stations have car-rental agencies, it's easy to combine rail travel with rural exploration by motorcar.

The jewel in the crown of France's public transport system, alongside the Paris *métro,* is its extensive rail network, almost all run by the state-owned **SNCF** (☎ 3635; www.sncf.com).

Since its inauguration in the 1980s, the pride and joy of SNCF – and the French – is the world-renowned high-speed **TGV (Train à Grande Vitesse; www.tgv.com),** pronounced 'teh zheh veh', which zips passengers along at speeds of up to 320km/h (198mph).

The four main TGV lines head due north, due east, southeast and southwest from Paris:

TGV Nord, Thalys & Eurostar These link Paris' Gare du Nord with Arras, Lille, Calais, Brussels, Amsterdam, Cologne and, via the Channel Tunnel, Ashford, Ebbsfleet and London St Pancras.

TGV Est Européen Inaugurated in 2007, this new line connects Paris' Gare de l'Est with Reims, Nancy, Metz, Strasbourg, Zurich and Germany, including Frankfurt and Stuttgart. At the time of research, super-high-speed track stretched only as far east as Lorraine but it's supposed to reach Strasbourg in 2012.

TGV Sud-Est & TGV Midi-Méditerranée These lines link Paris' Gare de Lyon with the southeast, including Dijon, Lyon, Geneva, the Alps, Avignon, Marseille, Nice and Montpellier.

TGV Atlantique Sud-Ouest & TGV Atlantique Ouest These link Paris' Gare Montparnasse with western and southwestern France, including Brittany (Rennes, Brest, Quimper), Nantes, Tours, Poitiers, La Rochelle, Bordeaux, Biarritz and Toulouse.

In order to make train travel both affordable and hip for the iPod generation, the SNCF has launched a new website, www.idtgv.com, which sells tickets for as little as €19 for TGV travel on 20 routes to/from Paris.

For details on especially scenic train routes all around France, see www.trains touristiques-ter.com.

Long-distance trains sometimes split at a station – that is, each half of the train heads off for a different destination. Check the destination panel on your car as you board or you could wind up very, very far from wherever it was you intended to go.

CLASSES & SLEEPING CARS

Most French trains have both 1st- and 2nd-class sections. Full-fare tickets for the former cost 50% more than the latter.

On overnight trains, the 2nd-class couchette compartments have six berths, while those in 1st class have four. Certain overnight trains have 1st-class *voitures-lits* (sleeping cars), which provide private facilities for one or two people and a

SNCF DISCOUNTS

The SNCF's most heavily discounted tickets are known as Prem's. They can be booked on the internet, by phone, at ticket windows and from ticket machines a maximum of 90 days and a minimum of four days before your travel date, though the very cheapest seats often sell out early on. Once you buy a Prem's ticket, getting your money back or changing the time is not allowed.

Corail fares that require neither a discount card nor advance purchase but get you 25% off include Loisir Week-End rates, good for return travel that includes a Saturday night at your destination or involves travel on a Saturday or Sunday; and Découverte fares, available for low-demand 'blue-period' trains to young people aged 12 to 25, seniors and the adult travel companions of children under 12. Mini Groupe tickets can save lots for three to six people travelling together, provided you spend a Saturday night at your destination.

Reductions of at least 25% (for last-minute bookings), and up to 40%, 50% or even 60% (if you reserve ahead or travel during low-volume 'blue' periods), are available with several discount cards, valid for a year:

Carte 12-25 (www.12-25-sncf.com, in French; €49) Available to travellers aged 12 to 25.

Carte Enfant Plus (www.enfantplus-sncf.com, in French; €65) For one to four adults travelling with a child aged four to 11.

Carte Sénior (www.senior-sncf.com, in French; €55) For travellers over 60.

Carte Escapades (www.escapades-sncf.com, in French; €85) For people aged 26 to 59. Gets you discounts on return journeys of at least 200km that either include a Saturday night away or only involve travel on a Saturday or Sunday.

The new Bons Plans fares, a grab bag of really cheap options on a changing array of routes and dates, are advertised on www.voyages-sncf.com.

Certain French *régions* (eg Basse Normandie and Alsace) offer great deals on intraregional TER transport for day trips or weekend travel.

An **InterRail One Country Pass** (www.interrailnet.com), valid in France, entitles non-residents of France to unlimited travel on SNCF trains for three to eight days over the course of a month. For three/four/six/eight days, the cost is €189/209/269/299 for adults, and €125/139/175/194 for young people aged 12 to 25 years.

continental l breakfast. Some couchette
compartments are reserved for women
travelling alone or with children.

COSTS
Full-fare tickets can be quite expensive
– for instance, a one-way low-/peak-period
trip by TGV from Paris to Lyon will drain your wallet of €61/79.50. Full-fare return passage costs twice as much as one-way fares. Children aged under four travel for free; those aged four to 11 pay half price.

TICKETS & RESERVATIONS
Large stations often have separate ticket windows for *international*, *grandes lignes*

(long-haul) and *banlieue* (suburban) lines, and for people whose train is about to leave *(départ immédiat or départ dans l'heure)*. Nearly every SNCF station has at least one *borne libre-service* (self-service terminal) or *billeterie automatique* (automatic ticket machine) that accepts both cash and computer-chip credit cards. Push on the Union Jack for instructions in English.

Using a credit card, you can buy a ticket by phone or via the SNCF's internet booking site (www.voyages-sncf.com, in French) and collect it from any SNCF ticket office or from train-station ticket machines.

Before boarding the train, you must validate *(composter)* your ticket by time-stamping it in a *composteur,* one of those yellow posts located on the way to the platform. If you forget (or don't have a ticket for some other reason), find a conductor on the train before they find you – otherwise you can be fined.

In general, reserving a place on a specific train – something you can do by phone, on the internet or at stations – is optional, although there are exceptions:

- travel by TGV, Eurostar, Thalys, Lunéa or Téoz
- couchettes (sleeping berths; €18 for 2nd class)
- travelling during peak holiday periods

For trains that do not require reservations (eg Corail Intercités and TER trains), full-fare tickets are usable whenever you like for 61 days from the date they were purchased. Like all SNCF tickets, they cannot be replaced if lost or stolen.

If you've got a full-fare Loisir Week-End ticket, you can change your reservation by phone, internet or at train stations for no charge until the day before your departure; changes made on the day of your reserved trip incur a charge of €10 (€3 for tickets bought with a discount card). Pro tickets (eg TGV Pro, Téoz Pro) cost extra and allow full reimbursement up to the time of departure and, if you're running a bit late, let you board the next train to the same destination up to an hour after your scheduled departure. Very cheap promotional tickets (eg Prem's) cannot be modified and are nonreimbursable.

↘ GLOSSARY

(m) indicates masculine gender, (f) feminine gender and (pl) plural

alimentation (f) – grocery store
AOC – *appellation d'origine contrôlée;* system of French wine classification
arrondissement (m) – administrative division of large city; abbreviated on signs as 1er (1st arrondissement), 2e (2nd) etc
auberge (m) – inn
auberge de jeunesse (f) – youth hostel

bastide (f) – medieval settlement in southwestern France, usually built on a grid plan and surrounding an arcaded square; also a country house in Provence
billet (m) – ticket
billetterie (f) – ticket office or counter
bouchon – Lyonnais bistro
boulangerie (f) – bakery or bread shop
brasserie (f) – restaurant usually serving food all day (original meaning: brewery)
bureau de change (m) – exchange bureau
bureau de poste (m) or **poste** (f) – post office

carnet (m) – a book of five or 10 bus, tram or metro tickets sold at a reduced rate
carte (f) – card; menu; map
cave (f) – wine cellar
chambre (f) – room
chambre d'hôte (f) – B&B
charcuterie (f) – pork butcher's shop and delicatessen; the prepared meats it sells

cimetière (m) – cemetery
consigne or **consigne manuelle** (f) – left-luggage office
consigne automatique (f) – left-luggage locker
couchette (f) – sleeping berth on a train or ferry
crémerie (f) – dairy or cheese shop

dégustation (f) – tasting
demi (m) – 330mL glass of beer
demi-pension (f) – half-board (B&B with either lunch or dinner)
douane (f) – customs

église (f) – church
épicerie (f) – small grocery store

fête (f) – festival
FN – Front National; National Front
fromagerie (f) – cheese shop
FUAJ – Fédération Unie des Auberges de Jeunesse; France's major hostel group

galerie (f) – covered shopping centre or arcade
gare or **gare SNCF** (f) – railway station
gendarmerie (f) – police station; police force
grand cru (m) – wine of exceptional quality

halles (f pl) – covered market; central food market
hôtel de ville (m) – city or town hall

jardin (m) – garden
jardin botanique (m) – botanic garden
jours fériés (m pl) – public holidays

maison de la presse (f) – newsagent
marché (m) – market

marché aux puces (m) – flea market

marché couvert (m) – covered market

mas (m) – farmhouse in southern France

menu (m) – fixed-price meal with two or more courses

mistral (m) – incessant north wind in southern France said to drive people crazy

musée (m) – museum

navette (f) – shuttle bus, train or boat

palais de justice (m) – law courts

parvis (m) – square

pâtisserie (f) – cake and pastry shop

péage (m) – toll

pensions de famille (f pl) – similar to B&Bs

pétanque (f) – a game not unlike lawn bowls played with heavy metal balls on a sandy pitch; also called *boules*

piste cyclable (f) – bicycle path

place (f) – square or plaza

plage (f) – beach

plan (m) – city map

plan du quartier (m) – map of nearby streets (hung on the wall near metro exits)

plat du jour (m) – daily special in a restaurant

pont (m) – bridge

port de plaisance (m) – marina or pleasure-boat harbour

porte (f) – gate in a city wall

poste (f) or **bureau de poste** (m) – post office

préfecture (f) – prefecture (capital of a *département*)

presqu'île (f) – peninsula

pression (f) – draught beer

quai (m) – quay or railway platform

quartier (m) – quarter or district

région (f) – administrative division of France

rez-de-chausée (m) – ground floor

rive (f) – bank of a river

rond point (m) – roundabout

sentier (m) – trail

service des urgences (f) – casualty ward

SNCF – Société Nationale des Chemins de Ferstate railway company

SNCM – Société Nationale Maritime Corse-Méditerranée ferry company linking Corsica and mainland France

sortie (f) – exit

spectacle (m) – performance, play or theatrical show

syndicat d'initiative (m) – tourist office

tabac (m) – tobacconist (also selling bus tickets, phonecards etc)

table d'orientation (f) – viewpoint indicator

taxe de séjour (f) – municipal tourist tax

télécarte (f) – phonecard

téléphérique (m) – cableway or cable car

TGV – *Train à Grande Vitesse;* high-speed train or bullet train

tour (f) – tower

tour d'horloge (f) – clock tower

vallée (f) – valley

v.f. (f) – *version française;* a film dubbed in French

vieille ville (f) – old town or old city

ville neuve (f) – new town or new city

v.o. (f) – *version originale;* a nondubbed film with French subtitles

voie (f) – train platform

VTT – *vélo tout terrain;* mountain bike

winstub – traditional Alsatian eateries

⬊ BEHIND THE SCENES

THE AUTHORS
NICOLA WILLIAMS

Coordinating Author, This is France, France's Top 25 Experiences, France's Top Itineraries, Planning Your Trip, Lyon & the French Alps, France In Focus

Lonely Planet author and independent travel writer Nicola Williams has lived in France and written about it for over a decade. From her hillside house on the shores of Lake Geneva, it's an easy hop to France's hot south, the French Alps and beyond, where she has spent endless years eating her way around the country and revelling in its extraordinary art heritage and landscapes.

Author thanks Thanks to the French experts who shared their best addresses: Patricia Wells in Paris and Provence; Champagne correspondent for *The World of Fine Wines* magazine, Michael Edwards *(merci* Wink Lorch of winetravelguides .com); man of a thousand magical tales and Mont St-Michel walking guide, Jack Lecoq; Chamonix-based Eric Favret; French *Euronews* journalist Lise Pedersen; radio presenter Elizabeth Lewis; and celebrity advocate of Bordelaise cuisine Jean-Pierre Xiradakis. In/around Paris thanks to a trio of press attachés: Marion Benaiteau (Louvre); Hélène Dalifard (Versailles); and Elsa Sauvé (Chambord). Kudos to the ever gracious Lúfkens boys; to Twitter and FB friends who rose so gallantly to my French music challenge; and to my fellow France authors whose skilled and stylish prose I slashed so ruthlessly.

OLIVER BERRY
The Loire & Central France

Oliver has been travelling to France since the tender age of two, and over the last decade his writing has carried him from the rural corners of the Lot Valley to the snowy hump of Mont Blanc and the chestnut forests of Corsica. Having worked on several editions of the *France* guide, for this title he plumbed the depths of prehistoric caves in the Vézère Valley, wandered the hallways of obscure Loire châteaux, and clambered to the top of dormant volcanoes in the Massif Central. When he's not out on the road, Oliver lives and works in Cornwall as a writer and photographer.

LONELY PLANET AUTHORS

Why is our travel information the best in the world? It's simple: our authors are passionate, dedicated travellers. They don't take freebies in exchange for positive coverage so you can be sure the advice you're given is impartial. They travel widely to all the popular spots, and off the beaten track. They don't research using just the internet or phone. They discover new places not included in any other guidebook. They personally visit thousands of hotels, restaurants, palaces, trails, galleries, temples and more. They speak with dozens of locals every day to make sure you get the kind of insider knowledge only a local could tell you. They take pride in getting all the details right, and in telling it how it is. Think you can do it? Find out how at lonelyplanet.com.

STEVE FALLON   Paris & Its Day Trips, Champagne & the Northeast

Steve, who has worked on every edition of *France* except the first, visited the 'City of Light' for the first time at age 16 with his half-French best friend. They spent a week drinking *vin ordinaire* from plastic bottles, keeping several paces ahead of irate café waiters demanding to be paid, and learning French swear words that shocked even them. Despite this inexcusable behaviour, the PAF (border police) let him back in five years later to complete a degree in French at the Sorbonne. Now based in East London, Steve will be just one Underground stop away from Paris when Eurostar trains begin departing from Stratford. *C'est si bon…*

EMILIE FILOU   Lyon & the French Alps, The South of France

Emilie was born in Paris but spent most of her childhood holidays roaming the south of France and the Alps. Bigger summits beckoned when she turned 18 and she spent a year in Nepal before going to university. She read geography at Oxford, where she had to endure colouring-in jokes for three years but managed to bag a field trip to Niger for her dissertation on nomadic tribes. More travel in French-speaking Africa, Southeast Asia, Australia and New Zealand ensued. She now works as a business and travel journalist in London.

CATHERINE LE NEVEZ   Brittany & Normandy, Bordeaux & the Southwest

Catherine's wanderlust kicked in when she lived in and road-tripped throughout France aged four. She's been road-tripping here at every opportunity since, completing her Doctorate of Creative Arts in Writing, Masters in Professional Writing, and postgrad qualifications in Editing and Publishing along the way.

Catherine's writing on France includes Lonely Planet's *France, Paris Encounter* and *Provence & the Côte d'Azur* guidebooks, newspaper and radio reportage covering Paris' literary scene, and several hundred Lonely Planet online accommodation reviews nationwide. When not scouting out hidden corners of France, Catherine has followed Lonely Planet travel writing assignments to neighbouring Italy, Germany, Belgium and (across the pond) Ireland, among others.

DANIEL ROBINSON   Champagne & the Northeast, Brittany & Normandy,
                        The Loire & Central France, Directory & Transport

Over the past two decades, Daniel's articles and guidebooks – published in nine languages – have covered every region of France, but he has a particular fondness for those bits of the Hexagone in which Celtic, Romance and Germanic cultures have mingled for over two millennia. Seeking out enchanting corners of rust-belt France is a long-time hobby, and he takes particular interest in the creativity and panache – and foresighted public-transport initiatives – of dynamic northern cities such as Lille, Nancy and Strasbourg.

Daniel grew up in the US and Israel and holds degrees from Princeton University and Tel Aviv University. He is based in Tel Aviv and Los Angeles.

MILES RODDIS   The South of France

Miles studied French at university, where he spent an idyllic sandwich year in Neuville-sur-Saône, a place quite rightly overlooked by the best guidebooks, including the one in your hand. Living over the Pyrenees in Valencia, Spain, he and his wife, Ingrid, cross the mountains to France for work or fun at least once a year. He has travelled the length of Languedoc, and usually Roussillon too, on seven occasions for Lonely Planet guidebooks, each time returning home several kilos and a case of fine red wine heavier.

Miles has written or contributed to more than 30 Lonely Planet titles including *France, Brittany & Normandy* and – most satisfyingly of all – *Walking in France*.

THIS BOOK

This 1st edition of *Discover France* was written and coordinated by Nicola Williams, and researched and written by Oliver Berry, Steve Fallon, Emilie Filou, Catherine Le Nevez, Daniel Robinson and Miles Roddis. This guidebook was commissioned in Lonely Planet's London office, and produced by the following:

Commissioning Editors Caroline Sieg, Paula Hardy, Suzannah Shwer
Coordinating Editor Alison Ridgway
Coordinating Cartographer Amanda Sierp
Coordinating Layout Designer Kerrianne Southway
Managing Editor Liz Heynes
Managing Cartographers Adrian Persoglia, Herman So
Managing Layout Designer Sally Darmody
Assisting Editor Victoria Harrison
Assisting Cartographers Xavier Di Toro, Birgit Jordan, Ross Macaw
Cover Naomi Parker, lonelyplanetimages.com
Internal image research Aude Vauconsant, lonelyplanetimages.com
Project Manager Chris Girdler
Language Content Annelies Mertens
Thanks to Sasha Baskett, Glenn Beanland, Yvonne Bischofberger, Stefanie Di Trocchio, Eoin Dunlevy, Ryan Evans, Suki Gear, Joshua Geoghegan, Mark Germanchis, Michelle Glynn, Brice Gosnell, Imogen Hall, James Hardy, Jane Hart, Steve Henderson, Lauren Hunt, Laura Jane, Chris Lee Ack, Nic Lehman, Ali Lemer, Alison Lyall, John Mazzocchi, Anna Metcalfe, Jennifer Mullins, Wayne Murphy, Darren O'Connell, Piers Pickard, Howard Ralley, Lachlan Ross, Julie Sheridan, Jason Shugg, Caroline Sieg, Naomi Stephens, Geoff Stringer, Jane Thompson, Sam Trafford, Tashi Wheeler, Clifton Wilkinson, Juan Winata, Emily K Wolman, Nick Wood

Internal photographs
p4 Cannes, Côte d'Azur, Richard I'Anson; p10 Pasture, Mont-St-Michel, Normandy, John Elk III; p12 Louvre-Rivoli metro station, Paris, Will Salter; p31 Eiffel Tower, Paris, Lee Foster; p39 Champagne route sign, Juliet Coombe; p3, p50 Limousine arriving at Palais Garnier, Paris, Barbara Van Zanten; p3, p101 Champagne route sign, Neil Setchfield; p3, p129 Poppy fields, Normandy, Diana Mayfield; p3, p167 Vineyard, Loire Valley, Alice Grulich-Jones; p3, p203 Hiker, Vanoise National Park, French Alpes, John Elk III; p235 Lavender fields, Provence, David Tomlinson; p3, p287 St Émilion, Bordeaux, John Elk III; p3, p320 Valley d'Aure, Pyrenees, Greg Johnston; p371 Marseille, Provence, Bethune Carmichael.

All images are copyright of the photographer unless otherwise indicated. Many of the images in this guide are available for licensing from Lonely Planet Images: www.lonelyplanetimages.com.

ACKNOWLEDGMENTS

Many thanks to the following for the use of their content:

Paris Metro Map © 2009 RATP

↘ INDEX

000 Map pages
000 Photograph pages